Roberto Simanowski, Jörgen Schäfer, Peter Gendolla (eds.)
Reading Moving Letters

The series "Medienumbrüche | Media Upheavals" is edited by Peter Gendolla.

ROBERTO SIMANOWSKI, JÖRGEN SCHÄFER, PETER GENDOLLA (EDS.)
Reading Moving Letters
Digital Literature in Research and Teaching. A Handbook

[transcript] Medienumbrüche | Media Upheavals | Volume 40

Bibliographic information published by the Deutsche Nationalbibliothek
The Deutsche Nationalbibliothek lists this publication in the Deutsche Nationalbibliografie; detailed bibliographic data are available in the Internet at http://dnb.d-nb.de

© 2010 transcript Verlag, Bielefeld

All rights reserved. No part of this book may be reprinted or reproduced or utilized in any form or by any electronic, mechanical, or other means, now known or hereafter invented, including photocopying and recording, or in any information storage or retrieval system, without permission in writing from the publisher.

Cover layout: Kordula Röckenhaus, Bielefeld
Cover illustration: Daniel Howe: Text Curtain (2005), © canazon2010
Copy editing by Patricia Tomaszek
Layout & Typeset by Georg Rademacher, Jörgen Schäfer, Patricia Tomaszek
Printed by Majuskel Medienproduktion GmbH, Wetzlar
ISBN 978-3-8376-1130-4

Distributed in North America by

Transaction Publishers
New Brunswick (U.S.A.) and London (U.K.)

Transaction Publishers   Tel.: (732) 445-2280
Rutgers University   Fax: (732) 445-3138
35 Berrue Circle   for orders (U.S. only):
Piscataway, NJ 08854   toll free 888-999-6778

Contents

Roberto Simanowski, Jörgen Schäfer and Peter Gendolla
Preface 9

Part One: Reading Digital Literature

Roberto Simanowski
Reading Digital Literature
A Subject Between Media and Methods..15

Noah Wardrip-Fruin
Five Elements of Digital Literature 29

John Zuern
Figures in the Interface
Comparative Methods in the Study of Digital Literature.......................59

Jörgen Schäfer and Peter Gendolla
Reading (in) the Net
Aesthetic Experience in Computer-Based Media....................................81

Karin Wenz
Storytelling Goes On After the Credits
Fanfiction as a Case Study of Cyberliterature.......................................109

Raine Koskimaa
Approaches to Digital Literature
Temporal Dynamics and Cyborg Authors...129

Astrid Ensslin
From Revisi(tati)on to Retro-Intentionalization
Hermeneutics, Multimodality and Corporeality in Hypertext,
Hypermedia and Cybertext..145

Alexandra Saemmer
Digital Literature—A Question of Style 163

María Goicoechea
The Reader in Cyberspace
In Search of Digital Literature in Spain 183

Janez Strehovec
Alphabet on the Move
Digital Poetry and the Realm of Language 207

Part Two: Teaching Digital Literature

Roberto Simanowski
Teaching Digital Literature
Didactic and Institutional Aspects 231

Noah Wardrip-Fruin
Learning to Read Digital Literature 249

John Zuern
Pop Spells, Hermetic Lessons
Teaching on the Fringes of the Literary 261

Peter Gendolla, Jörgen Schäfer and Patricia Tomaszek
Net Literature in the Classroom
Teaching Practice at the University of Siegen 273

Karin Wenz
Digital Media@Maastricht University
Problem-Based Learning as an Approach to Digital Literature 291

Raine Koskimaa
Teaching Digital Literature through Multi-Layered Analysis 299

Astrid Ensslin and James Pope
Digital Literature in Creative and Media Studies 311

Alexandra Saemmer
Digital Literature—In Search of a Discipline?
Teaching Digital Literature in France: A Short Overview 329

María Goicoechea
Teaching Digital Literature in Spain
Reading Strategies for the Digital Text..345

Janez Strehovec
In Search for the Novel Possibilities of Text-Based Installations
Teaching Digital Literature within New Media Studies in Slovenia................367

Contributors 377

Preface

Increasingly, as cinema once did, digital media are finding their way into the research of the humanities and by now a number of books on digital literature and art in general have been published. While some current collections of essays discuss how new media shape human relations and generate new genres of art (Landow; Lunenfeld; Hayles, *Writing Machines*), others discuss in detail the new forms of literature (Bolter; Aarseth; Douglas; Ryan; Simanowski; Heibach; Block, Heibach and Wenz; Gendolla and Schäfer; Funkhouser; Hayles, *Electronic Literature*). Although these books include discussions regarding terminological and aesthetic questions, they do not offer much information about the educational and pedagogical impact of digital literature and the institutional aspects of its incorporation into existing curricula. Neither do studies dedicated to specific questions of digital technology and digital literacy, since they are mostly focused on general discussions (such as programming skills, hybridity, authorship, virtuality, ephemerality, copyright, digital divide, surveillance) rather than on the close reading of a specific work of digital literature, or its teaching practice (Tuman; Barrett; Boschmann; Landow; Schäfer and Schubert). In addition, some of these and the aforementioned books contain assumptions (i.e., about the role of the author and the reader as well as the value of interaction), which in more recent discussions have been criticized, rejected, or at least put into a contemporary perspective. Although some studies (Douglas; Ryan; Simanowski) do present chapters on close readings as do some more recent publications (Hayles; Looy and Baetens; Ricardo), they do not discuss how a more thorough engagement with the aesthetic specifics of examples of digitale literature helps to introduce the subject into the classroom. While we have a number of impressive theoretical texts about digital literature, we as of yet have little in the way of resources for discussing the down-to-earth practices of research, teaching, and curriculum necessary for this work to mature.

Reading Moving Letters addresses this need on an up-to-date basis and provides examinations in an international comparative perspective: terminological considerations, close readings, institutional aspects, pedagogical concerns, experiences, and solutions shared by authors from different academic backgrounds. This book brings together contributions by nine scholars and teachers who illustrate their approaches to the study and teaching of digital literature. Grounded in substantial methodological questions that are examined thoroughly in this book the specific interest of this publication lies in the discussion of the definitions and methods available to approach digital literature and art. Additionally, the collection of essays presents the lessons learnt from conceivable obstacles that have to be taken into account for curricular planning and prepares teachers with valuable insights in international syllabi.

The contributions are divided into two sections: Part One, *Reading Digital Literature*, provides definitions of digital literature as a discipline of scholarly treatment in the humanities and presents the contributors' main focus in the field of digital literature. Part Two, *Teaching Digital Literature*, asks how and why we should teach digital literature and conduct close readings in the classroom. Central to this chapter are respective institutional considerations necessary to take into account when implementing digital literature into curricula.

Expanded by additional contributions, this book is based on the lecture series *Digital Literature in Research and Teaching* organized by Roberto Simanowski at Brown University in fall 2004 and spring 2005. This lecture series was part of a Transatlantic Cooperation initiated in 2004 between Roberto Simanowski from the German Studies Department at Brown and Peter Gendolla and Jörgen Schäfer from the research group "Literature on the Net/Net Literature" at the University of Siegen (Germany).

This book benefited from the work of many people. Our special thanks go to Brigitte Pichon and Dorian Rudnytsky for translating some of the texts into English and for checking the others for their linguistic correctness. Patricia Tomaszek provided invaluable assistance in unifying quotations and bibliographic information. We are also indebted to her for proof-reading the manuscript and for her assistance in finalizing the typesetting of this book. We are also grateful to Georg Rademacher for his support. Noah Wardrip-Fruin was an important interlocutor in the initial phase of the book's conceptualization.

We want to thank the Alexander von Humboldt Foundation for generously supporting our cooperation in its "TransCoop" program. This funding enabled us to establish a strong transatlantic link between Providence, RI and Siegen, of which this book is only one of several fruitful results.

Special thanks to Daniel C. Howe for giving permission to use a capture of his installation *Text Curtain* on the book cover.

Providence, RI and Siegen, September 2009
Roberto Simanowski, Jörgen Schäfer and Peter Gendolla

Works Cited

Aarseth, Espen J. *Cybertext: Perspectives on Ergodic Literature*. Baltimore: Johns Hopkins UP, 1997.

Barrett, Edward, ed. *Sociomedia: Multimedia, Hypermedia, and the Social Construction of Knowledge*. Cambridge, MA: MIT P, 1992.

Block, Friedrich W., Christiane Heibach and Karin Wenz, eds. *p0es1s: The Aesthetics of Digital Poetry*. Ostfildern: Hatje-Cantz, 2004.

Bolter, Jay David. *Writing Space: The Computer, Hypertext, and the History of Writing*. Hillsdale: Lawrence Erlbaum, 1991.

Boschmann, Erwin, ed. *The Electronic Classroom: A Handbook for Education in the Electronic Environment*. Medford: Learned Information, Inc. 1995.

Douglas, Yellowlees J. *The End of Books—or Books without End: Reading Interactive Narratives*. Arbor: U of Michigan P, 2000.

Funkhouser, Christopher T. *Prehistoric Digital Poetry: An Archaeology of Forms, 1959-1995*. Tuscaloosa: U of Alabama P, 2007.

Gendolla, Peter, and Jörgen Schäfer, eds. *The Aesthetics of Net Literature: Writing, Reading and Playing in Programmable Media*. Bielefeld: Transcript, 2007.

Hayles, N. Katherine. *Writing Machines*. Cambridge, MA: MIT P, 2002.

———. *Electronic Literature: New Horizons for the Literary*. Notre Dame: U of Notre Dame P, 2008.

Heibach, Christiane. *Literatur im elektronischen Raum*. Frankfurt a.M.: Suhrkamp, 2003.

Landow, George P. *Hypertext: The Convergence of Contemporary Critical Theory and Technology*. Baltimore: Johns Hopkins UP, 1992.

Landow, George P., ed. *Hyper/Text/Theory*. Baltimore: Johns Hopkins UP, 1994.

Looy, Jan Van and Jan Baetens, eds. *Close Reading New Media: Analyzing Electronic Literature*. Leuven: Leuven UP, 2003.

Lunenfeld, Peter, ed. *The Digital Dialectic: New Essays on New Media*. Cambridge, MA: MIT P, 1999.

Ryan, Marie-Laure. *Narrative as Virtual Reality: Immersion and Interactivity in Literature and Electronic Media*. Baltimore: Johns Hopkins UP, 2001.

Ricardo, Francisco J., ed. *Literary Art in Digital Performance: Case Studies and Critical Positions*. New York: Continuum, 2009

Schäfer, Jörgen, and Sigrid Schubert, eds. *E-Learning und Literatur: Informatiksysteme im Literaturunterricht*. Siegen: Universi, 2007.

Simanowski, Roberto. *Interfictions: Vom Schreiben im Netz*. Frankfurt a.M.: Suhrkamp, 2002.

Tuman, Myron C., ed. *Literacy Online: The Promise (and Peril) of Reading and Writing with Computers*. Pittsburgh: U of Pittsburgh P, 1992.

Part One:
Reading Digital Literature

Roberto Simanowski

Reading Digital Literature

A Subject Between Media and Methods

1 Defining Digital Literature

With the new media affecting basically every sector of individual and social life, even literary studies cannot proceed in their accumstomed way. Literary communication has fundamentally changed through the effects of the computer-based and networked media upon which it is based. Apart from the old—and with Amazon's "wireless reading device" *Kindle* renewed—threat the electronic book presents to print culture, literature is produced, distributed, perceived and discussed to an increasing extent online. Of course, most of it would fit well between two book covers and a great amount of the literature online is in fact written with the desire to become part of the realm of print. Such texts are not the subject of this book. They trigger questions about the economic and social dimension of literature, or, paraphrasing Pierre Bourdieu, about how cyberculture affects the "literary field." This book, however, investigates literary innovations with respect to new ways of aesthetic expression triggering questions such as those Jörgen Schäfer and Peter Gendolla list in their contribution to Part One of this book: Is there a new quality of literariness in digital literature? What are the terminological and methodological means to examine it? The subject of this book is not conventional literature disguised as "digital literature" or "digital publishing," as Raine Koskimaa names the production and marketing of literature with the aid of digital technology. The subject of this book concerns "digitally born" literary artifacts written *for* digital media, as Koskimaa puts it, or, as Noah Wardrip-Fruin states: "literary work that requires the digital computation performed by laptops, desktops, servers, cellphones, game consoles, interactive environment controllers, or any of the other computers that surround us."[1]

It should be underlined that the condition of "digital computation" is not fulfilled by the banal way of being created on a computer. What text is not created on a computer nowadays where pen and typewriter are rarely seen writing tools? The condition of "digital birth" points to the more existential characteristic of carrying the features of the "parents" such as connectivity, interactivity, multimediality, non-linearity, performativity and transformability. While many texts can easily migrate to the book page, "real" digital literature cannot live without digital media—just as a film cannot live without a screen. Considering temporality as a significant but, as Koskimaa claims, undertheorized dimension of digital literature, one may say that digital literature is to mere *digitized* literature like film is to photography.[2]

Such a definition, however, would include any "digitally born" text. With respect to the second term in the phrase *digital literature*, it is necessary to pay attention to the specific use of language described as the *literary*. Schäfer and Gendolla consider this specific use as the production of an alternative reality; Zuern notes as *sine qua non* of the specifically literary text the figurative as opposed to the literal deployment of language; Janez Strehovec refers to Russian Formalism defining literariness as the sum of special formal properties, as deviations from "ordinary" use of language, as defamiliarization and estrangement.

Of course, such a quality is also characteristic of conventional literary works hypertextually annotated and multimedially furnished, which Koskimaa considers an extra category of digital literature: *scholarly literary hypertext editions*. However, the figuration and estrangement those texts present are specific in their use of language and not in the digital technology used for editorial purposes. Such texts are not written *for* digital media and do not represent the aesthetic means of digital media. The question important to us is: What are the equivalent strategies of figuration and estrangement when literature is digitally born? Strehovec is certainly right in maintaining that the concept of defamiliarization needs to be applied beyond the realm of linguistics to the entire cyber'language', including visual and acoustic material as well as genuine features of digital media such as intermediality, interactivity, animation and hyperlink. A more general definition therefore characterizes the literary as the arranging of the material or the use of features in an uncommon fashion to undermine any automatic perception for the purpose of aesthetic perception. However, the question remains: How can we identify the "unusual" in a realm of expression not yet old enough (and growing too fast) to have established the "common?" How do we look at experimental writing in new media that, as Koskimaa points out, are trying to create new conventions rather than to break the established ones? In addition, we may also ask how the unusual can intentionally be designed by the author if the work is based on interactivity (with the reader) and performativity (by the computer). We will come back to these questions when discussing the literariness of the link below in section three.

No matter how we eventually define the specific "literariness" of digital literature, it is evident that it undermines the identity of digital literature as *literature*. In addition to the *sine qua non* of literariness, there is another *sine qua non* regarding the essence of digital literature; namely, in that it is more than literature defined in the traditional way. By definition, digital literature has to go beyond the employment of letters and it has to make an *aesthetic* use of the features of digital media. In digital literature, computation is, as Zuern holds, essential not only to the text as a particular kind of physical artifact, but also to the specifically literary properties of the text. The implication of such a notion is of a fundamental nature: If the features of digital technology are essential to the literary properties of the text, they inevitably more or less undermine the dominant status of the text. Similar to concrete poetry, where the meaning consists of a combination of the linguistic signification as well as the way this signification (i.e., the letters) appears, the appearance and meaning of digital literature consists of the linguistic (and visual/sonic) utterances as well as of the specific way these utterances are manifested and performed.

Paradoxically, undermining the prevalence of text as a linguistic dictum also undermines the digital nature of digital literature. This becomes clear if we take into account that texts consist of alphabetic letters—i.e., a small set of distinct, endlessly combinable symbols. With respect to the semiotic paradigm of the material (the distinct units), literature has, as Schäfer and Gendolla remind us, always been the result of digital coding. If the production of the letters is based on the binary code—as the operational paradigm of digital media—literature becomes digital in a double way. However, if we agree on the criterion that digital literature uses digital technology in order to be more than regular text, if we agree that in the case of digital literature writing exceeds the writing of text and includes the generation of visual, sonic and performative elements (which in contrast to letters do not appear as distinct units), then the second layer of being digital (within the medium computer) undermines the first (within the material). To put it another way: If literature in digital media only consists of letters as digital units, then it is not digital literature, for it does not apply the specific features of digital media. "Real" digital literature proceeds beyond the linguistic layer of digitality.

Going beyond the linguistic digital unit implicitly and potentially moves the subject at hand from the realm of literature towards the realm of the arts. The question of when to call a specific aesthetic phenomenon digital *art* rather than digital literature may be accompanied by the question of how much text such a phenomenon must contain in order to still call it *literature*. However, the counting of words or letters may not be the most sufficient means for deciding this question since there are many works that provide a lot of words and letters but nonetheless can be perceived without any reading. Hence, a more appropriate question may be how the audience engages with a piece that contains letters without being reduced to pure text. If the piece still requires reading as a central activity, we may call it digital literature. If it allows playing with the letters as mere visual objects—as is the case in *Text Rain* by Camille Utterback and Romy Achituv as well as *Re:positioning Fear* by Rafael Lozano-Hemmer—we may consider it digital art. As the mentioned works exemplify, the choice can be left to the audience and can, as in the case of *Listening Post* by Mark Hansen and Ben Rubin for instance, also be switched within the moment and place of perception.[3] However, in academic research the demarcation between digital literature and digital art is, as N. Katherine Hayles notes, "often more a matter of the critical traditions from which the works are discussed than anything intrinsic to the works themselves" (12) and, we may add, their likely or observed way of perception.

Hayles' assumption about the role of the researchers' individual preferences and prejudices seems to be confirmed by Maria Goicoechea's observation within the context of Spain that some critics (Goicoechea calls them *technosceptics*) still consider language the actual material of digital literature and hence expect digital literature to retain the domain of the word over other signifying elements, while others (the *technophiles*) expect digital literature to transcend the realm of the word in favor of a hypermedia genre following experiments in literary history such as language art and concrete poetry. With respect to experiments in the history of literature and the arts, Schäfer and Gendolla point to the precursors of certain phenomena in the realm of digital media but also warn against oversimplified contextualization considering the completely different technological and inter-relational (artist-work-audience) settings of seemingly similar artifacts in classical avant-garde and contemporary digital arts: "What, on the surface, seem to be resemblances or analogies of new media art to the modernist tradition, are symptoms of a radical change in media technologies whose mid- and long-term consequences we are only beginning to realize." The risk of explaining digital literature inaccurately from the logic of parenthood should of course (as Koskimaa is pointing out in his essay in Part Two) not prevent anyone from beginning a course on digital literature with lectures on classical avant-garde (Futurism, Dadaism, Surrealism) and later experimental writing such as mail-art, concrete poetry, sound poetry, and Oulipo. The overall task, it seems, is to be aware of the historic continuities as well as discontinuities that materialize in digital literature or art respectively.

Going beyond the traditional use of letters as signs with a linguistic value has not only consequences for the definition of the literary in digital literature but also for the historic contextualization of digital literature. It is obvious that digital literature is partaking of the literary tradition as well as of the developments in other art genres and hence ought to be discussed including this broader spectrum. Such multiple partaking places digital literature among different media and, consequently, among different academic disciplines. The subject, whose central feature Schäfer and Gendolla define as connectivity, is interconnected in a very complex net of different academic disciplines among which are not only aesthetic ones such as literary studies, performance studies and visual arts, but also computer science and, focusing on the aspect of networks and connectivity in a more general way, sociology and neuroscience. This specific characteristic and history of digital literature naturally makes it difficult to find the right institutional location for this subject. The contributions to Part Two in this book report on these difficulties, which I will discuss in the second section of my introduction to this part. The following section, however, explores the consequences the specific characteristics of digital literature have for the methodological approach to this subject.

2   Reading Digital Literature

While early scholarship discussed digital literature primarily against the background of contemporary theories such as post-structuralism and postmodernism, this book intends to discuss, beyond the meta-theoretical component, the aesthetic effects of the new phenomenon. A starting point is certainly an enhanced differentiation of the various forms of digital literature and a greater specificity about the forms and roles of computation involved in the works we are considering. Wardrip-Fruin, claiming such differentiation and specificity, for example distinguishes between "computationally variable" and "computationally fixed" digital literature depending on whether the computation is defined in a manner that varies the work's behavior (as in random text generation or interactive work) or does not lead to variation (if the narrative appears repeatedly in a predetermined way). The earlier can be further differentiated between those works that vary with or without input from outside the work's material. Within the works affected by outside input (Wardrip-Fruin speaks of "*interactive* variable digital literature"), one can distinguish yet again between those that are modified by human or by non-human input.

Such a formalistic approach may avoid the generalization known from early scholarship regarding digital literature. However, it may also obstruct the attention to the single work if it is still understood as an object of technology rather than as an act of creative expression. Though the study of digital literature, no doubt, ought to take into account non-linguistic features of the text (navigational, interactive, performative, multimedial aspects) that are no less definitive of its literariness, it should not, as Zuern underlines, emphasize medial specifics at the expense of the concrete object. Zuern warns of what in post-structural criticism is called "thematic" reading and which often also appears with respect to the underlying technology of digital literature. While we should pay attention to the underlying technology and the presupposed predecessors of digital literature, we must, Zuern holds, not reduce the specific example of digital literature to becoming a representative of digital media, "cyberculture," or what Hayles calls "legacy concepts." Zuern's notion presents a methodical approach quite different from Wardrip-Fruin's and is certainly appropriate if it does not mean neglecting the historic context and medial determination of a specific artifact. While we must not be indifferent to the specificity of the genre of digital literature, we also should not be indifferent to the particularity of its concrete examples. To put it in this way: In contrast to general theoretization, rigorous close reading starts with looking at the trees rather than at the forest.

But what are the techniques of close reading that account for the media-specific and cross-media figuration of digital literature? What might be a useful framework for thinking about the elements and contexts of works of digital literature? "What do we need to read, to interpret, when we read digital literature?", Wardrip-Fruin asks himself. His answer: We must read both data and process; the data of a work being words, images, and sounds, and the process being algorithms and calculations carried out by the work. Wardrip-Fruin then expands his model and includes interaction, surface, and context, the first signifying change to the work coming from the outside, the middle being the site of the work's presentation (and any interaction), and the last signifying the technological context (the software used to access data and process) as well as the social context of the recipients. Such a five-part model covers the different aspects of a work of digital literature contributing to its overall meaning and it seems to be a good point of departure for a systematic close reading.

Worth considering is also the two-perspective model by Koskimaa which by aiming at the perceiver rather than at the work raises the question "Is the code part of the work?" From the perspective of the user, Koskimaa notes, most works don't need any knowledge (beyond the ability to install a work).[4] The situation is different from the perspective of the researcher and teacher who may be unable to undertake a systematic analysis of a work and to establish an accurate description of it without understanding the basics of programming. This model reflects the real situation of the encounter with digital artworks; namely, that most people in the audience will not know how the work is programmed and, even if they did, would not know what difference it makes. It seems obvious that it is the job of the researcher and teacher to recognize the difference in a similar way as the professional critic of a painting, sculpture or conventional literary text does whose knowledge of art or literary history allows her to recognize and point out the intertextuality and connotations of the work. But is it really the same? Is the equivalent to the specific code used in the case of digital art really art history in the case of painting?

Isn't the counterpart to code rather paint, material or technique (i.e., woodcut, etching, drawing, watercolor, fresco, oil)? While we are unsure how much the professional art critics (need to) know about paint, we are certain that the technique used in any visual art defines how the visual appears and this definitely has to be factored into the interpretation. The technique, we may say, is part of the message; the woodcut is not purely by chance one of the prevalent techniques in Expressionism. Hence, when Koskimaa talks of the possibility that the work generates new contents during the reading process or imitates loop-effects through certain circular structures, we may either (as users) interpret these phenomena as such, or (as researchers/teachers) interpret with respect to the program language (technique) within which it is carried out. In the first case we will rather look for meaning; in the second we will first of all acknowledge virtuosity. Thus, Koskimaa's two-perspective model appears to be not simply about different depths in the perception and reading of a work but about different directions and even conceptualizations of art. It remains to be discussed what consequences this kind of "double aesthetic" has for the author/programmer of digital art and how the researcher/teacher should position herself (in contrast or accordance to the user).[5]

An approach to digital literature without focusing on materials or techniques but rather on art history is the approach from the perspective of a specific genre as exercised by Schäfer and Gendolla, who discuss the matter of narrative coherence and reading pleasure with respect to the detective story in digital media. While to a certain extent readers always act like detectives trying to figure out the meaning of a text by collecting "evidence," it can be said that particularly with respect to interactive digital literature the reader duplicates the investigation of the detective reconstructing the story by reconstructing the text. However, it is obvious that the specific structure of the hypertext and the unstable text of permutative literature contradict the central aesthetic elements of this genre: suspense and the discovery of carefully hidden information. The problem is not necessarily that the reader's interactivity inevitably interrupts her immersion into the story. As long as the reader's exact observation of the text and reasoning about the data revealed is rewarded with access to the next segment of text, she can still feel like a real detective coming closer and closer to the solution of the case as demonstrated by the discussed computer game *Sherlock Holmes: The Case of the Silver Earring*. The problem occurs when information is disclosed at the wrong time as can be expected in alternatively navigable hyperfictions.[6] One conclusion is to "discipline" the hypertext by forcing it to reveal information into the desired, predetermined order which can be ensured by "conditional links" linking only after certain requirements (like visiting other text segments first) are fulfilled. Among the interesting results of Schäfer's and Gendolla's discussion is the fact that literature does not work if it intends to work like "real life." This becomes clear when Jean-Pierre Balpe justifies the fact that his generative crime novel *Trajectoires* does not provide the reader with the same clues again if she returns to the same page for a second time, remarking that this is exactly what a cop would experience in real life: You met a concierge who told you something, you see her again three hours later and she does not tell you the same thing again. This may reflect the everyday working situation of detectives and policemen, Schäfer and Gendolla comment on Balpe, but it infringes on the narrative trajectory of the detective novel.

Interesting in this context is also Karin Wenz' account of the relationship between computer games and fanfiction pointing to the narratological characteristics of computer games: the fact that the roles of the protagonist of the narrative and the player often conflate and that the protagonist's (or avatar's) character remains flat since its functionality in the game world is more important than its fully developed personality. This specific trait of the computer game genre stimulates and allows the fans' further development of the game's characters, which is why Wenz answers the old dispute whether games possess narrativity in a quite surprising way: "Games possess narrativity as they function as source for fanfiction." Apart from the narratological point and transmedial aspect (games as source for text), fanfictions—not only those based on computer games—also allow engaging in a political discussion of contemporary culture as they confront the paradox that blockbusters such as *Star Wars* and *Lord of the Rings* trigger a "productive reception" in which the "passive," allegedly distracted consumer appropriates the product of the culture industry (as Adorno would have said) by way of "poaching"—as Henry Jenkins defined this form of appropriation in his essay "Star Trek Rerun, Reread, Rewritten: Fan Writing as Textual Poaching" (37-60).

Another approach strongly indebted to the receptive and interactive implications of game studies is Astrid Ensslin's concept of cybersomatic criticism. Along with Hayles (118) and inspired by phenomenologists such as Mark B. Hansen and Maurice Merleau-Ponty, Ensslin focuses on the human body as an integral part of the reading process, which has been categorically neglected by reader-centered literary criticism. Especially in the case of Kate Pullinger et al.'s *The Breathing Wall* where the reader gains access to the text depending on her breathing, the reader's body becomes part of a cybernetic feedback loop. In this feedback loop, both machine and human operator engage in a perpetual process of stimulus and response, of mutual action and reaction, which seems to shift power away from the user to the machine, and creates a communicative circuit between biological/human and technological/digital organisms. This idea more generally calls out for an innovative focus on the physical and physiological situatedness of reading, which Ensslin initiates with her reading of *The Breathing Wall*.

Informed by traditional literary studies rather than by the poetics of a traditional genre is the methodical model provided in Zuern's close reading example that focuses on the figuration in digital and non-digital literature. Such a focus is common practice in literary analysis, though now figuration is analyzed not only in verbal but also in visual and procedural forms, comparing and discussing the material differences between conventional and digital literature. In his analysis of Rudy Lemcke's 2002 digital video piece *The Uninvited*—a combination of photography, poetry, animation, music, and display space that represents the hallucinatory thoughts of a homeless Vietnam war veteran, Zuern refers to Rainer Maria Rilke's 1902 poem "Autumn" for its thematic similarity: both texts transform and elevate the clichéd topos of autumn leaves into an emblem of ethical responsibility. Rilke's poem gradually transforms "falling" from a physical movement of dying leaves to a metaphysical condition of existence. Lemcke's video piece presents shadow puppets made of leaves that function as tropes not because of linguistic figuration (as in Rilke's poem) but because of the process of their production: the shadow puppets are photographs of three-dimensional puppets constructed from dried plants in San Francisco's Golden Gate Park, the images posterized with the software *PhotoShop* and animated, along with the text of the poem, in *AfterEffects*. According to Zuern, Lemcke's leaves, like Rilke's, have been poetically processed with the result that the literal signifiers refer to deviant, indeterminate signifieds. However, while Rilke's anthropomorphization of the leaves is carried out in the poem, Lemcke's anthropomorphization of the leaves is carried out in the process of producing the images used in the video, i.e., outside of the artifact itself. In order to make sure the leaves eventually function as trope, *The Uninvited* actually needs a paratext explaining the material background of the video's images. It goes without saying that the audience also needs to read this paratext. The comparison Zuern undertakes between the example of conventional literature and the example of digital literature leads to the conclusion that in digital literature the figuration is not only carried out with means other than linguistic ones but is also carried out outside of the artifact with the consequence that the audience not only can fail to understand the shift of the literal to the figurative signifier; it can also fail to understand being exposed to this shift at all.

Zuern's cross-media application of classical criteria in the analysis of literature bears the question to what extent other concepts used in classical rhetoric can be applied in the reading of digital literature. If, for instance, in conventional literature the notion of rhyme represents the repetition of identical or similar sounds in words, in the context of digital literature one may also take into account the repetition of identical or similar animation as a new way of creating paradigmatic relationships within elements of a kinetic text. In a similar way allegory, traditionally understood as a narrative representation of ideas and principles by characters and events, may now be carried out by the animation of words. Such questions are discussed systematically by Alexandra Saemmer, who illustrates with several examples from French and American digital literature the suitability of classical rhetoric terms for the study of digital literature. Saemmer is aware of the fact that the conventional taxonomy, developed to characterize *textual* phenomena, has only limited value when describing the stylistic devices of digital literature, which naturally include other semiotic systems such as the visual and the performative. Consequently, in her discussion of interfacial media figures, Saemmer develops her own terminology such as "kinaesthetic rhymes" and "kinetic allegory" or "transfiguration" (morphing a word into another), "interfacial antagonism" (where the media content provoked by the interactive gesture is contrary to the announced and expected content) and "interfacial pleonasm" (where the interactive gesture does not provoke the emergence of additional information). With this terminology Saemmer also offers a way to explore the literary qualities of a link, one of the main features of digital literature. Analagous to natural language, and similar to Strehovec with his reference to Russian Formalism, Saemmer holds, it is the undermining of established grammatical rules that constitutes literariness: the incongruous, seemingly "irrelevant" link. Insofar as such a discrepancy with common usage runs the risk of being perceived as a malfunction, the *literary* collides with media *literacy*. Saemmer concludes that only consistency between a detected incongruity and the context helps in deciding whether one is confronted with a bug or an intentionally created figure, thus demanding a stabilization of the destabilization. It will—this is the (pedagogic) consequence of such a theoretical perspective—be important to understand (and teach) that certain grammatical rules of digital language are creatively dismissed on behalf of the poetic function of the digital text.

There are other concepts used to describe the specific experience of digital literature and arts, sometimes illustrating certain feelings triggered in this experience already with the terminology employed. With respect to the collaboration between the human author and the machine and the creation of the work by the computer or the World Wide Web, Koskimaa discusses the position of the "cyborg-author." With respect to the hyperlink, Strehovec, for instance, speaks of "techno-suspense" and "techno-surprise": the uncertainty when the reader clicks on the link and the sensation when she arrives at the new unit after that click. With respect to the uncertainty and uncontrollability of the appearance of a coded work on computers with different hard- and software, Saemmer quotes Philippe Bootz' concept of an "aesthetics of frustration." It is worth noting how here the performativity of the computer leads to the (unconscious) appropriation of a concept known from performance studies. In her seminal essay *Performance and Theatricality: The Subject Demystified* (1982), Josette Féral notes that the absence of narrativity in performance art "leads to a certain frustration on the part of the spectator" (215). This "aesthetics of frustration" has been described by Randy Martin as a replacement of the "solitary authority of the symbolic with the polyphonous circulation of human feeling;" the performing body is—as *phenomenal* body—"resistance to the symbolic, which attempts to limit the meanings of action and the body, to channel the flows of desire" (175). In the case of Saemmer and Bootz it is the absence of a solitary appearance of the work that undermines the authority of the symbolic. While the performance artist not only accepts but intends such frustration, the author of a digital artwork tries, more or less successfully, to counteract the frustration resulting from the applied technology by coding the work in such a way that it reliably appears even on different technological platforms.

Nevertheless, the lack of narrativity and meaning, discussed by Féral and others with respect to performance art, is also an element of digital literature and arts. If we consider not the performative aspect of the computer but the allowed and required performativity of the audience within an interactive work, the symbolic is, more or less, replaced by "flows of desire," as Martin puts it for performance art. Interactive art—especially installations such as *Text Rain* and *Re:positioning Fear*—produces "space-times" of "inter-human experiences," where people can elaborate "alternative forms of sociability," as the French theorist and curator Nicolas Bourriaud points out (44). It is an art that attempts "not to tell (like theater), but rather to provoke" relationships between subjects, to apply Féral's statement on performance art (215) to interactive installations. The difference, however, is the shift from frustration to pleasure: Interactive art immerses the audience into the work and thus allows focusing on action and play rather than on interpretation. The work may require a proper understanding of all the information provided, be it the specific options of interaction or the facts of the story, in order to proceed with the interaction or to the next level of the computer game. Such understanding, however, is only functional and, if it fails, does not lead to the "semiotic frustration" attributed to the non-narrative performance art. However, it is also important to keep in mind—and some close readings in this book will help us do so—that even though a work of digital literature and art may be the unpredictable result of the audience's interaction with the work and with each other, the specific mode of interaction is designed and controlled by the artist; often symbolically enough to reflect its deeper meaning. It may be possible to dismiss any reflection without feeling frustrated if the interaction itself is perceived as interesting and rewarding enough. Since it would be frustrating from the perspective of a researcher and teacher if the aesthetic experience of this new form of art were limited to functional interaction, this book promotes a semiotic reading of this new art form and aims at providing such reading with the necessary theoretical and methodical tools.

Notes

1   What Zuern, Wardrip-Fruin and others (including myself) call "authentic" digital literature is called *cybertext* by Koskimaa due certainly also to the influence of Espen Aarseth's theoretical work in Scandinavia, though Koskimaa's doctoral thesis of 2000 was still entitled *Digital Literature: From Text to Hypertext and Beyond*. Astrid Ensslin, by contrast, refers to *cybertext* in the sense of a third generation of digital literature, which is characterized by the "empowered" text/machine, i.e. the machine code which takes over control of the reading process, thus turning it into a cybernetic performance. Schäfer and Gendolla prefer the term *net literature* which was especially popular in Germany where the discussion of digital literature only began after the arrival of the Internet (Simanowski, "Interactive Fiction und Software-Narration"), although in Schäfer's and Gendolla's adoption "net" is not restricted to the Internet but also includes feedback loops in stand-alone computers and the communications of a user with her computer. If in this introduction and the introduction to Part Two the term "conventional" or "traditional" literature is used, the aim is to differentiate it from "digital" literature as defined above and not to judge its poetic quality as conventional/traditional in contrast to advanced/avant-garde. Unless stated differently, references to contributors aim at their articles in Part One.

2   Such an analogy refers to temporality not in terms of narrativity (which distinguishes both conventional literature and film from media that capture a single moment such as photograph, painting and sculpture) but aims at the kinetic aspect of the material (the moving film and the altering text on the screen).

3   Cf. my case studies of *Text Rain* and *Re:positioning Fear* using the material's function more than its proportion to distinguish between the two forms "literature" and "art" (Simanowski 2010: chapter one). Since in the mentioned interactive installations text continues to be important as a linguistic phenomenon in order to understand the work (and can be accessed in-

dependently of the installation as conventional text on a web site), we may also consider it digital *literature* depending on how the audience engages with the work. In the case of *Listening Post* the option of perceiving the text as linguistic utterance or as audio-visual object exists at the exhibition venue and depends on the audience's physical distance to the work (cf. chapter six).

4   As an example that does require a more profound understanding of the software environment also from the user, Koskimaa mentions *code art*; i.e., poems written in a way that work as executable code in a certain programming language.

5   One consequence is implicitly alluded to by the distinction between the author and the programmer of a digital artwork with the author commonly conceptualizing what to do (what it could mean) and the programmer considering how to do it (how the code would be most effective, elegant, sophisticated).

6   It should be pointed out that hyperfiction is a specific way of structuring text which also may be considered a specific technique of presenting information, but should not be mistaken for what was defined as technique in terms of program language before; there are different techniques (program languages) to create the structure of a hypertext.

Works Cited

Aarseth, Espen J. *Cybertext: Perspectives on Ergodic Literature.* Baltimore: Johns Hopkins UP, 1997.

Bourriaud, Nicolas. *Relational Aesthetics.* Paris: Les presses du réel, 2002.

Féral, Josette. "Performance and Theatricality: The Subject Demystified." *Performance: Critical Concepts in Literary and Cultural Studies.* Ed. Philip Auslander. Taylor & Francis, 1982. 206-217.

Hansen, Mark, and Ben Rubin. *Listening Post.* Installation. 2000-2001.

Hayles, N. Katherine. *Electronic Literature: New Horizons for the Literary.* Notre Dame: U of Notre Dame P, 2008.

Jenkins, Henry. *Fans, Bloggers, and Gamers: Exploring Participatory Culture.* New York: New York UP, 2006.

Koskimaa, Raine. *Digital Literature. From Text to Hypertext and Beyond.* University of Jyväskylä. 2000. 20 Mar. 2009 <http://www.users.jyu.fi/~koskimaa/thesis/thesis.shtml>.

Lemcke, Rudy. *The Uninvited. Light F/X.* DVD. 2005.

Lozano-Hemmer, Rafael. *Re:positioning Fear.* Installation. 1997.

Martin, Randy. *Performance as Political Act: The Embodied Self.* New York: Bergin and Garvey, 1990.

Pullinger et al. *The Breathing Wall.* CD-ROM. 2004

Sherlock Holmes: The Case of the Silver Earring. CD-ROM. Frogwares, 2004.

Simanowski, Roberto. *Against the Embrace: The Recovery of Meaning Through the Reading of Digital Arts.* Minneapolis: U of Minnesota P, 2010. Forthcoming.

———. "Interactive Fiction und Software-Narration: Begriff und Bewertung digitaler Literatur." *Liter@tur. Computer/Literatur/Internet: Beiträge zu einer Theorie einer digitalen Literatur.* Ed. Torsten Liesegang and Hansgeorg Schmidt-Bergmann. Bielefeld: Aisthesis, 2001. 117-140.

Utterback, Camille, and Romy Achituv. *Text Rain.* Installation. 1999.

Noah Wardrip-Fruin

Five Elements of Digital Literature

1   Introduction

The terms "digital literature" and "digital art" are used frequently in our field, but rarely defined. When I use them, I mean something in particular by them. Let me begin by explaining how I use them.

A phrase like "digital literature" could refer to finger-oriented literature (fingers are "digits") or numerically-displayed literature (numbers are "digits") —but I mean "digital" in relation to computers, specifically as it appears in computer engineering phrases such as "stored program electronic digital computer." I mean literary work that requires the digital computation performed by laptops, desktops, servers, cellphones, game consoles, interactive environment controllers, or any of the other computers that surround us. I think that's what most of us mean, even if we've come to it in an ad-hoc way.

To take the other term in my initial phrase, "digital literature" could be used in the sense of "the literature" (the body of scholarly work on a topic) or it could mean particularly high-status writing—but I mean "literature" (and "literary") as a way of referring to those arts we sometimes call fiction, poetry, and drama (as well as their close cousins). I mean the arts that call our attention to language, present us with characters, unfold stories, and make us reflect on the structures and common practices of such activities. I should probably also say that I don't view the literary arts as a citadel, separate (and perhaps in need of defense) from, say, visual or performing arts. Much of the best drama, for example, brings together the literary, performing, and visual arts.

To me, "digital art" is the larger category of which "digital literature" is a part. It encompasses all the arts that require digital computation, not just the literary arts.

I write all this because, as an artist and scholar in the field of digital literature, I've begun to try to think more generally about the field of which I'm a part. I do this on one level because I'm curious about certain topics. For example: Where did this field begin? But at a deeper level I'm interested in questions of how we conceptualize what we make and study. The question that motivates my writing here is one of these: What might be a useful framework for thinking about the elements and context of works of digital literature? To put it another way: What do we need to read, to interpret, when we read digital literature?

2 Turing, Strachey, Love Letters

2.1 Turing Machines get Electronic

When I say that I mean "digital" as in "stored program electronic digital computer," what does that mean, more precisely?

In 1937 everyone who used the term "computer" knew what it meant. A computer was a person who calculated answers to mathematical problems.[1] These computers weren't expected to develop new, creative methods to prove outstanding mathematical problems. Rather, they were expected to follow a known and specified set of instructions which, together, formed an effective procedure for solving a particular kind of problem. We call such sets of instructions algorithms (from the name of Arabian mathematician al-Khwarizmi, Hillis 78).

But with the publication, in 1937, of Alan Turing's "On Computable Numbers" the world was quietly introduced to the mathematical thought experiment that we call a "Turing machine"—a concept that lay the groundwork for the kinds of non-human computers we have today. Turing's paper wasn't remarkable for imagining a machine that could carry out the work of human computers. In the 1930s there were already in operation a number of such machines (including Vannevar Bush's *Differential Analyzer*) and at least 100 years earlier (by 1837) Charles Babbage had conceived of an Analytical Engine, capable of mechanizing any mathematical operation.[2] Two things, however, separated Turing machines from all calculating machines in operation in the 1930s (and most of the 1940s) as well as all previous thought experiments (including Babbage's).

First, according to Turing's most prominent biographer, the Turing machine was developed in response to a mathematical question (posed by Hilbert) as to whether mathematics was decidable (cf. Hodges). That is, was there a method that could be applied to any assertion that would correctly determine whether that assertion was true? The Turing machine was a formalization that made it possible to discuss what could and couldn't be calculated—answering Hilbert's question in the negative, and establishing one of the primary foundations for computer science as a science (the investigation of what can and can't be computed).

Second, the imagined design of the Turing machine was in terms of a potentially implementable (if inefficient) mechanism. This mechanism was such that it could not only logically branch while following its instructions (doing one thing or another based on results to that point), and not only act as a universal machine (simulating the activities of any other calculating machine), but also store its instructions in the same read/write memory as the data on which it acted. This would make it possible, for example, for the machine to alter its own instructions while in operation. And it is from this type of capability that we get the words "stored program" in the phrase "stored program electronic digital computer." This lies at the heart of the computers we use each day.

This leaves us with the words "electronic" and "digital." The first of these can probably pass without definition—but the second is in need of clarification, especially given the mystifying ways in which it is sometimes used. Being digital, as it were, is not specific to computers, despite the fact that it's the word we've latched onto in order to represent computers. "Digital" information, as opposed to "analog" information, is represented by discrete rather than continuous values. It's actually related, according to the *Oxford English Dictionary,* to the sense of fingers and numbers as "digits." Each of the first nine Arabic numbers (or ten, if one includes zero) can be expressed with one figure, a digit, and these were originally counted on the fingers, or digits. Charles Babbage's Analytical Engine called for representing decimal numbers using ten-spoke wheels—which made it a design for a digital computer, because each of the ten wheel positions was discrete.[3] During World War II Konrad Zuse built the first program controlled digital computer that, instead of Babbage's decimal arithmetic, used binary arithmetic implemented in on/off electronics. This was a considerable simplification and made possible advances in increased speed and precision—important to our "digital" computers. Working independently (and very secretly) the British government cryptanalysis group of which Turing was part (and where he was instrumental in cracking the German Enigma code) created the *Colossus,* which has been characterized as the first fully functioning electronic digital computer.[4]

It was only after the war that a number of successful efforts were made toward stored program electronic digital computers. The first was the Manchester University *Baby* in 1948 (it used a CRT display for its storage) which was followed by a more complex Manchester prototype in 1949 and then replaced by an industrially manufactured version, the *Ferranti Mark I,* in 1951. Turing wrote the programming manual for the *Mark I* and constructed a random number generator that produced truly random digits from noise.[5]

2.2 Strachey's Next Step

Once there were stored program digital computers, all that remained (for our field to take its first step) was for someone to make literary use of one. I believe that—in 1952, working on the Manchester *Mark I*—Christopher Strachey was the first to do so.

Strachey went up to King's College, Cambridge, in 1935. While this is the same time and place where Turing was doing his fundamental work on computable numbers (as a recently-graduated junior research fellow) it is likely that the two knew each other only socially, and never discussed computing. Strachey worked as a physicist and schoolmaster after graduating from Cambridge, becoming increasingly interested in computing during the late 1940s. In January 1951 he was first exposed to a stored-program computer: the Pilot ACE computer under construction at the National Physical Laboratory. He began writing a program to make it play draughts (checkers), inspired by a June 1950 article in *Penguin Science News*.

That spring Strachey learned of the *Mark I* computer that had just been installed at Manchester—he had known Turing just well enough at Cambridge to ask for, and receive, a copy of the programmer's manual. He visited for the first time in July, and discussed his ideas for a draughts-playing program with Turing, who was much impressed and suggested that the problem of making the machine simulate itself using interpretive trace routines would also be interesting. Strachey, taken with Turing's suggestion, went away and wrote such a program, establishing his reputation immediately.

A year later, in June 1952, Strachey had wound up his responsibilities as a schoolmaster and officially began full-time computing work as an employee of the National Research and Development Corporation. That summer he developed—with some aesthetic advice from his sister Barbara, using Turing's random number generator, and perhaps in collaboration with Turing—a *Mark I* program that created combinatory love letters. This was the first piece of digital literature, and of digital art, predating by a decade the earliest examples of digital computer art from recent surveys (e.g., Paul).

Strachey described the operations of this program in a 1954 essay in the art journal *Encounter* (immediately following texts by William Faulkner and P. G. Wodehouse):

> Apart from the beginning and the ending of the letters, there are only two basic types of sentence. The first is "*My*—(adj.)—(noun)—(adv.)—(verb) *your*—(adj.)—(noun)." There are lists of appropriate adjectives, nouns, adverbs, and verbs from which the blanks are filled in at random. There is also a further random choice as to whether or not the adjectives and adverb are included at all. The second type is simply "*You are my*—(adj.)—(noun)," and in this case the adjective is always present. There is a random choice of which type of sentence is to be used, but if there are two consecutive sentences of the second type, the first ends with a colon (unfortunately the teleprinter of the computer had no comma) and the initial "*You are*" of the second is omitted. The letter starts with two words chosen from the special

lists; there are then five sentences of one of the two basic types, and the letter ends "*Yours*—(adv.) M. U. C." (26-27)

As Jeremy Douglass notes, the love letter generator has often been discussed in terms of queer identity, rather than in literary terms. Certainly there are reasons for this—Turing and Strachey were both gay, and at least Turing openly so.[6] It might also seem from the most widely-reproduced outputs of the generator (e.g., that found in Hodges, 477-478) that it was a love-letter generator that "could not speak its name" (the word "love" being conspicuously absent).[7] But I suspect that the primary reason for the lack of literary discussion of Strachey's generator is that the output simply isn't very compelling. Here, for example, are the two outputs reproduced in *Encounter*:

> Darling Sweetheart
> You are my avid fellow feeling. My affection curiously clings to your passionate wish. My liking yearns for your heart. You are my wistful sympathy: my tender liking.
> Yours beautifully
> M. U. C.

> Honey Dear
> My sympathetic affection beautifully attracts your affectionate enthusiasm. You are my loving adoration: my breathless adoration. My fellow feeling breathlessly hopes for your dear eagerness. My lovesick adoration cherishes your avid ardour.
> Yours wistfully
> M. U. C. (26)

I would like to suggest, however, that examination of individual outputs will not reveal what is interesting about Strachey's project. As he wrote in *Encounter*: "The chief point of interest, however, is not the obvious crudity of the scheme, nor even in the ways in which it might be improved, but in the remarkable simplicity of the plan when compared with the diversity of the letters it produces" (27). That is to say, Strachey had discovered, and created an example of, the basic principles of combinatory literature—which still lie at the heart of much digital literature today (and, less commonly, non-digital works). Combinatory techniques allow a relatively small number of initial materials to be arranged, following certain rules, into a vast number of possible configurations. In relatively unconstrained systems such as Strachey's, each individual output is more likely to induce a humorous reaction than deep literary consideration. In fact, Turing biographer Hodges writes of the love letter generator that "Those doing real men's jobs on the computer, concerned with optics or aerodynamics, thought this silly, but . . . it greatly amused Alan and Christopher" (478). In the amusing nature of individual outputs, Strachey's system could be said to anticipate Roger Price and Leonard Stern's non-digital *Mad Libs* (conceived in 1953, but not published until 1958, cf. Montfort, "Literary Games"), though the love letter generator's more restrained combinatory vocabulary made it possible for most (rather than only a few) words to change from output to output. It is clear, however, from Strachey's contribution to *Encounter*, that he also understood the other side of combinatory literature— the view of the system itself when one steps back from the individual outputs, the remarkable diversity that can be produced by a simple plan. The production from such a simple plan, as has been pointed out with other combinatory texts, of more potentially different outputs than any of us could run our eyes across in a lifetime devoted to reading its output (Aarseth, "Nonlinearity and Literary Theory" 67). It is a work that can only be understood, in fact, as a system—never by an exhaustive reading of its texts.[8]

And it is not surprising that Strachey's effort is mostly of interest in terms of how it operates, rather than in the text it produces. After all, designing interesting ways for computers to operate—algorithms, processes—is at the heart of what most computer scientists and creative programmers do, from Turing and Strachey's moment to this day. In many ways we are al-Khwarizmi's descendants.

3 Data versus Process

3.1 What's a Computer for?

ACM SIGGRAPH, the Association for Computing Machinery's Special Interest Group on Computer Graphics and Interactive Techniques, holds an unusual yearly meeting. Tens of thousands of people come to see a combined industry tradeshow, scientific conference, and art gallery. One thing that is particularly striking is the differing status of images—of the products of computer graphics—in different parts of the conference. In the conference portion of SIGGRAPH, dominated by paper presentations from computer scientists, images play the role of examples and illustrations. Images are there to help explain the real results being reported—which are novel techniques, algorithms, processes. In the art gallery, while there are a few talks, most of the presentations are of art works, and most of the works are prints hung on the wall. In these prints, the images are not aids to an explanation of results—they, themselves, are the results. This can lead to some tension, because the artists know it would be impolite to call the images made by the scientists naïve and uninspiring, and the scientists know it would be impolite to call the processes used by the artists trivial and uninteresting. And such tensions aren't unknown in the field of digital literature; for example, around the literary readings held at ACM Hypertext conferences. But they can also take a somewhat different form.

Let's take a step back. Writers over the last century have often wanted to exceed the limitations of black and white text printed and bound into a traditional codex book. For example, twenty years before William Faulkner's text preceded Strachey's in *Encounter,* the 1934 *Publishers' Trade List Annual* carried a listing for a book it had also listed in 1933, but which never appeared: a four-color edition of Faulkner's *The Sound and the Fury* (cf. Meriwether). Faulkner wanted four-color printing in order to make the time shifts in the first section of the book easier for readers to follow. He worried that alternation between italic and roman type might not be sufficient, and rejected suggestions from the publisher that he felt would break the flow of the language (e.g., space breaks). But such four-color printing would have made the book, even after it was a proven critical success, prohibitively expensive for many purchasers—especially during the 1930s U.S. economic depression. With a modern computer, of course, it wouldn't be. The additional cost of transmitting colored text over the Web (an HTML file made slightly larger by tags indicating sections that should be different colors) is negligible, and the ability to display color is already present. Combining images with one's text consumes a bit more transmission bandwidth, and sounds and moving images a bit more—but for those connecting to the Internet from businesses, universities, or high-speed home connections, the difference is barely worth comment. Finally, there may be some software cost—such as for a program like Flash or After Effects, if one wants the text itself to animate—but this is generally much less than the cost of the computer itself, and miniscule compared to color printing on paper or film. This has opened vast possibilities for writers, and taken literary approaches such as animated text poetry and fiction from occasional curiosities to international movements with communities in South and North America, Asia, and Europe. The results also, apparently, have wide appeal. For example, the 2002 *Dakota,* by Korean duo Young-Hae Chang Heavy Industries, has found an audience ranging from visitors to the Whitney Museum to browsers of popular online animation forums such as Albino Blacksheep.[9]

But from a computer science standpoint most of this work is utterly trivial. The vector animation techniques on display in *Dakota,* for example, are so well-understood that they are packaged into a mass-market tool like Flash. Other uses of computers by writers are similarly uninteresting on an algorithmic level. For example, take the area of email novels. While writers and literary critics may see a vast difference between the playful medieval sci-fi of Rob Wittig's *Blue Company* and the traditionally-structured titillating mystery of Michael Betcherman and David Diamond's *The Daughters of Freya,* on a process level they are exactly the same—human-written chunks of text sent to readers via email at timed intervals.[10]

For their part, computer scientists can claim some literary successes. The interactive character *Eliza/Doctor,* for example, was created by Joseph Weizenbaum at MIT in the mid-1960s—and has been continually read and ported to new computing platforms for four decades. Yet writers often find the work of computer scientists in digital literature quite puzzling. For example, while writers tend to assume that literary work focuses on the creation of language, Natural Language Generation (NLG) is only one area of interest for computer scientists working in digital literature.[11] Another is continuing the work on interactive characters begun with *Eliza/Doctor*—for which NLG may not be part of the research project, or which may not be experienced linguistically at all. Take, for example, the famous Oz project at Carnegie Mellon University. Their early 1990s *Lyotard* was a textual piece, presenting a simulated house cat with an intriguing personality living in a simulated apartment, in which the user read descriptions (to understand the world and the cat) and wrote them (in order to take actions and perhaps befriend the cat). While not a traditional form of writing, the output of the system is certainly recognizable to writers. But the Oz project's *The Edge of Intention,* which from a computer science perspective was part of the same research project on believable characters, featured no text at all—instead presented entirely as real-time animation (Bates). The same is true in the area of story generation. Some systems, such as Selmer Bringsjord and David Ferrucci's *Brutus,* are constructed with generation of literary text as an important part of their operations. But others focus entirely on generating story structures, with text output nothing more than a report on the structure, as is apparent in this simple example from Raymond Lang's *Joseph*:

> once upon a time there lived a dog. one day it happened that farmer evicted cat. when this happened, dog felt pity for the cat. in response, dog sneaked food to the cat. farmer punished dog. (139)

From this we could say that our stereotypes have been confirmed. Writers innovate on the surface level, on the reading words level—while computer scientists innovate at the process level, the algorithm level, perhaps without words at all. But as soon as this stereotype is expressed directly it also becomes apparent that it must be taken apart. And we have much more to point toward, for this purpose, than the work of those few writers who are also computer scientists.

We could begin, in fact, with the most cited example of combinatory literature: Raymond Queneau's *One Hundred Thousand Billion Poems* (1961). This work consists of ten sonnets, each of 14 lines. While one might expect, then, that this work would be more suitably titled *Ten Poems,* there is something in the construction of each poem that causes the number of potential poems to be much larger than ten. To wit: a reader can construct alternate poems by reading the first line of any of the original sonnets, followed by the second line of any sonnet, followed by the third line of any sonnet—and find that the whole work is artfully constructed so that any reading of this sort produces a sonnet that functions syntactically, metrically, and in its rhyme scheme. And here we see combinatory literature as (independently) discovered by a writer. Strachey's generator contains many more possible variations in each few lines of output, but there need be nothing artful in the selection of words—a thesaurus search for terms related to love will do the trick. Queneau's *Poems,* on the other hand, is a high-wire act of writing. He has created a process, but a process that only works when real attention is given to the words.

And Queneau, as a writer inventing processes—whether carried out by the reader or the writer—was far from unique. In fact, he was a co-founder of the Oulipo (Workshop for Potential Literature) in 1962, a larger group of writers and mathematicians that, to this day, continue such investigations. And we should not forget that, even before the Oulipo, 20th century literary practice already had been shaped by the process-heavy experiments of William S. Burroughs, the Surrealists, the Dada movement, and others. Clearly we need some way of framing these issues more accurately than "writers vs. computer scientists."

3.2   Crawford's "Process Intensity"

Chris Crawford, a noted computer game designer and theorist, writes about the concept of "process intensity":

> Process intensity is the degree to which a program emphasizes processes instead of data. All programs use a mix of process and data. Process is reflected in algorithms, equations, and branches. Data is reflected in data tables, images, sounds, and text. A process-intensive program spends a lot of time crunching numbers; a data-intensive program spends a lot of time moving bytes around.

For our purposes, this distinction between process-intensive and data-intensive maps nicely onto the inappropriate stereotype distinction between writers and computer scientists. Crawford's terminology is a more accurate and useful way of talking about these differences in approach to digital literature. When a work of digital literature emphasizes words, images, and sounds, those are all data. When it emphasizes algorithms and calculations, those are process.

And here, I believe, we come to the first part of an answer to the question posed in this essay's introduction: "What do we need to read, to interpret, when we read digital literature?" We must read both process and data. This is true, of course, not only for work in digital literature, and not only for the writers cited above for their innovation at the process level, but also for composers such as John Cage, artists such as those associated with the Fluxus group, and dramatists such as Augusto Boal.[12] In all of these cases, we are interpreting works that emphasize data and process to differing extents (and employ them in differing ways) and which cannot be fully interpreted from a sample output.

But this isn't all we need to interpret.

4 Interactions

4.1 Turing Test vs. Turing Machine

While the term "Turing machine" is quite famous in computer science circles, in popular culture Alan Turing's name is more often associated with the so-called "Turing test."

Turing, however, actually proposed a game, rather than a test. In a 1950 article in the journal *Mind*, he proposed the "imitation game." This game has three participants: "a man (A), a woman (B), and an interrogator (C) who may be of either sex." During the course of the game the interrogator asks questions of A and B, trying to determine which of them is a woman. A and B, of course, do their best to convince C to see it their way—the woman by telling the truth, the man by "imitation" of a woman. The proposed game was to be played over a teletype, so that nothing physical (tone of voice, shape of handwriting) could enter into C's attempt to discern the gender of the other players based on their performances.

Turing then asked, "What will happen when the machine takes the part of A in this game?" That is, what will happen when a machine, a computer, tries to "pass" as female—rather than a man attempting to pass in this way—under the questioning of the human, C? Turing proposed this as a replacement for the question, "Can machines think?"[13] (Turing 434)

Turing's paper is important for a number of reasons. One, as Nick Montfort has pointed out (Wardrip-Fruin and Montfort 49), is simply that it proposed a linguistic, conversational mode of computing at a time when almost everyone thought of computers as number crunchers. For philosophers, the primary audience of *Mind*, it provided a specific, phenomenological formulation of the "problem" of machine intelligence. For the not-yet-born field of Artificial Intelligence it provided inspiration. But for our purposes it provides something much more basic: an early, clear instance of digital media conceived as an interactive experience.

Remember, Turing machines give us a way of thinking about what is computable—that is, what questions can we pose and receive an answer? But, as Peter Wegner and others have pointed out in recent years, much of the computing we do each day is not of this form. Rather than a posed question to which we receive (or fail to receive) an answer, interactive computing assumes an ongoing set of processes, accepting and responding to input from the outside world, and in some cases (e.g., airline reservation systems) with any ending considered a failure. Or, as Wegner puts it:

> Claim: Interaction-machine behavior is not reducible to Turing-machine behavior.
> Informal evidence of richer behavior: Turing machines cannot handle the passage of time or interactive events that occur during the process of computation.
> Formal evidence of irreducibility: Input streams of interaction machines are not expressible by finite tapes, since any finite representation can be dynamically extended by uncontrollable adversaries. (83)

That is to say, there is a real, definable difference between a program like the love letter generator and a program for playing the imitation game. The generator runs and produces an output, using its data and processes, and is completely representable by a Turing machine. But to play the imitation game requires data, processes, and an openness to ongoing input from outside the system that results in different behavior by the system—interaction—something for which at least some computer scientists believe a Turing machine is insufficient.

4.2 Forms and Roles of Computation

Of course, many of the most significant forms of digital literature involve interaction of some sort. Confusingly, in common discussion of digital literature some of these interactive forms have been defined using terms that specify system behavior, while others have been defined in terms of user experience. For example, "hypertext" is specified at the level of system behavior. A hypertext is a text that—according to the term's coiner, Ted Nelson—will "branch or perform on request" (by links or other means) (cf. Wardrip-Fruin, "What Hypertext Is"). On the other hand, "interactive drama" is a term for interactive digital literature that produces for users an experience related to theatrical drama—and how the system behaves while producing this experience is not specified. In fact, there is no reason that the experience of interactive drama could not be produced through a system that presents users with hypertext. However, we might have trouble discussing this work in digital literature circles, because we have become so accustomed to viewing "hypertext fiction" and "exploration-based fiction" as synonymous, even though the system behavior of hypertext does not specify that the user experience be exploration based.[14]

To read digital literature well, we need to be specific about system behavior and user experience—and explicitly aware that data's impact on experience is at least as great as process and interaction. Films and codex books, for example, mainly have very similar forms of system behavior and user interaction, but differing data produces a variety of user experiences. And while it seems true that the link-based hypertext interaction of systems such as Storyspace lends itself to exploration-based fiction, we also have some evidence that quite different "locative media" technologies (such as those used in Teri Rueb's *Itinerant*) are good platforms for exploration-based fiction, and link-based hypertext has shown itself effective for utterly different experiences of fiction (such as in Scott McCloud's "Carl Comics").[15]

In grappling with the various forms of digital literature, I believe we would also benefit from greater specificity about the forms and roles of computation involved in the works we are considering. One approach to beginning this effort would be to propose different distinctions and see what organizations of the field result—both those that run along and those that cut across the grain of our current intuitions.

For example, we could distinguish (1) between (a) digital literary works for which computation is required only in the authoring process and (b) those for which it is also required during the time of reception by the audience. In this case, (a) includes Strachey's love letter generator, computer-generated stories and books of poetry, and any literary prints hung on the wall at SIGGRAPH. We might call it "digitally-authored literature." Conversely, (b) includes *Dakota* if viewed on a computer screen, *Eliza/Doctor* and all other interactive works, email novels, and any literary uses of virtual reality Caves, web browsers, cell phones, game consoles, and so on. We might call this "digital media literature."

A different approach would distinguish (2) between (a) those works in which the processes are defined in a manner that varies the work's behavior (randomly or otherwise) and (b) those that contain nothing within their process definitions that leads to variation. In this case (a) again includes Strachey's generator, and story generators, but also all interactive works, while (b) includes *Dakota,* most email narratives, and so on. A rather different arrangement, which we might refer to as "computationally variable" and "computationally fixed" digital literature.

Within category 2a we could make a further distinction (3) between those that vary (a) without input from outside the work's material and (b) with input from outside. Here (a) includes Strachey's generator, and most poem and story generators, while (b) includes pieces that change based on the day's news, or user interaction, or other inputs. We might call these "batch-mode" and "interactive" variable digital literature.

And within 3b we could distinguish yet again (4) between those that vary with input (a) other than from humans, aware of the work, and (b) from humans aware of the work. Interestingly, (a) includes few works of digital literature, though it is an active area of digital art, including works that vary with network behavior (clients for RSG's *Carnivore*), the weather (John Klima's *Earth*), and the stock market (Lynn Hershman's *Synthia*); while it is (b) that includes popular literary forms such as hypertext fiction (Stuart Moulthrop's *Victory Garden*), interactive characters (*Eliza/Doctor*), and interactive fiction (Marc Blank and Dave Lebling's *Zork*). We might call these "environmentally" and "audience" interactive digital literature. It should be noted, of course, that this distinction (unlike others above) is not exclusive. *The Impermanence Agent* (by Noah Wardrip-Fruin, Brion Moss, Adam Chapman, and Duane Whitehurst) is an example of digital literature that is both environmentally and audience interactive.[16]

There is the potential for these sorts of distinctions to be of use in our conversations about digital literature, especially in combination (or tension) with existing groupings based on perceived genre. They help us name more precisely, for example, how the computationally variable email messages delivered by Rob Bevan and Tim Wright's *Online Caroline* (which are part of a larger audience interactive system) differ from those of most email narratives (which are generally computationally fixed) though the messages themselves are not interactive in either case.[17] These distinctions may also help us understand the relationship between the body of work in digital literature and in the broader digital arts—as well as the relationship between digital literature and computational systems more generally. Finally, we may also begin to use terms such as "random" or "interactive" more specifically.

But I believe there remains more I need to learn to read, in order to read digital literature.

5 Context

5.1 Computation as Context

At this point, in order to continue to broaden our view of digital literature, we need to begin to consider works that I still, frankly, find a bit puzzling. Here is an example of the kind of question that puzzles me: How do we understand the difference between an email narrative such as *Blue Company* and Bram Stoker's *Dracula*? Both, after all, are epistolary stories. Neither is interactive or otherwise computationally variable. But *Blue Company*'s letters originally arrived in one's email reader, with appropriate datestamps, and the timing of their arrival determined the possible timings of one's reading experience. Does this mean that there would be no difference between them if *Dracula* were separated into pieces and sent by post, receiving appropriate postmarks? No, not quite. When I say that digital literature requires digital computation, understanding computation required as context (e.g., the email reader as necessary context) is one of the challenges.

And this isn't simply for email narratives, or blog fictions, or other obviously networked forms (though Jill Walker Rettberg has begun interesting work on these and related forms under the term "distributed narrative"). As discussed earlier, works such as *Dakota* could have been created as traditional animations, and distributed on film. The dramatic growth of work in such forms isn't, however, simply an outgrowth of the availability of computer animation tools. There is something about the network, and about the growth of network culture (especially forums for posting, finding, sharing, and rating works—from sites specific to particular animation aesthetics through the teeming heterogeneity of *YouTube*) that has been important to the development of this work. And something about the ability to browse for and view this work in a web browser, using the same machine used for work, during any brief break from work. Here it seems likely that those of us studying digital literature could learn from work undertaken by Rettberg's colleagues in the Association of Internet Researchers.

But we also have a tradition, in digital literature, of "artifactual" work—which presents itself as a collection of computer files or systems, rather than as a literary work. The operations of a piece such as John McDaid's *Uncle Buddy's Phantom Funhouse* (delivered as a box of digital and non-digital artifacts supposedly left behind by the reader's recently deceased uncle) have nothing to do with the network. As McDaid explains:

To be precise, in artifactual hypertext, the narrator disappears into the interface, with the logic of the hypertext becoming the "narration." Which is why, in cases where you are creating a fictional narrator who might be given to puzzles or games, such devices can be appropriate. But only within, and as aspects of, that narrating interface. (10)

Bill Bly, author of the artifactual *We Descend,* joins McDaid in suggesting that such work is not unique to digital forms, citing Milorad Pavic's *Dictionary of the Khazars* (36). Just as we may learn about how to interpret processes through the work of those who study artists such as Cage, we may learn techniques for approaching artifactual work from those who have interpreted print texts such as Pavic's or Ursula LeGuin's *Always Coming Home.* At the same time, the fact that some digital artifactual literature is interactive—that, for example, as McDaid suggests, there can be puzzles that, when solved, alter the operations of the work's processes—points to the limits of comparisons, as does the issue of context noted above in relation to email narratives.

5.2   Computation in Context

Just as the WIMP (Windows, Icons, Menus, and Pointers) interfaces of modern computers provide a context for much digital literature, it is also important to note that other digital literature embeds its computation and data in utterly different contexts. Perhaps it will help clarify the issues if we ask ourselves another puzzling question, such as one first posed to me by Roberto Simanowski: How do we understand the difference between Guillaume Apollinaire's "Il Pleut" and Camille Utterback and Romy Achituv's *Text Rain*? Apollinaire's poem is made up of letters falling down the page like rain. Utterback and Achituv's installation takes a video image of the audience standing before it and projects that image on the wall in front of the audience, with the addition (in the video scene) of the letters of a poem falling down like rain and resting on the bodies of their readers. Obviously, one difference is the passage of time in *Text Rain,* and another difference is that *Text Rain* is audience interactive (lifting up a hand on which letters rest causes them to be raised as well). But, at least as fundamentally, another difference is that *Text Rain* is situated in a physical space other than a printed page or a computer screen, in which the method of interaction is the movement of the readers' bodies (which are represented within the work itself). I would suggest that one way of conceptualizing this is through the idea of a work's *surface,* which gives the audience access to the results of its data and processes and through which any audience interaction occurs. The surfaces of "Il Pleut" and *Text Rain* are obviously radically divergent. Simanowski has begun to think through the issues we need to consider when interpreting digital literature of *Text Rain*'s sort from a literary perspective (cf. Simanowski), but the insights of disciplines such as performance studies will also be important as we investigate further.

There are a number of forms of digital literature for which space and the body are obviously essential to our consideration—including installation art such as *Text Rain* or Bill Seaman's literary installations, locative fictions such as *Itinerant,* dance and technology pieces such as Jamie Jewett and Thalia Field's *Rest/Less,* and literary virtual reality such as *Screen* (by Noah Wardrip-Fruin, Josh Carroll, Robert Coover, Shawn Greenlee, Andrew McClain, and Ben Shine).[18] But, as N. Katherine Hayles reminds us, we're not necessarily well served by ignoring the reader's body when interpreting other works of digital literature (Hayles, "Response"). It is worth attending to the ways that our bodies become trained in the unusual WIMP mousing behavior required to engage the surface of Talan Memmott's *Lexia to Perplexia* or in the combinations and timings of game console controller manipulations required to move through Jordan Mechner and Ubisoft's *Prince of Persia: The Sands of Time.*

Of course there is also another kind of context—social context—that we have not yet discussed. Another mildly puzzling question might help bring some of these issues to the fore: How do we understand the difference between an interactive fiction such as *Zork* and a MUD or MOO? An interactive fiction is a textually-described world which one can move through by typing commands: investigating spaces, acquiring objects, and interacting with characters. MUDs and MOOs share all these characteristics with interactive fictions—the primary difference, for a first time visitor, is that the characters in the space are often real people (other visitors, experienced participants, and even those involved in constructing the world). Torill Mortensen is one of the writers who has been thinking seriously about the pleasures of experiencing these textual worlds with other players, as they are shaped through time by the actions of other players (cf. Mortensen). In a related vein, T.L. Taylor has been writing about graphical environments such as *EverQuest* in a manner that foregrounds how interactions within the simulated world are shaped by networks of relation "outside" of it (cf. Taylor and Jakobsson). Work of this sort is necessary if we are going to understand player experiences, and the context in which the performative narrative interventions of "event teams" take place in worlds such as *EverQuest* and more recent massively-multiplayer games, as well as related forms such as alternate reality games (which, following Elan Lee and Sean Stewart's foundational project *The Beast,* often involve elaborate plots and puzzles, hundreds of documents, and thousands of simultaneous reader/players in communication).

But there is much more we might consider as social context. Take, for example, the case of *Eliza/Doctor*. Our interpretations of this work are likely to be a bit odd if we interact with it now in a graphical window (e.g., as a Java applet in a web browser) and never consider its original context. As Nick Montfort has pointed out, the project was developed on a system that not only wasn't a graphical screen—it wasn't a screen at all. Rather, the system's textual interactions (and the reader's replies) were printed on a continuous ream of paper fed through a teletype, a surface nearly forgotten in our contemporary world of digital media ("Continuous Paper"). I draw attention to this not simply in order to point out that a work's surface can vary as it is experienced in different computational environments. More importantly, *Eliza/Doctor*'s typewritten interaction was taking place in an environment in which people communicated with each other through the very same textual medium (much as many people communicate via instant messenger clients today). This is what made possible the famous story of the Bolt Beranek and Newman manager conducting an increasingly exasperated conversation with *Eliza/Doctor*, believing himself to be communicating with a subordinate. As Janet Murray has pointed out, the spread of this story (in several variations, some certainly apocryphal) mirrors that of the Paris audience that supposedly fled the theatre when the Lumière Brothers' film of an approaching train was first shown (65-66). It points to our anxiety that the representational power of a new medium might cause us to mistake its products for reality. In the world of BBS culture, where I first experienced *Eliza/Doctor*, it remained in a context of predominantly textual software experiences mixed with human-to-human textual communication that allowed it to retain much of its original impact.[19] But to interact with *Eliza/Doctor* now, even if running as a bot on an instant-messaging network, is to read the work in a context quite substantially different from that in which it was created and first experienced.

6 A Five Element Model

6.1 Expanding Aarseth's Models

Espen Aarseth's *Cybertext: Perspectives on Ergodic Literature* is one of the most important books for those interested in digital literature to consider. The two neologisms in the title are worth defining. "Ergodic literature" is literature in which "nontrivial effort is required to allow the reader to traverse the text" (1). This can include works, such as James Meehan's *Tale-Spin*, that have both interactive and non-interactive modes of operation—or even works that involve simple choices of eye movement, such as poems of Apollinaire's that involve reader exploration on the page (or Egyptian wall inscriptions connected in two dimensions). As for the other neologism, Aarseth writes on page 3, "A cybertext is a machine for the production of variety of expression." This includes works in which texts can be added by the reader, or in which texts can be generated differently from fixed initial materials, or in which connections between texts can change in different states of the work. It explicitly excludes, however, statically-linked hypertexts such as Stuart Moulthrop's *Victory Garden* (cf. 75 and fig. 3.2).

Aarseth's book provides two models, each with three parts, that have been widely used by those writing about digital literature (though neither of his models is in any way limited to digital literature). The first, in chapter 1, is of the "textual machine" as composed of verbal sign, medium, and operator. As Aarseth writes:

> As the *cyber* prefix indicates, the text is seen as a machine—not metaphorically but as a mechanical device for the production and consumption of verbal signs. Just as a film is useless without a projector and a screen, so a text must consist of a material medium as well as a collection of words. The machine, of course, is not complete without a third party, the (human) operator, and it is within this triad that the text takes place. (21)

Aarseth's second model appears later. He writes:

> A text, then, is any object with the primary function to relay verbal information. Two observations follow from this definition: (1) a text cannot operate independently of some material medium, and this influences its behavior, and (2) a text is not equal to the information it transmits. *Information* is here understood as a string of signs, which may (but does not have to) make sense to a given observer. It is useful to distinguish between strings as they appear to readers and strings as they exist in the text, since these may not always be the same. For want of better terms, I call the former *scriptons* and the latter *textons.* Their names are not important, but the difference between them is. In a book such as Raymond Queneau's sonnet machine *Cent mille milliards de poèmes,* where the user folds lines in the book to "compose" sonnets, there are only 140 textons, but these combine into 100,000,000,000,000 possible scriptons. In addition to textons and scriptons, a text consists of what I call a traversal function—the mechanism by which scriptons are revealed or generated from textons and presented to the user of the text. (62)

Aarseth then proposes seven variables that "allow us to describe any text according to their mode of traversal." These are: dynamics, determinability, transiency, perspective, access, linking, and user function. It is difficult to overstate the importance of Aarseth's contributions to thinking about digital, ergodic, and cybertext literature. But I have also found, in thinking through what I believe I need to interpret in order to read digital literature, that for my purposes Aarseth's models need some expansion. For example, works of digital literature carry out many processes—such as those determining the simulated emotional state of a virtual character—that are important to their literary functions but are not traversal functions for revealing or generating textons from scriptons (or can only be considered as such quite circuitously). Somewhat differently, Aarseth's model of the textual machine (often represented as an equilateral triangle) divides the work up into a "material medium" and "a collection of words." While we can easily expand Aarseth's collection of words to data of many types, a work's processes are as much a matter of authorial creation and selection as its data, and can hold steady while its surface varies.

Given this, I find myself more comfortable using the five-part model presented here, rather than either of Aarseth's three-part models, as my starting point for reading digital literature. I should emphasize, however, that I view my work here as an expansion of, rather than a rejection of, Aarseth's work. All that said, I would summarize the five-part model presented here as follows:

- *Data.* This includes text, images, sound files, specifications of story grammars, declarative information about fictional worlds, tables of statistics about word frequencies, and so on. It also includes instructions to the reader (who may also be an interactor), including those that specify processes to be carried out by the reader.

- *Processes.* These are processes actually carried out by the work, and are central to many efforts in the field (especially those proceeding from a computer science perspective). As Chris Crawford puts it: "Processing data is the very essence of what a computer does." Nevertheless, processes are optional for digital literature (e.g., many email narratives carry out no processes within the work) as well as for ergodic literature and cybertext (in which all the effort and calculation may be on the reader's part).

- *Interaction.* This is change to the state of the work, for which the work was designed, that comes from outside the work. For example, when a reader reconfigures a combinatory text (rather than this being performed by the work's processes) this is interaction. Similarly, when the work's processes accept input from outside the work—whether from the audience or other sources. This is a feature of many popular genres of digital literature, but it is again optional for digital literature and cybertext (e.g., *Tale-Spin* falls into both categories even when not run interactively) and for ergodic literature as well (given that the page exploration involved in reading Apollinaire's poems qualifies them as ergodic). However, it's important to note that cybertext requires calculation somewhere in the production of scriptons—either via processes or interaction.

- *Surface.* The surface of a work of digital literature is what the audience experiences: the output of the processes operating on the data, in the context of the physical hardware and setting, through which any audience interaction takes place. No work that reaches an audience can do so without a surface, but some works are more tied to particular surfaces than others (e.g., installation works), and some (e.g., email narratives) make audience selections (e.g., one's chosen email reader) a determining part of their context.

- *Context.* Once there is a work and an audience, there is always context—so this isn't optional. Context is important for interpreting any work, but digital literature calls us to consider types of context (e.g., intra-audience communication and relationships in an MMO fiction) that print-based literature has had to confront less often.

These are, of course, far from rigid categories, as well as deeply dependent on each other. To take an example, supporting particular interactions is, of course, dependent on using a surface to influence appropriate processes and data. Or, to look at things more formally, as Crawford points out, "Experienced programmers know that data can often be substituted for process. Many algorithms can be replaced by tables of data. . . . Because of this, many programmers see process and data as interchangeable." But I think such arguments generally grow from approaching the issues at the level of minutia, rather than an attempt to think about what is important in interpreting digital literature. As Crawford says of the case he mentions, "This misconception arises from applying low-level considerations to the higher levels of software design."

6.2   Reading Processes

In the end, however, it isn't important how one divides up the elements of digital literature, or how one defines digital literature, except in how it informs analysis and creation.[20] I think it is important to distinguish process and surface, rather than collapse both into the "medium," in part because I believe that a major next step for our field is to begin to interpret processes. As I argue above in the context of Strachey's work, there are works of digital literature we simply can't understand without investigating their processes. Further, there are at least three ways that processes recommend themselves to our attention. First, they are a powerful means of crafting media experiences. Second, they express relationships, through their designs, with schools of thought, histories of practice, and other configurations important to interpretation. Third, because the processes of digital literature often operate in terms of concepts of humanity and the world (e.g., language, character motivation) they can be seen as miniature, operationalized philosophies of these concepts. These philosophies can be worth investigating in their own rights, as well as in how they shape the audience experience—both during "normal" operation and in situations of breakdown (which are not uncommon in complex digital systems). My book *Expressive Processing* is an early attempt at reading processes in these ways. I propose the elements suggested here, in part, because I believe that more attention to process, and to each of the other elements as identified here, will enrich the field. As investigation moves forward, I hope that new organizations, focusing on other elements, will naturally replace this one.

Notes

1   To be precise, "computer" was a job title. As N. Katherine Hayles writes in the prologue to *My Mother Was a Computer*, "in the 1930s and 1940s, people who were employed to do calculations—and it was predominantly women who performed this clerical labor—were called 'computers.' Anne Balsamo references this terminology when she begins one of the chapters in her book *Technologies of the Gendered Body* with the line I have appropriated for my title: 'My mother was a computer.' Balsamo's mother actually did work as a computer, and she uses this bit of family history to launch a meditation on the gender implications of information technologies" (1).

2   The design of the Analytical Engine called for it to be programmed via punched cards such as those used for automated looms, making it possible for Babbage's collaborator Ada Lovelace to be called by some the first programmer of a universal computer, even though the Analytical Engine was never constructed. Lev Manovich, in *The Language of New Media*, has commented on this connection between looms and computers, writing: "Thus a programmed machine was already synthesizing images even before it was put to processing numbers. The connection between the Jacquard loom and the Analytical Engine is not something historians of computers make much of, since for them computer image synthesis represents

just one application of the modern digital computer among thousands of others, but for a historian of new media, it is full of significance" (22).

3   In contrast, many early 20th century computers used analog, continuous representations—such as varying electrical currents or mechanisms that turned at varying speed. These analog computers could perform some tasks very quickly. For example, adding two quantities represented by electrical currents could be accomplished simply by allowing flow onto particular wires, rather than by actually establishing the two values and numerically calculating their sum. However, because of the lack of discrete states, analog computers were inflexible in their orders of precision and prone to noise-induced errors.

4   Many other projects and incremental advances took place, and especially notable of these was the University of Pennsylvania ENIAC (believed, while the *Colossus* was still secret, to have been the first fully functioning electronic digital computer). A 1945 report of future design plans—based on insights from ENIAC designers J. Presper Eckert and John Mauchly, working together with John von Neumann—was very influential on the design of future stored program digital computers (leading to the perhaps inappropriate name "von Neumann architecture" for such systems).

5   Similar efforts include the University of Cambridge EDSAC (1949), the University of Pennsylvania EDVAC (1951), the MIT *Whirlwind I* (1949), and others.

6   It was only a few years later that Turing committed suicide—after arrest and conviction for homosexual activities, followed by a sentence of hormone injections that caused him to grow breasts.

7   However, David Durand's research in the Oxford Bodleian Library has unearthed the program's complete grammar and vocabulary, which included "love," "loves," "loving," "lovingly," "lovesick," and "lovable."

8   For more on the love letter generator, cf. "Digital Media Archaeology: Interpreting Computational Processes" (Wardrip-Fruin, forthcoming).

9   *Dakota,* according to its authors "is based on a close reading of Ezra Pound's Cantos I and first part of II" (Swiss)—but in decidedly modern language. For example, Pound's opening line "And then went down to the ship" becomes "Fucking waltzed out to the car." Stark black text about driving and drinking, guns and gangbangs and Elvis, appears on a white background in time to Art Blakey's jazz drumming, eventually accelerating into near-illegibility.

10   *Blue Company* is an email novel that was performed in 2001 and 2002, with the current news influencing how messages were sent. As succinctly described in the Electronic Literature Organization's "showcase" entry for the piece, "a 'new economy' worker who is sent back in time to the early renaissance tells the story of his corporate team, Blue Company, and their curious work as he writes e-mails on an illicit laptop to his inamorata." *The Daughters of Freya* is also delivered as a series of fictional email messages, but even in its form is quite different from *Blue Company*. For example, the work is not performed at particular times, but always available to new readers, who receive their first message a few hours after signing up at the project's website. Also, while *Blue Company* maintains a close correspondence between the messages sent by the characters and those received by readers, *The Daughters of Freya* often includes messages from multiple characters in a single email received by readers, with datestamps driven by the story's timeline rather than the time of reading. And the two stories are also quite different, with that of *The Daughters of Freya* focusing on a reporter investigating a California sex cult and, eventually, a murder.

11   Natural Language Generation is an area of computer science research that focuses on the production of "natural language" (e.g., English). Tools employed range from formally-described grammars to word frequency statistics. A small number of researchers focus specifically on the generation of text with a particular stylistic approach or other literary parameters.

12   Cage is notable for using "chance operations" in his compositions, and also for scoring processes (such as the tuning of radios) that would reveal sound data that could not be determined in advance. Fluxus works include those that are purely process specifications (lists of instructions) as well as performances and other works built on process models. Augusto Boal's dramatic work is largely in the construction and use of his participatory theatre techniques (such as "forum theatre") with new actor/writers and "spect-actor" audiences.

13   Though, in common usage, the term "Turing test" usually drops the imitation game and gender aspects of Turing's description—focusing instead on whether a human judge believes a textual conversant to be human or machine. Artworks such as Mark Marino's *Barthes's Bachelorette* and Greg Garvey's *Genderbender 1.0* playfully recover some of these aspects.

14   This may be due, in part, to the descriptive vocabulary developed for hypertext systems. While Michael Joyce's distinction between "exploratory" and "constructive" hypertexts is certainly useful when trying to explain different types of hypertext systems and user positions, it's important

to remember that hypertexts that function in what Joyce would call an "exploratory" manner may not have exploration as their primary user experience.

15 *Itinerant* (2005) is a site-specific sound installation in Boston, Massachusetts. It invites people to take a walk through Boston Common and surrounding neighborhoods to experience an interactive sound work delivered via handheld computer and driven by GPS satellite information. During a walk which may last for more than two hours, visitors explore the area, finding fragments of a personal narrative of family and displacement, interspersed with passages from Mary Shelley's *Frankenstein*—the classic tale of a technoscientific monster and the family love he witnesses voyeuristically, but cannot share. It is an exploration-based narrative, but there are no links to click. "The Carl Comics," on the other hand, use links for purposes other than exploration. For example, *Original Recipe Carl* (1998) tells the story of Carl's death in an auto accident. Clicking links allows the reader to expand or contract the number of panels it takes from when Carl promises not to drink and drive until we end at his tombstone—from two panels to fifty-two panels. In essence, links change the level of detail of the story, making it like a comics version of one of Ted Nelson's original non-chunk hypertext concepts: "stretchtext." *Choose Your Own Carl* (1998-2001), on the other hand, is a crossword-style comic (branching and recombining) on the same subject, which is composed of frames drawn based on the suggestions of more than a thousand readers. Here, link-clicking operates to reveal the original suggestions considered for each frame. The result, as McCloud puts it, is a "Fully Interactive, Multiple Path, Reader-Written, Death-Obsessed Comics Extravaganza."

16 *The Impermanence Agent* (1998-2002) is not interactive in the sense that the audience can, say, click on the work. This piece launches a small browser window and tells a story of documents preserved and lost, of impermanence, within it. While this story is being told, the work is also monitoring the reader's web browsing of other sites. Parts of sentences and images from the reader's browsing are progressively collaged into the story, using a variety of techniques. This results in a different experience for every reader—one which is environmentally interactive in that it draws its material primarily from websites created without the work in mind, but is audience interactive in that readers can choose to alter their browsing habits in order to provide the work with different material to consider for collage into the story (cf. Wardrip-Fruin and Moss).

17 *Online Caroline* (2000, 2001) not only sends the reader email messages—it expects a response. The responses don't come by writing email, but by

visiting the website of the reader's online friend, Caroline. At the website readers communicate with Caroline via a simulated webcam, enter details about themselves via web forms, and experience the unfolding of a 24-part drama. Each email sent to a reader is a fixed block of text, but these texts are customized based on what is known about the reader from website visits (e.g., whether the reader has children). Also, the sequence of messages is not fixed. If a reader goes too long without visiting the website, after the receipt of one of Caroline's email messages, the character will begin to send reminders and eventually break off the "relationship" with a message that includes the words: "I won't mail you any more. I'll assume you're away, or busy . . . or maybe you're just fed up with me."

18   *Rest/Less* brings poetry together with dance, music, and technology. A collection of grid-shaped poems by Field become the space over which five dancers choreographed by Jewett move—triggering spoken language, bells, wind, and video images of the handwritten poems. The performance system, developed by Jewett, does not require sensors or tracking aids to be placed on the dancers' bodies, leaving them free to interact lyrically with the grid made visible to the audience on the floor of the performance space. *Screen* was created in Brown University's "Cave," a room-sized virtual reality display. It begins as a reading and listening experience. Memory texts appear on the Cave's walls, surrounding the reader. Then words begin to come loose. The reader finds she can knock them back with her hand, but peeling increases steadily.

19   BBSes, or Bulletin Board Systems, were computers that accepted connections from other computers over regular phone lines, using modems. Often run by individuals as a community service (though there were also commercial BBSes) these machines usually had a small number of dedicated phone lines that allowed users to upload and download files, take part in asynchronous discussions on "bulletin boards," make moves in turn-based games, exchange real-time messages with the users currently connected to the other phone lines, and interact with programs like *Eliza/Doctor*. A vibrant culture in the 1980s, they disappeared almost overnight as public access to the Internet expanded.

20   In fact, the elements presented in this essay are ones selected for the purpose of my argument here—and I have used others on different occasions.

Works Cited

Aarseth, Espen J. "Nonlinearity and Literary Theory." *Hyper/Text/Theory.* Ed. George P. Landow. Baltimore: Johns Hopkins, 1994.

———. *Cybertext: Perspectives on Ergodic Literature.* Baltimore: Johns Hopkins UP, 1997.

Bates, Joseph. "The role of emotion in believable agents." *Communications of the ACM* 37.7 (1994).

Betcherman, Michael, and David Diamond. *The Daughters of Freya.* 2005. 10 Aug. 2009 <http://www.emailmystery.com/dof/index.php>.

Bevan, Rob, and Tim Wright. *Online Caroline.* 2001. 10 Aug. 2009 <http://www.onlinecaroline.com>.Bly, Bill. "Learn navigation: doing without the narrator in artifactual fiction." *SIGWEB Newsletter* 9.1 (2000): 34-37.

Bringsjord, Selmer, and David A. Ferrucci. *Artificial Intelligence and Literary Creativity: Inside the Mind of Brutus, a Storytelling Machine.* Lawrence Erlbaum Associates, 2000.

Campbell-Kelly, Martin. "Christopher Strachey 1916-1975: A Biographical Note." *Annals of the History of Computing* 7.1 (1985).

Crawford, Chris. "Process Intensity." *Journal of Computer Game Design* 1.5 (1987).

Douglass, Jeremy. "Machine Writing and the Turing Test." Presentation in Alan Liu's Hyperliterature seminar, University of California, Santa Barbara. 2000. 10 Aug. 2009 <http://www.english.ucsb.edu/grad/student-pages/jdouglass/coursework/hyperliterature/turing/>.

Field, Thalia, and Jamie Jewett. *Rest/Less.* 2005. Performance.

Hayles, N. Katherine. "Response to Simon Penny." Riposte. *Electronic Book Review* (2004). 10 Aug. 2009 <http://www.electronicbookreview.com/thread/firstperson/haylesr1>.

———. *My Mother Was a Computer: Digital Subjects and Literary Texts.* Chicago: U of Chicago P, 2005.

Hershman, Lynn. *Synthia.* 2002. 10 Aug. 2009 <http://www.lynnhershman.com/synthia/>.

Hillis, W. Daniel. *Pattern on the Stone: The Simple Ideas That Make Computers Work.* New York: Basic Books, 1999.

Hodges, Andrew. *Alan Turing: The Enigma.* New York: Walker, 2000.

Joyce, Michael T. "Siren Shapes: Exploratory and Constructive Hypertexts." *Academic Computing* 3 (1988).

Klima, John. *Earth*. 2001. Installation.

Lang, R. Raymond. "A formal model for simple narratives." *Narrative Intelligence: Papers from the 1999 AAAI Fall Symposium,* Technical Report FS-99-01. Ed. Michael Mateas and Phoebe Sengers. AAAI Press, 1997.

Lebling, Dave, and Marc Blank. *Zork*. Computer Game. 1977.

Guin, le Ursula K. *Always Coming Home*. Berkeley: U of California P, 2001.

Manovich, Lev. *The Language of New Media*. Cambridge, MA: MIT P, 2001.

McCloud, Scott. *The Carl Comics*. 1998-2001. 10 Aug. 2009 <http://www.scottmccloud.com/1-webcomics/carl/index.html>.

McDaid, John. "Luddism, SF, and the Aesthetics of Electronic Fiction." *New York Review of Science Fiction* 69 (1994): 1; 8-11.

Meriwether, James B. "Notes on the Textual History of The Sound and the Fury." *Papers of the Bibliographical Society of America* 56 (1962): 285-316.

Montfort, Nick. "Literary Games." *Poems that Go* 14 (2003). <http://www.poemsthatgo.com/gallery/fall2003/print_article_games.htm>.

———. "Continuous Paper: The Early Materiality and Workings of Electronic Literature." *Modern Language Association Conference*. 2004. <http://www.nickm.com/writing/essays/continuous_paper_mla.html>.

Mortensen, Torill. "Flow, Seduction and Mutual Pleasure." *Other Players Conference Proceedings*. Center for Computer Game Research, ITU Copenhagen, 2004.

Moulthrop, Stuart. *Victory Garden*. CD-ROM. Cambridge, MA: Eastgate, 1991.

Murray, Janet H. *Hamlet on the Holodeck: The Future of Narrative in Cyberspace*. New York: Free Press, 1997.

Paul, Christiane. *Digital Art*. London: Thames and Hudson, 2003.

Queneau, Raymond. *Cent Mille Milliards de Poémes*. Paris: Gallimard, 1962.

Rueb, Teri. *Itinerant*. Installation. 2005.

Simanowski, Roberto. "Holopoetry, Biopoetry and Digital Literatures: Close Reading and Terminological Debates." *The Aesthetics of Net Literature: Writing, Reading and Playing in Programmable Media*. Ed. Peter Gendolla and Jörgen Schäfer. Bielefeld: Transcript, 2007. 43-66.

Strachey, Christopher. "The 'Thinking' Machine." *Encounter* 3.4 (1954): 25-31.

Swiss, Thom. "Distance, Homelessness, Anonymity, and Insignificance: An Interview with Young-Hae Chang Heavy Industries." *The Iowa Review Web*.

2002. 10 Aug. 2009 <http://www.uiowa.edu/~iareview/tirweb/feature/younghae/interview.html>.

Taylor, T. L., and Mikael Jakobsson. "The Sopranos Meets EverQuest: Socialization Processes in Massively Multiuser Games." *Digital Arts and Culture::2003::Streaming Wor(l)ds*. Melbourne, 2003.

Turing, Alan M. "On computable numbers with an application to the Entscheidungsproblem." *Proceedings of the London Mathematical Society* 2.42 (1936).

———. "Computing Machinery and Intelligence." *Mind: A Quarterly Review of Psychology and Philosophy* 59.236 (1950).

Young-Hae Chang Heavy Industries. *Dakota*. 2002. 10 Aug. 2009 <http://www.yhchang.com/DAKOTA.html>.

Walker-Rettberg, Jill. "Distributed Narrative: Telling Stories Across Networks." *The 2005 Association of Internet Researchers Annual*. Ed. Mia Consalvo, Jeremy Hunsinger, and Nancy Baym. New York: Peter Lang, 2006.

Wardrip-Fruin, Noah. "What Hypertext Is." *Proceedings of the Fifteenth ACM Conference on Hypertext and Hypermedia*. ACM, 2004.

———. *Expressive Processing: Digital Fictions, Computer Games, and Software Studies*. Cambridge, MA: MIT P, 2009.

———. "Digital Media Archaeology: Interpreting Computational Processes." *Media Archaeologies*. Ed. Erkki Huhtamo and Jussi Parikka. Berkeley: U of California P. Forthcoming.

Wardrip-Fruin, Noah, and Nick Montfort, eds. *The New Media Reader*. Cambridge, MA: MIT P, 2003.

Wardrip-Fruin, Noah, and Brion Moss. "The Impermanence Agent: Project and Context." *Cybertext Yearbook 2001*. Ed. Markku Eskelinen and Raine Koskimaa. Jyväskylä: Research Centre for Contemporary Culture, 2002. 14-59.

Wardrip-Fruin, Adam Chapman, Brion Moss, and Duane Whitehurst. *The Impermanence Agent*. 1999. 10 Aug. 2009 <http://www.impermanenceagent.com/agent/>.

Wardrip-Fruin et al. *Screen*. 2002. 10. Aug. 2009 <http://www.noahwf.com/screen/index.html>.

Wegner, Peter. "Why Interaction is More Powerful than Algorithms." *Communications of the ACM* 40.5 (1997): 80-91.

Weizenbaum, Joseph. *Computer Power and Human Reason: From Judgment to Calculation.* San Francisco: W.H. Freeman, 1976.

Wittig, Rob. *Blue Company.* 2002. 10 Aug. 2009 <http://www.robwit.net/bluecompany2002/>.

John Zuern

Figures in the Interface

Comparative Methods in the Study of Digital Literature

For more than a decade, scholars of electronic literature have been searching for theoretical models and critical practices that can adequately account for the specific properties of digitally born literary artifacts. During the same period, their next-door neighbors in the field of comparative literature have been attending to the difficult rebirth of their own discipline, redefining their objects of study and reassessing the fundamental concepts and assumptions that have guided their research for over a century. In 2006, the publication of the collection *New Media Poetics: Contexts, Technotexts, and Theories*, edited by Adalaide Morris and Thomas Swiss, made a major contribution to scholarship on digital literature; in the same year, *Comparative Literature in an Age of Globalization* released the results of a "state of the discipline" review conducted by a collective of leading comparativists (cf. Saussy).[1] These volumes are only two examples of a burgeoning culture of self-reflection, retrospective as well as prospective, in both areas of inquiry. Though the two fields have different foci, with digital literature largely emphasizing relationships across media and comparative literature concentrating primarily on relationships among linguistic, cultural, and historical contexts, both have been compelled to define "literature" in ways that counter deeply entrenched presuppositions: for the former, the dominance of print-based conceptions of literary production, and for the latter, the dominance of national (and nationalist) conceptions of literary culture and, more recently, the dominance of Euroamerican languages and literary traditions over those of other parts of the world. For each field, moreover, a retooled definition of literature has served as an organizing principle for innovative research projects, determining to a large extent scholars' choice of primary materials, theoretical frameworks, and critical methodologies. In terms of their place within academic institutions that offer an increasingly flimsy shelter to the study of literature and the humanities as a whole, both the digital and the comparative modalities of literary scholarship face challenges to their survival that make their task of self-definition and disciplinary legitimation particularly urgent.[2]

In this chapter I want to suggest that these two ongoing initiatives in literary studies, proceeding in parallel time but rarely intersecting, have something to learn from each other. My objective is twofold. First, in order to determine whether an explicit emphasis on *figuration* is essential to a functioning definition of digital literature, I want to bring to the fore an ago-old question to which comparativists have given a great deal of attention: does the trope, the figurative as opposed to the literal deployment of language, represent the *sine qua non* of the specifically *literary* text, regardless of the language (or, we must now add, the medium) in which the text is instantiated? Assuming an affirmative answer to this question, at least for the time being, my second aim is to argue that if we want to develop a procedure for the *close reading* of digital literary texts, a method we can pursue in our scholarship and cultivate in our students, we must endeavor to show how identifiable qualities of the medium in which a text is produced, displayed, and disseminated intersect *constitutively* with identifiable strategies of figuration that make the text recognizable as "literature." The operative (and tendentious) term here is "constitutively" the strictures of such an approach would demand that we ask ourselves, in each instance of close reading, whether computation as such is essential to the specifically literary properties of the text or essential only to the existence of the text as a particular kind of physical artifact. This distinction between literary and artifactual properties of texts is routinely blurred in current critical discourse on computer-based literary art. This confusion, I will argue, is structurally analogous to the confusion comparative literature has struggled to overcome: the blurring of the line between the specific "literariness" of a text (features that lend themselves to comparison with other instances of literariness across a broad spectrum of texts), and the text's presumed linguistic, cultural, and national-political specificities (features that lend themselves largely to contrasts with "foreign" texts and clubby assimilation to others of its putative kind).

I am by no means implying that scholarship in digital literature has neglected comparative approaches. Many of the leading critics in the field of digital literary studies, among them N. Katherine Hayles, John Cayley, Jessica Pressman, and Brian Kim Stefans, undertake approaches that explicitly involve detailed comparisons across time, media, and literary traditions.[3] From its beginnings, the field has worked productively across national and linguistic boundaries, as the international scope of this present volume illustrates. I do, however, want to suggest that the history of comparative literature's emergence contains an important caveat for the developing field of digital literary studies. For comparative literature, the "national language" continues to pose a dilemma: it represents, on the one hand, a set of linguistic skills that all serious students of literature must master and, on the other, a category that is far more ideological than it is "natural" and thus one that we hold in suspicion as a means of configuring our research agendas. My discussion in this chapter is guided by the heuristic hypothesis that we can establish an analogy between the vexed status of the "national language" for comparative literature and the status of the "digital" for scholars undertaking research on computer-based literary texts. Clearly we must endeavor to learn as much as we can about the codes and processes that comprise digital textuality; such knowledge is analogous to the language mastery required of the traditional literary critic. Roberto Simanowski is correct in his early recognition that the interpretation of digital cultural productions requires the "Entwicklung einer *Hermeneutik der Tiefeninformation,* die eine *Hermeneutik der Interaktion,* als den eingeplanten Faktor der Zeichenkonstituierung, einschließen muß" ('development of a *hermeneutics of deep information* that must include a *hermeneutics of interaction* as the integral factor in the constitution of signs') (121). The detailed studies of the materiality of electronic texts that Matthew Kirschenbaum conducts in *Mechanisms: New Media and Forensic Imagination* and Chris Funkhouser's technically precise account of the emergence of computer-based literature in *Prehistoric Digital Poetry: An Archaeology of Forms, 1959-1995,* both illustrate the importance of a solid grasp of the technology for the foundational woxrk of literary criticism, from establishing coherent bibliographic categories to categorizing and preserving individual artworks. Noah Wardrip-Fruin's work, including his contribution to this collection, powerfully exemplifies the value of fluency in computer programming for artists and critics alike. Yet in terms of *reading* these texts, an activity that attempts to demonstrate and conserve their meaning and cultural relevance, a preoccupation with media specificity threatens to override our attention to aspects of digital texts that are analogous, if not simply identical, to aspects of print documents, and thus to thwart critical and pedagogical projects that trace comparisons across differently formatted texts. Special pleading for the digital impedes our access to each artwork's "literary singularity," a quality that in Derek Attridge's terms "may be said to derive from—though it is much more than—the verbal particularity of the work: specific words in a specific arrangement (which may include spatial arrangement on the page or the use of pauses and other articulating devices in oral delivery)" (65). This oversight, in turn, limits the potential of our studies of digital literature to make meaningful contributions to the study of literature broadly conceived as an academic discipline, one that is increasingly downsized and sidelined in the American university system, and as an intellectual responsibility to the reading public.

 In the following section I describe what recent debates in comparative literary studies, with their emphasis on the text's figurative dimensions, might contribute to the elaboration of definitions, theories, and methods appropriate for the critical treatment of digital literature. I then offer a brief demonstration of how a close reading practice for electronic texts that stresses their comparability with printed texts might come to terms with the problems I identify in current critical orientations within digital literary studies. My example aligns a conventionally "readable" print poem, Rainer Maria Rilke's "Herbst" ('Autumn') (1902), with a digital video poem produced a century later, Rudy

Lemcke's *The Uninvited* (2005). I show how an orientation to the study of digital literature that takes into account the digital literature's departure from the print tradition, an orientation that finds one of its most sophisticated and compelling exemplars in N. Katherine Hayles's "intermediation," can open our eyes to vital, perhaps even definitive dimensions of the digital literary artwork. At the same time, I try to indicate how these approaches can lead us to overlook other features of the text, in particular its specific tropology, that are no less definitive of its literariness and that call for methods stressing the crossmedia comparability of literary forms.

Deviant by Definition:
Comparative Literature's Defense of the Figure

As Hayles notes in the opening of *Electronic Literature: New Horizons for the Literary*, the definition of "electronic literature" developed by a committee of the Electronic Literature Organization (ELO) has the virtue of a broad compass, but it also begs the question of what "literary" actually means: in the ELO's terms, "electronic literature" comprises "work with an important literary aspect that takes advantage of the capabilities and contexts provided by the stand-alone or networked computer" (qtd. in Hayles 3). The capaciousness of this definition affords individual artists and critics alike considerable latitude in developing projects. In its inclusiveness, it also resonates compellingly with Susan Bassnett's recent argument about how the discipline of comparative literature ought to reconfigure itself:

> The future of comparative literature lies in jettisoning attempts to define the object of study in any prescriptive way and in focusing instead on the idea of literature, understood in the broadest possible sense, and in recognising the inevitable interconnectedness that comes from literary transfer. No single European literature can be studied in isolation, nor should European scholars shrink from reassessing the legacy they have inherited. (10)

Bassnett's emphasis on interconnectedness and, especially, on the reassessment (but not, presumably, the abandonment) of our literary legacies corresponds in important ways with the thrust of current efforts to stake out the intellectual territory of electronic literature studies. A leader in this endeavor, Hayles has noted that "as we work toward critical practices and theories appropriate for electronic literature, we may come to renewed appreciation for the specificity of print" (*Writing Machines* 33). The critical agenda Hayles terms "intermediation," though it foregrounds the interaction between "human and machine cognition" (*Electronic Literature* X), is careful to acknowledge the connections between digitally born texts and their print forebears: "When literature leaps from one medium to another . . . it does not leave behind the accumulated knowledge embedded in genres, poetic conventions, narrative structures, figurative tropes, and so forth" (*Electronic Literature* 58). How, though, can critics mobilize these "legacy concepts" (84) in their work on digital texts without overlooking the specificity of the media and simply accommodating these new forms to older conceptions of literature? In the remainder of this section, I will pick up one of these inherited concepts—the "figurative trope"—and suggest that it can serve as a fulcrum for a robust comparative method for digital literary studies, in part by making the specificity of the media relative to the figural dimensions of literary textuality.

For comparative literature, the "tropical" nature of literary language has served as a key common ground for a study of literature that extends its scope beyond the confines of national cultures and traditions. In her appeal for a renewal of the comparative project in *Death of a Discipline*, for example, Gayatri Chakravorty Spivak emphasizes rhetoric as a distinguishing feature of literature and of literature's distinctive effect on human consciousness: "The literary text gives rhetorical signals to the reader, which lead to activating the readerly imagination. Literature advocates in this special way. These are not the ways of expository prose. Literary reading has to be learned" (22). The trope introduces a kind of difficulty into the text, a departure from straightforward decoding that demands that readers exert their imaginations. One of the earliest theoretical accounts of figuration in Western rhetorical theory emphasizes this operation of estrangement. In a remarkable passage in the *Rhetoric*, Aristotle compares the reader's experience of a figure of speech with an encounter with a foreigner:

> . . . to deviate [from prevailing usage] makes language more elevated; for people feel the same in regard to *lexis* as they do in regard to strangers compared with citizens. As a result, one should make the language unfamiliar, for people are admirers of what is far off, and what is marvelous is sweet. (221)[4]

Working out of a tradition of poetics that can be traced back to Aristotle, Spivak upholds literature's capacity to stage an encounter with otherness, an encounter that appeals to the reader's ethical imagination, as a crucial desideratum of a new comparative literature:

> In order to reclaim the role of teaching literature as training the imagination—the great inbuilt instrument of othering—we may, if we work as hard as old-fashioned Comp. Lit. is known to be capable of

doing, come close to the irreducible work of translation, not from language to language but from body to ethical semiosis, that incessant shuttle that is a "life." (Spivak 13)

Spivak's suggestion that the text's impact on the imagination ought to be the focal point of comparative studies provides a valuable corrective to the preoccupations with "media specificity" that have taken a firm hold on digital literary scholarship. While our critical practices must still pay scrupulous attention to the qualities of electronic literature as *electronic* literature, this attention will result in richer and less circular interpretations if we ask ourselves how these medium-specific elements *figure*—in all senses—in the reader's imaginative, ethical engagement with the text.[5]

The work of another major contributor to the revitalization of comparative literature, J. Hillis Miller, goes a long way toward imagining a comparative literature that might encompass digital forms. Though he has primarily concentrated on how the digitalization of printed texts can "teach us to see earlier works of literature in a different way" (137), his affirmation of the "materiality" of literature can supplement—and productively redirect—the corresponding emphasis in the study of digital literary artifacts. Miller calls upon the comparative tradition for models of "genuine reading" that can counter the "mimetic, representational, descriptive methodology" he associates with the identity politics that have informed cultural studies in the U.S. academy (147). In pursuit of laudably progressive political aims, Miller suggests, critics too often treat literary texts as if they offered transparent representations of cultural identities, social practices, and ethical-political problems. The tendency of these critics to overlook the mediating and displacing role of language in literary representations frequently means that in their enthusiasm to diversify the curriculum with non-English-language materials, they tend to overlook the additional mediations, displacements, and even misrepresentations that come with translated texts. Opposing such approaches, Miller's "'genuine reading' always must have recourse to the original language of the work, however awkward and time-consuming this may be" (151). Miller's insistence on reading in the original is, he argues, only the most visible version of a need, even in studying works in the

> same language as that of the critic, to get behind thematic reading and pay attention to what might be called the materiality of the work. The work's force as an event bringing cultural value or meaning into existence depends on a certain performative use of language or other signs. Such a reading must attend to what is internally heterogeneous, contradictory, odd, anomalous about the work, rather than pre-

supposing some monolithic unity that directly reflects a cultural context. (153)

While we must not jump to sloppy analogies between the human languages studied by comparatists and the programming languages and design protocols that shape the digital texts we seek to understand, Miller's demand that we read texts in the original reminds us of the essential but often arduous task of digging through the strata of source codes, scripts, file formats, release dates, and all the other technical data that make up the digital artwork's original "language" as well as its materiality. His emphasis on the performative and tropological dimensions of literary text, however, directs our gaze toward those aspects of texts that differ from and "other" their native cultures and languages, whatever they may be, far more than they reflect them or confirm their stability. Even if we don't fully take on board the habits of mind of poststructuralist critics like Miller, his effort to call into question the ideological presuppositions with which many literary scholars approach their objects of study might draw our attention to the foregone conclusions that shape our critical reception of digital texts. How often do we find in any given computer-based literary artifact only what we've learned to look for? How often do our analyses merely confirm the digital format's difference from—and implicit superiority to—the print format? How often, regardless of the text's specific thematics, do we delegate it a representative of "cyberculture" or a reflection of the *Zeitgeist* of the Late Age of Print? Despite our appeals to the digital text's innovativeness, how often do we allow it truly to surprise us?

If we place undue emphasis on what appear to be large differences between the printed and the digital, we will overlook the edgier and more edifying little differences that can be identified only through applying to individual texts the rigorous close reading strategies that have been a mainstay of comparative literature's critical methods. Our cross-media comparativism cannot simply serve to reinforce the priority of digital forms, nor should it accommodate its objects to the critic's presuppositions about experimentalism or innovativeness. Furthermore, we need not limit our focus to those particular printed texts—Concrete or Language poetry, for example, or the typographically complex works of fiction Hayles frequently treats—that appear to share an aesthetic (or a production process) with works of digital literature. As Nathan Brown argues, "[t]he challenge that we might thus pose to any art form, not insofar as we are indifferent to its particularity, but rather *insofar as it is specific to its medium,* is this: can it configure an assemblage whose force of resistance to what we already live is sufficient to *seize us*--into thought" ("The Function of Digital Poetry"). Insofar as a reaffirmation of figuration, and of figuration's potentially transformative appeal to the reader's imagination, has served comparative literature as a way of pursuing its disciplinary aims without falling into the traps of nationalist and identitarian essentialism, the same reaffirmation can guide digital literary studies out of the confines of an essentialist "digitalism." In the next section, I endeavor to sketch out such a path by way of a comparison of two poems, one printed and one digitally produced, both of which push at the limits of their respective media in order to fashion complex, compelling, and ethically fraught figures.

Rilke's "Autumn" and Lemcke's *The Uninvited*

An exegetical tradition spanning at least two millennia has taught us how to read—and how to teach others how to read—literary artifacts like Rainer Maria Rilke's well-known poem "Autumn," originally published in 1902 in the first volume of *Das Buch der Bilder* [*The Book of Images*], which will serve here as an object lesson in "classic" literary figuration. We are only beginning to develop techniques of close reading that can account for the cross-media figurations in the kind of literary artifact the San Francisco artist Rudy Lemcke offers us in his digital video piece *The Uninvited*, first exhibited in 2002, which combines photography, poetry, animation, music, and display space to represent the hallucinatory thoughts of a homeless Vietnam war veteran. The following comparison of "Autumn" and *The Uninvited* takes as its starting point a simple thematic similarity: both texts take up the image of autumn leaves, one of the most banal and sentimental images in all of poetry, and through a process of figuration both poems transform and elevate this clichéd *topos* into an emblem of ethical responsibility. I will first conduct a more or less standard explication of Rilke's poem, as if I were discussing it in a class, and then I will try to adapt these close-reading techniques for an examination of Lemcke's work.[6]

The first half of the first line of "Autumn" launches the poem with a declarative statement of fact which is immediately followed by two similes that introduce a "counterfactual" element into the description: "Die Blätter fallen, fallen wie von weit / als welkten in den Himmeln ferne Gärten" ('The leaves are falling, falling as if from far away / as if distant gardens were withering in the skies'). The doubling of "falling" in the first line inaugurates a pattern of *polyptoton*, the repetition of a word in different grammatical forms, which makes up a conspicuous structure of the poem. In "Autumn" this repetition is marked by an intensification of figuration. The next line anthropomorphizes the leaves: "Sie fallen mit verneinender Gebärde" ('They're falling with gestures of denial'), and the poem's remaining stanzas gradually transform "falling" from a physical movement to a metaphysical condition of existence.

The second stanza shifts from the human-scale image of the falling leaves to a cosmic-scale image of planetary movement, an image that shifts, in turn, from concrete heavenly bodies to an abstract state of alienation: "Und in den Nächten fällt die schwere Erde / aus allen Sternen in die Einsamkeit" ('And in the nights the heavy earth is falling / From all the stars into solitude'). From this all-encompassing perspective, the stanza that follows zooms back to the humans who occupy this "heavy earth," introducing a moral dimension into the motion of falling that has now been established as the poem's central theme: "Wir alle fallen / Diese Hand da fällt / Und sieh dir andre an: es ist in allen" ('We're all falling / This hand falls there / And take a look at others: it's in them all'). From the movements of the dying leaves, the poem itself moves to the orbit and rotation of planet Earth and then on to the movements of a collective humanity and its individual hands. The curiously detached reference to "this hand" prepares for the key image of hands that concludes the poem, an image that further complicates "Autumn's" elaborate metaphysics by invoking an unnamed but benevolent agency: "Und doch ist Einer, welcher dieses Fallen / unendlich sanft in seinen Händen hält" ('And yet there's One who holds this falling / Infinitely tenderly in his hands'). As we will see, the capitalized indefinite pronoun "One" serves as the catalyst for this poem's entrainment not only of our conscious attention but also of our ethical imagination.

A responsible teacher of this poem would insure that students have some inkling of its biographical and literary-historical contexts. Anyone familiar with Rilke's uneasy relationship with his Romantic forebears will recognize "Autumn" as a riff on the metaphysical nature poem; anyone familiar with Rilke's religious preoccupations is likely to hypothesize that the "One" in the last stanza refers to the elusive, yet awe-inspiring divinity who appears in so many of Rilke's poems. The poem is also replete with rhetorical figures that any undergraduate student of literature should be able to identify. Rilke employs end-rhyme (*Gebärde/Erde; fällt/hält*), assonance (*ferne/Gärten/schwere/Sternen; unendlich/Händen/hält*), alliteration (*Gärten/Gebärde*), apostrophe (the direct address to the reader in "take a look at others"), and a primarily iambic meter to fuse the poem into a densely articulated semantic, rhetorical, sonic, rhythmic, and visual object. Through its figural language, the poem effects a kind of "motion capture," seizing the kinetic image of "falling" and propelling it through a sequence of grammatical and tropical transformations that culminate in the strange indefiniteness of the last stanza's pronoun: if this "One," the guardian of this "falling," is indeed God, why doesn't Rilke just say so? Elsewhere he does not shrink from naming God, as he does, for example, in the opening of "Herbsttag" ('Autumn Day'), a companion poem in the same collection. A second glance at the ending should provoke us to ask who, after all, is this "One?"

In an effort to resolve the dilemma in terms of Rilke's own poetic practice, we might recall the famous imperative direct address to the reader in the last line of Rilke's "Archarischer Torso Apollos" ('Archaic Torso of Apollo'): "Du mußt dein Leben ändern" ('You must change your life'). We might also refer to his lesser-known poem "Der Leser" ('The Reader'), also included in *The Book of Images*, which gives a sensuous description of the physical experience of reading a book that grows heavier as the reader tires. Is it possible, then, that the hands at the end of "Autumn," with their infinite tenderness, belong to *me*, the reader, who holds the poem—"*dieses Fallen*," this cascade of figurative iterations of falling—literally in my hands or figuratively in my attentive gaze? Could it also refer to the hands of the poet, whose manual and moral effort have brought this specific instance of "falling" into being?

Concluding with this ambiguity, the poem tropes on its own materiality as a hand-held text-display device. In doing so, it loops its figurative play with language through its own physical existence as an object, an existence that impinges upon *my* own corporeal, agential being. "Und sieh dir andre an" ('Take a look at others'), the poem has demanded; its last line implies that I must now look directly at myself, at my hands, recognizing that I am called upon to be responsible to the "others" with whom I am conjoined in a precipitous, precarious existential "falling." In the course of ten lines, "Autumn" unfurls from a humdrum remark about the falling leaves into an ethico-aesthetic-theological conundrum. We need not choose only one among the alternative antecedents of "One." In fact, holding them all in suspension intensifies the poem's philosophical density. Furthermore, in terms of what Spivak identifies as "the role of teaching literature as training the imagination," the poem requires a kind of "fault tolerance" in our interpretative efforts, simulating the necessity for tolerant, imaginative judgments in other spheres of our social lives.[7]

Rudy Lemcke's animated poem *The Uninvited*, one of the video experiments in Lemcke's series *Light F/X,* enacts another deviation from the cliché of autumn leaves, another kind of poetic motion capture, and another ambiguous ethical appeal to the reader by way of its specific materiality. Exhibited at the Stonybrook University Art Gallery in Stonybrook, New York, in the last months of 2002, the single-channel video is designed for display on a gallery wall. A little over thirteen and a half minutes long, the piece plays in a continuous loop, allowing no intervention on the part of the viewer. Appearing in white letters against a burnt-orange background, single lines from the poem fade in and out, accompanied by a brash, almost wailing arrangement for gamelan and voice. What appear to be shadow puppets made of leaves and plant material, their elongated limbs reminiscent of the articulated stick-puppets in the Indonesian tradition of *wayang kulit*, move gracefully across the screen behind the words of the poem, duplicating and overlapping to form dense patterns (fig. 1).[8]

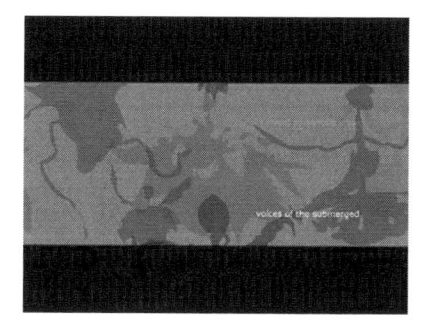

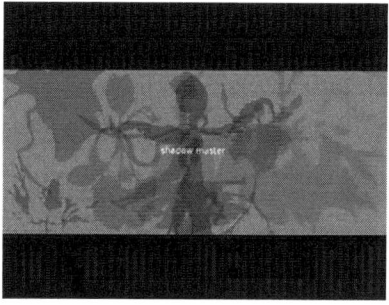

Fig. 1. Rudy Lemcke. Screenshots from *The Uninvited* (2005). Single-channel video.

As a text in which "sight is in-mixed with sound, texture with vision," *The Uninvited* clearly requires the kind of "synesthetic" reading Hayles exemplifies in her examination of Michael Joyce's *Twelve Blue* (*Electronic Literature* 64). The words of Lemcke's poem are meant to be *read* as well as "looked at" as visual details in the overall ensemble of images, yet their transient appearance before our eyes makes a stringent demand on our attention, and they must compete for that attention with the choreography of the much-larger animated images that dominate the screen.[9]

The most conspicuous visual elements of *The Uninvited*, the leaf-puppets are also the locus of the work's most intense figuration. Whereas the cascade of tropes in Rilke's "Autumn" issues from the declarative statement "the leaves are falling," Lemcke's tropology departs from actual leaves and plants; the images in *The Uninvited* are digital photographs of three-dimensional puppets Lemcke constructed from dried plants he gathered in San Francisco's Golden Gate Park. Lemcke posterized the image files in PhotoShop, then composited and animated them, along with the text of the poem, in AfterEffects. Thus Lemcke's leaves, like Rilke's, have been poetically *processed*, submitted to an artistic procedure that redirects the literal signifiers that refer to them—the word "leaves" and the photographic images of leaves—toward deviant, indeterminate signifieds. Anthropomorphism confers on Rilke's leaves the capacity to make "gestures of denial." Lemcke anthropomorphizes his leaves by sculpting them into abstract humanoid bodies, abstracting them further through photography and editing, and animating them. At times Lemcke's text appears to refer to these figures directly, but the reference is never explicit; the wraith-like images do not so much illustrate the verbal text as they extend and complicate its connotations. In this regard they are more symbolic than they are iconic, "figurative" in the sense of "tropological" rather than "representational."

The opening stanzas identify the poem's speaker as a homeless person who dreams of "going home" but suspects that the home he dreams of "could have been / something I saw on TV / I guess I don't remember clearly / my america." An outcast in American society, he lives "under those bushes / the ocean isn't very far." References later in the poem to "napalm," "the children of Saigon," and "the Mekong" suggest that he is a veteran of the war in Vietnam. He may be an amputee, and he is certainly suffering from psychological distress induced by the trauma of his experience in combat. One stanza of the poem makes the "phantom pain" of an amputated limb into a metaphor for the speaker's sense that he may already be dead, that his entire existence is only a lingering, illusory anguish:

> I am alive
> maybe not
> phantom pain: the doctor calls it
> after a limb has been severed from
> the body
> I am dead
> and this is all just some fucking phantom pain

Like the kinetic image of falling in Rilke's "Autumn," the psychosomatic image of phantom pain provides one of the guiding metaphors for *The Uninvited*. Lemcke's poem consists of a hallucinatory monologue in which the speaker relives incidents from the war, including the suicide of a platoon mate who "shot himself in the head one night." He seems confused about when and where this particular event occurred; "it happened over there," he says, apparently referring to Vietnam, then "no / just there," which seems to indicate a place in the speaker's present environs. The traumatic past event, like the missing limb, retains its painful immediacy.

Describing this conflation of past and present in the speaker's mind, the verbal text of *The Uninvited* alludes directly to the work's visual and musical components:

> the shadow of his body in the moonlight
> joins the other shadows
> ". . . I in their midst."
>
> and the sound of gamelan music in the wind
> this paradise

Although these lines seem to suggest that the shadow-puppets represent the "uninvited" specters of dead comrades who haunt the speaker's memory, the poem as a whole resists any definitive alignment of its words and images. Rather than merely offering a "visualization" of the verbal text's meaning, the animation serves dynamically to stage a range of possibilities for signification, providing an example of what Talan Memmott ingeniously refers to as a "*mise en écran*" whereby "the media/medium makes intentionality, poiesis, and poetics negotiable, rendered through various sensual and experiential stimuli rather than limited to the word" (304).[10] Like the indefinite "One" in Rilke's poem, Lemcke's animated leaves are the locus of an ambiguity that keeps our interpretive options in play. The anthropomorphic shapes of the shadow puppets allow them to operate like indeterminate yet nonetheless *personal* pronouns, stand-ins for the assembly of unnamed and politically "unrepresented" human others—"the uninvited"—on behalf of whom the poem solicits our compassion.

As is the case in "Autumn," the ambiguity in *The Uninvited* also serves to invoke some sort of super-human, if not divine, agency. The line ". . . I in their midst" quotes Jesus's words in Matthew 18:20: "where two or three are gathered together in my name, there am I in the midst of them." Although we might easily read this citation from the gospels as an ironic indictment of American society, which relentlessly claims Christian values even as it routinely betrays them, the inclusion of this precise passage, describing a human fellowship into which the godhead comes essentially "uninvited," complicates the frame of reference of the work's title. Evoking the zero-degree of social collectivity ("two or three"), the scrap of scripture allows us to interpret the small cast of puppets as the emblem of the *polis* to which the poem's speaker and the poem's reader belong by default, but within which they must negotiate the terms of their gathering ("in my name"). *The Uninvited* does not preach a Christian ethics, but its compositing of this particular text from the Christian tradition into its array of signs compels us to introduce the themes of mutuality and responsibility into our effort to assemble a coherent meaning from its component parts.

As does "Autumn," *The Uninvited* employs its particular material configuration to call our attention to the potential moral agency of our own hands. Lemcke originally conceived his poem as an interactive Flash piece in which each of the puppets would serve as a clickable link to parts of the poem, but he ultimately rejected this idea in favor of the uninterrupted flow of the poem and the continuous, painstakingly choreographed movement of the images.[11] The decision to exclude interactivity has the effect of intensifying the implication of its adaptation of shadow-puppet form. Moving "on their own," propelled by some invisible impetus (unlike *wayang kulit* puppets, these have no tell-tale stick indexing the hand of the puppeteer), Lemcke's puppets implicitly raise the question of agency. Like Young-Hae Chang Heavy Industries' aggressively non-interactive Flash pieces, *The Uninvited* makes its very lack of interactive options a dimension of its overall aesthetic and of the "ethical semiosis" it stimulates in its audience. We might take the risk of arguing that Lemcke's work imaginatively "disables" its viewers, and in doing so demands that its audience re-imagine the ethical and political abilities it does posses but does not always exercise. The ambiguity of agency—the question of who controls the puppets, in the poem and in our social lives—is posed with particular intensity in the final lines, in which the speaker apparently becomes at once an active "master" and a passive "memory" of the shadow-play:

> strange theater
> of shadows
> lingers
> a moment between
> chaos and absolute silence
> its sweet poisonous music
> this haunting
> and I
> shadow master
> its memory
>
> these uninvited

While the conclusion of Rilke's poem moves in the direction of generalized metaphysics, Lemcke's conclusion moves in the direction of a highly specific politics. Golden Gate Park has recently become the residence of a new cadre of homeless people who use laptops and public wireless hotspots to sustain viable alternative lifestyles, but Lemcke's speaker is by no means one of these "urban outdoorsmen."[12] He is not participating in the "consensual hallucination" of Gibson's cyberspace; his delusions have been induced by the technology of twentieth-century warfare. As the poem was produced and exhibited during the war in Afghanistan and the buildup to the U.S. invasion of Iraq in March 2003, its references to the Vietnam War cannot help but be drawn within the hermeneutic horizon of current American military operations in those countries. The "boxes of dead boys" represent the causalities of both past and present conflicts, and the devastating experience of the poem's Vietnam veteran also emblematizes the psychic and physical suffering of today's veterans. The prescience of Lemcke's vision of the similarities among these wars is sadly borne out in recent coverage of the disenfranchisement, and in some cases the homelessness, of men and women returning from combat in Iraq and Afghanistan.[13]

The Uninvited reminds us of something that critics of digital literature too often appear to be in danger of forgetting: that literary texts have on the whole tended to concern themselves with topics other than their own material conditions of possibility. Even those texts that make references to their own physical nature—Rilke's gesture toward the hand-held printed page, Lemcke's gestures toward his "strange theater of shadows"—do so in order to trope on this physicality, engaging figuration to apply literal, material means to poetic and often ethical ends. Our critical practice must keep up with this movement of the properly literary beyond literature's now breathtakingly expanded means of production, or it will lose sight of literature's still far more expansive aesthetic and ethical ends.

What *matters* in both these works, in terms of their status as literary objects, is the juxtaposition of verbal, visual, and auditory components that produce complex multimodal figures: metaphoric fusions, metonymic contiguities, tantalizing and philosophically compelling ambiguities. While Hayles' definition of materiality as "an emergent property created through dynamic interactions between physical characteristics and signifying strategies" unquestionably applies to texts in general (*My Mother Was a Computer* 3), when we seek to apply the definition to specifically *literary* texts, must we not isolate a subset of these "signifying strategies" (3) that are specifically figural, even if they are not specifically digital? Hayles and the critics who follow her example are hardly blind to figural language, yet the role of the trope as a distinctive feature of the literary tends to get eclipsed by their detailed, provocative assertions of the distinctiveness of the text's machinic substrate and of the revolution in reading borne out by the partnership of intelligent, literate humans and purportedly intelligent, literate machines in the processing of the text's layered codes. In the case of Lemcke's digital video work, the programming and machine-language codes that contribute to its constitution are, as Cayley has put it, "largely sublinguistic, or on the outer margins of paratext" ("Time Code Language" 314). In his production of *The Uninvited*, Lemcke certainly required photo-editing and animation software to accomplish the text's figural nuances, yet it is this figuration rather than computation that takes the literary upper hand.

Conclusion

Works such as Lemcke's *The Uninvited* qualify as "electronic literature" because they estrange the practices of digital photography, text animation, and visual display from their conventional applications in industry and commerce in ways that compare to the "making strange" of language's declarative, information-bearing functions in more traditional modalities of literary discourse. Groundbreaking though they may be in terms of form, digital texts are no less rooted in this fundamental dimension of the literary. In human-computer interfaces made literarily deviant, we certainly find an opportunity for reflection on the hyper-mediated world in which now we live our lives and engage with the lives of others, but we are also sent back to the deep and richly varied history of our practices of reading and writing, which are bound up with the perennial conundrums of our curiously human being-in-language.

The close reading practices that have developed within comparative literature demand that critics, grounded in a knowledge of the text's codes, look closely at the linguistic specificity of a given work and at the same time look across a broad set of works, taking a synoptic view that allows them to make inferences about literature's functions and values. Maintaining this broad perspective without lapsing into pat generalities has required a constant negotiation with pre-determined categories and entrenched critical prejudices. Comparatism always entails relativism; some aspects of the text's totality will take a back seat to whatever dimensions the critic chooses to privilege. To a large extent, we assess the validity and relevance of critical interpretations by weighing the costs of these choices. Throughout this chapter I have tried to stress the expense of passing over the problem of figuration, whether it occurs in verbal, visual, or procedural forms, in order to emphasize the material differences between digital and non-digital literature.

I have focused primarily on what comparative literature has to teach digital literary studies, but obviously arguments can be made in the other direction. Comparative literature is on the verge of being digitally remastered: as it continues to engage with the different human languages and cultures that have been its traditional focus, comparative literature will now have to cross the many systems of encoding and modalities of discourse that increasingly shape the production of literary texts in contemporary culture.[14] "We must learn to 'code-shift,'" as Sander Gilman puts it, "moving elegantly between a command of the language and culture of our object of study and an awareness of the purpose of that research for the culture in which we live, learn, and teach" (23). My emphasis here on the need for digital literary studies to maintain a focus on the conditions of figuration that pertain to the literariness of digital texts has its corollary in the need for comparative literature to become more attentive to the material conditions of textuality and their impact on figuration.

It is tempting to conclude with a prediction: it seems likely that we will find the results of our present-day efforts to establish a class of literary objects that are by definition "digital" to be no more philosophically sound or methodologically useful, in the long run, than were the results of the efforts of scholars a century ago to establish a class of literary objects that were by definition "German" or "French." Such an assertion obviously requires the invocation of *mutatis mutandi*: digital formats like hypertext and animation are not natural languages like Russian and Urdu, and the values driving the definitions and disciplinary formations appropriate for digital literature are for the most part untainted by nationalist chauvinism. Few critics have been so bold as to claim that the digital medium should be the only consideration when it comes to interpreting digital texts, and most recognize the complex interpenetration of digital forms and their printed precursors. Furthermore, it remains clear that in order to understand the historical development of digital literature, as Funkhouser does, and their complexity as material objects, as do Hayles and Kirschenbaum, a deep knowledge and close critical attention to the digital dimension of these artifacts is indeed essential to building the foundations of a robust field of literary study. Nevertheless, an insistence on the alleged "flatness" of print still pervades critical discussions of digital literature, and this recognition of the printed page's literal two-dimensionality frequently slips from a more or less empirical, more or less trivial observation about the materiality of printed documents to a denigration of the aesthetic and cultural potentials of literary language that happens to have been printed.[15] This over-emphasis on literature's material substrate seriously underestimates the dimensionality introduced into all properly literary texts by way of the diverting, distancing, layering, and deepening operations of figuration. At stake here is hardly a defense of print, but rather a defense of the virtuality of the trope, the deviancy and illusionism that constitute the defining characteristic of the literary. By the time print finally disappears, no one is likely to shed a tear for it. By the time figuration disappears, we will have taken leave of a fundamental capacity of our linguistic and ethical existence as human beings, a departure we might be wise to bewail in advance.

Notes

1   *New Media Poetics* is the outcome of the October 2002 New Media Poetry Conference at the University of Iowa. The American Comparative Literature Association assembled the review committee and gave it its charge in 2004; *Comparative Literature in an Era of Globalization* represents the final report on the review process.

2   For a discussion of the institutional challenges that are shaping the intellectual expansion comparatists are attempting to foster in the academy, see the essays in the 2006 issue of *Comparative Critical Studies* devoted to the future of comparativism, in particular Susan Bassnett's "Comparative Lit-

erature in the Twenty-First Century" and Jonathan Culler's "Wither Comparative Literature?" Sander Gilman's *The Fortunes of the Humanities* provides a cogent diagnosis of the imperiled state of humanistic study as a whole in the U.S. university system.

3   Hayles's extensive examinations of the connections between digitally born texts and print texts that leverage the capacities of their digital production is clearly comparative, although her work also demonstrates the tendency to fuse the questions "is it literary?" and "is it digital?" Other examples of careful comparative work in the field include John Cayley's "Writing on Complex Surfaces": which links his work in CAVE with Joan Retallek's ethopoetic practice and, in an inspired cross-medium move, Saul Bass's film-title design; Jessica Pressman's efforts to show how digital literature builds on the traditions of literary Modernism in her dissertation *Digital Modernism: Making it New in New Media;* and Brian Kim Stefan's attention to the legacy of experimental poetry in "Privileging Language: The Text in Electronic Writing," as well in as many of the essays in his *Fashionable Noise: On Digital Poetics*.

4   Countless efforts to define literary figurality have returned to this notion of the trope's strangeness; in the twentieth century, several important schools of thought have built on this notion that the literary is constituted by an estrangement of the instrumental operations of language. The best-known versions of this idea are the Russian Formalist conception of "ostranenie" ('defamiliarization') put forward by Victor Shklovsky and Bertolt Brecht's "Verfremdungseffekt" ('alienation effect'). Though their political investments in tropology are quite different, each of these theorists asserts that a text fulfills its properly "literary" function by way of a departure from naturalized protocols of linguistic usage.

5   Animation and kinesthesia are examples of medium-specific elements that can in some cases provide the basis for figuration. Literary texts that solicit physical responses on the part of the reader, whether in small-scale forms such as clicking a hyperlink to large-scale forms such as full-body immersion in virtual worlds exemplified by texts written for CAVE environments, certainly promise to effect something like a translation "from body to ethical semiosis" (Spivak 13). In *Writing Machines,* for example, Hayles includes "kinesthetic involvement" in her list of features of electronic literary texts that distinguish them from print (20). Cf. also Dene Grigar's "Kineticism, Rhetoric, and New Media Artists," and in particular the extensive treatment of embodiment in relation to digital literature and art in Mark B. N. Hansen's *New Philosophy for New Media* and *Bodies in Code.*

6   The translation of Rilke's poem is mine; it is an "occasional" translation aimed at highlighting Rilke's figural language and clearly conveying the poem's central images rather than at offering a definitive rendering. Despite the awkwardness of the presentation, I provide the original German to preserve the language-specific details of its stylistics and to allow readers of German to cross check my English version.

7   I understand Spivak to be claiming that in our serious engagement with the simulated, "virtual" reality of a literary text we acquire a certain kind of skill: insofar as literary reading often confronts us with difficulties, uncertainties, and ambiguities that nonetheless demand an effort to make meaning, we gain from it a capacity to fashion provisional, qualified, but nonetheless *active* responses to real people and in the face of real ethical and political problems. The important point is that we do not draw "morals" from exemplary situations depicted in the text, but rather that we build up our ethical capacities by way of our encounter with textual alterity and through the heavy lifting of interpretive work.

8   The entire text of "The Uninvited" and a clip of the third section of the video are available on Lemcke's web site at <http://www.rudylemcke.com/Pages/VideoPages/UninvPg.html>.

9   In *Words to Be Looked At,* Liz Kotz gives a detailed account of experimental artworks of the 1960s that incorporate text in ways that make the words' semantic values relative to their visual impact as images. Both Brian Kim Stefans in "Privileging Language: The Text in Electronic Writing" and Warren Batten in "Poetics in the Expanded Field: Textual, Visual, Digital . . ." address the influence of this artistic tradition on the attitudes regarding words-as-words and words-as-images in contemporary digital literature.

10 Though I certainly affirm Memmott's formulation as it applies to Lemcke's text, as well as to a great many digital works that integrate text with images, animation, and sound, we must acknowledge that it applies equally well to other non-digital multimedia art forms that put verbal language into play alongside other signifying systems (opera is an often-cited example). The phrase "limited to the word" (304) and the mysterious suggestion that words are not sensual, is symptomatic of the effort to establish a "digital difference" (304) at the expense of precision.

11 "I'm really aware of the choreography of it," Lemcke reported in a 2006 interview, "and I really think of it as dance. I spent hours and hours with it, trying to get the motion the way I wanted it. The slowness of the piece, but not so slow, slow enough to be moving at a kind of elegant breathing

pace, exhale and inhale on the screen at a very gentle pace." Animation and video-editing software has made the "writing" component of the terms "choreography" and "cinematography"—dance-writing and movement-writing—even more literal; Lemcke's composition of the kinetic dimension of "The Uninvited" compares to Rilke's careful attention to the sounds and rhythms of words as much as does his composition of the poem's verbal text.

12 Cf. C. W. Nevius's article on Tom Sepa, a self-described "urban outdoorsman" who holds down a full-time job as a telemarketer while living in Golden Gate Park.

13 Cf., for example, "Surge Seen in Number of Homeless Veterans," in which *The New York Times* reports that by the end of 2007 "[m]ore than 400 veterans of the Iraq and Afghanistan wars have turned up homeless." <http://www.nytimes.com/2007/11/08/us/08vets.html?_r=1&oref=slogin>.

14 Though it was completed before the explosion of literary creativity in digital forms that followed the expansion of the Internet and the emergence of the World Wide Web, the 1993 American Comparative Literature Association report, "Comparative Literature at the Turn of the Century," contains a premonition of this transformation in recommending "that comparative literature turn from a concentration on literature to the study of cultural productions or discourses of all sorts" (Culler 87).

15 I have in mind Hayles's "Print is Flat, Code is Deep" and Cayley's "Writing on Complex Surfaces."

Works Cited

Aristotle. *On Rhetoric: A Theory of Civic Discourse.* Trans. George A. Kennedy. Oxford: Oxford UP, 1991.

Attridge, Derek. *The Singularity of Literature.* London: Routledge, 2004.

Bassnett, Susan. "Reflections on Comparative Literature in the Twenty-First Century." *Comparative Critical Studies* 3.1-2 (2006): 3-11.

Brown, Nathan. "The Function of Digital Poetry at the Present Time." 22 Mar. 2009 <http://www.newhorizons.eliterature.org/essay.php?id=11>.

Cayley, John. "Time Code Language: New Media Poetics and Programmed Signification." *New Media Poetics: Contexts, Technotexts, and Theories.* Ed.

Adalaide K. Morris and Thomas Swiss. Cambridge, MA: MIT P, 2006. 307-333.

———. "Writing on Complex Surfaces." *Dichtung Digital* 2 (2005). 22 Mar. 2009 <http://www.dichtung-digital.org/2005/2-Cayley.htm>.

Culler, Jonathan. "Wither Comparative Literature?" *Comparative Critical Studies* 3.1-2 (2006): 85-97.

Funkhouser, Chris. *Prehistoric Digital Poetry: An Archaeology of Forms, 1959-1995*. Tuscaloosa: U of Alabama P, 2007.

Gilman, Sander L. *The Fortunes of the Humanities: Thoughts for After the Year 2000*. Stanford: Stanford UP, 2000.

Grigar, Dene. "Kineticism, Rhetoric, and New Media Artists." *Computers and Composition* 22.1 (2005): 105-112.

Hamill, Sean D., Michael Parrish, and J. Michael Kennedy. "Surge Seen in Number of Homeless Veterans." *The New York Times*. 7 Nov 2007. 22 Mar. 2009 <http://www.nytimes.com/2007/11/08/us/08vets.html?_r=1&oref=slogin>.

Hansen, Mark B. N. *Bodies in Code: Interfaces with Digital Media*. London: Routledge, 2006.

———. *New Philosophy for New Media*. Cambridge, MA: MIT P, 2004.

Hayles, N. Katherine. *Electronic Literature: New Horizons for the Literary*. Notre Dame: U of Notre Dame P, 2008.

———. *Writing Machines*. Cambridge, MA: MIT P, 2002.

———. *My Mother was a Computer: Digital Subjects and Literary Texts*. Chicago: U of Chicago P, 2005.

———. "Print is Flat, Code is Deep." *Poetics Today* 25.1 (2004): 67-90.

Kirschenbaum, Matthew. *Mechanisms: New Media and Forensic Imagination*. Cambridge, MA: MIT P, 2008.

Kotz, Liz. *Words to Be Looked At*. Cambridge, MA: MIT P, 2007.

Lemcke, Rudy. Web Site. 22 Mar. 2009 <http://www.rudylemcke.com>.

———. Personal Interview. 14 July 2006.

———. *The Uninvited. Light F/X*. DVD. 2005.

Memmott, Talan. "Beyond Taxonomy: Digital Poetics and the Problem of Reading." *New Media Poetics: Contexts, Technotexts, and Theories*. Ed. Adalaide K. Morris and Thomas Swiss. Cambridge, MA: MIT P, 2006. 293-306.

Miller, J. Hillis, and Manuel Asensi. *Black Holes/J. Hillis Miller, or Boustrephodonic Reading.* Stanford: Stanford UP, 1999.

Nevius, C. W. "Park Nomad, Laptop in Tow, Calls Bushes Home." *San Francisco Chronicle.* 31 July 2008. 22 Mar. 2009 <http://www.sfgate.com/cgi-bin/article.cgi?f=/c/a/2008/07/31/BAPB1227KF.DTL>.

Pressman, Jessica. *Digital Modernism: Making it New in New Media.* Diss. Yale, 2007.

Rilke, Rainer Maria. "Herbst." *Gedichte.* Vol. 2. Leipzig: Insel, 1927. 53.

Saussy, Haun. *Comparative Literature in an Age of Globalization.* Baltimore: Johns Hopkins UP, 2006.

Saussy, Haun. "Exquisite Cadavers Stitched from Fresh Nightmares: Of Memes, Hives, and Selfish Genes." *Comparative Literature in an Age of Globalization.* Ed. Haun Saussy. Baltimore: Johns Hopkins UP, 2006. 3-43.

Simanowski, Roberto. *Interfictions: Von Schreiben im Netz.* Frankfurt a.M.: Suhrkamp, 2002.

Shklovsky, Victor. "Art as Technique." *Russian Formalist Criticism. Four Essays.* Ed. and trans. Lee T. Lemon and Marion J. Reis. Lincoln: U of Nebraska P, 1965.

Spivak, Gayatri C. *Death of a Discipline.* New York: Columbia UP, 2003.

Stefans, Brian K. *Fashionable Noise: On Digital Poetics.* Berkeley: Atelos, 2003.

———. "Privileging Language: The Text in Electronic Writing." *The Electronic Book Review.* 5 Nov. 2005. 22 Mar. 2009 <http://www.electronicbookreview.com/thread/firstperson/databased>.

Watten, Barrett. "Poetics in the Expanded Field: Textual, Visual, Digital . . ." *New Media Poetics: Contexts, Technotexts, and Theories.* Ed. Adalaide K. Morris and Thomas Swiss. Cambridge, MA: MIT P, 2006. 335-370.

Jörgen Schäfer and Peter Gendolla

Reading (in) the Net

Aesthetic Experience in Computer-Based Media

In his empirical theory of literature *Filozofia Przypadku* [*Philosophy of Chance*] that Stanislav Lem published in 1968, he sketches a sort of creative process between the brain of the writer and the paper he is using. It is

> eine Bahn im semantischen Raum. . . . Die "Absicht" liegt gewissermaßen halbwegs zwischen der ständigen "Problematik" des Schriftstellers und dem konkreten "Thema" des Werks. . . . Es geht um gewisse "ständig aktivierte Gradienten," "Pole" im semantischen Raum, sich gewissermaßen kreisförmig wiederholende Prozesse von emotional wirksamen Erinnerungen und Erregungen; das, was die Absicht darstellt und schon den thematischen Keim des Werks bildet, gruppiert sich gewissermaßen um jene Zentren, die bestimmte Inhalte, Beobachtungen, Urteile zu erfassen und teilweise zu ordnen scheinen und ihnen dadurch eine "latente" Geschlossenheit verleihen. (80ff.)

> a track in semantic space. . . . The "purpose" lies, so to speak, halfway between the constant "set of problems" of the writer and the concrete "subject" of the work. . . . It is a question of certain "constantly activated gradients," "poles" in semantic space, in a sense circularly repeating processes of emotionally effective memories and states of agitation; the elements pertaining to the purpose of the work and that already create its thematic core are virtually grouped around those centers that seem to grasp (and in part also to order) certain contents, observations, and judgments, thereby lending them a "latent" closure.

Even if Lem is deducting this description from the comparison of ideas, drafts and finished novels in the sense of a process between an individual person's brain and an environment, one can definitely read it as a current description of the brains connected through computer-based media that continue communicating with the purpose to enter another "second world" which we continue to call "literature" for lack of a more suitably fitting name. The difference to literary communication in printed media consists in the fact that it is not only one person who is writing and the others who are only reading. In computer-mediated communications, the world of simulation starts, and this means that the drafts in which aesthetic intentions are turned into short poetic texts or long narratives are realized in a still quite unexplored, open and multiple recursive process between "writers" and "readers" whose writing and reading activities often are transformed by "autonomous" programs, "agents," etc.

This essay tries to give a brief outline of our theoretical and methodological approaches for analyzing such changes in *literary* communication triggered by computer-based and networked media. This leads to questions such as: Can we discover a new quality of literariness? What are the terminological and methodological means to examine these literatures? How can we productively link the logics of the play of literary texts and their reception in the reading process? What is the relationship between literary writing and programming? Is there a unique *aesthetic difference* regarding literature in computer-based and networked media?

After one hundred years of ongoing avant-garde "revolutions" in the arts, it seems about time to reassess which of all the innovative artistic practices are today interesting only for historians—and which, on the other hand, have had a lasting and enduring effect on contemporary arts. At present, indeed, various elements, structures and procedures of 20th century avant-garde continue to have a strong impact on visual arts, music and, last but not least, literature in computer-based media. For example, Marcel Duchamp's *ready-mades* or William Burroughs' *cut-ups* are apparently being taken up in works such as Noah Wardrip-Fruin's "textual instruments" *News Reader* or *Regime Change*.

But if we do a double take, things turn out to be more complicated: What on the surface seem to be resemblances or analogies of new media art to the modernist tradition are symptoms of a radical change in media technologies whose mid- and long-term consequences we are only beginning to realize. If we approach computer-controlled processes in the context of industrial production from the producer's point of view, we could argue that manual work has been replaced by industrial work and automation technologies. This can also be observed in the arts: Whereas the Cubists and Dadaists had to work with paper, scissors and paste, contemporary artists trust in fast word processing, communications, image editing, graphics, animation and motion tracking software. Tristan Tzara's instruction how to make a Dadaist poem or Burroughs' cut-up poetics—to name only two examples—have turned into cut-and-paste or "StorySprawl" tools, and Mail Art is being succeeded by web logs and wikis. From the point of view of a reader, spectator or listener, we could argue that these tools demand a much higher grade of activity than the coughing, snorting and hawking which John Cage activated in his famous composition *4'33"*. As regards the work of art, it seems as if the individual piece with beginning, middle and end had actually vanished from the scene or—to put it more mildly—had been transformed into an open and recursive process between producers, programs, and readers/spectators/listeners.

However, these considerations will not suffice to comprehend the pivotal changes imposed on the arts by the latest developments in information technologies. We would like to suggest thinking about literature in computer-based and networked media from a wider perspective: Many participants, human as well as non-human "actants," collaboratively create structures, forms and patterns that none of them has ever intended to produce—nor have any of them foreseen the horizon, the aim or even the meaning of the emerging phenomena. Literature has always been a medium in which intelligence and stupidity, understanding and misunderstanding, causes and consequences of love and power discourses have been *aesthetically* reflected, i.e., it is this particular *aesthetic difference* which must also be taken into account when art and literary theory turn to analyzing projects in computer-based and networked media. The following considerations introduce some basic ideas, key hypotheses and interim results of our recent research which, under a broader transdisciplinary perspective, aims at analyzing social and cultural changes caused by the dissemination of computer-based and electronically networked communications systems. As regards literature, the moot question is whether a "new" literature is arising, i.e., whether those aesthetic communications in computer-based media that we still regard as "literature" retain the aesthetic difference essential for traditional print literature.

Language, Semiosis and Media

Various methodological approaches have been introduced and different terms have been proposed for many good reasons since literature in computer-based media has attracted the interest of many scholars all over the world. This includes such influential theories as "hypertext" and "hyperfiction" (Bolter; Landow; Suter and Böhler), "E-Poetry" (Glazier), "cybertext" and "ergodic literature" (Aarseth), "interfictions" (Simanowski, *Interfictions*), or "literature in electronic space" (Heibach) and—last but not least—"electronic literature" (Hayles) and "digital literature" (Simanowski, *Digitale Literatur*; Wardrip-Fruin, "Five Elements of Digital Literature"), which have turned out to be sort of umbrella terms.

We, however, prefer *not* to talk of "electronic" or "digital" literature but of "net literature" as an abbreviatory term for "writing in networked and programmable media" (Gendolla and Schäfer).[1] This is not for desperately adding another label for its own sake but because we think that there still is a continuous misunderstanding about both the etymology and meaning of "digital," which has serious consequences for the scholarly discourse. Speaking of "digital literature" is a tautological argument that ignores the peculiarities of human perception and cognition. By reading a text, human beings only perceive *discrete alphanumeric signifiers,* which could have been encoded in *any* sort of medium previously (Schäfer, "Sprachzeichenprozesse").

We consider the existence of information feedback loops between humans and sign processing machines as the major modification caused by computers in literary communication. Sense or meaning emerges from networked literary processes quite explicitly only through multiple "writing back" or "overwriting" activated textual elements or lines, as Ludwig Jäger has conceptualized it in his theory of recursive transcriptivity for all mediated processes of linguistic signs (29ff.). In local-area as well as in global computer networks every single bit of data can be processed at any point, so that, under the conditions of "permanent mutability" (Chaouli 68), every reading is just a temporary glimpse at a text in flux. The supposed "digitality" of computers, however, does not provide further assistance in explaining these processes. We do also insist that the "digital" should not be confused with binary code and that it is not necessarily tied to computer technologies. For defining the digital, binary coding is contingent, arbitrary, and independent of the medium (Pflüger 66ff.), and we do not need electronics to build a computer.[2] The crucial advantage of the binary code is that it can *easily* be electrified, thus allowing the calculation of every bit-serial, that is to say the processing of signifiers or symbols by programs. It does not need any further explanation here that the computer as a universal programmable machine is not a specific medium in itself but can potentially simulate every other medium. Hence computers are nothing else but temporary programming devices, a processing of a logical machine connected to analog input devices such as keyboards, microphones, mouses, motion sensors, and output devices such as screens, virtual reality environments or mobile phone displays.

Secondly, and this is of equal importance, a literary text has always been the result of digital coding. Literature operates with letters in the basic medium we call language, i.e., it is nothing else but a peculiar combination of discrete, discontinuous and arbitrary signs. It should not be forgotten that the etymological origin of "literature" can be traced back to the Latin *littera* (letter) that initially denoted all kinds of written texts. In a strict sense, it does not make much sense to talk of digital media regarding the storage and transmission of information.

However, we are not pretending that it does not make any difference whether literary texts are stored and transmitted in print or electronic media. That is why we would like to make clear now why we regard the aspect of computer-aided net-operations, the "net" as a multi-source feedback system for literary or other signs as the essential difference to literature in print media. It is not surprising that early discussions of literature in computer-based media to a large extent were focused on functions and semantics of the printed book. Although this is not in the focus of our interest, we would like to note that the transmission of linguistic signs via electronic networks represents the replacement of the well-established distribution system of the book culture that was based on the printing press and the book market. This position is currently being taken by a system with a completely different structure in which the feedback channel between producer and recipient is in principle open.

As regards literature, this also allows for a fresh perspective on the difference between offline and online projects. What we call "net literature" is not necessarily restricted to the Internet or the World Wide Web—even though the effects we briefly touched on are expanding in the global network in a very literal sense. But in our perspective it is crucial to keep in mind that feedback loops are a basic feature of the stand-alone computer itself as well as of communications of a user with his computer or communications of many users via computer networks.

These recursive transcriptions—and especially the enrichments or losses of meaning occurring there—cannot be fully recorded, let alone understood at present. But notably to the extent to which human sensory channels are linked to electronic sensor technology—and at present this is happening more and more densely and frequently—it is becoming more urgent to understand them better. In the run-up to such terminological and theoretical awareness, already today projects of net literature are reacting; they perceive the short-lived effects as well as the long-lived consequences, the positive and the negative possibilities of these transcriptions.

Thus, the *Assoziations-Blaster* by Alvar C.H. Freude and Dragen Espenschied already since 1999 represents the potentially unlimited possibilities of linking in the World Wide Web by processing the limitless, permanent white noise of the communication currents thereby documenting the pure "being-online-to-participate." But the fact that from the elements of such information currents sense can be generated by using combinatorial procedures poetry already has known since antiquity. Since that time it has always played with these possibilities and has discovered—since the first attempts of the "Stuttgarter Gruppe" ('Stuttgart Group') or the French group Oulipo in the 1960s—computer-aided media as ideal tools for this kind of production. The creation of such elementary sense can be observed by any user of quite simple poetry generators, for example on the *Internet Anagram Server*—and the generators can of course primarily be used by him- or herself (Wordsmith).

Barbara Campbell, who has allowed us to participate in her *1001 Nights Cast*, is also showing how a lasting effect can be gained from the never ending flow of news in the World Wide Web today—in other words, how complete and to-be-continued narratives can be built around the subject "survival-by-narration" as already did the oldest narratives from *A Thousand and One Nights*. Campbell attempts—analogous to the frame narrative of the oriental collection—to reactivate the motivation for narratives from out of the will to survive of the fictitious narrator (whose husband has died), and thus to reactivate also the thematic fascination for the Orient even under the changed conditions of computer-based and networked communication. Every morning she is looking in the daily papers for current articles on political events in the Middle Eastern countries; she gathers terms or fragments of sentences from them that might contain a generative potential for possible inside narratives in the context of the frame narrative. In other words, they are supposed to serve other authors as stimuli for the contribution of such an interesting and entertaining story that it is able to help the protagonist of the frame story to get over her loss, motivating her to continue her fictitious journey. Campbell presents this fragment on the site as so-called "prompt word/phrase," quasi as an appeal for potential authors to create texts of their own.

This collaborative writing project in principle offers an open entry for narrators of inside narratives or embedded stories within the frame that Campbell has provided as the initiator of the project. In this way, the project "describes" quite literally reflexive and sensory consequences of the novel links between body and spirit with social agents, devices and institutions. Thus, we can ask for the interplay of freedom and constraint, of indeterminateness and determination through formal directives induced as much by technical parameters and temporal constraints as by connections to historical genre conventions and the attribution of social roles. By asking these questions, the project permits *aesthetic* perception as literature always has done.

What then needs to be done in research on literature in computer-based media? In our opinion, two issues need to be given priority: First of all, a theory of literary human-machine communication is to be elaborated, and secondly, such an approach needs to be amended by an aesthetic theory of literature in computer-based and networked media.

Networks and Human-Machine Communication

The creative processes operating between the ideas of writers, the reactions and interventions of users, and the "autonomous" part of the machine have so far been neglected not so much by computer studies but certainly by literary studies. These heterarchical, distributed, and mutual connections between "writers," "works," and "readers" need to be taken into closer consideration.

Computers and networks should not be misunderstood as mere channels for the transmission of messages. In contrast to print media that—generally speaking—aim at storing and transmitting its input, computers are able to process signifiers according to a program and thus generate an output that can neither be predicted nor kept fully under control by writers or by readers.

We provisionally distinguish three parameters of communication:

- *Human-human communication,* i.e., various people co-operate in computer networks and thus become co-authors of a collaborative work, as, for example, in Claudia Klinger's *Beim Bäcker* ('At the Bakery') or the Austrian installation *Lichtzeile* ('Light Line'). Such *collaborative projects* are rooted in Dadaist and Surrealist cooperative works and in networked collaborative works that have been realized in the respective current communication networks (telephone, fax, radio broadcasting, satellite TV, e-mail, "Minitel," World Wide Web, mobile phones, SMS, etc.).

- *Human-machine communication,* i.e., literary texts that originate from computer-controlled processing of signifiers; the "creativity" is (partly) transferred to the machine in projects such as David Link's *Poetry Machine 1.0* or in the text generators documented in Christopher T. Funkhouser's eminent monograph *Prehistoric Digital Poetry*. Such automatic text generators generate literature by calculating new character strings. This means that the counting with a random number replaces the execution of a literary idea. They have a long previous history in the diverse forms of combinatory poetry experimenting with the fact that the literary text is also determined by technical levels of programming and processes (Schäfer, "Gutenberg Galaxy Revis(it)ed").

- *Human-machine-human-machine-etc. communication:* These are potentially endless collaborations of writers, readers, and computer programs. Before, during, *and* after its production, transmission and reception/consumption this "literature" is affected in many ways by the processing of computers. What traditionally has been called "intersubjectivity" enters into a new dimension when automatic and autonomous transcriptions of intended and realized texts do not only affect their design but also have a strong impact on the meaning of a text, on its semantics. Thus, the environment furnished with electronic sensors and the direct linking of the bodies with networked systems are playfully interacting through or reflecting each other in the different literary projects. The installation *Text Rain* by Camille Utterback and Romy Achituv for example initially disassembles the elements of its own basis, namely the poem by Evan Zimroth "Talk, You" on the difficulties of communication and physical nearness, at the outset dissolving it into letters and words falling from up above with which the viewers then can "play" with their hands, arms, legs, and the silhouettes of dark objects: they can catch them, gather them, divert them and hold onto them. One could also say: they "read-out" the elements and reconnect them in an altered way into meaningful and sensible or senseless "words," into ephemeral successions of signs that for a short while seem to have "meaning" that, however, can directly dissolve again.

It is our key hypothesis that it cannot definitely be decided *who or what* is at the origin of such a process of signification. This definitely calls the conceptions of "author," "work of art" and "reader" into question—with far-reaching aesthetic but also very severe legal consequences. A work of art or a literary text thus can no longer be regarded as the materialization of a finalized creative process of a gifted person (Rohrhuber). It is just an ephemeral, transitory or mutable stage of a potentially never-ending process of creation, a sort of computer-based *ars combinatoria*.

We thus believe that an enhanced *model of literary human-machine communication* has to be worked out starting from the assumption that there are various layers that mutually influence each other in new media or are influenced by new media. The French theorist and artist Philippe Bootz has already developed initial ideas for such a model. He differentiates the functions of writing, processing and reading:

> From a semiotic point of view, we can separate the classical and general semiotic notion of text (the text is the object of interpretation) into three different parts that do not act in the same space. Program and data (in high-level forms) constitute the *texte-auteur* ("author-text" or "text-of-inscription"). This is a sign that is only accessible by the author. . . . The second sign is constituted by what will be considered as "the text" by the reader. It is the *texte-à-voir* ("text-to-be-seen" or "text-of-visualization"). It is a part of the observable transient event that can differ from a reader to another . . . The physical process itself is a function. From a semiotic point of view, it transforms the *texte-auteur* into the *texte-à-voir*. (93ff.)

Between writing and reading a text, there are various encoding and decoding procedures on distinct human and machine levels, which mutually "read" and "write" onto each other. The role of the arts in general and of literature in particular may be seen in an *aesthetic perception and reflection* of transitions, disturbances, associations between these levels, identifying the crucial junctions of decisions between humans and machines.

For this approach, the definitions and conceptions of "nets" and "networks" are decisive. It is quite useful to realize that the word fields open up lots of seemingly incompatible definitions from fishing nets to traffic systems, from neural nets to energy supply grids, from soccer goals to spider webs. At first glance, it may not be obvious what all these different sorts of nets may have in common. We thus refer to the philosopher Hartmut Böhme, the sociologist Manuel Castells and the network theorist Albert-László Barabási who—among others—coined very broad definitions, which nonetheless may be helpful. Böhme defines nets as follows:

> *Netze sind biologische oder anthropogen artifizielle Organisationsformen zur Produktion, Distribution und Kommunikation von materiellen und symbolischen Objekten. . . . Netze bilden komplexe zeiträumliche dynamische Systeme. . . . Sie tun dies nach stabilen Prinzipien, doch in instabilen Gleichgewichten, selbstgenerativ, selbststeuernd, selbsterweiternd, also autopoietisch und evolutionär.* (19)

Nets/networks can be regarded as biological or man-made, artificial organizations for the production, distribution and communication of material and symbolic objects. . . . Nets create complex dynamic systems in time and space. . . . Their bases are stable regularities but instable balances, they are self-generating, self-controlled, and self-expanding, that is to say: they are autopoietical and evolutionary.

According to Castells, a network is a set of interconnected nodes with a node being a point with a curve intersecting itself. This implies that networks are *open* structures that are able to expand beyond all measure and thus integrate new nodes—it does not matter on this general level whether these are brain cells, human beings, machines or societies.

These arguments have two consequences: First of all, they imply that all these nodes must be able to communicate within the network, which means that they either need to share the same communication code or that these codes can be translated into each other (Castells 470f.). That is why networks may be regarded as topological configurations, which are well suited for explaining the increasing complexity of interactions and the emergence of non-predictable developmental patterns as a result of generic "creative" processes. Secondly, this approach connects the self-organizing dynamics of mental processes with that of computers producing hitherto unpredictable configurations. Computer-based media and electronic networks permit and require an increasingly far-reaching modularization of production processes, which potentially are always under construction. Due to the structural congruence of stand-alone computers and computer networks—the German media theorist Hartmut Winkler, for example, claims that it is telegraphy which is operating both inside and outside the single computer—(213), the principles of storing, processing and transmitting signifiers potentially expand without any limit.

According to Barabási, networks are generally not random; particular nodes are being favored. They form so-called "hubs," i.e. nodes with an extraordinarily large number of links: "Hubs appear in most large complex networks. . . . They are ubiquitous, a generic building block of our complex, interconnected world" (63). Whenever various elements are connected to networks, the so-called "connectors," i.e., "nodes with an anomalously large number of links" (56), either immediately or gradually develop a strong attraction to energies, to information or to communication. Similar processes are tuning in with one another, enhancing mutual feedbacks, canceling dissimilar processes.[3]

Another corresponding conception has been repeatedly brought forward by the German philosopher Hans Blumenberg, namely that of *simultaneousness*. Blumenberg argues that at any point the most banal and the most important things happen at the same time. The relation between occurrences that we regard as significant and those that we regard as completely insignificant derives only from this simultaneousness. According to Blumenberg, the simultaneity of various major events, minor occurrences and subjective trains of thought amalgamate to a sort of joint "horizon of meaning" (Blumenberg) which is the ultimate pre-condition for any emergence of meaning.

A model that has been intensely developed in the research done on artificial intelligence in recent years and that certainly can be connected to these ideas—namely the so-called *connectionism*, or better the theory of connectionist systems going far beyond the actual AI—is based on the assumption that a multiplicity of heterogeneous but effectively connected units of processing can be networked into a system. Through this networked interconnection, the individual elements permanently influence each other in their functions. It is true that this approach, as far as we can see, cannot yet be directly applied to literary procedures and especially not to the new procedures developed in computer-based networks of literary communication. However, it clearly lends itself as a comprehensive model for the constantly occurring, split-second, automatically coupled or specifically and intentionally planned multimedial and multimodal links between man and machine. We thus think that for working out a revised theory of literature, especially of "net literature," those four conceptions we mentioned should be taken into further consideration:

- attraction in networks ("hubs");

- synchronizations by resonances;

- narratives as means of creating meaning from coincidental actions and occurrences;

- connections of texts, images and sounds as multimodal operations between the central nervous system, physical-sensual interfaces and computers.

Why that? On an abstract level, literature has always been a mode of connecting contingent events to more or less meaningful strings of signifiers—to stories, poems or drama—or in the words of the French philosopher Paul Ricœur: to an *intrigue*. It was Ricœur who once drew our attention to the etymological source of "intrigue," which derives from the Latin *intricare*, "tying things together". Literary texts emerge from connecting or coupling coincidental, simultaneous, similar, etc., occurrences and ideas which seem to happen by chance to a meaningful chain of events—no matter whether they are thrilling, tragic, amusing or boring. For doing this, cultures throughout time invented various literary genres and canonical models which—this has been the basic idea of all theories of "intertextuality" from Mikhail Bakhtin to Julia Kristeva and others—eventually constitute the realm of literature as a whole by interacting through various cultural and media systems.

This is what different approaches of critical theory such as hermeneutics, systems theory or reader-response theories have in common: There are nothing but signifiers referring to signifiers, symbols referring to symbols, communications referring to communications—which eventually constitute networks of texts: of "great" classics as well as of minor adaptations, of pulp fiction as well as of diaries of amateur writers.

If, however, "writers" *and* literary texts *and* "readers" are connected through computer-based electronic networks, these theories, formal constraints and cultural practices prove to be insufficient and need to be complemented by the physical laws and technical procedures mentioned above:

- attraction of certain themes, motives, and methods simply for reasons of accumulation: elements often copied or repeated must be important; text generators based on technical linkages create automatic associations or completions of net literature;

- effects of synchronizations and resonances during the processing of texts in the net, including "net poetry" or "net literature."

This does not immediately lead to great narratives, and the long-awaited "Ulysses of the Internet" is still to come. But we can certainly observe some clusterings, some patterns, or some focal points of attention. Under present-day cultural and technological conditions, there apparently is nothing like a "work of art" which has been finalized by its creator, a solitary, complete and unique piece to which nothing can be added or from which nothing can be taken away. Instead, we can only observe mutable and transitory effects on screens or other display media: a constantly transforming Web of signifiers that may constitute a *"net-work."*

Aesthetic Difference and Literariness

However, from our point of view, such a theory of communication cannot be regarded as a sufficient theoretical model for describing the peculiarities of the *literary* system. As literature in general can be regarded as a medium of *testing action* of interactions and its consequences, it should be worthwhile to apply *aesthetic criteria* to literary human-machine communications in networked media. From this point of view, literature has been a medium of *virtual realities* long before modern computer technologies developed. The alphabetic script, i.e., discrete and alphanumeric code, has proved to be the most successful medium of storing, processing and transmitting information in/from the human mind to storage devices such as stone, wood, papyrus, leather or paper to date. If we regard literature as a sort of meta-medium, a commentary to the consequences of the exteriorization of imagination and ideas by producing an alternative reality, the specific *literariness* of texts needs to be put at the center of attention of research. In our opinion, in most studies this has not been done so far: This even applies to such important books like Espen Aarseth's seminal study *Cybertext* or Christiane Heibach's *Literatur im elektronischen Raum* [*Literature in Electronic Space*] which claims to focus on what she calls "Sprachkunst" ('art of language') in its varying medial surroundings but avoids any answer to the crucial question whether there is a unique *aesthetic difference* regarding literature in computer-based and networked media.

In order to illustrate what is meant by *aesthetic difference* let us return to Utterback and Achituv's *Text Rain*: The poem by Evan Zimroth as the basis of the installation talks of the wish for communication, and in a literal sense: as a wish of the body transferred into speech, into words:

> I like talking with you,
>   simply that: *conversing,*
> . . .
> At your turning,
> each part of my body turns to verb.

And it is just that which is declared impossible in the poem, a turning into nothingness, empty chatter:

...we are synonyms
for limbs' loosening of syntax,
and yet turn to nothing:
It's just talk. (40)

Here, from the conflict between the writing surface and imagination, between the two-dimensional medium of letters on a surface—on the page of the book, the monitor or the projection screen—and the multidimensional imaginative realm of the reader, develops *aesthetic difference*. This conflict, indissoluble in the traditional space of the medium book now, in the three-dimensional space of the installation is solved in a quite specific way by returning the words back to the bodies. However, the conflict on this level is also renewed: The body or the bodies may move as they like; they are unable to reassemble the poem *as a whole*. *Aesthetic difference* as a perceptional conflict or tension between the senses and sense in this installation has been transcribed into the electronic-organic coupling.

What then are the methodological consequences for research in net literature? First of all, the established theories of literature such as hermeneutics, formalism, reader-response theory, systems or discourse theories need to be critically reviewed. How do they conceptualize literariness? What do they regard as specific aesthetic qualities of texts? Are any of their key terms and conceptions such as "defamiliarization" (Shklovsky), "horizon of expectation" and "aesthetic experience" (Jauß), "gaps" and "implied reader" (Iser), "interdiscourse" (Jürgen Link), "autopoiesis" and "communication" (Luhmann), and so on relevant for analyzing "net literature?"

The question remains whether a radically new literary quality is developing: Is it possible to amalgamate the openness of networked communications with the claims of traditional aesthetic theories for perfection, consistency and harmony of finalized texts or works of art? Texts in computer networks can only be described as transitory effects of human-machine-human-etc.-communication. Consequently, we argue that the reassessment of some important epistemological and aesthetic categories may provide a theoretical foundation for the key question about the specific aesthetic qualities of literature under the conditions of permanent mutability of signifiers.

- *Intentionality vs. chance:* How do intentional actions of the persons involved—particularly those of writers—coincide with computer-based chance operations? How can the consequences for traditional conceptions of "authorship" be described? Unlike print literature, the initial and intentional idea of the author—for example Umberto Eco's desire of "poisoning a monk" (509) when he wrote *The Name of the Rose*—is being refracted or transformed by both human and machine "agents" in net literature. It is only effective in particular time segments, for example when an author lays down his initial idea or when some other participants are actively contributing to the text; in other time segments, computer programs are "writing." Hence every primordial intention is being split up spatially as well as temporally: It does not emanate from one exceptionally talented mind but is being agglomerated step by step from recursive processes between minds and computers.

- *Performativity/performance:* How can the relations between the hidden processing of algorithms and the performance of transitory texts on various interfaces be described? This hidden processing can only be perceived—and then be manipulated—when its output (as pixels, sound waves, touch or smell signals) is projected onto various interfaces. There is nothing like the progression from manuscript to the printed book but writing itself becomes performative, and this performance is in part defined by software (Kamphusmann).

- *Emergence:* How can the shift of the emergence (of meaning), which once used to be an element of text alone, be described as something that now is generated in processes between human and machine agents? The emerging meaning can no longer be regarded as part of the finished work of art, but it is generated in recursive actions between writer(s), readers and computers.

- *Game/Play:* Does it make any sense to examine new forms of "net literature" using terminologies and concepts of various theories of play? It may be helpful to analyze all those new forms, procedures and objects that become manifest in net literature by taking up the new approaches of game studies and ludology.

The specific "virtuality" of literature has never been primarily dependent on its relation to nature, society, etc., but above all on its *self-reflective relation to the literary tradition* (this may be called first-order virtuality). In computer-based and networked media, literary forms have emerged that can no longer be produced, stored or transmitted by traditional materials and media. It is only these forms that now could be called "virtual" with some validity. In terms of "virtuality," these forms then would allow for forms of second- or third-order virtuality—or even virtualities of n-dimensional order corresponding to the grade of explicit or implicit self-reflectivity.

A prominent example of *first-order virtuality* can be seen in Cervantes' *Don Quijote* who is continuously virtualizing knightly romances. American and European Literature of the 19th and 20th century continued with these procedures of reflexivity by inventing metaphors, introducing the montage of advertising materials in Alfred Döblin's *Berlin Alexanderplatz* or by using "stream of consciousness" in James Joyce's *Ulysses*.

By playing with functional or mechanized communications net literature on the one hand assembles an aesthetic difference—that is to say a difference in the perception of our world. On the other hand, media technologies are giving important impulses in the evolution of literature, and only in the interplay of that difference and these media technologies are the literary forms emerging. We would like to distinguish this essential virtuality—i.e., the first-order virtuality—from procedures of virtualization of the second, third or n[th] order.

A first, rather simple example for *higher-order virtuality* is a text adventure like Thomas Holz' *Murder Without Escape*, which on the one hand is a murder mystery, while on the other is a game using elements and modules of crime stories (crime, murderer, victim, rooms, trails, circumstantial evidence and so on). The key issue for our argument is that the *implicit* mental position of crime stories—the (murderous) imagination of the reader—is turned into an *explicit* combination of reading and acting: into reading, clicking and, potentially, writing.

Narrative Models and Story Elements: An Exemplary Case Study

Processes or "works" of net literature fundamentally pose all those questions once more that can be asked of printed texts as well. Therefore, the comparison to book-literature promises to provide interesting information on continuities and discontinuities. Given that a migration of literary forms from printed texts into computer-aided media apparently is taking place, there must be invariant structures that only enable us to speak of "literature" as a single field. Our assumption is that the semantics of literary concepts therefore need be more durable than the pragmatics of communicative acts. Among those concepts, literary genres still play an important role since they reflect core aspects of literariness. For reasons of space we would like to illustrate this with an example of only one narrative genre, namely crime fiction, which continues to be popular to this day—maybe because it is structured in a comparatively conventional way.[4] As common features between crime fiction in books and computer-based media we can note three basic elements that, according to Ulrich Schulz-Buschhaus, can be identified in all crime novels, films, TV drama, hyperfictions or computer games:

1. *Mystery:* In the beginning, there always is a mystery that the detective has to solve during the course of his investigation. It is both the precondi-

tion *and* the continuing antinomy of the detective's investigation that eventually lead to a—usually unexpected and surprising—solution of the case and to the revelation of the culprit.

2. *Analysis:* The reader competes with the detective in making observations, analyzing the testimonies of witnesses and suspects, assessing evidence, setting up hypotheses, and so on.

3. *Action:* This category describes the plot of the story; it covers all the narrative elements such as the committing of the crime itself, the detection, the escape and chase of suspects, and so on (Schulz-Buschhaus 3).

At the beginning of *A Scandal in Bohemia* (1891), the first ever Sherlock Holmes story, the detective is described as "the most perfect reasoning and observing machine" (Doyle 1). His systematic investigation of the crime competes against the criminal's strategy of obscuration that allows the reader to draw conclusions about his intentions. These mutually determining strategies constitute a narrative model in which—due to the antinomy of revelation and obscuration—*visibility* serves as a fundamental structural principle. Every criminal action leaves a number of clues at the crime scene. The detective thus has to be attentive for the most ephemeral, heterogeneous and disparate clues—in particular small or even microscopic objects such as hair, blood spots, fingerprints, ashes or DNA traces. According to K. Ludwig Pfeiffer, the investigative work thus requires a "semiotische Empirisierung der imaginativen Analyse" ('semiotic empiricizing of the imaginative analysis') (251). It is based upon the interpretation of indexical signs in order to recover the existential link between the signifier, the signified and the referent, which is the starting point for uncovering hidden connections and for reconstructing the chain of events.

The pleasure of reading such a novel derives from its *hysteron-proteron*-structure, a particular reversal of the chronological order: Since the detective who is gathering evidence and fitting them to his hypotheses advances into the past in order to examine the interplay of causes and effects which led to the crime, the initial event—the criminal action—is only told in detail at the end of the story. Whereas the plot of an adventure story is arranged on a narrative trajectory in the temporal order of *events,* the plot of a crime story follows the order of *discoveries.*

In our context, the crucial question arises whether this specific tension in crime fiction can be transferred to computer-based media. Is there any equivalent to the narrative trajectory of traditional crime novels in print media? Do hypertext fictions and games, in which the plot is separated into a multitude of narrative threads, also satisfy the criterion of narrative coherence? Have the elements of "mystery," "analysis" and "action" survived the transferral into a different media dispositive? If yes, then how have their interrelationships changed?

Using crime fiction, it therefore is possible to illustrate our thesis that computer-based media demand an explicitly active engagement with the plot of narratives. This again points to the question to what extent *games* are "narrative"—and on the other hand, to what extent *stories* can be playful. If the "narrativity of games is not an end in itself but a means toward a goal" (Ryan 349), we have to be aware of the latent conflict between the writer's or game designer's aim to preserve narrative coherence and the reader/player's desire for *interactivity*.

This indicates a crucial difference between detective stories in books and those in net literature or in computer games: In crime fiction, all the necessary clues have to be revealed but, at the same time, the mystery has to be strictly preserved until the end of the story in order to sustain the suspense. While the coherence of the story and the complete process of induction, abduction, and deduction remain under the author's control, in games as well as in net literature, however, the solving of the mystery has to be subdivided into a series of minor challenges which the reader/player has to pass one by one in order to advance.

This leads us back to our introductory assumptions that, firstly, applying narratives to computer-based media increasingly requires a *modularization* of processes, and that, secondly, the *implicit* mental position of crime stories is turned into an *explicit* combination of *perceiving and acting*. In games and in net literature, the detective's investigation has to be realized as a *series of solvable problems*. The entire case thus is subdivided into a number of autonomous missions that have to be completed in a successive order. The key question is whether—as a result of this modularization—there is a general and unavoidable tendency to prematurely unravel the mystery—or at least to reveal important clues too early. If this in principle is the case, this raises the further question whether there are strategies to compensate for this loss of narrative coherence, and, if yes, by which means either an equivalent or a different form of narrative trajectory can be implemented.

On the *pragmatic* level, the analysis centers on the user participation, i.e., on *interactivity* and *reactivity*. We consider readers/players' actions as *hybrids* of both narrative and playful moments. This can paradigmatically be seen in *mystery games*, which have adapted the motives and devices of crime fiction to computer-based media. According to Ryan,

> this genre allows greater narrative sophistication than the others because it connects two narrative levels: one constituted by the actions

of users, as they wander through the fictional world in search for clues, and the other by the story to be reconstructed. Since the story on this second level is independent of the actions of users, it can be as fully controlled by the author/designer as the plot of a novel. (352)

If the story emerges as an output of a series of readers/players' actions, the *abductive* process of evaluating clues and of developing hypotheses about what has really happened stimulates the reader/player's imagination in a very similar way to that of the reader of a novel. The suspense is maintained by "the taking together of both past and future horizons, which consciousness spans" (Rankin 4), or, in the terms coined by Husserl and Ricœur: by *"retention"* and *"protention."* In both stories and games, readers or players organize events into successions by reassessing their past experiences and hypotheses and by looking forward to possible future developments.

The deductive element of the detective's method, however, which, in print media, is to provide a surprising solution of a case only at the end of a story, has in principle been maintained in computer-based media—but with far-reaching modifications. In games and net literature, the mystery is unraveled if—and *only if!*—the readers/players' actions, which have been inspired by their imaginative analysis in the course of the reception, turn out to be in accordance with pre-scripted solutions that have been programmed by the game designers and implemented into the rules and computer operations. There is no way for the reader/player to keep up the suspense without constantly surmounting challenges, i.e., without complementing the imaginary activity of perceiving what is happening on the screen with explicit actions such as, for example, choosing between different links in a hypertext fiction or by controlling an avatar in a virtual world.

In the computer game *Sherlock Holmes: The Case of the Silver Earring*, which is full of allusions to the long tradition of Sherlock Holmes novels and movies, players are strongly encouraged not to miss out on any of the dialogue options, because these interrogations give meaningful evidence, and because—which, at some point is even more significant—sometimes talking about one subject opens up possibilities for others. Of core importance is Holmes' notebook in which, most importantly, all the testimonies of the characters in the game the player (as Holmes or Watson, his assistant) has spoken to, as well as the reports and documents such as newspaper clippings, postcards, pictures, etc., that have been uncovered, are collected. Hence, everything the player needs in order to solve the mystery is gathered in the inventory in the course of the investigation.

It is of eminent importance not to neglect any object or testimony, because otherwise it is impossible to advance to the next level of the game. Thus, even the minutest clue has to be discovered and all interrogations have to be conducted before Holmes and Watson note that all their tasks on this day of their investigation, i.e., on this particular game level, have successfully been performed and that it is about time to return to their quarters. The return to their lodgings always indicates that the player has to take a *quiz*, in which s/he has to answer "yes" or "no" to each question and to provide evidence from the notebook to justify the answers given. Hence the deduction, the third and last element of the detective's method, is implemented into an abstract game in which success depends on correctly answering questions.

Most notably, *The Case of the Silver Earring*, like mystery games in general, is a "progression game," but its hybridization with both "emergence game" elements and narrative cut-scenes helps to resolve the paradoxical relationship of narrative and game elements. On the one hand, there is always a link between playtime and fictional time in games, which Juul described as "projection": "Projection means that the player's time and actions are projected onto the game world where they take on a fictional meaning" (143). The chronology of the fictional time must be strictly respected in games, because both flash-forwards and flashbacks in interactive media would inevitably end up in the paradoxical situation that player's actions on one time level may render the fictional world on another time level impossible. On the other hand, the narrated story often requires different time levels. Therefore, two strategies of correlating different time levels are applied in the game: Firstly, the player only gets to the next level if he/she has correctly answered all the quiz questions—in other words, Sherlock Holmes can only carry on with his investigations on the following day if the player has succeeded in the quiz game. Secondly, the narrative coherence of the mystery game can only be controlled if additional information about the fictional world is again and again introduced to the player.

Frank Klötgen's hyperfiction *Spätwinterhitze* demonstrates that it is by no means simple to create the agonal tension of crime fiction while at the same time opening up interactive possibilities. The reader neither has many opportunities to influence the progression of the story by deciding for multivariant plot lines, nor is he authorized to actively contribute to the story. In most parts of the story, he can only click from one link to the other, from "footprint" to "footprint"—in a literal sense the "footprints" are links to the following point of the story—and thus come across one clue after the other. Having in mind that there is a conflict between the reader's desire for narrative coherence and the permanent mutability of signifiers in computer-based media, Klötgen may have been aware that

> it is simply not possible to construct a coherent story out of every permutation of a set of textual fragments, because fragments are

implicitly ordered by relations of presupposition, material causality, psychological motivation, and temporal sequence. (Ryan 341)

There are only a few points that permit a certain degree of interactivity: At one point, the reader has to choose—in a multiple-choice test with pre-scripted answers—between different options in order to get on with the investigation. At this point, the interplay of abduction and deduction is implemented into a combination game that assesses the reader's comprehension of the story up to this point. He can only read on after having opted for the right combination of statements, which is only possible if the reader has followed the development of the story very carefully and has remembered the key situations (of course, he/she can also solve the puzzle by testing all possible combinations). At this point, *Spätwinterhitze* offers something like the nucleus of an "interactive narrative." It points at the crucial difference between reading a detective story in a book and "reading" it from a multimedia device: The imaginary tension between expectation and disappointment is disturbed or disrupted by the game features; the imaginary theater of the reader/detective is interrupted by the action of the player and his "agent." Therefore, the tension oscillates between the reader's reflections and his actions, so that the imaginary rapture of the reader and the player's immersion into the virtual world pale in comparison to his agency if linear narrative and interactive game features are brought together in one moment/situation.

If we regard literature as a specific mode of perception, as a sort of explicit "interface" for conflicts between an individual's subjective desires and social demands, in particular between the subjective and the collective unconscious, then media technologies add a sort of "technological unconscious," the forms and structures of which always have to be taken into consideration. In computer-based and networked media, code, scripts and programs represent the "technological unconscious." The complex feedback loops between individuals, society and technology are being reflected in net literature—ranging from consciously controlled to random processes.

Jean-Pierre Balpe's interactive and generative crime novel *Trajectoires* may serve as an example for the impact of algorithmic text generation on literary genres. It starts with a plot identical for every reader: On August 1st, 2009, in the region of Gâtinais, 24 persons receive an anonymous e-mail. Who is the "Raven" threatening to kill them? What is the difference between the psychological terror that he inflicts today and the political terror of 1793? The singularity of Balpe's project is based on the fact that it allows combining not just text, sound, pictures—stills as well as moving pictures—or interactive programs, but also computer codes (which are an integral part of the piece) for creating computer-aided literature.

Trajectoires could have been a perfect example for supporting our assumption insofar as Balpe does not only confront the mail recipients'—and the reader's—subjective desire to survive the threat with collective social restrictions (which Balpe calls the "sous-univers" ('sub-universe'))—the intimidating power of terror in this case—but, in addition, these conflicts are technologically organized by computer software. Although this program can be influenced to a certain degree by the reader, s/he constantly has to cope with the arbitrary output of the text-generating computer.

Therefore, the emphasis is on "*could* have been:" although Balpe claims his piece to be a crime or terror story, he does not observe the rules of the genres. In particular, he disregards the requirement to carefully intensify and dissipate suspense by foreshadowing, postponing or misdirecting possible outcomes (what we earlier described as interplay of "protention" and "retention"). Instead, *Trajectoires* only offers variations of the same basic patterns that all too soon make reading and intervening rather boring—just like a game of dice without any chance of winning.

In contrast to Balpe's assertion, the reader does *not* become an essential element of this fiction because there are too many variations possible between random and intentional operations. Balpe argues as follows:

> The narrative is not totally built in advance but put together from a variety of virtualities that are—or are not—actualizing themselves in the course of reading. This reading is then fundamental and tends to substitute itself to the diegetic axis. Each new reading—actualizing the narrative in a new way, built on what I call micro-fictions—creates its own diegesis, which is not a predetermined but an undetermined diegetic axis. This really means: Any reader A needs to develop a unique hypothesis giving him an idea of the narrative that is different from that of any reader B. . . . One novel can thus be constituted by one or an infinite number of texts and no reader reads the same number of texts. There is no structure of the narrative, only an idea of a virtual one built by the reading itself. ("Principles and Processes" 313)

This, however, is contrary to the genre conventions of crime fiction. An imagination that creates nothing but variations cannot be held together by a larger narrative trajectory. It only provides opportunities to make free *associations,* but it certainly does not create anything like a narrative *reality.* Therefore, Balpe's idea that "generative literature's only pretension is to enrich the text's potentialities" (315) is too vague: Literature can only be expanded if it is *constrained* at the same time, as regards stylistic or plot variations.

When asked in an interview how the reader should cope with the possibility of not finding the same clues again if he/she returns to the same page for a second time, Balpe argues: "Exactement comme si vous étiez un policier! Vous avez rencontré une concierge, elle vous a dit quelque chose, vous la rencontrez trois heures après, elle ne vous dira pas la même chose. . . ." ('Exactly as if you were a cop! You met a concierge who told you something, you see her again three hours later and she no longer tells you the same thing. . . .') (qtd. in Sadin). This may reflect the everyday working situation of detectives and policemen. The narrative trajectory of the detective novel, however, tends to follow a strictly defined pattern that is being narrated in reversed temporal order. *Trajectoires* would be a good example of narrative in computer-based media,

- if Balpe would have integrated the modules of the story into a narrative trajectory, at least a game-like one which is subdivided into various segments or a fragmentary one, for example one in which modules 1 to 24 are indispensable;

- if the text generator would be able to do more than just produce impressions or descriptions, namely *tell a story*—and this would necessarily require an intelligence that could anticipate and construct a story with an end in mind;

- or, if the reader could collaborate with the text generator in producing her or his own narration. In this case, however, the generator would be nothing but a sort of creative-writing tool.

Instead, the text/image generator enables the reader/user to generate lots of varying descriptions of characters, settings and situations that offer a vivid impression of the intimidating terrorist atmosphere—but it certainly is not what it claims to be: an interactive networked *crime* story. Markku Eskelinen, however, has imagined further new subgenres of crime fiction, for example stories whose genre or mode will change "based on how the text is being read—let's say the faster you read a detective story the faster it becomes a horror story to slow you down with gruesome details" (189), or a detective story may be turned "into a hypertext and boost its epistemological structures with conditional links, hiding the evidence so to speak, and then turn this ergodically static hypertext into an ergodically dynamic cybertext that after a certain time starts playing with both its own and its users' time and begins to destroy its static scriptons, that is, its very evidence" (191).

Conclusion

The examples discussed here for reasons of space were only able to give a brief overview of the questions with regard to literatures in computer-based media.

A lot of in-depth studies of net literature need to be conducted before our initial questions whether there is a "new" literature emerging and what this literature tells us about the state and the future of our societies will be satisfyingly answered. The first question can certainly be affirmed by now; the second question, however, whether this aesthetic reflection allows us to forecast how societies whose members are connected via computer networks will develop, whether their collaborations will eventually result in a state that deserves to be described as swarm intelligence rather than swarm stupidity, remains to be seen.

Translated by Brigitte Pichon and Dorian Rudnytsky

Notes

1   Our reserve against the aforementioned terms coincide with those that John Cayley as one of the most important writers, programmers and scholars in the international "electronic literature" community has formulated: "When I scratched around for a name to describe what I had been doing and continue to do, I rejected or badly needed to qualify those terms that had begun to circulate—hypertext, cybertext, hyperpoetry, cyberpoetry, elit(erature), epoetry, etc.—as either meaningless or misdirected. I still refer to what I do as 'writing in networked and programmable media' and I baulk at shortening this to electronic or digital writing.... Despite their association with a particular moment in cultural history, the 'new' of new media, the 'hyper' and 'cyber', the 'digital' and 'electronic', all these prefixes and the characterisations they encourage have the effect of removing history and locatedness. They substitute a fixation with the dehistoricised 'new' and an over-emphasis on delivery media-as-technology that overwhelms the determinations of formal and compositional technique." (605).

2   As Florian Cramer once put it, "computers can be built from broomsticks—and computer networks via shoestrings or bongo drums—if digital data, including executable algorithms, can be printed in books and read from them back into machines or, alternatively, executed in the mind of the reader, there is no reason why computer network poetry couldn't or shouldn't be printed as well in books" (267-269).

3   Such resonances and synchronizations have been traced by Michel Foucault in the chapter "The Four Similitudes" of his *The Order of Things*. It has been said that such pre-modern ways of thinking have prevailed in

most cultures, and that they may be a sort of blueprint for theories of aesthetics as sensory perception, as a sort of interpretation or countermovement against pure rationalism.

4 Our considerations on continuities and discontinuities in poetry and drama have been published elsewhere. (Gendolla; Schäfer, "Looking Behind the Façade").

Works Cited

Aarseth, Espen J. *Cybertext: Perspectives on Ergodic Literature.* Baltimore: Johns Hopkins UP, 1997.

Balpe, Jean-Pierre. *Trajectoires.* 2001. 31 July 2009 <http://www.trajectoires.univ-paris8.fr/>.

———. "Principles and Processes of Generative Literature: Questions to Literature." *The Aesthetics of Net Literature: Writing, Reading and Playing in Programmable Media.* Ed. Peter Gendolla and Jörgen Schäfer. Bielefeld: Transcript, 2007. 309-317.

Barabási, Albert-László. *Linked: The New Science of Networks.* Cambridge, MA: Perseus, 2003.

Blumenberg, Hans. *Lebenszeit und Weltzeit.* Frankfurt a.M.: Suhrkamp, 1986.

Böhme, Hartmut. "Netzwerke: Zur Theorie und Geschichte einer Konstruktion." *Netzwerke: Eine Kulturtechnik der Moderne.* Ed. Jürgen Barkhoff, Hartmut Böhme and Jeanne Riou. Cologne: Böhlau, 2004. 17-36.

Bolter, Jay D. *Writing Space: The Computer, Hypertext and the History of Writing.* Hillsdale: Erlbaum, 1991.

Bootz, Philippe. "The Problem of Form: *Transitoire Observable*, a Laboratory for Emergent Programmed Art." *The Aesthetics of Net Literature: Writing, Reading and Playing in Programmable Media.* Ed. Peter Gendolla and Jörgen Schäfer. Bielefeld: Transcript, 2007. 89-103.

Campbell, Barbara. *1001 Nights Cast.* 2005-08. 31 July 2009 <http://www.1001.net.au>.

Castells, Manuel. *The Rise of the Network Society.* Vol. 1. Cambridge, MA: Blackwell, 1996.

Cayley, John. "Screen Writing: A Practice-based, EuroRelative Introduction to Electronic Literature and Poetics." *Third Text* 21.5 (2007): 603-609.

Chaouli, Michel. "Was bedeutet: Online lesen? Über die Möglichkeit des Archivs im Cyberspace." *Digitale Literatur.* Ed. Heinz L. Arnold and Roberto Simanowski. Munich: Text + Kritik, 2001. 65-74.

Cramer, Florian. "Digital Code and Literary Text." *p0es1s: The Aesthetics of Digital Poetry.* Ed. Friedrich W. Block, Christiane Heibach and Karin Wenz. Ostfildern: Cantz, 2004. 263-275.

Doyle, Arthur C. *The Sherlock Holmes Illustrated Omnibus.* Vol. 1. London: Murray, 1978.

Eco, Umberto. *The Name of the Rose.* Trans. William Weaver. Fort Washington: Harvest, 1994.

Eskelinen, Markku. "Six Problems in Search of a Solution: The Challenge of Cybertext Theory and Ludology to Literary Theory." *The Aesthetics of Net Literature: Writing, Reading and Playing in Programmable Media.* Ed. Peter Gendolla and Jörgen Schäfer. Bielefeld: Transcript, 2007. 179-209.

Foucault, Michel. *The Order of Things: An Archeology of the Human Sciences.* Trans. A. M. Sheridan Smith. New York: Pantheon, 1970.

Freude, Alvar C.H., and Dragan Espenschied. *Assoziations-Blaster.* 1999. 31 July 2009 <http://www.a-blast.org/>.

Funkhouser, Christopher T. *Prehistoric Digital Poetry: An Archaeology of Forms, 1959-1995.* Tuscaloosa: U of Alabama P, 2007.

Gendolla, Peter. "Artificial Poetry: On Aesthetic Perception in Computer-Aided Literature." *Literary Art in Digital Performance: Case Studies and Critical Positions.* Ed. Francsico J. Ricardo. New York: Continuum, 2009.

Gendolla, Peter, and Jörgen Schäfer. "Playing With Signs: Towards an Aesthetic Theory of Net Literature." *The Aesthetics of Net Literature: Writing, Reading and Playing in Programmable Media.* Ed. Peter Gendolla and Jörgen Schäfer. Bielefeld: Transcript, 2007. 17-42.

Glazier, Loss P. *Digital Poetics: The Making of E-Poetries.* Tuscaloosa: U of Alabama P, 2002.

Hayles, N. Katherine. *Electronic Literature: New Horizons for the Literary.* Notre Dame: U of Notre Dame P, 2008.

Heibach, Christiane. *Literatur im elektronischen Raum.* Frankfurt a.M.: Suhrkamp, 2003.

Holz, Thomas. *Murder Without Escape.* 2000. 31 July 2009 <http://www.suspicion-of-murder.com/crime/e/book11.htm>.

Iser, Wolfgang. *The Act of Reading: A Theory of Aesthetic Response*. Baltimore: Johns Hopkins UP, 1978.

Jäger, Ludwig. "Transkriptivität: Zur medialen Logik der kulturellen Semantik." *Transkribieren: Medien/Lektüre*. Ed. Ludwig Jäger and Georg Stanitzek. Munich: Fink, 2002. 19-41.

Jauß, Hans R. *Aesthetic Experience and Literary Hermeneutics*. Trans. Michael Shaw. Minneapolis: U of Minnesota P, 1982.

Juul, Jesper. *Half-Real: Video Games between Real Rules and Fictional Worlds*. Cambridge, MA: MIT P, 2005.

Kamphusmann, Thomas. "Performanz des Erscheinens: Zur Dramatisierung des Schreibens unter den Bedingungen des Internet." *Zeitschrift für Literaturwissenschaft und Linguistik* 39.154 (2009): 31-53.

Klinger, Claudia. *Beim Bäcker*. 1996-2000. 31 July 2009 <http://www.claudiaklinger.de/archiv/baecker/index.htm>.

Klötgen, Frank. *Spätwinterhitze: Ein interaktiver Krimi*. CD-ROM. Dresden, Leipzig: Voland & Quist, 2004.

Landow, George P. *Hypertext 2.0: The Convergence of Contemporary Critical Theory and Technology*. Baltimore: Johns Hopkins UP, 1997.

Lem, Stanislaw. *Philosophie des Zufalls: Zu einer empirischen Theorie der Literatur*. Vol. 1. Berlin: Volk und Welt, 1990.

Lichtzeile. 1996-present. 31 July 2009 <http://www.lichtzeile.at>.

Link, David. *Poetry Machine 1.0*. Installation. 2001-2002.

Link, Jürgen. "Interdiscourse, Literature, and Collective Symbols: Theses towards a Theory of Discourse and Literature." *Enclictic* 8.1-2 (1984): 157-165.

Luhmann, Niklas. *Art as a Social System*. Trans. Eva Knodt. Stanford: Stanford UP, 2000.

Oulipo. *La littérature potentielle: Créations, re-créations, récréations*. Paris: Gallimard, 1988.

Pfeiffer, K. Ludwig. "Mentalität und Medium: Detektivroman, Großstadt oder ein zweiter Weg in die Moderne." *Poetica* 20 (1988): 234-259.

Pflüger, Jörg. "Wo die Quantität in Qualität umschlägt." *HyperKult II: Zur Ortsbestimmung analoger und digitaler Medien*. Ed. Martin Warnke, Wolfgang Coy and Georg Christoph Tholen. Bielefeld: Transcript, 2005. 27-94.

Rankin, Jenny. "What is Narrative? Ricœur, Bakhtin, and Process Approaches." *Concrescence* 3 (2002): 1-12.

Ricœur, Paul. *Time and Narrative*. Transl. Kathleen Blamey and David Pellauer. 3 vols. Chicago: U of Chicago P, 1990.

Rohrhuber, Julian. "Implications of Unfolding." *Paradoxes of Interactivity: Perspectives for Media Theory, Human-Computer Interaction, and Artistic Investigations.* Ed. Uwe Seifert, Jin Hyun Kim and Anthony Moore. Bielefeld: Transcript, 2008. 174-191.

Ryan, Marie-Laure. "Will New Media Produce New Narratives?" *Narrative Across Media: The Languages of Storytelling.* Ed. Marie-Laure Ryan. Lincoln: U of Nebraska P, 2004. 337-359.

Sadin, Eric. "Les Trajectoires de Jean-Pierre Balpe." 20 Apr. 2009 <http://www.manuscrit.com/Edito/invites/Pages/MarsMulti_TrajectoiresBalpe.asp>.

Schäfer, Jörgen. "Sprachzeichenprozesse: Überlegungen zur Codierung von Literatur in 'alten' und 'neuen' Medien." *Analog/Digital: Opposition oder Kontinuum? Zur Theorie und Geschichte einer Unterscheidung.* Ed. Jens Schröter and Alexander Böhnke. Bielefeld: Transcript, 2004. 143-168.

———. "Gutenberg Galaxy Revis(it)ed: A Brief History of Combinatory, Hypertextual and Collaborative Literature from the Baroque Period to the Present." *The Aesthetics of Net Literature: Writing, Reading and Playing in Programmable Media.* Ed. Peter Gendolla and Jörgen Schäfer. Bielefeld: Transcript, 2007. 121-160.

———. "Looking Behind the Façade: Playing and Performing an Interactive Drama." *Literary Art in Digital Performance: Case Studies and Critical Positions.* Ed. Francsico J. Ricardo. New York: Continuum, 2009.

Schulz-Buschhaus, Ulrich. *Formen und Ideologien des Kriminalromans: Ein gattungsgeschichtlicher Essay.* Frankfurt a.M.: Athenaion, 1975.

Sherlock Holmes: The Case of the Silver Earring. CD-ROM. Frogwares, 2004.

Shklovsky, Viktor. *Theory of Prose.* Trans. Benjamin Sher. Normal: Dalkey Archive P, 1991.

Simanowski, Roberto, ed. *Digitale Literatur.* Munich: Text + Kritik, 2001.

———. *Interfictions: Vom Schreiben im Netz.* Frankfurt a.M.: Suhrkamp, 2002.

Suter, Beat, and Michael Böhler, eds. *Hyperfiction: Hyperliterarisches Lesebuch: Internet und Literatur.* Basel: Stroemfeld, 1999.

Utterback, Camille, and Romy Achituv. *Text Rain.* 1999. 31 July 2009 <http://www.camilleutterback.com/textrain.html>.

Wardrip-Fruin, Noah. "Five Elements of Digital Literature." In this book.

Wardrip-Fruin, Noah, with David Durand, Brion Moss, and Elaine Froehlich. *News Reader. Regime Change.* 2004. 31 July 2009 <http://www.transition.turbulence.org/Works/twotxt/>.

Winkler, Hartmut. "Medium Computer: Zehn populäre Thesen zum Thema und warum sie möglicherweise falsch sind." *Das Gesicht der Welt: Medien in der digitalen Kultur.* Ed. Lorenz Engell and Britta Neitzel. Munich: Fink, 2004. 203-213.

Wordsmith. *Internet Anagram Server.* 31 July 2009 <http://www.wordsmith.org/anagram/advanced.html>.

Zimroth, Evan. "Talk, You." *Dead, Dinner, or Naked poems.* Chicago: Northwestern UP, 1993. 40.

Karin Wenz

Storytelling Goes On After the Credits

Fanfiction as a Case Study of Cyberliterature

This contribution will introduce fanfiction as a case study. Fanfiction has been discussed as an example of cyberliterature, a term used by Viires, which includes digital literature as well as digital games but also digitized literature, printed literature made available online. Cyberliterature is then used as a generic term including very different forms of literature and art. Fanfiction is a specific case chosen with two goals in mind:

1. As a form of popular (net) literature fanfiction will be discussed in relation to concepts like digital literature, net literature, and cyberliterature. Especially the case chosen here, fanfiction based on the digital game *Zelda,* makes it necessary to also discuss the relation of digital games and narrativity.

2. The dynamics of fan communities, the cooperative writing and the impact of the networked group of authors writing fanfiction are examples to introduce the methodology used here, which can best be described as a combination of virtual ethnography with a semiotic analysis of the texts chosen.

Fanfiction is a case study which contradicts the complaints, ubiquitous in society these days, about the development of teenagers and young adults, who seem to lack literacy and knowledge about their cultural heritage. But in contrast to these complaints, this new generation publishes a huge amount of texts online. One specific narrative fan practice, *fanfiction,* is the focus of this article. Under narrative fan practices, I understand a broad range of texts and activities that are based on existing narrative texts (source texts). Fans are continuously transforming source texts into new ones. They engage with a text not only by reading and discussing it; they also want to explore the fictional world of their beloved text further, expand it and share their interpretation with other fans. I use the concept "text" in a broad semiotic sense, thereby referring to sign systems in general, including, e.g., written texts, movies, games and theatrical performances. Fan narrative is the generic term including fanfiction, fan comics, fan videos/machinima, but also performances as for example cosplay, in case it includes a narrative and is not only a costume show on a catwalk. The fans' interpretation and engagement with a source text lead to the creation of narrative texts produced by fans that clearly relate to one source text, mostly a well-known text of popular culture.

We can observe new forms of literacy. Through narrative fan practices, a canon of popular culture is established as we find core texts of popular culture used by fans as source material: *Star Wars* and *Lord of the Rings*, for example, but also computer games such as *Zelda* or *World of Warcraft*, to name just a few. While the discourse on a decrease of cultural literacy exposes the worries concerning the established canon, a new canon is being established not by critics and institutions but by the consumers themselves. A question discussed on the web site <www.fanfiction.net> revealed the deviance in regard to a classical canon: "What is your favorite classic?" The answers ranged from Dante's *Inferno* and Shakespeare's works to contemporary popular literature and movies. The question of high culture and of a (literary) canon needs revision when we take such a broad range of examples into consideration. Classics—something we consider part of a literary canon—are indeed mentioned besides those "classics" which are part of a canon of popular literature. Fans participate actively in the production of narratives but also in the construction of a general consensus about a source-text. Fan narratives are heavily linked to the fan community and its interpretation and evaluation of a text and the related fan practices. In fan communities, fans are not only authors, but also critics and readers. At some point these identities may conflict. Being a fan with specific interests influences the way one looks at other fan texts and products. Fanfiction writers discuss the fanfiction as follows:

> Would a fan of the series . . . think "those are the demons from my series"? Or would they think "those are LIKE the demons from my series"? The second means you are writing original fic. [fiction] The first means you are writing fanfic. (Naheniel, "Qualify as fanfic?")[1]

A simple reference to another narrative would not be considered fanfiction. Fanfiction is using the setting and/or the characters and/or the storyline of another source text. Fanfiction wants to be a transformation or extension of the source text and does not claim to be independent of its source. The narratives written by fans have not been described as part of digital literature. What is the relation of fanfiction to concepts discussed in the context of digital textuality? Dependent on the concept, fanfiction seems to be a part of it or excluded from it. Below, I will discuss the concept net literature, cyberliterature and digital literature, and will position the texts produced by fans and published in most cases online in relation to these concepts.

Net Literature, Cyberliterature and Digital Literature

Digital media are networked media nowadays. Therefore, Gendolla and Schäfer suggest the term "net literature": "The medium always inscribes itself into the contents" (27). Fanfiction is one example elucidating the way in which the medium and its networked communication inscribe themselves into the medium. Fanfiction published online usually does not simply use the internet as a distribution platform, but as a possibility to write fiction, discuss it with other fans, rewrite it, react to the comments, and transform it anew. Other authors do not only refer to the source texts but also to examples of fanfiction in their own narratives. The dynamics created through the community of authors of fanfiction has an impact on the texts. The final result could simply be called digitized literature, as the medium then is the publication platform on which an author then starts to write the next chapter or the next fanfiction. The process, however, which can be observed on the web sites, can be compared to cooperative writing projects which depend on networked computers for their production but not for the execution. Even though Gendolla and Schäfer do not mention fanfiction as an example of net literature and their statement that "literature is—as are all the arts—engaged in individual aesthetization rather than social 'anesthetization'" (Gendolla and Schäfer 29), made me wonder whether they would include popular literature under the concept of net literature. Of course, authors of fanfiction also discuss style, grammar and content and support each other to improve their writing. However, the individual aesthetization is less important as the reference to a source text lies at the centre of the interest of an author of fanfiction. The source texts are part of popular culture as well and they do not claim to be part of high culture. In the discussion on narrative and digital textuality, Marie-Laure Ryan talks about a split condition. On the one hand we have digital literature, which she considers part of a literary avant-garde. She uses the metaphors of the "North Pole" vs. the "Tropics" ("Narrative and the Split Condition" 257). While the North Pole is the place where the avant-garde can be situated, which she describes as the cool intellectual and conceptual art forms, the Tropics would be the place to find the hot masses and products of popular culture. Digital games are an example she positions at the hot extreme of her scale. While print literature has a middle spectrum where she places authors such as Tony Morrison, Michel Tournier, Umberto Eco and others, digital textuality does not seem to have such a middle spectrum yet. Popular genres such as detective stories would have to be situated rather close to the Tropics. Ryan tried to avoid the political implication the use of metaphors such as right and left would evoke; however, north and south also evoke a political implication as the digital divide between those who have and are educated versus the have-nots (also commonly described as a north vs. south division). Concerning the population of authors and of readers, her distinction is well thought of as indeed the cold North Pole is sparsely populated, while the Tropics are inhabited by many. I will consider fanfiction as an example of popular net literature, of which some texts belong to the tropics and others reach a middle spectrum.

A definition of cyberliterature with the goal of including fanfiction can be found in Viires (154-155). He uses the concept "cyberliterature" in a generic way to refer to all forms of literature published digitally. His definition includes the concept of digital literature, for him a subordinate concept, which he discusses under the terms "hypertext literature and cybertexts." For him cybertexts—concurring with Aarseth (*Cybertext*)—are multimedia artifacts, "merging literature, visual arts, film, music" (Viires 155). The term corresponds with concepts such as "e-poetry" (Glazier), "new media poetry" (Kac) or "digital literature" (Simanowski, Block et al.). Cybertext applies to artistic projects that deal with media changes in language and language-based communication in computers and digital networks. Digital literature, as one specific form of cybertext, refers to a creative, experimental, playful, and also critical language art involving programming, multimedia, animation, interactivity, and net communications. The attribute "digital" emphasizes its semiotic nature, which influences the culture of computer technology in a specific way. Digital literature is based in its production, execution and reception on the use of the computer as a medium.

This is not the case for cyberliterature. For Viires, cyberliterature includes all literary texts available on the Web and therefore also forms that have explicitly been excluded from the field of digital literature: digitized versions of print literature and online literature magazine, as well as all non-professional literary texts available on the Web such as fanfiction, texts based on role-playing, and others. While for digital literature the computer (and especially the Web) is not only a tool for distributing literary texts—since those texts are already dependent on the digital medium in the processes of production and execution—this does not hold true for the two latter examples of digitized print literature and fanfiction. While the term cyberliterature includes fanfiction, it does not distinguish it from other literary forms published digitally.

In the case of fanfiction based on a digital game, we could argue that it can be considered a case of digital literature as the production of the text is dependent on the digital medium in so far as the playing of the game on which the text is based is a necessary precondition for the production of the text. The distribution of fanfiction is not necessarily dependent on the computer, as fanfiction had been published and still is published also in printed fanzines or booklets sold or distributed for free at fan conventions. The application of the term digital literature to the field of fanfiction therefore seems not convincing.

Neither is the production of the literature dependent—strictly speaking—on the computer. Even though playing the game is a precondition in the case of fanfiction dependent on digital games, this does not hold true for all other forms of fanfiction, such as those based on a novel, a comic or a movie. Digital literature seems to be a concept rather applied to the digital "North Pole" and not to the specificity of fanfiction, which is situated in or close to the "Tropics." Most texts produced by fans are not dependent on the computer as a medium of production and execution but on the distributive potential of digital media only. Narrowly understood, they are not part of digital literature and only in the broader concept of net literature can they be included as an important part of the field. Net literature seems to be the concept most adequate here in case we specify that we are dealing with a popular variant of net literature.

With the massive distribution of this kind of literature online on web sites such as fanfic.net and others, the literature has been made accessible to a broader public and the discussion about and interpretation of the source texts can be shared within a fan community worldwide. The accessibility and acknowledgement of fanfiction (and other fan practices) has lead to a discussion about fan culture.

Fan Culture

The line between fans and non-fans used to be more clear-cut. A fan was an enthusiast, a fanatic, an intensive reader, spectator or player who liked to express his affinity and loyalty to a certain source text. User participation online allows for a more active, constructive audience. Fan cultures, which inhabited niches and whose publication possibilities were limited, are now visible and accessible to everyone, from young teenagers, who write for friends, to professionals. The distinction is not always easy to make, as most publishers of fanfiction use a screen name which does not tell us who the person is behind it. Fans used to include the enthusiast and the active audience. This has changed since the growth of the internet and especially since the development of Web 2.0, as the general audience is invited to participate. Fan practices are slowly becoming mainstream practices. Jenkins comments ironically on this change: "The old ideal might have been the couch potato; the new ideal is almost certainly a fan" ("Afterword" 361). Fan practices have become more visible as fans no longer live in niches but use distribution channels online that are accessible to a broad public.

Fans engage with a text, a movie or a computer game not only by reading and discussing it; they also want to explore the fictional world of their beloved text further, expand it and share their interpretation with other fans. The fans' interpretation and engagement lead to the creation of fan narratives produced by fans that clearly relate to one source text, mostly a "critically acclaimed" text of popular culture. Fan practices play with narratives of popular culture, which are part of a shared culture, establishing intermedial relations in a surprising and often ironical way. Fanfiction is based on existing texts and transforms them into new ones, thereby expanding the texts into a larger network. Fanfiction can be understood as an hommage to a source text and at the same time as an expansion: fans rewrite storylines from different perspectives, add something untold or unseen in the source text, or add an entirely new storyline. The Web enables the distribution but also the discussion and evaluation of fanfiction. As long as an author of fanfiction uses a disclaimer referring to the source text and its copyright, he or she is free to publish the text. In the example of fanfiction based on a digital game, there is not one author of the source text but a group of game designers and the narrative implemented in the game is only one element of the game world. Authors of fanfiction based on a digital game do not only treat the digital game as a source text but additionally include their playing experience of the game. This means that the fanfiction refers to the gameplay itself and not only to the gameworld of which a storyline is one part. The experience of playing the game and understanding the game's rules as well as the inconsistencies experienced while playing are used as a topic in fanfiction, as the quote by user Zeldagirl91 "That' just the way Nintendo made it" shows.

Literature and Game Studies

According to Viires, digital games can be considered a part of cyberliterature. I would not agree but rather support the approach that games often include narratives, which does not automatically make them a new narrative. For the case study of fanfiction based on digital games, the narrative potential of games is crucial. Following Ryan, we can distinguish between narrative potential on the one hand and being a narrative on the other. Games have a narrative potential as the gaming experience can be used as a basis for a narrative about the game. Games often include narratives or follow one big narrative line as in *Zelda*. However, understanding a game as a narrative only ignores the importance of the gaming activity. The debate whether games are narratives is also a methodological debate. Digital games have been studied by narratologists assuming that they are narratives as a text, while ludologists analyze them as games. For Marie-Laure Ryan games belong to the digital tropics, which means she understands them as texts but clearly points out the differences between narratives and games ("Narrative and the Split Condition"). Opposite to the approach to digital games as texts and narratives, ludologists study the game as an activity (Dovey and Kennedy). The ongoing debate between narratologists and ludologists testifies to a shift in paradigms; while narratologists would like to stick to the long-established research tradition as reflected in narrative analyses of media content, ludologists would propose to overthrow this paradigm and replace it with a new one instead.

"Game studies" is a distinct term used for the same research interests as ludologists have formulated. However, in contemporary game research, game studies cover a broader field than ludology. In an interview Torill Elvira Mortensen, a scholar of media and game studies clearly states that "the study of games is larger than ludology" for "ludology is the study of games as games, not as anything else" and describes game studies as an inherently interdisciplinary field.

Joost Raessens and Jeffrey Goldstein, the editors of the *Handbook of Computer Game Studies*, point to the fact that in order to study computer games, an extensive collection of scientific disciplines must be included, such as cognitive sciences, artificial intelligence, psychology, history, film studies, cultural studies and philosophy, which also includes narratology.

According to Jesper Juul, the first reason for neglecting a narrative approach towards games rests in the fact that games do not belong into the narrative media ecology. The problem lies in the impossibility of translating a story into the framework of a game. Taking a different point of departure, it can be said that translating a movie into a novel or vice versa is much more convincing than doing the same with the game. A narrative cannot be translated into a game the way it could be translated from a linear medium to another such as novels or movies (Juul, "Games telling stories?"). In a movie or a novel some event occurs, e.g., the protagonist solves a problem. It is a closed sequence of events resulting in the same outcome every time the movie is viewed or the novel is read. In a game, however, the result varies: the first time the game is played the protagonist (here represented by an avatar played by the player) might not be able to solve the problem. Through several play sessions, the player might be able to find out how to solve the problem and finish the game. Dependent on the player's choices, the sequence of events can change dramatically. One could speak of an open sequence of events. This openness challenges fans in their narratives. The story can be retold in different ways as the play sessions can vary. While a narrative interpretation of the game as a research method to understand a digital game fully is criticized by ludologists, the narrative openness and dynamics of a game seems to support the creation of a wide array of fan narratives. Even though they are not adaptations of the game that try to be true to the original, the critique that a transformation of a digital game into another medium is not possible has to be revised.

The discussion of differences regarding time in games and linear narratives is an important aspect as well. Time in narratives is structured according to story time and discourse time; the former refers to the time in which events told in the story happen chronologically, whereas the latter refers to the time and ordering of the narrative, e.g., the novel, the movie and the ordering of the events during the telling. While the distinction between story and discourse and its application to digital games has been criticized, the fan narratives take the gaming experience of a player as story, while the fanfiction is one possible discourse. The distinction between story and discourse for a game itself is difficult as the story partly evolves through the playing of the game and is therefore indistinguishable from the discourse. Several stories might be potentially possible—or one story with several endings and plotlines. Only the discourse gives an insight into the underlying story. The discourse in a computer game might be dynamic as different play sessions might end up with different results. As for linear narratives for which story time is prior to discourse time, the same holds true for fanfiction even though it is based on different dynamic discourses, which are taken as the underlying story for the new product.

Furthermore, the analysis of an application of narrative theory to digital games is based on the difference between a reader or spectator and a player. Games need the player to actively engage with the game world and thereby construct the discourse. This is a difference to the function of a reader or spectator. The player's actions will always have an impact on the game environment, whereas the reader of a novel cannot influence the course of events. For Marie-Laure Ryan "[t]he narrative element of computer games is therefore typically subordinated to the playing action" (*Narrative Across Media* 350). Playing includes the change of perspectives and the manipulation of the environment. Furthermore, the roles of the protagonist of the narrative and the player are conflated in digital games. The game sometimes refers to the player as a fictional character, sometimes as a player.[2] This double role of the player, as an observer and thus external to the fictional world, and as the main protagonist and therefore internal to the fictional world, is blending. The game's narrative is dynamic. For that reason players often have to fill in gaps in the narrative with their own imagination. Next to narratives based on the gameworld, fans can also refer to their individual experiences within the game or connect a narrative from another setting to the game, thereby expanding the intermedial relation of their fan narrative by adding their own personal experiences within the game. The reason for this extension of the narratives to personal experiences lies in the fact that the avatar (the game character to play with) remains a flat character, even in examples as *Zelda* in which the avatar is an established character functioning as the protagonist. The functionality of the avatar in the game world is more important than its fully developed personality. This asks for a further development of the character and allows for many different modifications. In the digital game *Zelda*, the main protagonist has the task to save princess Zelda. Zelda and her relation to Link, the main protagonist, are developed further in many narratives written by fans, e.g., fanfiction describing a love story between them, which is not part of the narrative of the source text.

Aarseth used the concepts "anamorphic text" and "metamorphic text" to describe different functions of digital texts (*Cybertext* 179-81). The anamorphic text is a text in which a player has to change the text from an unsolved text to a solved text. This holds true for digital games. The player is usually confronted with a conflict (e.g., to save the princess) and has to find a solution during his play session. Narrative and interaction are interdependent, as the player's actions constitute the narrative. The narrative of a computer game establishes a conflict with a recursive structure. While background information given introduces the conflict, the solution has to be found in the interaction with the game. When the solution has been found, the problem is solved and the text is changed to a solved text. Digital games usually include several unsolved problems, which are all part of one major problem. The constant problem solving is what keeps a player active and engaged. Metamorphic text, however, is transforming endlessly. The term metamorphic text is used by Aarseth to describe digital, dynamically changing texts. The whole net of fan narratives based on one source text can be described as metamorphic. Each fan narrative in itself is static. The whole web of fanfiction, the constant meta-discussion on the fan narratives and the discussion about the source text can be understood as a metamorphic whole. An understanding of the net of fanfiction as metamorphic underlines the processual aspect of the cooperative production of these texts.

Marie-Laure Ryan asks: "Can games be narratives or possess narrativity?" (*Avatars of Story* 267). Fanfiction clearly answers the second part of the question. When they possess narrativity, they have the potential to evoke narratives or the narrative potential as Ryan calls it. Games possess narrativity as they function as the source for fanfiction. Some game genres as, e.g., most adventures and role-playing games, also include narratives; however, they are more than a narrative transposed into a digital medium.

Methodological Reflections

The introduction of the relation between narratologists and ludologists has been put forward to show that in the case of an approach to popular net literature a narrotological or semiotic analysis of the content of the text itself will also lead to a one-sided result, as is the case when digital games are analyzed with semiotic methodology only. The content of the texts and the relation to their source texts is important, which means that a semiotic analysis is necessary to elucidate the intermedial relations and come to a better understanding of the content of fan narratives. However, not only the content of the narrative of the source text has to be taken into consideration when fanfiction is based on a digital game, but also the gaming experience, the rules of the game and its structure. Fans comment on these gaming elements as well and include them into their fanfiction. This means that a familiarity with the source text does not mean that a summary of the narrative(s) of the gameworld is enough for an understanding. The game has to be understood in its totality. The game mechanics need to be known for an analysis and understanding of fanfiction based on games as well. Furthermore, the metadiscussions and cooperations between writers are important because they show which source texts and topics are important for fanfiction writers. To get an impression of the meta-discussion on fanfiction forums and their impact on the text, the discussions on forums have to be studied as well and the development of fan narratives as result of these discussions has to be followed. This means that besides a content analysis and an understanding of intermedial relations, the method of virtual ethnography (Hine 2000; 2005) is necessary additionally. In cases in which net literature is based on networked cooperative writing, a combination of both methods is important to achieve an insight into the different layers at work in the practice and production. The case study of fanfiction based on *Zelda* can give only a first insight into the different layers.

Fanfiction Based on *Zelda*

Fanfiction based on digital games has been described as a metagaming activity of players (Salen and Zimmermann 540). It is a sign of the intimate knowledge of the game and of the desire to imprint oneself into the text. Fan narratives rely heavily on the source text, which means that a reader of a fan narrative needs to know the source text at least to some degree. In the case of a digital game, this does not only mean that the reader needs to know the main characters and the background story but that he or she also needs to know about the game mechanics and rules. A fan text does not necessarily use the same setting and genre as the source text. While *Zelda* is a role-playing game set in a fantasy world, some of the fan narratives use a different literary genre as, e.g., drama or poetry or different subgenres of fiction such as science fiction, mystery, or horror. Others keep the setting, time and genre of the original. Besides referring to different genres, a fan narrative can refer to different source texts of popular culture at the same time—the so-called crossover—by, e.g., combining protagonists and events from *Zelda* with a storyline and characters based on *Lord of the Rings* as in the following example:

> . . . Link was dropped on the said dwarf. The sudden appearence caused the rest of the counsil to draw their weapons. The stranger rubbed his head, and muttered, "magic should be able to provide a softer landing," before opening his eyes. Link was surprised to find several arrows, swords and axes aimed at him.
> "Uuh, hi?" he said weakly.
> "Who are you, and how did you appear in the halls of Rivendell."
> Link tried to answer but the dwarf he landed on, decided his live was more than being a pillow, "GETOFF."
> Link quickly stood up, "I am so sorry, I never meant to land on you, sir, I come from the land of Hyrule."
> "The land of I RULE?" a other dwarf said, "He is nuts." (Alex phoenix Wing, "Ring of Darkness")

After this sudden introduction of Link into a scene of *Lord of the Rings*, his presence is taken for granted by the characters. Link applies his specific magic in the situations the group encounters in the following while the storyline follows the one of *Lord of the Rings*. Productive receptions such as fanfiction give an insight into the mechanics of interpretation, which is always a form of appropriation: Fanfiction highlights the way in which reading is a transformation of the original as has been debated by reader-response criticism. Interpretation is a key term here. Problematic when dealing with source texts is that the established textual content can be deduced from several sources and can also be interpreted in different ways as the example above shows. These discussions as well as the source texts chosen by fans give insights into the underlying cultural canon they refer to. The canon can be investigated by analyzing the discussions of the fans themselves. Does the fan narrative stay true to the original text? Is the fan's interpretation convincing? Which other source texts are used in the fan's narrative? The web site <http://www.fanfiction.net> with its links to crossovers shows clearly which different sources the narratives based on *Zelda* rely upon. *FanFiction.net* names 191 crossovers connecting *Zelda* and other sources such as *Harry Potter, Lord of the Rings, Final Fantasy, Transformers, Naruto*. Crossovers can be named from media such as novels, comics, movies, TV-series but also other computer games.

As fan narratives are texts which are constantly enriched with new storylines and told or retold through various media, we face all aspects of intermediality. Intermedial relations exist between the source text(s) and the fan narrative, but they exist also between different fan narratives that are used as source text(s) as well. However, not only is the content of source texts used and appropriated; we also find relations to the rules of the source texts as in the following fanfiction:

> "Link, you played the Song of Storms. . . of COURSE it's going to start raining you idiot!" Navi yelled, shaking her head in disappointment. "Well, when I play the Song of Storms in Lon Lon Ranch, it never rains. How come it only rains when I play the song in Kakariko Village?" Link asked, completely dumbfounded. Navi sighed. "That' just the way Nintendo made it Link. SO STOP ASKING STUPID QUESTIONS!" (Zeldagirl91, "Haunting Memories")

The "Song of Storms," as other songs played by Link in *Zelda*, has a magical effect. Strangely enough, this effect does not work in the place called Lon Lon Ranch. Whether this was intended by the game designers or is a "bug" of the game can be questioned. It seems to be inconsistent regarding the game mechanics and is therefore a topic discussed by players.

Another remark in a fanfiction refers to the impact the player can have on the story:

> "Oh, hold on for a sec, guys," called an ominous, loud voice from the sky. Everyone looked up. "Who is that?" demanded Krypton. "Oh, just me, the *Ocarina of Time* player. Listen, I decided that I don't like Buttwipe's name, so I'm restarting the game. Sorry, guys," the player announced before the screen went black. When the screen came back into focus, Buttwipe was gone. (Igor Lollipop, "The Epic Adventure")

This example refers to the possibility a player has to start the game anew and thereby change the name of the avatar the player is playing with. In the case of *Zelda*, even though the avatar always looks like Link, the player can give him a name freely. These two examples show how authors of fanfiction do refer to the game's rules and play conditions in their narratives. With these references, a metafictional level is created, a contradiction between the fictional world of the game and the fanfiction on the one hand and the extra-fictional reality of the game designers and the player on the other.

On a third layer, the meta-discussions of fans about their fan narratives add another intermedial relation, which is highly self-reflexive. Fans participate actively in the production of narratives but also in the construction of a general consensus about a source-text. Fan narratives are heavily linked to the fan community and its interpretation and evaluation of a text and the related fan practices. In fan communities fans are not only authors, but also critics and readers. At some point these identities may conflict. Being a fan with specific interests influences the way one looks at other fan texts and products. Many comments of readers are praising the texts, supporting the author of the fanfiction and asking for a sequel. It seems that a badly written text does not receive any comment rather than a lot of bad reviews.

The genre categories used by *FanFiction.net* are only partly comparable to traditional literary genres. The categories used here reflect an understanding about genres by the fanfiction community and not a standard genre subdivision. Genres used by the community include drama, horror, sci-fi but also categories such as angst, family, hurt/comfort, which can be compared more to tags given by users to their narrative than to a genre description. Additionally, fanfiction authors have to add information about the age of the reading group. There are narratives written for very small children from 1 year onward designed to be read to them by a parent but also pornographic narratives for a group of readers aged 18 and older. At the moment, only the categories between 5+ and 16+ are in use on the fanfiction web site. The differentiation between genres and also age groups helps in locating a narrative one might be interested in; alone *Zelda* fans published over 14,000 texts[3] already on the web site. The web site also uses a comment function (under the tag "reviews"), which gives every reader the possibility to interact with the author. Those comments range from positive feedback to concrete suggestions how to improve the text. Additionally for all categories, beta readers are available who offer help before an author decides to publish a text on *FanFiction.net*.

The whole network of *FanFiction.net* is constantly changing. Fan narratives are updated and modified, texts are added daily but additionally a forum is used by its users to stay in touch, talk about their interests or organize meetings at fan conventions.

Fanfiction and the related texts produced build a whole hypertextual universe that includes narratives, theoretical discussions about the interpretation of the source texts, discussions about the role of the producers of fanfiction or the relation of fanfiction to other fields as the question by user Amber "What does philosophy have to do with fanfiction?" shows. The last question debated on *FanFiction.net* led to the following answer:

> Philosophy has very little to do with fanfiction (unless an author is somehow incorporating it, of course). However, several individuals mistook X's comments about Schrodinger's Cat for philosophy, when in reality it is a thought experiment that helps explain a key idea behind quantum mechanics. The conversation on this topic digressed from there, up to A.'s astute question. To answer the question this

explanation will raise, quantum mechanics has nothing to do with fanfiction either. However, unrelated concepts can still be used to make a point on another subject altogether, which is what X was doing. He simply used an analogy that went over most heads. (TempleMaster17, "But sometimes")

A thread on the forum with the title "but sometimes "bad" fanfictions are just not bad" had caused a debate about the relation of fanfiction to philosophy. The example of Schrödinger's Cat was mentioned and at that point the debate reached an abstract level which could not be followed by all participants of the discussion anymore. This was a moment when the question "What does philosophy have to do with fanfiction?" came up. Debates like the one mentioned above can be observed from time to time as the authors of fanfiction define their own field of interest, discuss several stylistic topics as well as narrative structure, genre or the creation of characters. In relation to precursors of print culture, we can compare those web sites to critical editions of texts, which also include comments and guidelines for interpretation of the source text beside the collection of fanfiction, but they can also be compared to textbooks for creative writing. In relation to forms of digital literature, they are similar to collective writing projects and are an example of net literature. As Gendolla and Schäfer have stated, we can observe the impact of communication within the net itself as much as that of traditional literary texts (27).

Discussion

Fanfiction has been described as an example of popular net literature. Web sites such as *FanFiction.net* and the publication of fanfiction as well as the comments and discussions we find there are examples of networks of fans contributing to this constantly expanding and changing universe of texts. The intermedial aspects of this network of texts shall be discussed briefly.

The concept of intermediality is based on (1) aesthetics: a discussion on intermedia art (Higgins) and (2) cultural sciences: the academic discourse on intertextuality (Eco; Kristeva). Digital technology provides us with the possibility to integrate all media and combine them freely, thereby creating new possibilities such as, e.g., sampling. Intermediality has not only been described as one important feature of digital literature, but also in the description of digital media and their hybridity. Simanowski describes intermediality as the "conceptual coexistence of medial elements" (50); he thereby follows Higgins' aesthetic understanding of intermediality. From this perspective, fanfiction is not intermedial as the texts rarely include other media as images, sound or video. In case images are included, they function rather as illustrations and are therefore multimedial and not intermedially integrated. If we understand intermediality not in the sense that the work includes and integrates several media but in the sense that several media lie at the basis of the production of the fan's narrative—which is the perspective of cultural sciences—fanfiction is intermedial. The concept of intermediality as deduced from intertextuality has been introduced to refer to the appropriation of content from one source medium to another. I use intermediality as a generic concept including intramedial and transmedial relations. While intermediality in a narrow sense means the migration of content from one medium to another, I suggest including intramediality and transmediality as subordinate concepts. Intramediality stands for an integration of content from a source text into another one using the same medium. Transmediality stands for a multiplication of one and the same content using different media. The use of intermediality as a generic term is based on an understanding of the concept medium not only as technically but primarily as culturally determined, based on semiotic codes. Intermediality in this broad understanding allows for tracing source content as well as describing media specificity. Intermedial relations are the fundament of fan practices. This seems to be self-evident. However, the intermedial relations are a source to investigate the co-existence of canons and gain an insight into the dynamics between a critically acclaimed canon and a new, transformative one, as is the case in the example of fan narratives. The intermedial relations of fanfiction are made visible by the categories fanfiction authors follow at *FanFiction.net*. They explicitly state through the chosen category or additionally in their disclaimers which sources they refer to. Some sources, which are not mentioned explicitly, are discussed in the reviews by their readers. As the attachment to the source texts is the connecting bond of the fan community, the intermedial relations are at the center of their interest. The list of source texts and the number of fanfiction published in relation to each of them shows a ranking. It is easy to see which texts have been chosen as source by how many authors. This ranking gives an insight into the new canon established by fan communities.

Transmediality has been discussed in the context of intermediality and aesthetics (Meyer et al.) and of convergence culture (Jenkins). While the aesthetic approach to transmediality as well as to intermediality is in the focus of research, especially in Germany (e.g., Müller; Paech; Spielmann), I will open up the discussion regarding cultural dynamics and transformations following Jenkins. According to Jenkins, a convergence culture has already been shaped in the last decades. Also, stories have been performed anew time and again in the past in processions and (religious) sermons, and both, convergence as well as intermediality, have far-reaching historical roots. However, with digital media we can observe a change since digital media are the role model for all convergent media. I relate convergence to intermediality as media convergence includes intermedial relations. The concept of transmediality, which I introduced as a subordinate concept of intermediality, refers to media industries and their impact on users. These concepts do not only gain new meaning by reframing them on the background of a convergence culture but they are also deconstructed and refined anew on the basis of fan practices.

Notes

1 The quotations from *FanFiction.net* are used without any comments on typographic or grammatical errors. Provided are only the usernames that are alphabetized by their first letters in the list of works cited. Following the link, interested readers will find the whole discussion/fanfiction.
2 Cf. also Burns who observed the same for *final fantasy* or Carr for *Baldur's Gate*.
3 Web site checked in June 2009.

Works Cited

Alex phoenix Wing. "Ring of Darkness and the Sword of Evil's bane." *Fanfiction.net*. 9 Aug. 2008. 23 July 2009. <http://www.fanfiction.net/s/2519642/2/Ring_of_Darkness_and_the_sword_of_evils_bane>.

Aarseth, Espen J. *Cybertext: Perspectives on Ergodic Literature*. Baltimore: Johns Hopkins UP, 1997.

———. "Computer Game Studies, Year One." *Game Studies* 1.1 (2001). 23 July 2009 <http://www.gamestudies.org/0101/editorial.html>.

Bailey, Steven. *Media Audiences and Identity: Self-Construction in the Fan Experience*. New York: Palgrave, 2005.

Block, Friedrich W., Christiane Heibach, and Karin Wenz, eds. *p0es1s: The Aesthetics of Digital Poetry*. Ostfildern: Cantz, 2004.

Burns, Andrew. "Playing Roles." *Computer Games: Text, Narrative, and Play*. Ed. Diane Carr et al. Cambridge: Polity P, 2006. 72-87.

Busse, Karen, and Kristina Hellekson, eds. *Fan Fiction and Fan Communities in the Age of the Internet*. London: McFarland, 2006.

Carr, Diane. "Games and Narrative." *Computer Games: Text, Narrative, and Play.* Ed. Diane Carr et al. Cambridge: Polity P, 2006. 30-44.

Castells, Manuel. *The Rise of the Network Society.* 1996. Oxford: Blackwell, 2000.

Mul, de Jos. "The Game of Life: Narrative and Ludic Identity Formation in Computer Games." *Handbook of Computer Game Studies.* Ed. Joost Raessens and Jeffrey Goldstein. Cambridge, MA: MIT P, 2005. 251-266.

Dovey, Jon, and Helen W. Kennedy. *Game Cultures. Computer Games as New Media.* New York: Open UP, 2006.

Eco, Umberto. *The Open Work.* 1962. Cambridge, MA: Harvard UP, 1989.

Gendolla, Peter, and Jörgen Schäfer, eds. *The Aesthetics of Net Literature: Writing, Reading, and Playing in Programmable Media.* Bielefeld: Transcript, 2007.

Gitelman, Lisa. *Always Already New: Media, History, and the Data of Culture.* Cambridge, MA: MIT P, 2006.

Glazier, Loss P. *Digital Poetics: The Making of E-Poetry.* Tuscaloosa: U of Alabama P, 2001.

Gray, Jonathan, Cornel Sandvoss, and C. Lee Harrington, eds. *Fandom: Identities and communities in a mediated world.* New York: New York UP, 2007.

Higgins, Dick. "Intermedia." *Something Else Newsletter* 1 (1960): 11-29.

Hine, Christine. *Virtual Ethnography.* London: SAGE, 2000.

———, ed. *Virtual Methods: Issues in Social Research on the Internet.* Oxford: Berg, 2005.

Igor Lollipop. "The Epic Adventures of Potassium & Krypton." *Fanfiction.net.* 24 May 2009. 23 July 2009. <http://www.fanfiction.net/s/5083359/1/The_Epic_Adventures_of_Potassium_Krypton%3E>.

Jenkins, Henry. *Convergence Culture: Where Old and New Media Collide.* New York: New York UP, 2006.

———. *Fans, Bloggers, Gamers.* New York: New York UP, 2006.

———. "Afterword: The Future of Fandom." *Fandom: Identities and Communities in a Mediated World.* Ed. Jonathan Gray, Cornel Sandvoss, and C. Lee Harrington. New York: New York UP, 2007. 357-364.

Juul, Jesper. "Games telling stories?" *Game Studies* 1 (2001). 23 July 2009. <http://www.gamestudies.org/0101/juul-gts/>.

———. *Half-Real: Video Games between Real Rules and Fictional Worlds.* Cambridge, MA: MIT P, 2005.

Kac, Eduardo, ed. "New Media Poetry: Poetic Innovation and New Technologies." *Visible Language* 30.2 (1996): 184-212.

Kristeva, Julia. *Desire in Language: A Semiotic Approach to Literature and Art.* New York: Columbia UP, 1980.

Meyer, Urs, Roberto Simanowski, and Christoph Zeller, eds. *Transmedialität zur Ästhetik paraliterarischer Verfahren.* Göttingen: Wallstein, 2006.

Mortensen, Torill E. "Humans Playing World of Warcraft: or Deviant Strategies?" *Digital Culture, Play, and Identity. A World of Warcraft Reader.* Ed. Heide G. Corneliussen and Jill Walker Rettberg. Cambridge, MA: MIT P, 2008. 203-224.

———. Interview with Daria Kuss. 26 Mar. 2008.

Müller, Jürgen E. *Intermedialität.* Münster: Nodus, 1996.

Naheniel. "Does this qualify as fanfic?" *Fanfiction.net.* 11 Jan. 2009. 23 July 2009. <http://www.fanfiction.net/topic/2872/12325053/1/>.

Paech, Joachim. "Zur theoretischen Grundlegung von Intermedialität." *Intermedialität: Theorie und Praxis eines interdisziplinären Forschungsgebiets.* Ed. Jörg Helbig. Berlin: Erich Schmidt, 1998. 14-30.

Raessens, Joost, and Jeffrey Goldstein, eds. *Handbook of Computer Game Studies.* Cambridge, MA: MIT P, 2005.

Ryan, Marie-Laure. *Narrative as Virtual Reality: Immersion and Interactivity in Literature and Electronic Media.* Baltimore: Johns Hopkins UP, 2001.

———. *Avatars of Story.* Minneapolis: U of Minnesota P, 2006.

———. "Narrative and the Split Condition of Digital Textuality." *The Aesthetics of Net Literature: Writing, Reading, and Playing in Programmable Media.* Ed. Peter Gendolla and Jörgen Schäfer. Bielefeld: Transcript, 2007. 257-280.

Ryan, Marie-Laure, ed. *Narrative Across Media.* Lincoln: U of Nebraska P, 2004.

Salen, Katie, and Eric. Zimmerman. *Rules of Play: Game Design Fundamentals.* Cambridge, MA: MIT P, 2004.

Simanowski, Roberto. "Holopoetry, Biopoetry, and Digital Literature: Close Reading and Terminological Debates." *The Aesthetics of Net Literature: Writing, Reading, and Playing in Programmable Media.* Ed. Peter Gendolla and Jörgen Schäfer. Bielefeld: Transcript, 2007. 43-66.

Simons, Jan. "Narrative, Games, and Theory." *Game Studies* 7.1 (2007). 23 July 2009 <http://www.gamestudies.org/0701/articles/simons/>.

Spielmann, Yvonne. *Intermedialität: Das System Peter Greenaway.* Munich: Fink, 1998.

TempleMaster17. "But sometimes 'bad' fanfictions are just not bad." *Fanfiction.net*. 22 Jan. 2006. 23 July 2009. <http://www.fanfiction.net/topic/4844/87927/1>.

Viires, Piret. "Literature in Cyperspace." *Folklore* 29 (2008): 153-174. <http://www.folklore.ee/folklore/vol29/cyberlit.pdf>.

Zelda. The Legend of Zelda Series. Nintendo. 1986-2009.

Zeldagirl91. "Haunting Memories." *Fanfiction.net*. 25 June 2009. 23 July 2009. <http://www.fanfiction.net/s/2557143/1/Haunting_Memori.

Raine Koskimaa

Approaches to Digital Literature

Temporal Dynamics and Cyborg Authors

In this article I will first briefly describe what I mean with the concepts of digital literature and cybertext. There are two aspects of cybertextuality, and digital culture in general, which I consider as especially important to discuss. *Cyborg author* deals with the complex combination of human and machine jointly producing texts with literary qualities. In this context, the networked computer cannot be seen only as a tool for writing, but rather as a partner in creative processes. *Temporality* of cybertexts is another significant but under-theorized area. Through analyses of temporal experiences of dynamic cybertexts, we should be able to better grasp the temporality of the digital culture we are living in. Together these issues shed light on how we experience not only digital phenomena, but also the whole fully technologized world around us.

1   Digital Literature and Cybertextuality

To begin with, it is necessary to define what I mean by "digital literature." It is possible to distinguish at least three quite different meanings for this designation:

1. *Digital Publishing.* This is a perspective that focuses on the production and marketing of literature and books with the aid of digital technology. It includes such phenomena as eBooks (for Kindle and other devices), Print On Demand, AudioBooks as MP3 files, etc.

2. *Scholarly literary hypertext editions* for educational and research purposes. This category includes hypertextually annotated literary works, as well as multimedia implementations of classics.

3. *Writing for Digital Media.* Digital texts are always *programmed* texts; on one level they are computer code. This opens up a limitless field for literary play and experimentation, as texts can be programmed to behave in a more or less dynamic way. I call these works cybertexts, following Espen Aarseth (*Cybertext*). Cybertextuality is a general textual theory, a perspective on all textual communication foregrounding the functional aspects of texts (often almost invisible to us, because they are so wholly conventionalized). Cybertext, in its turn, is more limited in scope as it refers to

those text types which foreground the functional aspect. It is an umbrella term comprising of such various types as hypertexts, kinetic texts, generated texts, texts employing agent technologies, etc. Cybertext may refer to both literary and non-literary texts, but if we explicitly limit the focus on literary cybertexts, then we seem to be dealing with essentially the same concept as Noah Wardrip-Fruin's digital literature (in this same volume). The slight difference exists because cybertext is indifferent to the distinction between digital and other electronic text types; literary cybertext could be used synonymously with electronic literature (which is a somewhat broader concept than digital literature).

All these categories are important fields in themselves, but in this paper I limit our attention mainly to the third category, "cybertextuality." Before going to that, however, I want to underline that when we talk about digital literature, we are not talking about digital literature alone. Rather, all of this is relevant to more traditional forms of print literature as well. Even if certain contemporary works look exactly like older literary pieces in their formal, structural and semiotical aspects, they are nevertheless written and read in a new context. Writing and reading strategies as well as our cognitive-emotional engagement with literature are quite different today than during previous periods of history. The challenge facing teaching literature could be described as a need for "media-specific analysis" of literary works, as argued especially by N. Katherine Hayles (*Writing Machines*). This is a twofold task: First, there is a need to understand the character of literary discourse, based on the material conditions of its existence and on the new conventions developed around it; second, we need to acquire an understanding of the overall media landscape, as well as related user-spectator-audience behaviour, and to see literature as a medium operating amongst others. Literary works may also reflect the new media forms in their own structuring. The e-mail novel, for example, is a natural descendant of the traditional epistolary genre, but with the wholly new temporal perspective of real-time, online communication (cf. Keskinen). It is an important task for basic research in literary studies to recognize how notions of everyday life, changing by the growing role of information and communications technologies, are reflected in literature, and what consequences this has for narratological, semiotic, cognitive and other structures in literature.

All digital works are in a very concrete sense *experimental writings*. First of all, the authors are experimenting with the new media, trying to find out what is possible in digital textuality, what the limits are of literary expression in programmable media. It is a question not so much of experimenting to break down established conventions, as it is of experimenting *trying to create new conventions*. Because the new digital technology plays such a crucial role in cybertextuality, we may refer to the works in this emerging field as "technological avantgarde." Stepping into this new field means that the authors have to learn to write anew, from a novel set of premises. This holds true not only for authors, while the readers also have to learn to read in a new way not governed by the conventions of print literature. This double challenge is a factor slowing down the development of the cybertextual field, but at the same time it creates a peculiar kind of close connection between the authors and readers of cybertextual literature as they experiment together with the possibilities offered by this new field of textuality.[1]

Roughly speaking, cybertexts can be located within the triangle:

literature

cinema games

They employ techniques such as hypertextuality, interactivity, and programmability, and there is a grey area where clearly literary cybertexts give way to works more naturally classified as games or (interactive) cinema. I do think, however, that there is much to gain in keeping the literary world open to these new developments, and in acknowledging the fact that "literature" is a historically changing concept, rather than strictly sticking to the traditional forms of literature.

There is always a computer code involved on some level of the work. An interesting question is then: is the code part of the work? This may be reformulated as: where lies the border between text and code? As we examine cybertextual literary works, how "deeply" do we need to search?

From a user's ("reader's" in the traditional parlance) point of view, we may detect three main scenarios:

1. There are many works for which you don't need programming knowledge at all; all you need to know is the basic usage of a computer (like using a web browser) to be able to read and enjoy the work.

2. There are works that only require installing.

3. There are works that require a more profound understanding of the software environment. These include, for example, poems written in such a way that they work as executable code in a certain programming language. These works can be catagorized as a literary branch of "software art" or "code art."

Even though most cybertexts do not require advanced computer skills from the reader, the situation is somewhat different from the perspective of a researcher or a teacher.[2] Systematic analysis of a given work requires an understanding of the specific nature of cybertextuality and the logic of the work. Without this sort of understanding, it is impossible to establish an accurate description of the given work (for example, if the work is dynamic only in combinatorial sense, or if new content may be generated during the reading process, or if the work is trapped in a loop or just imitates loop-effects through certain circular structures). For this, one needs to know the basics of programming. This does not necessarily mean the mastery of specific programming languages, but rather more general understanding of how computer programs are put together and what they are capable of doing. Michael Mateas ("Procedural Literacy"), for example, has talked about the necessity of teaching "procedural writing and thinking" as a part of education in new media, and Noah Wardrip-Fruin has further elaborated on this train of thought in the present volume.

1.1 Textons, Scriptons, and User Functions

In cybertext theory, texts are seen as machines for meaning production (Aarseth 21). This has to be understood in quite concrete terms and not only as a metaphor. As machines, texts have to be used in certain ways—and this also holds true of traditional print texts. A book is a specific type of interface for textual content and it has to be manipulated in a certain way if the reader wants to get access to its content. With books and other print texts, these manipulation techniques are conventionalized in such a way that we usually do not notice them anymore. Cybertextuality, then, offers a perspective on all literature (both print and digital texts), which directs the attention to these functional (and consequently, also material) aspects. The dynamic inherent in cybertextuality is based on the two-layered structure of texts (62):

- *Textons*: building blocks, deep structure, text as it is in the system; with hypertextual work this refers to the text material (and possible audio-visual content) stored in the computer memory

- *Scriptons*: appearance, surface structure, text as it appears to the reader; again, with hypertextualwork this refers to the text chunks (like web pages) the reader sees on her screen[3]

In addition, a mechanism to turn textons into scriptons is needed, and that is called the *Traversal Function*. By analyzing the nature of textons and scriptons and their relation to each other, as well as the characteristics of the traversal function, will give us quite a useful understanding of a specific work. We are still talking about a rudimentary level, and to acquire a deeper insight some more concepts are needed. Aarseth introduces his textual typology with seven variables and their possible values (62-65). These are:

1. *Dynamics*: static (*scriptons* are constant), intratextonic dynamics (the number of *textons* is fixed, the *scriptons* may change), textonic dynamics (the number and content of *textons* may vary).

2. *Determinability*: determinable (the same response to a given situation will always produce the same result), indeterminable (the results of responses are unpredictable).

3. *Transiency*: transient (mere passing of user's time causes *scriptons* to appear), intransient (*scriptons* appear only through user's activity).

4. *Perspective*: personal (requires the user to play a strategic role as a character in the world described by the text), impersonal (reader not involved as a participant).

5. *Access*: random (all *scriptons* are readily available to the user at all times), controlled (some *scriptons* are available only when certain conditions are met).

6. *Linking*: explicit, conditional, none.

7. *User function*: explorative, configurative, interpretative, textonic.

This textual typology produces 576 different combinations or genre positions, which all differ from each other at least regarding the value of one of the variables. The notion of genre is somewhat problematic here. It is certainly true that we lack adequate classifications of digital text types, but the abundance of almost 600 distinct genres does not appear to be a viable solution. It might be possible to form "meta-types" by grouping certain combinations that bear a significant resemblance to each other. These meta-types would then serve as digital genres.[4] The list of variables is not necessarily exhaustive, and what is certainly lacking here is the notion of hybridity—parts of a certain text may employ certain values of variables, whereas (an)other part(s) of the same text may have different values. Also, it is possible that the value of some variable in a text changes over time, so that the text does not need to stay in just one genre position. As Aarseth himself has stated, this typology is best understood as a heuristic device; it helps us to detect characteristics in texts that we might not otherwise notice and furthermore, it may point towards new text types (only a small part of all the possible positions has been experimented with so far, after all). The temporal aspect is here underdeveloped; that is quite obvious, and I'll elaborate on that issue below.

Here it is enough to briefly describe the user functions (using Aarseth's definition) as four types of activity, usually referred to simply as "interactivity." Interpretation is something we do with all possible text types as soon as we engage in something that may be called reading. Through interpretation we make the text mean something to us. Here information flows from the text to the reader. It is possible that a text offers (or requires) ways to choose her path through the text to navigate or explore it, which is typical of hypertexts. In communicating her choices to the system via the keyboard, mouse or other pointing device, the reader sends information back to the system, completing the feedback loop consisting of the text-system and the reader. If the text employs a configurative user function, then the reader has a chance to configure the text in various ways (to change its appearance: for example, as in customization). Finally, if the reader is allowed to add new text or permanently delete parts of it, the text employs the textonic user function. Interpretative function is always present, and the other three functions (explorative, configurative, textonic) may or may not be present, and they may also coexist. To further specify the nature of a given text, it may be necessary to describe which of the user functions is the dominating one. As a central term for Aarseth, ergodicity refers to the extra effort required from the reader in addition to the interpretation. Ergodic texts are such types requiring nontrivial efforts from the reader.

The cybertext framework is clearly a tentative one, and several improvements—even whole competing models—have been put forth since its initial release. It seems to us, however, that it still serves as an important heuristic model that offers powerful tools to analyze the spectrum of texts, especially new digital text types; print texts as well. Even at the points where the framework fails, it manages to bring forth important aspects of textuality and textual communication. In what follows I will take this discussion into two various directions which are at the heart of our current research activities: The pondering of the temporality of digital texts, and the nature of the cyborg authorship related to the use of complex software and data networks in creative writing processes.

2   Temporal Issues

Temporal dimension is the most underdeveloped part of the cybertext theory. There is the distinction between user-controlled time (transient texts), and text-controlled time (intransient texts), and also dynamics (both in intratextonically in textonically dynamic texts), which necessarily implies temporal change, but they offer only rudimentary starting points for pondering the temporality of cybertexts.[5]

One way to classify temporal possibilities in programmed texts is the following:

- *Limiting reading time.* Text appears on screen only for a limited period of time. The period may be long enough for a thorough, focused reading, but it may also be used to challenge the reader, force her to read on the edges of apprehension.

- *Delaying reading time.* Whereas it is practically impossible to implement means to hinder the reader of a print book from browsing through the pages with a pre-determined speed, or to jump over dozens of pages on one turn, it is extremely simple in digital cybertext to force the reader to wait for a fixed time before it is possible to proceed from one text passage to another.

- *Limiting the reading opportunities.* The text may only be accessible at certain times, or only for a limited period of time. An extreme case here would be what Gonzalo Frasca has termed "one-session game of narration," which, as the self-explanatory phrase describes, can be accessed and read only once; after that the text either erases or changes itself. Another hypothetical example (borrowed from Eskelinen, *Digitaalinen avaruus*) would be a text which can only be accessed during office hours, or a text which is different if either on day-time or night-time. Some of these possibilities are such, that the reader does not necessarily even notice them, if she does not read the text several times under different circumstances or, if the text is not explicitly reflecting on them.

- *Temporally evolving texts.* This category includes texts that evolve continuously through additions posted by the author or the readers, or both. The addition or modifications may also be programmed according to certain variables outside of the text (stock marker rates, environmental factors, etc.), so that no authorial intrusion is needed after the initiation of the text (even though it may be quite hard to guarantee that feeds from external web sources would stay in existence for longer periods).

The ideas above mainly refer to the reading time, but the time within the textual work—the fictional time—may be even more interesting in theoretical terms. Temporality in traditional print texts is a highly problematic notion. It is possible to use direct temporal points of reference that situate the events described in some specific historical period, but often these are not available. The truly problematic issues, however, are duration and speed. The relation between the time used for narrating certain events and the time those events lasted cannot be precisely determined. Gérard Genette has proposed a solution through the concept of *pseudo time*: the amount of text used to describe an event as measured in lines of text determines the speed of narration. Thus, if the events of a lifetime are recounted in a few pages, we have the feeling that narration is sped up, that the discourse time is faster than the story time. Or in another direction, if a simple event like choosing a proper tobacco pipe from a rack is recounted in twenty pages, we have the feeling that the discourse time is slower than the story time. Somewhere in between, there is the balance where discourse time and story time are seen as approximately the same. It should be noticed that pseudo time is really not a temporal measure at all, but a spatial one: pseudo time is counted in number of words, sentences, and pages used to describe certain event(s).[6]

With temporally dynamic cybertexts, however, we need also to take into account the measurable true time, as we can, for example, define the duration for each node (for example, in Stuart Moulthrop's *Hegirascope*, each node gives way to the next one in 30 seconds). Thus, we have at least the following four temporal levels for cybertexts with narrative content:

1. *User time* (the time the user spends reading the cybertext)

2. *Discourse time* (the time of the narrative discourse)
   - pseudo time
   - true time[7]

3. *Story time* (the time of the narrated events)

4. *System time* (the time of the cybertext system states)

One more aspect of temporality deals with simultaneity. There are two issues involved: Events which occur as a temporal sequence are all present in the form of the whole text simultaneously, and they are all equally accessible to the reader, but on the other hand, simultaneous events are rendered sequential in narration (simultaneity being established with such notions as "At the same time . . ."). It seems to us that one of the most promising areas of research within digital literature is the reorganization of these temporal issues through the dynamics of system time (the succession of the processor cycles pacing the execution of the code), reading time, and textual (fictive) time. When we enter the code level of cybertext, we face issues such as genuine simultaneity enabled by parallel processing, and apparent simultaneity based on the fact that system time is divided into such small units that a human perceiver is experiencing as simultaneous applications which are actually handled sequentially. Also, cyclical and linear time both play a role here, as code is typically using loop structures, but the system clock is ticking linear timing as lapses from the moment when the processor was started. It may be technically possible to consider the various temporal levels separately, but on the experiental level they merge together in a novel way. Trying to grasp the temporality of cybertext bears crucial implications for the wider notions of temporality within digital culture.

As examples of cybertextual works that might prove fruitful as subjects for this sort of temporal analysis, I could mention John Cayley's *Speaking Clock* (which is an overt reflection on time keeping) or *The Impermanence Agent* by Noah Wardrip-Fruin and others. The *Speaking Clock* translates current time into short poems, based on the text materials forming the round clock shape (fig. 1). *The Impermanence Agent* is a combination of a narrative text with illustrations and an agent-program monitoring the WWW traffic within the machine presenting the piece. The narrative is a biography; the memoirs of Wardrip-Fruin's grandmother written down by him and illustrated with pictures taken from the family album. This memoir is shown in a small window supposed to be open on top of a web browser (and possibly other running applications). The text progresses automatically, calmly paced, new "pages" appearing in set intervals. While the program is running and the text proceeding, the agent-program is constantly scanning the WWW traffic within the computer. Following a certain procedure, the program selects some of the webpages the reader/user has recently visited, cuts out parts of those pages (fragments of either text or images), and pastes these fragments onto the memoir text (fig. 2 and fig. 3). Thus, the longer *The Impermanence Agent* has run, the more of the original memoir is replaced by materials borrowed from the webpages visited by the reader. As I have mentioned elsewhere ("Cybertext Challenge"), *The Impermanence Agent* can be seen as a sort of cybertextual response to Marcel Proust's *The Remembrance of Things Past*. As I am referring to a fledgling research area here, it suffices to say that with *Speaking Clock* it is worth paying attention to the dialectics of cyclical and linear time—which may also be phrased as the question between emergence and repetition. And then, focusing on *The Impermanence Agent*, one can, for example, pay attention to the questions of accessibility of temporally divergent materials, or the relation of (technologically enhanced) memory and time that are currently under scrutiny.

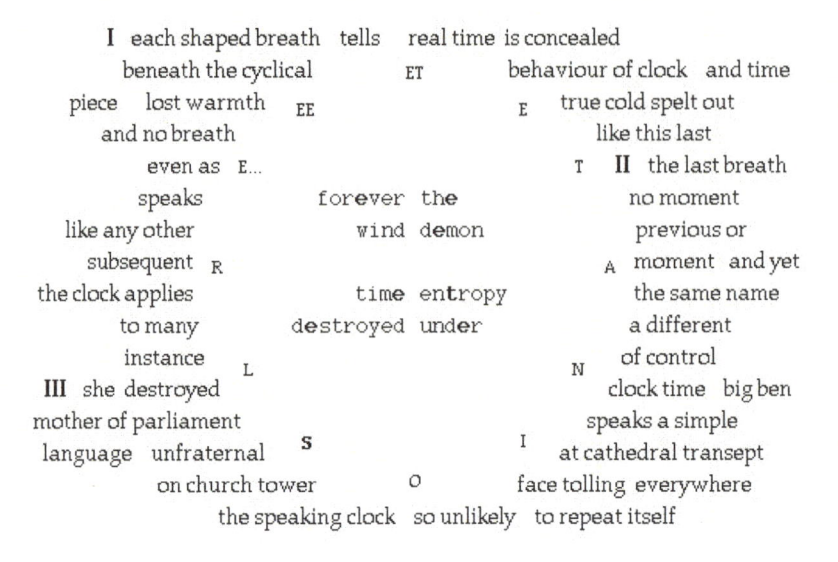

```
         I  each shaped breath  tells      real time  is concealed
            beneath the cyclical       ET           behaviour of clock   and time
      piece   lost warmth    EE                  E    true cold spelt out
         and no breath                               like this last
            even as   E...                        T   II  the last breath
         speaks             forever  the              no moment
      like any other         wind  demon              previous or
         subsequent   R                            A  moment  and yet
      the clock applies           time  entropy        the same name
         to many            destroyed  under           a different
            instance    L                           N    of control
      III  she destroyed                                clock time   big ben
      mother of parliament                              speaks a simple
         language   unfraternal    S             I      at cathedral transept
            on church tower           O             face tolling  everywhere
            the speaking clock   so unlikely  to repeat itself
```

Fig. 1. A screenshot from *The Speaking Clock* by John Cayley.

Figs. 2 and 3. Screenshots from *The Impermanence Agent* by Noah Wardrip-Fruin et al.

3   The Cyborg Author

In the following chapter I will discuss digital literature in the context of the "cyborg author," as defined by Aarseth (129-141). Here the focus is especially on the creative processes undertaken in collaboration between a human actor and a machine.

The term "cyborg," an abbreviated form of "cybernetic organism," was coined by Manfred E. Clynes and Nathan S. Kline in their highly influential paper "Cyborgs and space." They defined cyborg as an "exogenously extended organizational complex functioning as an integrated homeostatic system unconsciously" (30-31). The framework for the paper was the preparation for manned space flights, including the idea to refashion astronauts as cyborgs, in order to enable them to survive the harsh conditions of space travel. The construction involved mechanisms to automatically inject drugs and other chemicals into the astronaut's body.

From this very specific origin, the cyborg began to have a life of its own, especially in two distinct fields. In academic discussions, the cyborg attained a central role—especially in Donna Haraway's feminist theory, where the concept was extensively expanded from its technological origin to include various sorts of transgressive figures (*Simians, Cyborgs, and Women*). The transgressions, a combining of two disparate elements, usually imply a resulting monstrosity. Other notable transformations of the cyborg can be found, for example, in N. Katherine Hayles' discussion on the "posthuman" (*How We Became Posthuman?*). The other field where cyborgs emerged was in popular culture. In science fiction, Philip K. Dick especially problematized the existential condition of the cyborg, or android, as he called it. More mainstream recognition was gained via the cyborg protagonist of the TV series *The Six Million Dollar Man*. Later on, the *Terminator* films have brought easily recognized cyborg characters into popular culture. As with Haraway's transgressive figures, the popular culture cyborg is never far from a threatening monstrosity.

In regards to digital literature, we may use the concept of "cyborg author" to refer to the combination of human and machine producing texts with literary qualities. Whereas the concept of cyborg has been stretched to its limits by counting a person with glasses as one, the aim here is not to claim that a writer hacking away with her typewriter is a cyborg author. Rather, I am concentrating on more complex and more flexibly functioning tools: Especially the WWW and various software tools enable a new type of collaboration between the human author and the machine. This is a significant phenomenon in at least two ways. First, it opens up possibilities for wholly new types of expressions and literary communication. Second, the computer programs help the human author to reflect language from a new perspective, and to investigate the new (digital) environment (Montfort). As a consequence, the (networked) computer cannot be seen only as a tool for writing; rather, it is a partner in the creative process of digital writing. The significant aspect of this sort of man-machine relationship is that it is very hard—maybe even impossible—to exactly define who is responsible for the final outcome, and it is this combination I call the cyborg author.

It is possible to classify types of cyborg authorship according to the phases of the creative production where the man-machine interaction takes place (Aarseth's *pre-processing, co-processing*, and *post-processing*[8] (135), but that is not the point I am interested in here. Rather, it is the idea of the "World Wide Web as Cyborg Author" I find especially intriguing (Wall). With most of the well-known text (poem/story/dialogue) generators like *Eliza/Doctor, Tale-Spin, Racter, Brutus,* etc., the fundamental limitation lies in the fact that there is a predetermined set of materials out of which the output is generated. Also, despite possible randomness in the composition, the outcome is rarely surprising. The later generators may be somewhat more refined than Richard Strachey's love-letter generator discussed by Wardrip-Fruin in this volume, but they essentially follow the same format. With the addition of the WWW to the formula, the situation changes dramatically. Suddenly, there is a never-ending flow of materials to which the generator (or an authoring tool) may be tapped. The WWW plays a dual role here; it serves as a medium to connect the millions of web users to create this potential cyborg author; it also concurrently plays an active role in structuring, filtering, and combining the continuous data flow.

From a psychological perspective, creative processes are not too well understood, but one aspect, which seems to be central for creativity, is the unconscious. One could argue that the biggest problem with text generators has been their lack of the unconscious, but the WWW seen as a cyborg author may be overcoming that obstacle. On one level highly organized, on another fully chaotic: the plethora of WWW communications seems to be a close enough approximation of the human unconsciousness to serve as a source of machinic creativity. Here again I refer to The *Impermanence Agent* as an interesting sample case, where the WWW as a network environment participates on a (partially) unconscious level in the creative activity initiated and structured by Wardrip-Fruin et al., and pieced together by each individual user and the occasional instantiation of the WWW. The deeply intriguing composition of *The Impermanence Agent* manages to address the question of the unconscious on two fronts simultaneously, as it also deals with the user's (human) unconsciousness: following the paradigm of the critical technical practices, it makes the (at least partially unconscious) routine web browsing habits visible for the user through foregrounding aspects of pages recently browsed in new contexts (and also concretizing the fact that all browsing activities are monitored, something the web user knows but does not often actively think about).

Douglas Engelbart was one of the first to explicate the potential in computer-based information processing (in his early work on hypertext system) to extend the human mental capabilities. Marshall McLuhan famously declared media as an extension of the human nervous system. Along that trajectory we may state that the cyborg author is bound to produce a mental change in humanity. This change can only be compared to the invention of writing: "More than any other single invention, writing has transformed human consciousness" (Ong 78). Through the analyses of works like *The Impermanence Agent* we might be able to catch glimpses of what sort of transformations in human consciousness and unconsciousness is taking place through the introduction of digital, networked media.

In order to address those types of issues, we need to understand the logic of the cybertextual processes, and for that we still have a lot to do in establishing the necessary concepts and models. Adalaide Morris has paid attention to the same issue by stressing the discrepancy between "what we do and see" in the current digitalized world, and "the representational conventions through which we think." We have to be able to interpret the individual works, to make them mean something for us by combining our understanding of the underlying technical structure and the semiotic-cultural content. What we need then is nothing less than the ability to combine the results of the centuries of literary-hermeneutic studies with sensitivity to the new digital cultural context where the meanings are embedded.

Notes

1   I have discussed the role of hyperfiction authors in the development of hypertext theory in my PhD-thesis (*Digital Literature*).

2   It is possible to argue that instead of researcher and teacher it would be more relevant to talk about the ideal reader or implied reader. This would call for deeper pondering that is possible here, but it seems to me that the demands of systematical analysis put on a researcher are even stronger than may be required from the ideal reader.

3   An illustrative example from print literature would be Marc Saporta's *Composition No. 1*, which physically resembles a deck of cards. Each card has text print on its face; the reader is supposed to shuffle the deck, and then read the text in whichever order the cards happen to be. In this case the individual cards comprising the deck form the set of textons. Each time the reader shuffles the deck and reads the cards, she generates a new scripton out of this limited set (52 cards) of textons.

4   In any case, it would be necessary to establish different genre classifications depending on whether we are concentrating on content, technological choices, or cybertextual functioning, etc.

5   A recent, very thorough classification and analysis of temporal dimensions at work in cybertexts can be found in Eskelinen, "Travels."

6   These issues were already discussed in relation to practical authoring applications in Eskelinen and Koskimaa.

7   Comparable to screen time in film studies.

8   In pre-processing, the human operator programs and loads the generator with textual source materials and the machine is then free to generate new text according to its programming. In co-processing, the human and the machine jointly create the output, as is the case with dialogue programs like *Eliza/Doctor*. In post-processing, the machine is first generating output, out of which the human operator selects and edits the final product. Pre-processing is usually always present, and it may co-exist with either co-processing or post-processing. The latter two often seem to be mutually excluding, but there are cases where all three modes co-exist.

Works Cited

Aarseth, Espen J. *Cybertext: Perspectives on Ergodic Literature*. Baltimore: Johns Hopkins UP, 1997.

Cayley, John. *The Speaking Clock*. 1995. 28 Apr. 2009 <http://www.homepage.mac.com/shadoof/FileSharing9.html>.

Clynes, Manfred E., and Nathan S. Kline. "Cyborgs and Space." *Astronautics* (1960): 29-33.

Engelbart, Douglas. "Augmenting Human Intellect. A Conceptual Framework." *The New Media Reader*. Ed. Noah Wardrip-Fruin and Nick Montfort. Cambridge, MA: MIT P, 2003. 95-108.

Eskelinen, Markku. *Travels in Cybertextuality: The Challenge of Ergodic Literature and Ludology to Literary Theory*. Diss. Jyväskylä: U of Jyväskylä, 2009.

———. *Digitaalinen Avaruus*. Helsinki: WSOY, 1997.

Eskelinen, Markku, and Raine Koskimaa. "Discourse Timer. Towards Temporally Dynamic Texts." *Dichtung Digital* 3.3 (2001). 28 Apr. 2009 <http://www.brown.edu/Research/dichtung-digital/2001/05/29EskKosk/index.htm>.

Frasca, Gonzalo. "Ephemeral Games. Is It Barbaric to Design Videogames after Auschwitz?" *Cybertext Yearbook 2000*. Ed. Markku Eskelinen and Raine Koskimaa. Jyväskylä: U of Jyväskylä, 2001. 172-182.

Genette, Gérard. *Narrative Discourse: An Essay in Method*. Ithaca: Cornell UP, 1980.

Haraway, Donna. *Simians, Cyborgs, and Women: The Reinvention of Nature*. New York: Routledge, 1991.

Hayles, N. Katherine. *Writing Machines*. Cambridge, MA: MIT P, 2002.

Hayles, N. Katherine. *How We Became Posthuman: Virtual Bodies in Cybernetics, Literature, and Informatics.* Chicago: U of Chicago P, 1999.

Keskinen, Mikko. "E-pistolarity and E-loquence: Sylvia Brownrigg's *The Metaphysical Touch* as a novel of letters and voices in the age of E-mail communication." *Critique: Studies in Contemporary Fiction* 45.5 (2004): 383-404.

Koskimaa, Raine. "Cybertext Challenge: Teaching Literature in the Digital World." *Arts and Humanities in Higher Education* 6.2 (2007): 169-85.

———. *Digital Literature: From Text to Hypertext and Beyond.* Diss. Jyväskylä: U of Jyväskylä, 2000. 28. Apr. <http://www.cc.jyu.fi/~koskimaa/thesis>.

Mateas, Michael. "Procedural Literacy: Educating the New Media Practitioner." *On the Horizon* Special Issue: *Future of Games, Simulations and Interactive Media in Learning Contexts* 13.2 (2005): 101-11.

Morris, Adalaide. "New Media Poetics: As We May Think/How to Write." *New Media Poetics: Contexts, Technotexts, and Theories.* Ed. Adalaide Morris and Thomas Swiss. Cambridge, MA: MIT P, 2006. 1-46.

Montfort, Nick. "The Coding and Execution of the Author." *Cybertext Yearbook 2002-03.* Ed. Markku Eskelinen and Raine Koskimaa. Jyväskylä: U of Jyväskylä, 2003. 201-217.

Moulthrop, Stuart. *Hegirascope.* 1997. 28 Apr. 2009 <http://www.smoulthrop.com/lit/hgs/>.

Ong, Walter J. *Orality and Literacy: The Technologizing of the Word.* London: Methuen, 1982.

Proust, Marcel. *The Remembrance of Things Past.* 3 vols. New York: Vintage, 1982.

Wall, David. "The World Wide Web as Cyborg Author in the Postmodern Mold." Charlottesville: U of Virginia, 1994. 28 Apr. <http://www2.iath.virginia.edu/courses/encr481/wall.paper.html>.

Wardrip-Fruin, Noah et al. *The Impermanence Agent.* 1999. 28 Apr. 2009 <http://www.impermanenceagent.com>.

Astrid Ensslin

From Revisi(tati)on to Retro-Intentionalization

Hermeneutics, Multimodality and Corporeality in Hypertext, Hypermedia and Cybertext

1 Introduction

Since its inception in the late 1980s, digital literature has come a long way. It has seen groundbreaking technological changes and advances, which have taken it from a largely script-based, off-line medium to a prolific multimedia, interactive and ludic form of verbal and artistic expression, which is making use of a variety of online and offline forms of communication and representation. By the same token, genre boundaries are increasingly blurring between literature, art, digital film, photography, animation, and video game. That said, I contend that we can only use the term "digital literature" if and when the reception process is guided if not dominated by "literary" means, i.e. by written or orally narrated language rather than sequences of images—no matter how short and allusive text chunks, or lexias, may be.

Although in the UK digital literature has hitherto never fully entered the canon of English literature, various scholarly niches have opened up in the past few years, especially in the communities of stylisticians, narratologists, media and discourse analysts, largely represented by the Poetics and Linguistics Association (PALA) and its Special Interest Groups "Narrative" and "Narrative and Multimodality." Similarly, creative approaches to New Media writing have been taken by a number of experimental, hypermedia-savvy writers (e.g. Catherine Byron, John Cayley, Matthew Fuller, Pauline Masurel, Alan McDonald, Helen Whitehead and Tim Wright). That said, there has—to my knowledge—only been one true creative "hub" in the UK, forming around Sue Thomas, Kate Pullinger and Chris Joseph, first at Nottingham Trent's *trAce* Online Writing Centre (1995-2006) and, since 2006, at De Montfort University (Thomas, "Narratives of Digital Life at the trAce Online Writing Centre").

Not surprisingly, interest in close-reading various forms of digital fiction derives from the distinct narrative techniques used by digital writers, which reflect questions of textual fluidity, openness vs. closure, linearity, the creation and maintenance of suspense, narrative voices, text worlds, character development, transliteracy and multimodality. To give just a few examples, leading UK-based scholars of digital literature have been focussing on new forms of literacy required in the digital age (Thomas et al.), and new learning and teaching approaches resulting from them (cf. Ensslin and Pope in this book). An innovative approach to close-reading first generation hypertext is provided by Bell, who examines Storyspace hyperfictions against the backdrop of Possible Worlds Theory ("'Do You Want to Hear About it?'"; *The Possible Worlds of Hypertext Fiction*; "Ontological Boundaries and Conceptual Leaps"). Page and Taylor have been paying particular attention to blog narratives, and Thomas ("Canons and Fanons") has looked into fanfiction on the Web. An eclectic overview of close-reading approaches to various forms of digital narrative has been given by a recent special edition of *Dichtung Digital* (Ensslin and Bell), covering digital literature, blogs, narrative games and machinima.

This essay is based on my own research into hypertext and other forms of digital literature. It situates instances of digital literature along a techno-historical spectrum, which ranges from mainly typographic hypertext (in the sense of first generation hyperfiction, hyperdrama and hyperpoetry) through multimodal, transmedial hypermedia to machine-code-centred, textual performances as represented by cybertext (cf. Ensslin, *Canonizing Hypertext*; "Of Chords, Machines and Bumble-bees"). I argue that, from the vantage point of reader-response criticism, this spectrum (viewed diachronically) parallels a move from an aesthetic of revision and revisitation ("revis[itat]ion")—ultimately based within traditional hermeneutics—to an aesthetic of retro-intentionalisation (Ensslin, "Breathalyzing Physio-cybertext;" "From (W)reader to Breather;" "Respiratory Narrative"). To illustrate this phenomenological approach, I provide a short analysis of Kate Pullinger et al.'s *The Breathing Wall*, in which I demonstrate that corporeality in text reception cannot but interact with and thereby reinforce intentionality. Against this backdrop, I introduce a new critical approach, which I refer to as "cybersomatic criticism." It is inspired by literary forms of "physio-cybertext" yet may be taken beyond the boundaries of literature proper, into the realm of narrative games and Visual Novels.[1]

2 From Hypertext to (Physio-)Cybertext

In previous studies (e.g. Ensslin, *Canonizing Hypertext*) I have categorised digital literature in terms of three overlapping generations: hypertext, hypermedia and cybertext. Whilst, for the first decade following Michael Joyce's *afternoon*, this tripartite taxonomy proved to be appropriate on a largely diachronic scale, more recent forms show a distinct sense of generational synchronicity in the sense of combining, in multifarious ways, the technologies and narrative-poetic techniques that have become available over the years to produce unique and innovative creative artefacts. Before I exemplify this development, however, let me explain the three generations in more detail.

Hypertext refers to a largely typographic form of interactive computer-based literature, translating previously linear forms of writing into a macro-textually nonlinear format and thereby instigating multilinear reading processes.[2] The crucial structural and aesthetic component of hypertext is the hyperlink, which opens up to the reader various navigational possibilities. Some theorists refer to the earliest specimens of hypertext as "hyperfictions," thus failing to include hyperpoetry and hyperdrama, which emerged at around the same time, and to distinguish between fictional and non-fictional text. The first hypertexts were written by North-American literary and media scholars (e.g. Michael Joyce, Stuart Moulthrop, Deena Larsen and Jane Yellowlees Douglas), with the intention to demonstrate hypertext's potential to implement and thus verify central tenets of poststructuralism (e.g. the death of the author, the decentralization of textual meaning and coherence, the rhizome metaphor, multi-linearity, and the notion of the text chunk, or "lexia" (cf. Barthes; Landow). Therefore, it is not surprising that some early works emphasize, if not exaggerate, the meta-theoretical component, thereby neglecting the aesthetic effects necessary to attract a non-academic readership.

Taking into account that phenomena like "cognitive overhead," "lost in hyperspace" and "serendipity"[3] are commonly experienced by hypertext readers, one is inclined to suspect that they are deliberately employed by hypertext writers to draw readers' attention to processes of composition, decoding and other metafictional elements. Similarly, readers' expectations upon embarking on a hypertext need to be informed by the aesthetic effects implied by the semantic prosody[4] of hypertext as a deconstructivist literary genre. Clearly, confusion and disorientation can only reasonably be coped with and processed creatively by readers if they are recognised as generic characteristics. To a greater extent than readers of traditionally linear texts, which are structurally "un-marked" in the sense of not challenging the reader's conventional macro-structural expectations, hypertext readers are thus urged to reflect upon text-organizational strategies to approximate an overall idea of the text in front of them.

This approximation procedure involves a set of interwoven cognitive sub-processes of continual semantic construction, deconstruction and reconstruction, which ultimately undermine the conventional, mutually complementary interplay between bottom-up and top-down processing. Readers of Michael Joyce's *afternoon*, for instance, are led to revise perpetually their mental image of the protagonist, Peter, in terms of whether or not he was involved in or even caused the car accident that killed his son Andy. The ever-recurring sentence, "I want to say I may have seen my son die this morning," is charged with grammatical modality, thus underscoring the possibility rather than factuality of the propositional content. In the process of navigating through *afternoon*, readers are given contradictory textual cues, which cause them to revise their temporary mental models of the text incessantly, to maintain several alternatives simultaneously, to weigh them up, revise, refine and question them, and thereby revisit their readings repeatedly. This complex hermeneutic process is what I refer to in terms of an aesthetics of revis(itat)ion (Ensslin, *Canonizing Hypertext*), which is specific to literary hypertext and needs to be accepted as a receptive prerequisite (cf. Bell, *The Possible Worlds of Hypertext Fiction*, Douglas, *Print Pathways and Interactive Labyrinths*, "'How Do I Stop This Thing?'" and Liestøl).

Pictorial devices are employed sparsely if at all in prototypical hypertext, which emphasizes the kinship to conventional print literature. Typically, pictographic elements are limited to navigation maps and desktop icons (e.g. Deena Larsen's *Marble Springs* and Stuart Moulthrop's *Victory Garden*) and can represent additional layers of metaphorical meaning (e.g. the "brain map" and "body map" in Shelley Jackson's *Patchwork Girl*).

Early hypertexts were mostly edited and received in pre-web programmes such as NoteCards, HyperCard, GUIDE, Intermedia and Storyspace, which, to this day, remains Eastgate's major authoring and editing tool. More recent hypertexts, however, can also be found on the Web. With the emergence of HTML, the gap between hypertext and hyper*media* (cf. below) began to narrow because HTML allowed the combination of multiple semiotic systems into various forms of digital multimodality. Furthermore, the underlying mark-up, the "deep structure" of a hypertext, as it were, linguistically encodes its "surface structure," which again includes other para- and hypertextual features such as font design, paragraphing, backgrounds and hyperlinks.

Hypermedia, short for "hypertext multimedia" (Nielsen), is based on the aforementioned concept of digitally encoded multimodality. Its evolution was boosted by the 1993 invention of the Mosaic browser and the popularization of the World Wide Web. Hypermedia typically combines a variety of semiotic modes including typography, (scanned) handwriting, digitized speech, sound and music, pictographic and photographic images, animation and film.[5] Produced by means of HTML, JavaScript, Flash, and various graphics and web editors, hypermedia typically exhibits a variety of pastiche and collage techniques. Embedded interactivity (e.g. point-and-click and drag-and-drop mechanisms) enacts intermediality, and in some cases—even before the Web 2.0 era—online hypermedia allows direct reader participation via posts to the web site in question (e.g. Alvar Freude's and Dragan Espenschied's *Assoziations-Blaster*).[6]

From an aesthetic point of view, hypermedia readers are confronted not only with interlinked text lexias but a wider semiotic variety, e.g. image-text, image-image and text-image links as well as dynamic and interactive elements such as film clips and drag-and-drop mechanisms. As opposed to first generation hypertexts, which use images mainly as illustrative or decorative means, hypermedia writings form a coherent intertextual, intermedial and multimodal whole (Heibach, *Literatur im elektronischen Raum*; Kok), which is more than the sum of its constituent parts. Prototypical examples are concrete digital poems such as Ursula Menzer's and Sabine Orth's *Er/Sie*[7], Judd Morrissey's and Lori Talley's *My Name Is Captain, Captain* and Tone Avenstroup and Robert Lippok's *marbel + matrikel*.

Cybertext, finally, is a term coined by Aarseth, who sees hypertexts that are programmed in particular ways as autonomous "text/machines," which assume power over the reader by literally "writing themselves" rather than presenting themselves as an existing textual product. The concept of cybertext is based on Aarseth's alternative model of textual communication (21; cf. fig. 1), which places the "text/machine," a mechanical rather than metaphorical concept, at the centre of the communicative triangle. The text/machine is symbolically surrounded by the (human) "operator," the "verbal sign" and the material "medium" that disseminates the text. These three elements engage in a complex interplay with the text and each other, which results in a variety of different cybertextual subgenres, depending on which element is emphasized most strongly.

What Aarseth aims to communicate is a reversion of reader-response principles, which renders the operator a constitutive yet somewhat disempowered element of (cyber)textual performance. Put differently, readers become part of a cybernetic feedback loop, which operates on the basis of mutual stimulus and response between machine and operator. By flagging up this reciprocal contingency, however, Aarseth's model subliminally reconfirms the validity of reader-response theory, as the thus disempowered reader may be either discouraged from reading on, or indeed fill the metatextual gaps opened up by the text by reading cybertextual meanings into the text.

Interestingly, Aarseth omits two crucial elements contained within conventional communication models: first, the notion of reference, in the sense of Jakobson's extralinguistic "context," which would traditionally form an essential part of any communicative event, or even constitute the purpose of it. Secondly, the model disregards the crucial role of the author-programmer, who is ultimately responsible for the creation and "behavioral" mechanisms of the text machine. One is inclined to assume that the author is contained within the operator concept. However, this poses the nagging dilemma of not being able to distinguish between the elevated position of the programmer and the disempowered role of the user-player.

```
              operator
                 /\
                /  \
               /    \
              / text/\
             / machine\
            /_____\
      verbal sign    medium
```

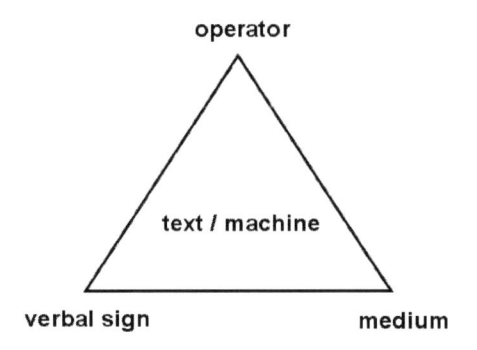

Fig. 1. Aarseth's "text/machine."

Inspired by other forms of (ludic) digital narrative, such as video games and MMPORGs (Massively Multiplayer Online Role-Playing Games), the cybertext generation uses the latest achievements in hypermedia technology combined with a variety of plug-ins, which add interactive, playful elements to the text. Early examples are Stuart Moulthrop's *Hegirascope* and Urs Schreiber's *Das Epos der Maschine*. In 2000, Auer predicted that, by virtue of such innovations, a more corporeal notion of interactivity, which directly responds to human emotions and physical conditions, may ultimately replace the hyperlink as the central aesthetic and structural feature of hypertext. In fact, as recent "physiocybertextual" (cf. below) developments have shown, Auer's vision has to a certain degree become reality. That said, hyperlinks are not generally replaced but rather combined with other creative technologies to produce literary and artistic novelties. As I shall demonstrate in the following section, Kate Pullinger et al.'s *The Breathing Wall* is a case in point.

The three generations of hypertext reflect stages of text transforming "into an intelligent object" (Heibach, "Conversations on Digital Aesthetics" 43). As I have argued at the beginning of this section, however, this is not to say that any digital literature phenomenon may be clearly categorized diachronically along generational lines. Nor does it mean that first generation hypertext will entirely disappear. As Kate Pullinger and Chris Joseph have shown in Episode 4, "Hometown," of their emergent digital narrative, *Inanimate Alice* (cf. Ensslin and Pope, this volume), hypertextual elements can be embedded in a largely linear hypermedia story so as to give readers different options and reading paths without, however, allowing them to get lost in hyperspace (fig. 2).

To conclude this section, I would argue that with the increase in hardware and software technologies as well as the participatory implications of the Web 2.0, the creative repository available to writers and artists has grown to such an extent as to enable them to use and experiment freely according to need and mood. By the same token, the ever-increasing possibilities of literary, artistic and ludic expression will, in the near and distant future, give rise to a widening range of new genres, which will increasingly cross boundaries between textual, ludic and pictorial phenomena.

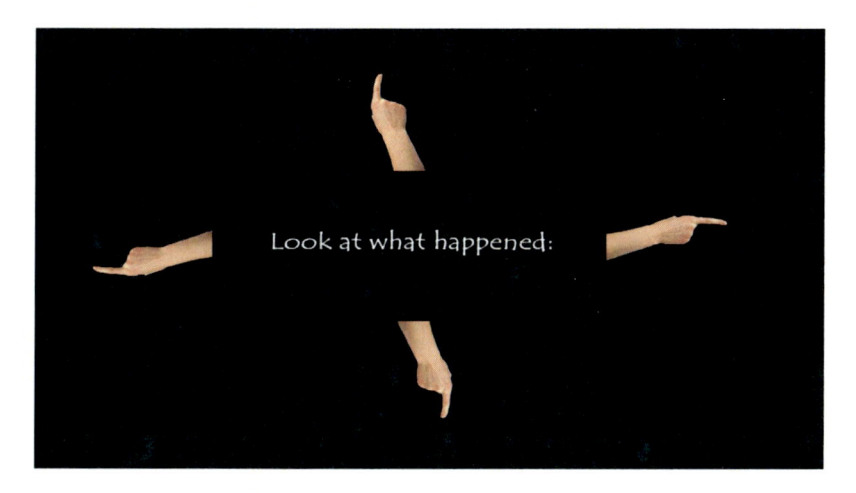

Fig. 2. *Inanimate Alice*, Episode 4, "Hometown;" Alice's options after the staircase has collapsed beneath her.[8]

3 Physio-Cybertext and Cybersomatic Criticism

In this section I shall focus on one particular development within third generation cybertext, which is closely linked to the physical interactivity found in games, yet takes us further into the critical realm of phenomenology. I refer to it as "physio-cybertext" and take it as a starting point to a new critical approach, which I shall provisionally call "cybersomatic criticism" as it pays particular attention to the corporeal mechanisms at play during the reading process (cf. Ensslin, "Breathalyzing Physio-cybertext;" "From (W)reader to Breather").

To begin with, we have to accept that our bodies are physically and physiologically situated, i.e. contingent upon a variety of external and internal influences which impact on our mental disposition. In fact, the two cannot be separated. What this means to literary analysts is what I envisage as a shift in focus from the primacy of readerly intentionality to the interplay of corporeal and psychological functions at work during the receptive process. In recent years, stylisticians and narratologists have placed an emphasis on cognitive and empirical aspects of reading and textual procedurality. Cognitive stylistics, on the one hand, uses the principles of cognitive science to investigate how textual elements evoke certain psychological patterns and cognitive effects in the reader's mind (cf. Semino and Culpeper; and Stockwell for a comprehensive overview of this approach and, more specifically, Emmott for narrative comprehension, Gavins for text world theory and Ryan for possible worlds theory). Empirical stylistics, on the other hand, applies empirical research methods to examine reading and response patterns and processes (cf. Miall and Dobson for an empirical investigation of hypertext reading).[9]

Both approaches are indebted to reader response theory in that they foreground the cognitive, in the sense of cortically controlled, dimension of reading. Involuntary, instinctive corporeal processes, which are subcortically controlled, however, are largely neglected. Whilst I do not question the importance and validity of reader response theory and its diverse ramifications, I would argue that literary criticism still lacks a significant degree of auto-physiological awareness to complement cognitive stylistics. In fact, I contend that readers are largely contingent upon physical (i.e. corporeal and environmental) circumstances, which impact cognitive processes and can only be controlled to a certain degree by cortical functions of the human brain, and that a new, more comprehensive anthropological focus is needed.

Such an inclusive approach needs to embrace both the psychological and the physical nature of text reception—especially in the area of New Media narratives, which are *per definitionem* embedded in the human-machine cybernetic feedback loop. To that end, I advocate turning to game theory, which largely dispenses with the body-mind division in what has been termed the "discourse of transcendence in writing about digital technology" (Dovey and Kennedy 106), i.e. the transgression of the Cartesian body-mind (and hence reader-text/player-game) dualism via the concept of bodily double-situatedness in New Media environments.

The double-situatedness of the body implies, on the one hand, that user-readers are "embodied" as direct receivers, whose bodies interact with the hardware and software of a computer in what could be called a mechanical, or electronic feedback cycle. On the other hand, user-readers are "re-embodied" through feedback which they experience in represented, mediated form, e.g. via avatars. Seen as a whole, the reader-text-medium apparatus may thus be conceived of in terms of a complex cybernetic feedback loop, which operates on the basis of the reader-user's physical, physiological and cognitive interaction with the text/machine.

I would argue that we can transfer both aforementioned dimensions of situatedness to the analysis of digital literature. Clearly, digital literature differs from games narratives in that as readers we categorically do not need a physical representation of our own subjectivity in the text world. That said, every work of literature assumes an implied reader,[10] and it is a major achievement of cybertext that this implied reader or "breather," as in the following example, can share his or her phenomenological physicality with the narrator, and/or hero of the story. The dialectic of double-situatedness in cyber-literature thus operates on the basis of phenomenological, embodied empathy with the protagonist rather than the semiotic representation of selfhood in the avatarian "other."

Along with other breath-driven New Media texts and installations (e.g. Lewis LaCook's reactive cyberpoem *Dirty Milk* and Char Davies's installation *Osmose*[11]), Kate Pullinger's, Stefan Schemat's and babel's physio-cybertextual murder mystery *The Breathing Wall* aesthetically implements both the double-situatedness of the reading body and, in close connection to it, the partly involuntary interplay between the physiological and psychological. More precisely, *The Breathing Wall* investigates creatively to what extent intentionality may be constrained through textual autonomy and the textually encoded emphasis of the perceiving body.

Running on a specially designed software called "Hyper Trans Fiction Matrix," *The Breathing Wall* uses the reader's respiratory system as driving force for revealing essential referential meaning, or, more precisely, "clues" to solving the "who-dunnit" or rather "how-did-it-happen" question. To "read" the text from CD-ROM or hard disk, a headset with attached microphone is required. Unusually, however, the microphone is placed under the reader's nose to measure his or her breathing rate (fig. 3).

Depending on the rate and depth of inhaling and exhaling, the text (in the combined sense of program code and audio-visual, interactive user interface) will release either more or less information. More precisely, the Hyper Trans Fiction Matrix will release a maximum number of textual clues only if and when the reader breathes as if he or she were asleep, i.e. deeply and slowly. In other words, the quality of reception depends largely on the reader's momentary physiological, psychological and spatio-temporal situatedness and their ability to "control" their own breathing. This is particularly interesting considering the fact that neurologists disagree about the extent to which breathing is an involuntary process. Even more intriguingly, human breath tends to accelerate when the organism is under any kind of stress; and although the average reader of *The Breathing Wall* may find him- or herself in a comparably relaxed condition, the fact that his/her intention to obtain textual clues puts him/her under a certain degree of stress has a potentially adverse effect on their depth and speed of breathing and, thus, their ability to move the narrative forward.

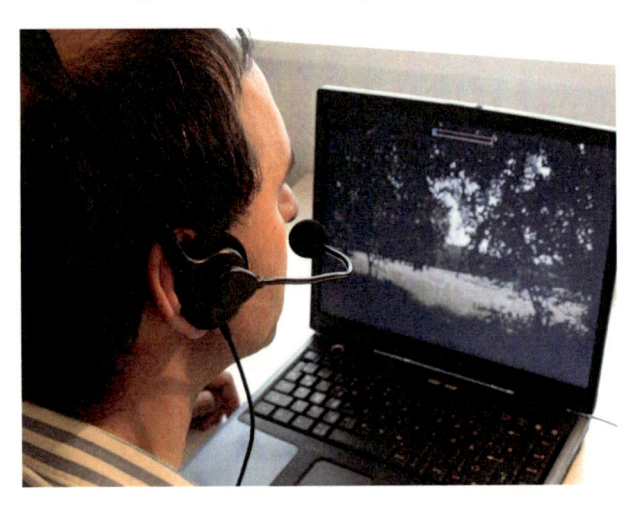

Fig. 3. Reading *The Breathing Wall*. The reader's depth of breath is displayed on the horizontal bar across the top of the screen.

The protagonist of the story is Michael, a young man who has been falsely convicted of murdering his ex-girl-friend Lana. When her body is spotted in the park, a note scribbled by him the day before is found (fig. 4), which is used as evidence against him.

The gothic atmosphere of the story is mainly evoked by the nocturnal appearances of Lana's voice in Michael's dreams, as she speaks to him through the prison "wall." In those audiovisual, animated "dreams," Lana gives Michael—and the reader/breather—phenomenological clues as to how she experienced the night of her murder. Depending on the extent to which the actual reader succeeds in "controlling" his/her respiratory mechanisms along the lines of an "implied breather," Lana's death experience will be conveyed more or less comprehensively through her ghostly analepses.

For example, in Dream 4, the climax of the story, Lana's ghostly voice gives away core information on how she perceived the last moments of her life. Against a visual and aural background that evokes the multisensory image of the park where she was murdered, as well as the hand of her murderer over her face, the successfully breathing reader hears—almost as in a cut scene from a computer game—Lana's whispering voice calling Michael's name intently, as if to draw his attention to her metaphysical death narrative.

By referring verbally to the "hand over [her] mouth" and "under [her] nose," the text draws the "breather's" attention back to his or her own physicality and the technological "extension" (McLuhan) that connects him or her cybernetically to the text world. Thus, by co-experiencing (with Michael) Lana's phenomenological death narrative, which merges her physical metamorphosis into "thin air" with the reader's breathing motor, the reader reaches a maximum level of psychosomatic union with the text machine and the characters within it. At the same time, however, he or she is again reminded of the fact that, without intentional interference in the sense of goal-directedness and perspectival focalization on the Intentional object, the body's unmonitored interaction with the software would not have yielded the same textual depth.[12]

The Breathing Wall purports to undermine the cybernetic accommodation process usually experienced in game-play. These appropriations, performed by the human body through repetitive use of the same "moves," is ultimately based on the workings of intentionality, in the sense of purposefulness and object-directedness, yet it does not usually re-direct the player's attention to the physical nature of the interaction. *The Breathing Wall*, however, does, by making the reader aware of the physical conditionality of text reception and the indispensable interplay of perceiving body and mind. The authors confront their readers with the entextualized threat of losing control of intention-driven textual decoding and inferencing, for the sake of a partly involuntary, cybernetically controlled process of information disclosure.

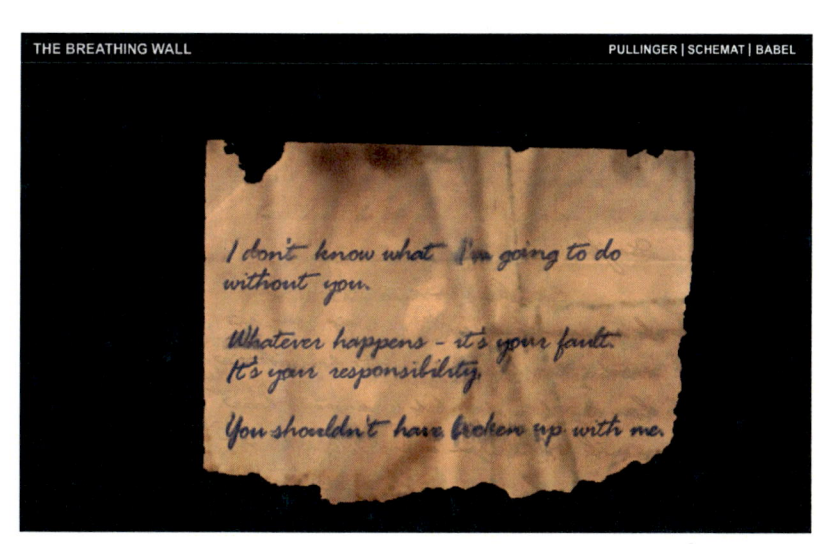

Fig. 4. Michael's note to Lana.

In conclusion, *The Breathing Wall* can be considered a prime example of physio-cybertext, as it not only focuses on body-machine amalgamation but in fact highlights the relative possibility of cortical control and, thus, readerly agency over material-corporeal interaction with the text. I refer to this process, which entails the reader's subconscious and conscious engagement with subcortical (involuntary) physiological processes versus cortical control and manipulation as "retro-intentionalization."[13]

The Latin term "retro" means "back" or "backwards." Used as a prefix, it is used to denote reversal and reaction as well as recursivity, retro-spectivity and reflexivity. My concept of retro-intentionalization involves all five of these notions: "reversal" because it reverses the direction of fit from the text back to the reading organism; "reaction" because the text requires perpetual reactive flexibility; "recursivity" because, by directing the reader's attention to the cybernetic feedback loop, textual understanding inevitably occurs at a metafictional, metamedial level; "retro-spectivity" because the reader is permanently made to remember how to breathe appropriately in order to retrieve more textual information; and "reflexivity" because the process of retro-intentionalization triggers off more general processes of meta-theoretical, meta-phenomenological contemplation.

My reading of *The Breathing Wall* serves as an example of cybersomatic criticism at work. Clearly, not every (cyber-)text operates along the same principles. Surely, breath is a suitable medium of input as it can be measured in terms of air pressure and processed by specially designed software. Other bodily functions, however, may be more difficult to link to a cybernetic feedback loop. That said, straightforwardly measurable elements such as body temperature, blood pressure and heart rate may form the "somatic" basis of a number of e-literary artefacts, which may well be in production or existence at the time of writing yet have not found their way into my critical network.

Notes

1 The so-called "Visual Novel"—a recent import from Japan—represents a digital cross-over between epistolary novel, interactive narrative, hypermedia, anime cartoons and adventure game. For more information, cf. <http://www.vndb.org/>.

2 "Multilinear" stands for "linear in multiple ways" and is a more suitable term than "anti"—or "non-linear" because reading is in itself a temporal and, hence, linear process.

3 According to Kuhlen (129), the term "serendipity" refers to the likelihood that readers will be distracted by one or more aspects of the plot (typically marked by a hyperlink) which they did not originally intend to pursue yet which suddenly seems more interesting than the previous aim of reading.

Consequently, readers may eventually obtain a large amount of information most of which is irrelevant to the initial focus of interest.

4   The term "semantic prosody" goes back to Sinclair. Its underlying assumption is that habitual collocates of a given word form or lemma "colour" its connotational meaning(s). Stubbs has expanded the concept to include the level of discourse in the sense of supra-lexematic semantic relations. In this essay I use "semantic prosody" at a text- or medium-generic level, which is inextricably interlinked with typical patterns of user behaviour and expectations.

5   Contrary to Conklin's predictions, tastes and smells have not yet been included in hypermedia's multisensory experience. Tactile interaction, on the other hand, is implemented via touch-screen technology, mouse and keyboard.

6   Collaborative creative writing projects are a digi-lit phenomenon that emerged alongside hypermedia. It heralded the read/write Web as early as the mid 1990s (e.g. Douglas Davis's *The World's First Collaborative Sentence*, Claudia Klingers's collaborative *Beim Bäcker*, and Teri Hoskin's and Sue Thomas's collaborative *Noon Quilt*) and is now spreading across the blogo- and wiki-sphere as well as social networking sites such as *Facebook*. For an in-depth discussion of collaborative writing projects, cf. Simanowski.

7   *Er/Sie* does not contain image-text, image-image and text-image links but uses text-text links as image, much as in conventional concrete poetry.

8   The reader is repeatedly taken back to the same interface until all directions, represented by pointing hands, have been explored. Afterwards the linear narrative continues.

9   Corpus stylistics is another branch of empirical stylistics, which, however, concentrates on textual patterns and occurrences rather than readerly behaviour.

10 I assume, along with award-winning British poet Carol Rumens (unpublished speech at Bangor University, 1 Nov. 2008) that every literary genre, including poetry, drama, and fiction, has at its basis narrative structures.

11 To quote from the *Osmose* web site, "Osmose (1995) is an immersive interactive virtual-reality environment installation with 3D computer graphics and interactive 3D sound, a head-mounted display and real-time motion tracking based on breathing and balance. . . . Immersion in Osmose begins with the donning of the head-mounted display and motion-tracking vest. The first virtual space encountered is a three-dimensional Cartesian Grid which functions as an orientation space. With the immersant's first

breaths, the grid gives way to a clearing in a forest. There are a dozen world-spaces in Osmose, most based on metaphorical aspects of nature. These include Clearing, Forest, Tree, Leaf, Cloud, Pond, Subterranean Earth, and Abyss. . . . Through use of their own breath and balance, immersants are able to journey anywhere within these worlds as well as hover in the ambiguous transition areas in between." <http://www.immersence.com/osmose/index.php>.

12 For a more detailed cybersomatic reading of *The Breathing Wall*, cf. Ensslin ("From (W)reader to Breather;" "Respiratory Narrative").

13 The notion of intentionality has been explored by leading scholars in philosophy, psychology and narratology since the early 1970s. I want to emphasize that I do not wish to confuse "intentionality" with either the critical concept of "intention" (the writer's or text's assumed purpose, or effect he, she or it is aiming at, cf. Richards, Hirsch, and de Beaugrande and Dressler). Nor am I referring to intentionality as propagated by Speech Act Theory (e.g. Austin, Searle), which denotes the communicative intention of the speaker in performing an illocutionary act successfully, as well as the hearer's recognition of this intention. Likewise, despite my fascination for Peter Brooks's *Reading for the Plot*, I do not share—in the present investigation—his specific idea of narrative intention, which, essentially, relates to the "motor forces" of plot or rather "plotting" and, hence, narrative meaning. In fact, most of the afore-mentioned theories associate intention and intentionality with either the author-producer's side or the text itself as an abstract static or dynamic concept. Conversely, my main interest lies in the receiver's side and to what extent we can uphold purpose-driven, goal-directed intentionality in a cybersomatic literary experience.

Works Cited

Aarseth, Espen J. *Cybertext: Perspectives on Ergodic Literature*. Baltimore: Johns Hopkins UP, 1997.

Ascott, Roy. "Gesamtdatenwerk: Connectivity, Transformation, and Transcendence." *Ars Electronica: Facing the Future: A Survey of Two Decades*. Ed. Timothy Druckrey. Cambridge, MA: MIT P, 1999. 86-89.

Auer, Johannes. "7 Thesen zur Netzliteratur." *Dichtung Digital* 2.12 (2000). 8 May 2009 <http://www.dichtung-digital.de/IASL-Forum/Auer-20Jun00.htm>.

Austin, John L. *How to Do Things with Words*. Oxford: Oxford UP, 1962.

Avenstroup, Tone, and Robert Lippok. "marbel + matrikel." 2002. 7 Aug. 2008 < http://www.marbelundmatrikel.de>.

Barthes, Roland. *S/Z*. Paris: Seuil, 1970.

Bell, Alice. "'Do You Want to Hear About it?' Exploring Possible Worlds in Michael Joyce's Hyperfiction, *Afternoon, a story*." *Contemporary Stylistics*. Ed. Marina Lambrou, Marina and Peter Stockwell. London: Continuum, 2007. 43-55.

———. *The Possible Worlds of Hypertext Fiction*. London: Palgrave, 2010. Forthcoming.

———. "Ontological Boundaries and Conceptual Leaps: The Significance of Possible Worlds for Hypertext Fiction (and Beyond)." *New Narratives: Theory and Practice*. Ed. Ruth Page and Bronwen Thomas. Lincoln: U of Nebraska P, 2009. Forthcoming.

Brooks, Peter. *Reading for the Plot: Design and Intention in Narrative*. New York: Knopf, 1984.

Conklin, Jeff. "Hypertext: An Introduction and Survey." *IEEE Computer* 20.9 (1987): 17-41.

Davies, Char. *Osmose*. 1995-2008. 5 Aug. 2009. <http://www.immersence.com/osmose/index.php>.

Davis, Douglas. *The World's First Collaborative Sentence*. 1994. 5 Aug. 2009 <http://www.artport.whitney.org/collection/index.shtml>.

Beaugrande de, Robert, and Wolfgang Dressler. *Introduction to Text Linguistics*. London: Longman, 1981.

Douglas, Jane Y. *Print Pathways and Interactive Labyrinths: How Hypertext Narratives Affect the Act of Reading*. Diss. New York U, 1992.

———. "'How Do I Stop This Thing?': Closure and Indeterminacy in Interactive Narratives." *Hyper/Text/Theory*. Ed. George P. Landow. Baltimore: Johns Hopkins UP, 1994. 159-188.

Dovey, John, and Helen Kennedy. *Game Cultures: Computer Games as New Media*. Maidenhead: Open UP, 2006.

Emmott, Catherine. *Narrative Comprehension: A Discourse Perspective*. Oxford: Oxford UP, 1997.

Ensslin, Astrid. *Canonizing Hypertext: Explorations and Constructions*. London: Continuum, 2007.

Ensslin, Astrid. "Of Chords, Machines and Bumble-bees: The Metalinguistics of Hyperpoetry." *Language in the Media: Representations, Identities, Ideologies.* Ed. Sally Johnson and Astrid Ensslin. London: Continuum, 2007. 250-268.

―――. "Breathalyzing Physio-cybertext." *Proceedings of the 18th ACM Conference on Hypertext and Hypermedia, Manchester, UK, September 10-12, 2007.* Alpha: Sheridan, 2007. 137-138.

―――. "From (W)reader to Breather: Cybertextual Retro-intentionalisation in Kate Pullinger et al.'s *Breathing Wall.*" *New Narratives: Theory and Practice.* Ed. Ruth Page and Bronwen Thomas. Lincoln: U of Nebraska P, 2009.

―――. "Respiratory Narrative: Multimodality and Cybernetic Corporeality in 'Physio-cybertext.'" *New Perspectives on Narrative and Multimodality.* Ed. Ruth Page. London: Routledge, 2009. 155-165.

Ensslin, Astrid, and Alice Bell. *New Perspectives on Digital Literature: Criticism and Analysis. Dichtung Digital* 9.37 (2007). 6 Aug. 2008 <http://www.brown.edu/Research/dichtung-digital/editorial/2007.htm>.

Freude, Alvar, and Dragan Espenschied. *Assoziations-Blaster.* 1999-2009. 8 May 2009 <http://www.a-blast.org>.

Gavins, Joanna. "Text World Theory in Literary Practice." *Cognition in Literary Interpretation and Practice.* Ed. Bo Petterson, Merja Polvinen, and Harri Veivo. Helsinki: Helsinki UP, 2005. 89-104.

―――. *Text World Theory: An Introduction.* Edinburgh: Edinburgh UP, 2007.

Guyer, Carolyn. *Quibbling.* CD-ROM. Cambridge, MA: Eastgate, 1993.

Heibach, Christiane. *Literatur im elektronischen Raum.* Frankfurt a.M.: Suhrkamp, 2003.

―――. "Conversations on Digital Aesthetics: Synopsis of the Erfurt Discussions." *p0es1s. Ästhetik digitaler Poesie/The Aesthetics of Digital Poetry.* Ed. Friedrich W. Block, Christiane Heibach, and Karin Wenz. Ostfildern: Cantz, 2004. 38-56.

Hirsch, Eric D. *Validity in Interpretation.* New Haven: Yale UP, 1967.

Hoskin, Teri, and Sue Thomas. *Noon Quilt.* 2000. 7 Aug. 2008 <http://www.tracearchive.ntu.ac.uk/quilt/info.htm>.

Inglis, Gavin. *Same Day Test.* 1999. 7 Aug. 2008 <http://www.bareword.com/sdt/>.

Jackson, Shelley. *Patchwork Girl.* CD-ROM. Cambridge, MA: Eastgate, 1995.

Jakobson, Roman. "Closing Statement: Linguistics and Poetics." *Style in Language*. Ed. Thomas A. Sebeok. Cambridge, MA: MIT P, 1960. 350-377.

Joyce, Michael. *afternoon, a story*. 1987. CD-ROM. Cambridge, MA: Eastgate, 1990.

Klinger, Claudia. *Beim Bäcker*. 2000. 5 Aug. 2009 <http://www.claudia-klinger. de/archiv/baecker/index.htm>.

Kok, Kum C. "Multisemiotic Mediation in Hypertext." *Multimodal Discourse Analysis: Systemic Functional Perspectives*. Ed. Kay L. O'Halloran. London: Continuum, 2004. 131-159.

Kuhlen, Rainer. *Hypertext: Ein nicht-lineares Medium zwischen Buch und Wissensbank*. Berlin: Springer, 1991.

LaCook, Lewis. *Dirty Milk*. 2003. 8 Aug. 2008 <http://www.lewislacook. org/dirtymilk/>.

Landow, George P. *Hypertext 2.0: The Convergence of Contemporary Critical Theory and Technology*. Baltimore: Johns Hopkins UP, 1997.

Larsen, Deena. *Marble Springs*. CD-ROM. Cambridge, MA: Eastgate, 1993.

Liestøl, Gunnar. "Wittgenstein, Genette, and the Reader's Narrative in Hypertext." *Hyper/Text/Theory*. Ed. George P. Landow. Baltimore: Johns Hopkins UP, 1994. 87-120.

Lyons, William. *Approaches to Intentionality*. Oxford: Polity, 1995.

McLuhan, Marshall. *Understanding Media: The Extensions of Man*. New York: McGraw, 1964.

Menzer, Ursula, and Sabine Orth. *Er/Sie: ein literarisches Internet-Projekt*. 2001. 7 Aug. 2008 < http://www.soyosigma.de/ersie/>.

Miall, David S. and Teresa Dobson. "Reading Hypertext and the Experience of Literature." *Journal of Digital Information* 2.1 (2001). 7 Nov. 2008 <http://www.journals.tdl.org/jodi/article/view/jodi-36/37>.

Morrissey, Judd, and Lori Talley. *My Name Is Captain, Captain*. CD-ROM. Cambridge, MA: Eastgate, 2002.

Moulthrop, Stuart. *Victory Garden*. CD-ROM. Cambridge, MA: Eastgate, 1991.

———. *Hegirascope*. 1995. (1996). 7 Aug. 2008 <http://www.iat.ubalt.edu/ moulthrop/hypertexts/hgs/>.

Nielsen, Jakob. *Hypertext and Hypermedia*. Boston: Academic P, 1990.

Page, Ruth. "Blogging on the Body: Gender, Narrative and Identity." *New Narratives: Theory and Practice*. Ed. Ruth Page and Bronwen Thomas. Lincoln: U of Nebraska P, 2009. Forthcoming.

Pullinger, Kate, and Chris Joseph. *Inanimate Alice*. 2005-2009. 7 May 2009 <http://www.inanimatealice.com>.

Pullinger, Kate, Stefan Schemat, and babel. *The Breathing Wall*. London: Sayle, 2004.

Richards, Ivor A. *Practical Criticism*. London: Kegan Paul, Trench, Trubner, 1929.

Ryan, Marie-Laure. *Possible Worlds, Artificial Intellingence, and Narrative Theory*. Bloomington: Indiana University Press, 1992.

Schreiber, Urs. *Das Epos der Maschine*. 1998. 7 Aug. 2008 <http://www.kunst.im.internett.de/epos-der-maschine/edmdiemaschine.html>.

Searle, John. *Speech Acts: An Essay in the Philosophy of Language*. Cambridge: Cambridge UP, 1969.

———. *Intentionality: An Essay in the Philosophy of Mind*. Cambridge: Cambridge UP, 1983.

Semino, Elena, and Jonathan Culpeper. *Cognitive Stylistics: Language and Cognition in Text Analysis*. Amsterdam: John Benjamins, 2002.

Simanowski, Roberto. *Interfictions: Vom Schreiben im Netz*. Frankfurt a.M.: Suhrkamp, 2002.

Sinclair, John. *Corpus, Concordance, Collocation*. Oxford: Oxford UP, 1991.

Stockwell, Peter. *Cognitive Poetics: An Introduction*. London: Routledge, 2002.

Stubbs, Michael. *Words and Phrases: Corpus Studies of Lexical Semantics*. Oxford: Blackwell, 2001.

Taylor, Claire. "Virtual Bodies in Cyberspace: Guzik Glantz's Weblog." *Latin American Cyberculture and Cyberliterature*. Ed. Claire Taylor and Thea Pitman. Liverpool: Liverpool UP, 2007. 244-256.

Thomas, Bronwen. "Canons and Fanons: Literary Fanfiction Online." *Dichtung Digital* 9.37 (2007). 7 Aug. 2008 <http://www.brown.edu/Research/dichtung-digital/2007/thomas.htm>.

Thomas, Sue. "Narratives of Digital Life at the trAce Online Writing Centre." *Computers and Composition* 22.4 (2005): 493-501.

Thomas, Sue, et al. "Transliteracy: Crossing Divides." *First Monday* 12.12 (2007). 8 Aug. 2008 <http://www.uic.edu/htbin/cgiwrap/bin/ojs/index.php/fm/article/view/2060/1908>.

Alexandra Saemmer

Digital Literature—A Question of Style

Traditions and Approaches of Digital Literature in France: A Short Overview

The rediscovery of the text as a graphic and plastic material undoubtedly found its ideal medium on the World Wide Web. Nevertheless, this new materiality was first experienced on traditional paper pages. From its spectacular creation at the end of the 1960s, many critics therefore have concentrated on the philosophical and literary contexts that have facilitated the emergence of technical, informational, communicational and literary "networks." It certainly constitutes an interesting and complex theoretical aim to determine which transformations of textual material into digital media could really be considered as a break with the paper media and which devices only continue the paper tradition in a more effective way: digital literature is continuously changing, gradually discovering its specific potential.

An evolution that began long before the establishment of the electronic Web continues today in multimedia creation: the layout, once confided to the publisher's and printer's care, acquires an essential role in the creative process. From Arthur Rimbaud to Stéphane Mallarmé, from Concrete poetry and Poesia visiva via the Surrealists, from the Dada movement to Oulipo (Workshop of Potential Literature)[1] the borders between the arts of the image and of the text have gradually become obliterated in 20th century French literature. The letter has become part of the iconography—texts are regarded as paintings and paintings can be read. The white space surrounding a text is worked on with as much attention as the words themselves; the letters become coloured, expanding beyond their standard default size or contracting. Books are cut into strips, enabling the reader to choose between multiple reading paths. The rectangular format is sometimes abandoned.

When French critics began to focus on new forms of literary writing on digital media, they often referred to texts prior to the existence and use of computers, but whose "pre-hypertextual" structures, as Jean Clément has pointed out in many of his articles, quite naturally seem to suggest hypertextual adaptations.[2] Bernard Magné notes: "Everything happens as if, with multimedia, literature had finally found the technical devices it suggested and required long before" (127).[3]

With the "Nouveau roman,"[4] French authors not only questioned the rigid format of books, but also the ability of traditional narrative structures to reflect the complexity of contemporary social, technological, political and historical processes. They no longer believed in the power of language to represent the world. The plots of "new" novels, therefore, take place while presenting the tools with which they have been manufactured, breaking all fictional illusion, sometimes even thematizing the "fictionality" of all speech, i.e., the fundamental transformation of things by speech. The author, once considered a priest-prophet inspired by supernatural forces, is partially deprived of his power.

From the moment that the importance of intertextual influences, the role of imitation and recombination, and even the role of chance in creative acts are clearly recognized and shown, why not confide a part of the creative process to a machine? Critics thus have often considered the combinatorial "games" by Raymond Queneau and Georges Perec, the experimental incises by Jacques Roubaud, and the combinatorial or hypertextual practices in digital literature as component parts of the same cultural context. Combinatorial literature in particular seems to offer, as Bernard Magné explains, a chance to take a stand "against the carefully maintained illusions of naturalism, which still hides its cultural dimension behind a very effective cover of evidence and common sense" (127). In order to demonstrate the importance of random processes in arts, the Oulipo authors broke up books, tore up the pages and cut poems into strips. Their desire to definitively transgress the bounds of rectangular pages and hardcover books naturally compelled them to consider new tools and devices. Members of the Oulipo as a result were among the first to focus on computers as creative supports. A "literary workshop assisted by computers" (ALAMO) was founded by Jacques Roubaud and Paul Brafort. In 1975, a pilot group presented the first computer-based literary creations at the Centre Georges Pompidou in Paris. Antoine Denize and Bernard Magné republished *One hundred thousand billion poems* by Raymond Queneau on a CD-ROM. All the combinatory writing and reading operations which were rather difficult to handle on the paper medium were thus realized by a simple click, giving the impression that literature finally found the tools, devices and supports it had been dreaming of for a long time.

More and more sophisticated textual generators have been created. A textual generator usually selects words in a prefabricated vocabulary. A grammar allows it to combine these elements in various ways: "Literary generation algorithms are based on a semantic grammar: they consider semantics and syntax as equivalent on all levels. The fundamental mode of operation is grammatical" (Balpe and Baboni-Schilingi 149). The richer the vocabulary and the grammar of a generator, the more surprising are the generated results. Some generators like *A response to Claude ADELEN* by *JP BALPE 1* even permit the manipulation of data by the reader. The first electronic text generators nevertheless seem tightly linked to the rules that human beings (e.g., authors or readers) impose on them. "What could be the style of a literary automaton?" therefore asks Italo Calvino. "I believe that its true vocation would be for classicism. The test of a poetic-electronic machine would be its ability to produce traditional works, poems with closed metrical forms" (12). In the years after those first experiences with textual generators, authors tried to transgress purely potential combinatorial concepts, to put in a "virtual," unpredictable dimension into their works.

In fact, this virtuality is always present in digital literature because of the instability of the device (changes caused by the operating system, the speed of the computer, software developments, etc.). Philippe Bootz and some other members of the group L.A.I.R.E.[5] and the *Transitoire observable*[6] emphatically theorized on the influence of this instability in digital creations. Considering the "intentionality of the computer," the author of a digital work, according to Philippe Bootz, always creates with the awareness of a failure ("The Problem of Form").

In fact, this failure awareness is also true for critics. When observing and analyzing the phenomena of meaning in digital literature on computer screens, we must always keep in mind that their operation is conditioned by the "intentionality of the computer." The exact scrolling speed of an animation, for example, undoubtedly influences the aesthetic impression. Bootz thus integrates the physical phenomenon of program execution as a fundamental component in his works; in his "aesthetics of failure," the machine with its bugs, its power of amendment, is fully included in the poem's signification process ("Ébauche de quelques notes"). The author is also experimenting with "processing figures" where the coherence between the involved media is based on exchanges between programs. The identification of these specific figures will constitute one of the aims of a future research project at University Paris 8.

Figures of Manipulation

For some time, as mentioned before, critics tried to circumscribe the "novelty" of digital literature in rather generalist terms, either taking into account its relation to literary avant-gardes or focalizing on its technical features; these theoretical approaches were often blind to contents. Now that digital literature seems more and more aesthetically convincing, the time has come to define its stylistic features with more precision.

In order to circumscribe the poetics of interaction, Jean Clément first tested the validity of the classical figures of style. In using terms like "animated metaphor" or "metalepsis," I tried in my book *Matières textuelles sur support numérique* [*Material Text on Digital Media*] to describe the phenomena of meaning in digital literature when animation enters in significant relationships with the linguistic content. It is, however, probably dangerous to use classical rhetorical terms intended to characterize *textual* phenomena, whereas the signs of digital text almost constantly refer to different semiotic systems (including the visual one). In the following pages of this article, I will sometimes continue to borrow from conventional taxonomies to describe the stylistic devices of digital literature, and I will try in other cases to invent a new terminology in order to avoid foolhardy analogies. It is not so much the character of an interactive gesture—touching or clicking, removal or rollover—that transforms interaction into a figure; rather, it is the relationship between the gesture, the media content on which this gesture is applied and the media content appearing after the performance of this gesture. When the relation between the content of an interactive medium, the manipulation gesture and the content of the media discovered or processed by the gesture appears surprising or even incongruous, when it thus destabilizes the reader's expectations, I would propose to call these phenomena *figures of manipulation*.

Most of the time in digital documents, the relationship between the manipulation gesture and the interacted media content complies with a certain number of increasingly stabilized grammatical rules. The activation of a keyword hyperlinked to a definition of a term, the entering of numbers giving access to a bank account, the manipulation of a textual or iconographic element enabling the reconstitution of a puzzle, do not seem incongruous: the manipulation gesture mainly facilitates rapid access to information—gesture and media contents are related according to the reader's expectations previously established by his habits.

The style of digital literature, however, is partly based on a discrepancy between the reader's expectations and the realized events on the screen. Thus, the figures I will try to identify and describe in this essay may be considered indicative of the *poetic fact* in electronic text. Since they diverge from standardized usage, creating resistance to the reader's expectations, the figures run the risk, however, of being first perceived as malfunctions, as "bugs." If we take into account the instability of the digital device discussed above and its influence on the updating of a poetic work, we can go even further and assume that a critic may sometimes mistakenly consider a phenomenon actually due to a bug as a figure! As I will further demonstrate, only the consistency between a detected incongruity and the context can help us to decide whether we are confronted by a bug or by a figure intentionally created by the author. Perhaps, we might therefore argue for the existence of two distinct "aesthetics of frustration": in the first case, the resistance of the work against the readers' habits/expectations is consciously pre-programmed by the author; in the second case, resistance would be caused unintentionally by the instability of the digital device.

While keeping in mind these general considerations, I will now try to identify some figures of manipulation in a panel of works relating to digital literature.

Many internal hyperlinks in the literary blog *tierslivre.net* by François Bon work in accordance with the reader's expectations: a keyword, a part of a sentence announces the following parts of the text, representing a textual unity that can be activated by a click. In the text entitled "Comment Internet multiplie la littérature" ('How the Internet Multiplies Literature'), the typographical highlight of the word "Malbreil" in the fragmented sentence "see Malbreil" invites the reader to click on the word; by activating the link, he browses through a collection of texts composed by Xavier Malbreil (just the same way as one might say to the reader: "Take your Saussure"). Such a link therefore controls the relations between strongly stabilized entities; primarily motivated by efficiency in a firmly established communicational context, it tells us nothing new about the organization of the world.

Some authors, however, attribute a function to the hyperlink that is contrary to the established practice:

> ce qui est fascinant, côté Internet, c'est le lien qu'on peut consituer de pair à pair (peer to peer), l'idée de <u>réticule</u> commence par une auto prise en charge: elle s'annonce déjà trop tardive. Internet ne peut fonctionner selon des utopies de maison commune: aussi parce qu'il s'ancre désormais sur des lieux de création singulière, dont le principe serait plutôt de <u>constellation,</u> et que ce qui s'y affirmera peu à peu comme contenu de littérature le fera depuis ces singularités, par quoi en chacune le langage va au monde. (Bon, *Le tiers livre*)

> [W]hat is fascinating about the internet is the peer to peer link that can be established; the idea of the <u>reticule</u> is set-off by way of a self-invested responsibility that, however, reveals itself only belatedly. The internet can not function according to the (administrative) utopias of "town-halls"—also because from now on it is anchored in spaces of singular acts of creativity whose guiding principles function rather like <u>constellations,</u> and those components that therein will gradually establish themselves as "literary" will accomplish this based on the very singularities that allow each of their forms of expression to spread throughout the world.

In French, the word "reticle" has a double meaning, designating a constellation of the southern hemisphere and at the same time a network of fine lines, dots, cross hairs, or wires in the focal plane of the eyepiece of an optical instrument. In the context of *tierslivre*, the hyperlink on the word "réticule" does not lead to a definition of the term, but to the blog *LittéRéticulaire* by Patrick Rebollar. The activation of the link on "constellation" allows the reader to discover a page of the website *Le Bloc-notes du désordre*: in the middle of a starry sky, a button is set with the legend "randomly Balthazar." All the small points of light can be triggered, guiding to other sites, giving substance to what has often been called metaphorically the "Internet galaxy" or the "cyberspace," and making significant and visible what the text affirms. When the manipulation gesture of the click thus brings to the forefront an element that enters with what is triggered and the activated media in an incongruous, surprising, metaphorical relationship, I propose the term *retroprojection* in order to characterize it.

However, is the argument of incongruity and surprise sufficient to define a figure? The "figures of speech" have often been considered as a difference, a reasoned change of meaning or language in relation to the ordinary and simple way of speaking (Quintilian, IX, 1, 11-13). Structuralism considers figures first and mainly as devices meant to emphasize the message. They are characteristic of the poetic function of the language: according to Gérard Genette, figures even constitute the way literature distinguishes itself. The semiotic approach has helped to refine the concept of incongruity essential in the definition of a figure.

According to Jean-Marie Klinkenberg (344-347), the generation of a figure takes place in four inextricably linked steps. The first step consists in locating an isotopy in the utterance. Each element of an utterance is included in a context created by the preceding elements. These elements set forth an expectation that can be met or disappointed by the following elements. In the case of the example quoted from *tierslivre* by François Bon, the context of the link "reticle" describes how the Internet functions according to the "peer-to-peer" principle; implementing a link on the word "reticle" seems to meet the reader's expectation for an illustration of this context. He logically expects a definition of the term.

The second step in the forming of a figure is defined as the identification of an allotopy, i.e., an irrelevance in the utterance. In classical poetry, for example, this allotopy may be based on an encyclopaedic incompatibility between the terms of a metaphor. In the context of *tierslivre*, it is the relationship between the content of the activated media (the word "reticule," defined as an optical device or a constellation), the manipulation gesture questioning this term, and the media content activated by the manipulation gesture (the blog *Le Journal LitteRéticulaire*), which proves to be allotopic.

A third step is intended to safeguard the general principle of cooperation between the cited elements in the utterance (it is primarily this third step that allows one to distinguish figures of manipulation from incongruities produced by the computer's intentionality). During this process, it is important to first identify exactly what part of the interactive utterance should be considered incongruous. It is the general isotopy that enables one to decide: François Bon described the way the Internet works according to "peer-to-peer" principles in his text. He neither spoke about optical devices nor about astronomy. Therefore, the word "reticle" constitutes a first allotopy (reminding of a classical metaphor). Since the rather unfamiliar word "reticle" is used and hyperlinked in the text, the grammatical rules of the digital document would have required the display of a definition; but the hyperlink leading to the blog *Le Journal Litteréticulaire* does not throw any direct light on its meaning—it leads neither to a starry sky, nor to an optical tool, thus constituting a second allotopy. At this "perceived degree" imposed by the utterance, a content is superimposed which is compatible with the rest of the context. It could be formulated as "the general functioning of the Internet, and particularly of peer-to-peer principles." Jean-Marie Klinkenberg calls this level "conceived degree 1."

In a final step, the compatible semantic components of the perceived degree and the conceived degree 1 are superimposed: The double semantic emanation of the word "reticle," which at the same time refers to a constellation of stars and to the precise aim you can perform with an optical device, can in fact be explored by the manipulation gesture on the word "reticle;" while illustrating the idea of the Internet as a *constellation* of web sites, it leads the interactor not to a page of links, but to a specific site, as if the reader had aimed at the site by clicking. *Retroprojection* is thus the first example of a figure of manipulation that I would like to present here, a figure based on mediation between the perceived and the conceived degree.

One of the most conventional relationships between a hyperlinked word, a manipulation gesture and an activated content consists in providing an explanation of the word. Already by its title, the poem "Explication de texte" ("Explication de texte") by Boris de Boullay seems to allude to this pragmatic use of hyperlinks. At the centre of a black surface appears, in green, a poem sprinkled with 27 hyperlinks:

Having clean hands for cross a bridge in the summer.
Crossing the bridge of Arcole with hands as big as pockets, with frogs in the belly, arms in the air to restore balance.
Balance is to risk the water of the Seine, green, thick, unreal, prohibited, abandonment, to make frogs find the green water.
Being a bag of water, floating, swollen with water.

Having <u>clean</u> hands and slender, <u>stretched</u>, long fingers, to <u>imagine</u> grasping the <u>guardrail</u>, to see, despite the <u>tremendous</u> <u>breadth</u> of the pavement.

Whenever one of the underlined words of the central poem is activated, new textual fragments are displayed around the poem in the black space. Often, they are hyperlinked again, creating long chains of associations. If we click, for example, on the word "summer" in the poem, the fragment "what, the summer?" emerges from the darkness around the poem, and a hyperlink can be activated on the question mark. Emphasis is placed on the performative potential of the hyperlink.

After a certain number of interactions, several associative chains end, however, on the word "maman" ('Mom'); whenever the reader clicks on this hyperlink, the same word appears on the screen, gradually sparkling over the entire black space around the central poem. When the manipulation gesture is invariably followed by the same effect, I call this figure an *involution*. Whereas the context of the poem incites the reader to discover the associations, or even the "explanations" of the central poem, his curiosity remains unsatisfied when he activates the link on "Mom." After having clicked several times on the same word, the reader discovers a fragment thematizing this stagnation, which is once again opposed to his expectations: "I heard that the day I was born, my mother bathed in the sea in Le Havre." No more hyperlinks can be activated on this fragment. The desire to return to this prenatal stage has been verbalized in the central poem as well. This context enables us to superimpose the perceived degree of this interactive utterance and the conceived degree: "Risking the water of the Seine, green, thick, unreal, prohibited." Floating in the water . . . as an embryo. The subject has never been so close to his drowning dream as on his birthday, when his mother, pregnant, bathed in the ocean. The baby was floating in the amniotic fluid, which was floating in the womb, which was floating in the salt water of the sea. Interactive reading turns into a regressive activity, recalling some pleasantly automatic gestures of early childhood. The repetitive use of hypertext links creates the illusion of a "recaptured past."

Progression or stagnation—in most interactive environments, something goes on when the reader activates hyperlinks. In *The Subnetwork* by Gregory Chatonsky, a click on a photo showing a subway corridor gives, quite conventionally, access to the work. The text emerging and disappearing, "When I took the subway, as a child, I was doing little shows to make passengers laugh," bathes the reader in a narrative universe. The reader expects to discover the content of these shows, the reactions of the other passengers. Activating certain points in the network and abandoning others paths, pointing and clicking, the interactor quickly creates a relationship between the metro branching, the neural network and the Internet: the branching of subway or bus maps has often inspired e-poets. Whereas in traditional hypermedia, navigation among fragments can be re-experienced and easily modelled by graphs and diagrams, the reader of *The Subnetwork* realizes that some changes occur in the interface regardless of whether he interacts or not; that some manipulations seem to have an impact on the interface without being instantly discernible.

A click on the words "first memory" in the sequence "map," for example, does not at first seem to produce visible effects on the interface. Yet, the interactor feels that multiple clickings on the link provoke reactions, such as the sequence of sounds gradually getting out of control. Processes apparently take place beneath the smooth surface of videos and animated graphics. Do they also influence the *visual* re-composition of the narrative fragments? In the sequence "reflects of the travellers," a click on the emerging words does not immediately alter the display of the background videos. If nothing happens immediately after a click, the reader will maybe forget his past interactions. In *The Subnetwork*, however, images and words seem changed when the reader returns to the same place after a few other explorations. According to the author, Gregory Chatonsky, it is the program that links the fragments of *The Subnetwork* according to prescribed parameters and variables. These variables are relayed via a statistical device based on navigation paths that former visitors had explored before. Interaction has thus consequences on the work's device. But these consequences are not always connected to the immediate, well-known interfacial reactions.[7] The relationship between the manipulation gesture, the activable and the activated media content proves to be strongly disturbed.

When the interactor clicks on the words "first memory" without creating any apparent interfacial reaction, this incongruous relationship between the gesture and its effect therefore constitutes the perceived degree of the figure. The projection of the conceived degree 1, built around the utterance "interactive exploration of the metro network and the author's memory," on the perceived degree (the impossible activation of the link on "first memory") makes us understand that some specific areas of *The Subnetwork* will forever resist manipulation. I propose to call this figure a *neantism*. When a manipulation gesture produces changes on the digital interface of a numerical creation, but these changes occur too late for the interactor to easily create a meaningful relationship between his gesture and the provoked changing, I would speak about an *incubation*. In *The Subnetwork*, neantisms and incubations contribute to building a complex metaphor, suggesting similarities between memory and digital network.

When the interactor clicks on a hyperlink, his gesture usually provokes either a page break, or the display of a new window that overlaps the initial one. This pop-up technique has proved to be particularly effective in the context of information searching. Whereas a page break may disturb the reader, the pop-up technique allows him to keep looking at the original context. But the pop-up technique is much less reassuring if, instead of a single window, multiplicities of windows invade the screen. Online advertising overuses this technique that so often irritates the reader. In *Crowds and Power* by Jody Zellen, the multiplication of pop-up windows becomes a figure of manipulation I would like to call *interfacial sporulation*. The activable images in *Crowds and Power* do not only show crowd movements invading public places, department stores, airports and railway stations; the activation of the hyperlinks also provokes a pop-up invasion; the reader has to fight the invaders by clicking over and over again. The "normal" functioning of digital documents, where a click provokes the display of a *single* pop-up window, constitutes the isotopy of this utterance; the multiplication of pop-up windows on the screenic surface can be considered allotopic. More specifically, it is the incongruous relationship between the manipulation gesture and the uncontrollable pop-up invasion that constitutes the perceived degree of this figure. The contents of the pop-up windows, thematizing the sensations of a person literally overwhelmed by multiplicity, however, allow for the superimposing of the perceived degree and the content compatible with the rest of the context. The identification and the application of semantic components compatible with the unpleasant invasion of the screen by crowds of pop-up windows, the manipulation gesture consisting in provoking *and* pushing back the invasion, and the content of the activated images showing crowds moving, permits us to describe the functioning of this figure of manipulation.

The manipulation gestures involved in media figures are not only limited to the click. In *Soleil amer* ('Bitter Sun') by Bruno Scoccimarro, for example, a rollover on the black background displays textual and iconographic fragments, making us dream about a meaningful entirety. However, each little fragment disappears as quickly as it springs up. Instead of reading, instead of recomposing an image, the interactor can only enjoy his gesture. A prolonged exploration of *Soleil amer* proves either to be motivated by the "dizzying" pleasure to observe the emergence and disappearance of light spots on the interface, or by the desire to recompose ephemeral entireties separated from media contents, or to play the interface like an instrument.

When the visitor takes pleasure in exploring the interface for itself, when the interface becomes the real object of semiosis, and when the interfaced content proves to be only an artefact for technical functioning, Philippe Bootz calls this figure an *"interfacial inversion"* ("Eléments d'analyse" 119). And this means that the contents of activable and activated media have lost their importance in the construction of meaning, and so we leave the field of "media" figures, moving on to an experimental, still largely unexplored field of "a-media" figures.

Figures of Animation

After dealing with the figures of manipulation, I will now try to identify and precisely define some figures of animation in digital literature. Whereas in the previous chapter I based my comments on several digital works, I will focus now on one particularly convincing example. *The Dreamlife of Letters*, a kinetic poem by Brian Kim Stefans, is one of the most frequently cited digital creations on the Web. Indeed, after a few initial moments of surprise when the reader tries in vain to interact with the words on the screen, he is quickly fascinated by the variety of these animations exploring a "dreamlife" of the alphabet. While applauding the great inventiveness of Stefans, most commentators, however, have made do with proposing only very general remarks about the poem's content and form. We can also note that the insertion of Stefans' work in a specific, existing poetical tradition has divided critics' minds. Whereas Edward Picot does not consider *The Dreamlife of Letters* as an avant-garde work ("Hyperliterature as a Product?"), James Mitchell argues that the methods of traditional literary analysis would not be effective to interpret this poem: its form is pertinently changing without the possibility for the reader to intervene ("A Modest 'Electronic' Proposal"). According to Marjorie Perloff, Stefans' poem should be considered as lettrist, belonging to a literary avant-garde based on onomatopoeia and ideographic signs used to repudiate meaning ("Screening the Page, Paging the Screen" 376 ff.). For Philippe Bootz, *The Dreamlife of Letters* simultaneously refers to kinetic poetry, abstract calligram and typographical animation ("Quelles sont les formes"). Lori Emerson thinks that the reader of this poem plays, above all, a passive role, having nothing to interpret since meaning would be entirely subsumed by movement. N. Katherine Hayles, on the contrary, asserts that the morphemes and phonemes of this poem are charged with an "eroticized graphic imagination," expressing a collective subconscious with its feelings and desire (*Electronic Literature* 28).

The great divergence of these comments has intrigued me as much as the fact that they often seem too general. In proposing a close reading of the first few minutes of *The Dreamlife of Letters*, I will try to identify some *figures of animation*. Purely kinetic, non-interactive poetry, referring not explicitly to the instability of the digital device in its poetic project, is primarily characterized by media figures, which create meaning on the surface of the screen between the legible, visible and audible components of a word. In the following analyses of *The Dreamlife of Letters*, I will at times continue to borrow from conventional taxonomies to describe the stylistic devices of digital literature, and in order to avoid indiscriminate analogies, I will try in other cases to invent a new terminology.[8] It seems particularly important to me that these terms mark the difference between rhetorical "figures" and technical processes used to *create* the animations: *morphing* or *fade-in effects*, for example, should not be considered as figures; these effects only become figures in relation to the media content to which they are applied.

Brian Kim Stefans initiated the project *The Dreamlife of Letters* during a virtual workshop on the topic "sex and literature." Inspired by a text written by Dodie Bellamy, the feminist writer Rachel Blau DuPlessis proposed, in a first step, a very personal, somewhat opaque reading often using puns. Brian Kim Stefans responded to DuPlessis by putting all the words of her text in alphabetical order and then, with some of these words, composing a series of poems he himself calls "concrete."[9] But the tradition of concrete poetry quickly seems too burdensome for him: he decides to explore the "dream life" of letters through text animation. According to the author, the final result of *The Dreamlife of Letters* is no longer entirely concrete. What has changed? Let us take a close look at what "happens" to the letters and words moving on an orange background in a small, square window.

The title of the poem appears in the middle of the window, briefly stabilizes, and disappears at the same pace. This event, produced by fade-in and fade-out effects, can only be considered as a figure of animation if it provides the word with an additional, surprising or incongruous meaning. I thus suggest the terms *emergence* and *eclipse*. The term *syncope* characterizes a temporary stabilization of the textual material. Some emergences and eclipses fall fully within the scope of rhetorical tropes. Let us, for example, consider the sentence "I am stable" exploding into thousands of pieces, and then analyze it according to the method proposed by Jean-Marie Klinkenberg already dealt with in the previous chapter. The isotopy in this utterance is constituted by the content of the words: a speaker asserts his stability. But the specific animation of the letters does not index on this isotopy, thus constituting an allotopy. The perceived degree of this figure is therefore based on the incongruity between the content suggesting stability and the movement of the words. The speaker in this utterance affirms his stability, but the animation contradicts his assertion—the purpose therefore becomes ironic, tropologic. However, in the title of *The Dreamlife of Letters*, the animation effect acts rather like a catachresis, a figure which has come into common use: without radically changing their meaning, the emergence and the eclipse of the words point out the poem's title.

In the following sequence, the multiplied letter "A" gradually occupies the entire surface of the window; when such a multiplication of letters "makes sense" in an incongruous way, I would call it an *animated sporulation*. In digital poetry, a sporulation sometimes suggests an act of fertilization. The movement insists on the substance of the text in a rather obsessive way. In *The Dreamlife of Letters*, the letter "A," emerging and sporulating, represents the background material for poetic imagination.

The letter "A" then slowly arises from the background, growing and turning on itself. This resizing effect, very common in digital poetry, cannot always be considered as a figure. But when the animated words acquire a new tropologic meaning, I call such changes of size *expansion* and *contraction*. In this sequence of *The Dreamlife of Letters*, we cannot really consider them as tropologic. To be more precise, the gradual evolution emphasizes the graphic potential of the letter "A," recalling how a "figure of diction" accentuates the sonorous materiality of language in classical poetry. Here, the legacy of concrete poetry is still very perceptible.

On the median bar of the letter "A" now appears the fragment "bilities," which needs other letters to become meaningful. Classical rhetoric calls an *aphaeresis* the significant loss of one or more phonemes at the beginning of a word. I will keep this term by adding the adjective *transitional*[10]: often based on effects of appearance and disappearance, aphaeresis in digital poetry is always conditioned by the instability of the device. When the phonetic transformation occurs at the end of the word, I propose the term *transitional apocope*. A phonetic change inside a word could be called a *transitional gash*. When the alteration of a word or a group of words is not based on the removal of phonemes, but on the moving and crossing of phonemes inside this word or that group of words, this figure could be called a *transitional metathesis*.

In *The Dreamlife of Letters*, Stefans remedies the aphaeresis on the word "bilities" by an *inclusion*: this figure characterizes a letter or phoneme graphically included in another. Here, the inclusion emphasizes the symmetrical, reassuring and protecting typographical aspect of the letter "A," recalling the form of a roof or a house. One could hold that the animation announces, through its figures, the general "topic" of the poem: the exploration of the sonorous and visual "abilities" of the letter, i.e., its abilities to produce meaning through its semantic and graphic potential.

The "protector A" gradually eclipses. Becoming once again a transitional aphaeresis, the fragment "bilities" leaves its stable position and descends to the edges of the window. Sometimes such an ascending or descending, diagonal, horizontal or vertical movement acts on the word or letter as a figure that I would call a *transposition*. Like emergences and eclipses, transpositions are often catachretic: scrolling names at the end of films, for example, obviously do not change the meaning of the words, but only make us understand that the film is finished. In other contexts, when a transposition transforms or nuances the meaning of a word, this figure can nevertheless gain a tropologic value.

Now, the word "all" appears, massively repeated around the horizontal centerline of the window. This repetition may be regarded as a tautology in a classical sense: while being multiplied, the word "all" does not really gain a new meaning; the animation rather emphasizes multiplicity, already signified by the word itself. The movement of all these "all"s constitutes a transposition before stabilizing in a partial syncope. The content of the word "all" can be considered as the isotopy in this animated utterance, whereas the animation constitutes the perceived degree. The identification and the application of semantic components compatible with the perceived degree and the conceived degree 1—which can be formulated as "the behaviour of individuals within a multiplicity of individuals"—enables us to interpret this animation: the chaotic movement of some components and the gradual stabilization of other elements resembles a crowd movement gradually calming down, finally entering in an almost militaristic order. Some "all"s stay unstable, as if they refused to submit to the order; a slight sporulation emphasises the impression of these specific communities being really different. Whereas the letters "l" connect in some places to form barriers, the disobedient "all"s already announce their future exit from the ranks.

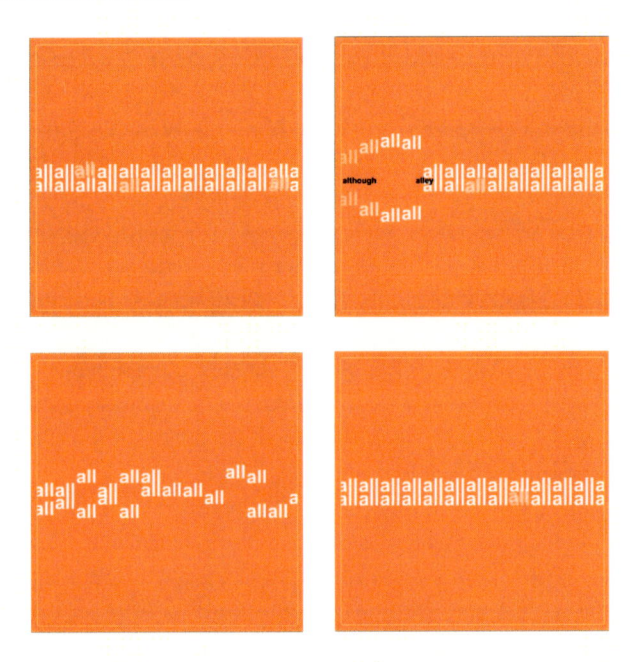

Fig. 1. Brian Kim Stefans: *The Dreamlife of Letters*.

When several figures merge to form a single tropologic system, I would call it a *kinetic allegory*: traditional allegory is based on a double meaning—literal and spiritual—through which one thought is presented through the image of another thought; here, this "other thought" is provided by animation, which not only makes the words more striking, but incites the reader to interpret a "story" that the content of words alone does not tell. Kinetic allegories should nevertheless not be confused with *movie-grams,* which express the same meaning by its letters and its movement.

The following animation in *The Dreamlife of Letters* enables us to clarify that difference: the rows of "all"s are separated by two new words racing through them. Their intrusion causes a momentary dispersal of the occurrences of the word "all"; this dispersal is not chaotic: a circle of words quickly forms around the incident. It is, in fact, the word "alley" that causes telescoping in this sequence, constituting indeed a movie-gram: "alley" literally paves the way. Thus, in this sequence of *A Dreamlife of Letters*, the relationship between animations and words tell a complex story about communities and the individual. Again, the term allegory seems well suited to characterize the interaction of all the figures involved in this sequence.

It is then the word "am" that is "sporulated" and animated by a vertical transposition, suggesting through the movement an existential feeling of instability; one "am" is black instead of being white; the loneliness of an individual in the midst of other individuals becomes literally visible. Imagine how the meaning of this animation would be different if "am" was alone and steady in the middle of the window! Sometimes, the sporulated word "am" seems able to merge. But this never becomes true. Again, the interactions of all these figures of animation constitute, therefore, a kinetic allegory.

The gradual emergence and repetition of the word "an" in the following sequence reminds the animation of the word "all." Unlike Janez Strehovec, who does not locate rhymes or verses in this poem ("Text as Loop"), I would therefore defend the existence of *kinaesthetic rhymes* in *The Dreamlife of Letters*: some animations are repeated throughout the poem and create paradigmatic relationships between the sequences.

In principle, the word "an" means "one." The repetition of the word in this sequence can therefore, with classical rhetoric, be called "paradoxic," paradoxism being defined as "an artifice of language by which usually opposed and contradicting ideas are combined in ways that, while pretending to combat and exclude one each other, create highly surprising agreement" (Fontanier 137).

For one last example, let us focus on a particularly significant sequence of *The Dreamlife of Letters*: the transitional aphaeresis of the word fragment "nder" is complemented by the arrival of a "c" and an "i", though both seem reluctant to stabilize in the window. By a morphing effect, the word "cinder" then transforms into "cixous." When a morphing effect influences the meaning of a word in an incongruous way, I suggest the term *transfiguration*. Here, the feminist writer Hélène Cixous, mentioned in the text written by DuPlessis, seems literally reborn from the ashes of writing.

With this quasi-mystical transfiguration, we are far from the "concrete" paper version of *The Dreamlife of Letters*! On paper, the words "cinder" and "cixous" are merely juxtaposed, calling to mind the origin of the poem, a cut-up of letters in the text written by DuPlessis and their arrangement in an alphabetical order: the two words have just become neighbours because of their proximity in the dictionary. We hesitate to put them together with an attempt at interpretation. In the animated version of the poem, the words "cinder" and "cixous" get into quite a different relationship: the delayed discovery of "cixous" emphasizes the materiality of the letters, telling a story about resurgence. The relationship between the two words is not due to chance. Whereas concrete poetry is reluctant to syntax links, we can remark that new links are created here, reminding of syntax.

The animated version of *A Dreamlife of Letters* therefore cannot be reduced to the enlargement of a "concrete" experiment. Brian Kim Stefans actually reinterpreted the poem. He filled the empty gaps of the concrete poem with meaning. He re-injected desire, expression, subjectivity, and the possibility of interpretation; he created a kinetic, a lyrical poem. Concrete Poetry generally emphasizes form and structure, and rejects the hedonistic and subjective expressiveness of lyrical poetry. In the kinetic poetry by Brian Kim Stefans, as N. Katherine Hayles is correct in saying, the words rediscover their power of seduction (*Electronic Literature* 28).

Far away from the Oulipo's "silent celebration of the algebra of language" (Burgelin 36), far away from the anti-lyrical beauty of the computer hosting kinetic poetry, the musical, rhythmic and literally graphic voice of digital "media" poetry, based on interactive and animated "figures," seems decidedly closer to the surrealist experiences than to concrete or Lettrist experimentations.

Notes

1   Cf. the very complete and well-informed article "Poésie et ordinateur" by Tibor Papp.

2   In 2008, a special edition of the journal *Passages d'encres* was entirely dedicated to Digital poetry (edited by Alexandre Gherban and Louis-Michel de Vaulchier). In their articles, Jean Clément and Serge Bouchardon and some other critics and poets insist again on this tradition, explaining them thoroughly.

3   French titles of books and articles, and quotations from French electronic literature have been translated by the author.

4   For example Claude Simon; Alain Robbe-Grillet Nathalie Sarraute; Jacques Roubaud.

5   Founded in 1989 at Paris.

6   "Transitoire Observable" is a group of digital artists. It was created on February 6th, 2003 by three numerical poets: Philippe Bootz, Alexandre Gherban and Tibor Papp. It has been joined by several other numerical artists. Each artist of the group has already known personal poetics. These artists are focusing on the global nature of systems which are using computers and not only in the forms of surface which can be observed on-screen." <http://www.transitoireobs.free.fr/to/>.

7   Alain Balseiro and Marida di Crosta show that the reader of *The Subnetwork* therefore is immerged in a state of "semiotic fuzziness:" he can no longer "conceptualize laws of contingency, namely the law that relies interaction to its effects" (92).

8   For a French version of this proposal, cf. Saemmer: "Figures de surface média."

9   Accessible at <http://www.ubu.com/contemp/stefans/dream/>.

10 This term is inspired by the French group *Transitoire Observable* already cited before <http://www.transitoireobs.free.fr/>.

Works Cited

Balpe, Jean-Pierre. "Réponse de J.P. BALPE à Claude ADELEN." *KAOS* 3/Action poétique 129/130 (1992): Hypercard/Mac.

Balpe, Jean-Pierre, and Jacopo Baboni-Schilingi. "Génération aautomatique ppoésie-mmusique." *Rencontresmédias* 1 (1996-1997). Ed. Jean-Pierre Balpe. Paris: BPI centre Pompidou, 1997. 148-156.

Balseiro, Alain, and Marida di Crosta. "Narration hypermédia et cognition." H2PTM'07." *Collaborer, échanger, inventer: Expériences de réseaux*. Ed. Imad Saleh et al. Paris: Hermès, 2007. 91-106.

Bon, François. "Comment Internet multiplie la littérature." *Le tiers livre*. 23 Feb. 2009 <http://www.tierslivre.net>.

Bon, François. *Le tiers livre*. <http://www.tierslivre.net>.

Bootz, Philippe. "Ébauche de quelques notes sur la forme programmée." *Transitoire observable*. 23 Feb. 2009 <http://www.transitoireobs.free.fr/to/article.php3?id_article=56>.

———. "Eléments d'analyse de l'interface sémiotique des sites Web." *H2PTM'07: Collaborer, Échanger, Inventer: Expériences de Réseaux*. Ed. Imad Saleh et al. Paris: Hermès, 2007.107-121.

———. "Quelles sont les formes de la poésie numérique animée?" *Leonardo/Olats* 2006. 23 Feb. 2009 <http://www.olats.org/livresetudes/basiques/litteraturenumerique/13_basiquesLN.php>.

———. "The Problem of Form: *Transitoire Observable*, a Laboratory For Emergent Programmed Art." *The Aesthetics of Net Literature: Writing, Reading and Playing in Programmable Media*. Ed. Peter Gendolla and Jörgen Schäfer. Bielefeld: Transcript, 2007. 89-103.

Bouchardon, Serge. "L'écriture interactive: Une rhétorique de la manipulation." *H2PTM'07: Collaborer, Échanger, Inventer: Expériences de Réseaux*. Ed. Saleh et al. Paris: Hermès, 2007.155-170.

Burgelin, Claude. "Esthétique et éthique de l'Oulipo." *Le Magazine littéraire* 398 (mai 2001).

Calvino, Italo. "Cybernetics and Ghosts." *The Uses of Literature: Essays*. Ed. Patrick Creagh. San Diego, CA: Harcourt, 1982. 3-27.

Chatonsky, Gregory. *Sous terre/The Subnetwork*. 2001. 23 Feb. 2009 <http://www.incident.net/works/sous-terre/>.

Clément, Jean. "Du texte à l'hypertexte: Vers une épistémologie de la discursivité hypertextuelle." *Hypertextes et hypermédias—Réalisations, Outils, Méthodes*. Ed. Jean-Pierrre Balpe, Alain Lelu, and Imad Saleh. Paris: Hermès, 1995. 23 Feb. 2009 <http://hypermedia.univ-paris8.fr/jean/articles/discursivite.htm>.

De Boullay, Boris. *Explication de texte*. 23 Feb. 2009 <http://www.lesfilmsminute.com/explication/>.

De Jonckheere, Philippe. *Le Bloc-Notes du Désordre*. 23 Feb. 2009 <http://www.desordre.net/blog>.

Denize, Antoine, and Bernard Magné. *Machine à écrire*. CD-ROM. Paris: Gallimard, 1999.

Emerson, Lori. "On Materialities, Meanings, and The Shape of Things." Rev. of *The Shape of The Signifier: 1967 to the End of History*, by Walter Benn Michaels. *The Electronic Book Review* (2005). 23 Feb. 2009 <http://www.electronicbookreview.com/thread/endconstruction/significant>.

Fontanier, Pierre. *Les Figures du discours (1821-1830)*. Paris: Flammarion, 1977.

Genette, Gérard. *Figures 1*. Paris: Seuil, 1966.

Gherban, Alexandre, and Louis-Michel De Vaulchier, ed. *Poésie: numérique*, revue *Passages d'encres* 33 (2008).

Hayles, N. Katherine. *Electronic Literature: New Horizons for the Literary*. Notre Dame, IN: U of Notre Dame P, 2008.

Klinkenberg, Jean-Marie. *Précis de sémiotique générale*. Louvain-la-Neuve: De Boeck, 1996; Paris: Seuil, 2000.

Magné, Bernard. "Machines à écrire, machine à lire." *Études françaises* 36.2 (2000): 119-128. 23 Feb. 2009 <http://www.erudit.org/revue/etudfr/2000/v36/n2/005258ar.pdf>.

Mitchell, James. "A Modest 'Electronic' Proposal." 23 Feb. 2009 <http://www.edgewise-magazine.com/nov2007LiteratureProposal.html>

Papp, Tibor. "Poésie et ordinateur." *Transitoire observable* (12 Mar. 2005). 23 Feb. 2009 <http://www.transitoireobs.free.fr/to/article.php3?id_article=59>.

———. "Queneau, Raymond. Cent mille milliards de poèmes." *Alire* 1 (1989).

Perloff, Marjorie. "Screening the Page, Paging the Screen: Digital Poetics and the Differential Text." *Contemporary Poetics*. Ed. Louis Armand. Evanston: Northwestern UP, 2007. 376-392.

Picot, Edward. "Hyperliterature as a Product?" 2003. 23 Feb. 2009 <http://www.edwardpicot.com/papertiger2.html>.

Queneau, Raymond. *Cent mille milliards de poèmes*. Paris: Gallimard, 1961.

Quintilian. *The Institutio Oratoria X*. 1920. *The Orator's Education*. Ed. and trans. Donald A. Russell. Cambridge, MA: Harvard UP, 1996.

Saemmer, Alexandra. "Figures de surface media." *Protée : Revue internationale de théories et de pratiques sémiotiques* 36.1 (2008): 79-90.

———. *Matières textuelles sur support numérique*. Saint-Etienne: Publications de l'Université, 2007.

Scoccimarro, Bruno. *Soleil amer*. 23 Feb. 2009 <http://www.mandelbrot.fr/SoleilAmer.html>.

Stefans, Brian Kim. "The Dreamlife of Letters." *Electronic Literature Collection* 1.1 (2006). 23 Feb. 2009 <http://www.collection.eliterature.org/1/works/stefans_the_dreamlife_of_letters.html>.

Strehovec, Janez. "Text as Loop: On Visual and Kinetic Textuality." *Afterimage* 31.1 (2003). *BNET* 23 Feb. 2009 <http://www.findarticles.com/p/articles/mi_m2479/is_1_31/ai_113683509/pg_4>.

Transitoire observable. 23. Feb. 2009 <http://www.transitoireobs.free.fr/to/.>

Zellen, Jody. "Crowds and Power." *The Iowa Review Web*. 2002. 23 Feb. 2009 <http://www.uiowa.edu/~iareview/tirweb/feature/zellen/jody%20zellen_crowds%20and%20power/crowdsandpower_website/index.html>.

María Goicoechea

The Reader in Cyberspace

In Search of Digital Literature in Spain

1   Introduction

Today digital literature in Spain is a nascent reality connected to the university sphere. Most of the authors are unknown to the general public, but their names appear recursively in discussions about Spanish digital literature, which means that they have left some interesting trails in the work they have published online (Santiago Ortiz, Edith Checa, Dora García, Ainara Echaniz, etc.). Authorship is generally shared between the story writers and the computer designers. In quite a few cases the digital literature works are created by students of Media and Communication Degrees in the context of a university course project under the guidance of a teacher. The predominant style of these texts seems to suit the taste of young Spanish readers: There are collages of chats, e-mails, sms; images are mixed with words and music; the influence of the comic is strongly felt. The themes and characters also reflect young people's problems and interests, involving identity, solitude and isolation, falling in and out of love, social conflict, etc. These recent creations also use very varied generic frames: blognovels, e-mail stories, hypertext fiction, holopoetry, interactive and adventure game fiction, etc. It is possible to find a decent repertoire of digital literature in Spanish and critical commentary in the work of Dolores Romero (341).

Even if Spain is considerably less prolific in terms of digital literature production when compared with the United States, it has nevertheless developed a profuse response of critical interpretations and thought about technology and literature. In the Spanish context, reflections on the phenomenon of digital communication in general, and on the new literary forms in particular, have grown considerably in the last decade, advancing from different academic fields. Some of the most outstanding contributions in the international context come from the sociologist Manuel Castells, the philosopher of science Javier Echeverría, and the journalist and narrative fiction writer José Antonio Millán, author of important publications on the impact of the Internet on the Spanish language. Among historians, we must highlight the reflections of Antonio Rodríguez de las Heras regarding the transformation of the book as a technology of cultural transmission in the digital world. Midway between academic research and political activism, we find the studies of Andoni Alonso and Iñaki Arzoz.

From the perspective of literary studies and the academic field, an outstanding figure is the poet Jenaro Talens, whose pioneer considerations as culture theorist and his work as editor of "Documentos de trabajo" of the academic journal *Eutopías* (from the University of Valencia), have contributed to make known some of the most important authors of different critical interpretations of electronic culture.

Another important point of reference emerging from the university field is the open space provided by the electronic journal *Espéculo* (from the University Complutense of Madrid). Its editor, Joaquín Aguirre, is one of the most sensible cyberculture theorists in Spain. He has managed to create a virtual space alive with literary criticism and philological research, which hosts an up-to-date debate (theoretical, critical, and creative) through the section "Hipertulia." This section has also been coordinated by Susana Pajares, whose works on hypertextual writing are a landmark in the Spanish Cyberculture.

With respect to interactive media and narrative, the Audiovisual University Institute of the University Pompeu Fabra of Barcelona, where Xavier Berenguer is the main researcher, offers a series of interesting resources.

From the field of comparative literature and literary theory we find the research group and its electronic journal *Hermeneia* (at the University of Barcelona). The works of Laura Borràs Castanyer (director of *Hermeneia*) and Joan-Elies Adell are a place of reference for Spanish researchers of digital literature, and their web page is a compulsory stop <http://www.hermeneia.net/eng/index.html>. One of the most useful resources available on their web page is a digital literature anthology, which provides an eclectic sample of works of authors from all over the world.

Also emerging from the field of comparative literature and cultural studies comes the research group "Leethi" ("Spanish and European Literatures: From Text to Hypertext") at the University Complutense of Madrid. Their web page <http://www.ucm.es/info/leethi> offers a series of reading guides that aim to explore the didactic use of hypertext for the teaching of different languages, literatures and cultures.

One of the most enthusiastic technophiles of Spanish cyberculture is José Luis Orihuela, from the Department of Culture and Audiovisual Communication at the University of Navarra. He is the main researcher and promoter of the Digital Laboratory, and teacher of one of the first Spanish university courses dedicated to the study of digital literature, called "Non-linear Writing." His web log about Cyberculture, Media, eCommunication and Blogging, *eCuaderno v.3.0* <http://www.ecuaderno.com> has also become an important reference point for the study of Spanish Cyberculture.

In the field of academic encounters celebrated around the topic of literature and cyberculture, we can underscore the one organized by the Spanish distance learning university UNED in 1994, which was a true call of attention to the field and which served to inaugurate subsequent conferences and symposiums that made their appearance around the country. The publication of conference proceedings helped to disseminate the work of young researchers in this field (for example the volume extracted from the First Congress of Internet and Language, organized by the University Jaume I of Castellón in 2003, *Internet in Linguistics, Translation and Literary Studies*).

From this explosion of interest in the topic has emerged a recent collection of books about digital literature, such as *Literatura hipertextual y teoría literaria* (2003), edited by María José Vega, *Literatura y Cibercultura* (2004), edited by Domingo Sánchez-Mesa, *Literatura Digital: El paradigma hipertextual* (2004), written by Susana Pajares Tosca, and *Textualidades Electrónicas: Nuevos escenarios para la literatura* (2005), edited by Laura Borràs Castanyer. To this collection we could add the book *Literatura e hipermedia* (2000), written from a hybrid profile between philology and computer science by Nuria Voullaimoz, who has provided one of the most useful syntheses of the transformations of the literary system in its encounter with hypermedia.

Out of this interdisciplinary corpus, we will attempt to provide in this article an overview of current Spanish criticism regarding the literariness of digital texts. From the most enthusiastic Technoromantics to the most effervescent Luddites, we will expose the different appraisals that Spanish critics have made of the reconfiguration of literary conventions in the advent of digital literature. The main focus is placed on contesting definitions of digital literature, hypertext, intermediality, interactivity and intertextuality. Throughout the presentation, special attention is paid to the role of the reader, whose new interpretative tasks appear to be more adequate for a "cyborgic" ideal reader yet to come than to the malleable memory of the human word processor.

2 Trends in Spanish Criticism of Digital Literature

In broad terms, we could simplify the conflict posed by the new technologies in the field of literature to the debatable tendency to privilege the technical aspect of literary communication (for example, the position of N. Katherine Hayles in *Writing Machines*) to the detriment of its more traditionally literary, social and cultural aspects. Spanish critics tend to approach the literary innovations of cyberculture with the conviction that it is the social, economic, and cultural history (and therefore also the literary history) that illuminates the technical history, and not the other way around. Therefore, there is a general tendency to highlight a humanist tradition, and to see literary events in a continuous flow of influences rather than as an accumulation of discrete changes or technological revolutions. Thus, it is not surprising that many Spanish critics have adopted George Landow's categorization, which attributes the materialization of postmodern qualities to the digital texts, since it is firmly grounded on French theory and its dependence on the intertext as a privileged mode of reading. As in other parts of the world, hypertext theory was the predominant paradigm of the 1990s in the field of digital textuality and aesthetics, but nowadays even its most fervent proponents, like Susana Pajares, have realized that they had been "for too long concentrating on a very small part of the picture" ("Ludology" 53). Some Spanish authors, however, are still devoting their writing to its conceptualizations since they perceive that the Spanish academia has still not accepted the canonical digital literature criticism as part of the most recent developments of literary history. Anxo Abuín and Teresa Vilariño's volume, *Teoría del Hipertexto: La literatura en la era electrónica* (2006) presents translations of seminal articles on hypertext theory by, among others, Paul Delany, Michael Joyce and George P. Landow to Spanish readers.

This manoeuvre of transposing postmodern theory to the digital sphere becomes necessary in a strongly technophobic academic environment, still tied to chalk and paper. However, it imposes certain restraints in the type of approach these new electronic textualities receive, since there is the artificial imposition of measuring virtual texts with the structures of the past.

Spanish critics, such as Teresa Gómez Trueba and Juan Carlos Fernández Serrato, also tend to evaluate digital literature from the perspective of their own literary heritage, emphasizing a Hispanic literary tradition of ergodic texts, or, as they are more traditionally called, "the difficult forms of the literary *acumen*" (for example, works by Cervantes, Max Aub, Cortázar, Borges). It is symptomatic of this tendency that Dolores Romero, for example, perceives the connection between the Spanish digital literature creators and the university world as a natural one, as she refers back to other moments in the literary history in which change emerged from the university circles: The *mester de clerecía* ('craft of clergy'), which gave rise to the first universities and developed a new type of poetry, the humanists during the Renaissance, the 18th century innovators, or the avant-garde intellectuals of the 20th century (334-335).

In his book *Neo-Baroque: A Sign of the Times* (1992), the semiologist Omar Calabrese has presented from the field of semiotics another alternative route with deep European roots to assign the digital text a space inside literary history. The neo-baroque combines the visual, the auditory and the textual, with a dynamism, polycentrism, and lack of respect for the limits of the frame that parallel the characteristics of seventeenth century baroque form in technologically and culturally new ways. Some critics from the Hispanic world, such as

Jaime Alejandro Rodríguez, already discussed in 1999 the advantages of deviating the discussion on modernity/postmodernity towards the debate regarding a supposed return of the baroque (and to situate there the discussion on hypertext), since this move offers the critic a more long-term view; it allows him or her to visualize other connections and convergences in contemporary culture (93).

With respect to the "literariness" of these new forms of literature, there is a division among critics. Not everybody agrees with the idea that digital literature actually exists, either because it has not reached a certain quality or because its identity as literature is put into question. For Fernando Cabo Aseguinolaza, for example, the expressive possibilities of the digital medium have still not been exploited to the extent to which the digital work can be considered a work of art or literature.

As critics searching for digital literature, we indirectly come to realize the set of expectations that a specific work needs to meet in order for us to recognize it as "digital literature." We demand an acceptable degree of "traditional" literary quality from the text (a quality which is immediately calibrated by our own naturalized standards: A fine equilibrium between interpretative effort and gained insight, originality, sensitiveness without sentimentality, etc.), at the same time that we expect the potential of the new medium to be exploited (intricacy of programming effects, visual impact of design, adaptation of theme to the other multisensory "signifying components" of the electronic text, etc.).

After assessing the scarce repertoire of Spanish digital texts, we perceive that the literary quality does not always match the technical, intrinsically digital, virtuosity, and *vice versa*. This new technical dimension is not always accepted as part of the literary identity of the text, as there is not a consensus among critics regarding the classification of these new forms of texts in the environment of the arts in general and of literature in particular.

Although the boundary between different literary genres in electronic textuality is very imprecise, criticism continues to offer similarities between these texts and the three great classical genres: poetry, prose and theatre. For some authors (Abuín; Orihuela; Vega), digital literature still refers mainly to hypertext, which is perceived as a new literary genre bent to the impositions of the medium (use of shorter sentences and paragraphs, fragmentary, non-linear construction, etc.). In recent years, however, the concept of digital literature has expanded to comprise a more varied repertoire of genres: kinetic concrete poetry (mainly using *Flash* animations), interactive installations, blognovels, e-mail, chat and sms-fiction, computer game narratives, etc.

The value of these creations and their position inside the literary tradition depends on the critic's intuition of what constitutes "literature" in the first place. For technosceptics, literature is a form of cultural expression that uses language as its raw material and, therefore, digital literature should retain the domain of the word over other signifying elements. From this perspective, for a virtual performance or installation to be considered digital literature it is necessary that demands be made of the viewers to interact with the works in ways that involve some literary aspects; generally a certain amount of reading should be made possible. Technophiles, on the other hand, think that digital literature should transcend the realm of the word and evolve into a truly hypermedia genre, a tendency also present in previous literary traditions. Their reconstruction of literary history emphasizes the coexistence of the word with other types of signs (iconic, indexical) in pre-digital texts, and assumes hypertext as a logical evolution in which the postmodern postulates find their realization. From this perspective, the main potential of the digital medium is considered to be its interactive and intermedial nature, with its ensuing blurring of boundaries between the traditional roles of reader and writer. In this respect, some critics believe that the authorial role of the writer will always be retained, while others think that the author will allow the reader to tell the story to himself, relinquishing previous functions to act as a mere guide. Finally, some critics, Vega among others, consider the new digital literary forms as an incipient new art, which is still in its prehistory, but which will develop as an independent artistic manifestation, without displacing literature.

Independently of the type of conceptual frame that is used to approach the digital text, the same division between technophile and technosceptic or Luddite critics that has emerged in other parts of the world has also developed in Spain. The technophile position of some critics, such as José Luis Orihuela, is characterized by a predominance of computer science conceptualizations, which influence the critic's perception of notions such as text, reader, writer, information, memory, interactivity, intertextuality, actualization, immersion, etc. The language of machines and their users, as it is adapted to the analysis of cultural artefacts, contrasts strongly with the language of purely literary critics, who dwell in a world of symbolic representations and communication involving at least two human minds. The conflict that ensues from the encounter of these two perspectives implies a high degree of mutual misinterpretation. Misunderstandings are due, in large part, to the different definitions that each group attributes to key concepts in the debate, such as the nature of the electronic text and the reading process, involving discussions on intertextuality, interactivity, and intermediality as we will see further on.

3   Some Considerations Regarding Hypertext

"Electronic literature," "digital literature," "hyperliterature," "interactive fiction," "hyperfiction," "hypertext," "cybertexts," are some of the terms that coexist and overlap in meaning in discussions about this new form of literature, born out of the hybrid mixture of literature and computer science. Spanish researchers normally borrow the English terms and translate them literally. Some terms, however, are preferred over others. Susana Pajares, for instance, privileges the umbrella term "digital literature" over "electronic literature" since, in her opinion, it is the digital nature of the medium that is really significative, rather than the type of energy required to make the computer and its circuits function. Also, the term "electronic literature" seems to place greater emphasis on form rather than on content, as in "electronic publishing" or "e-books," whereas "digital literature" appears to "apuntar al contenido y la materialidad (o inmaterialidad) de dicha literatura, que no se creó para el papel, sino para la pantalla" ('point towards the content and materiality (or immateriality) of such literature, which was not created for paper, but for the screen') (*Literatura Digital* 20). The Spanish language is also less apt to use abbreviated prefixes such as "e-."

The seminal work of Pajares in Spain has spread the use of "digital literature" as a generally accepted rubric. She has also popularized the notion of the "hypertextual paradigm" to approach digital literature, even though in recent years she has concentrated on the discussion of other potential properties or axes belonging to digital literature—such as the multimedia convergence allowed by the digital medium, and ludology as an alternative paradigm.

In general, definitions of hypertext found in Spanish essays do not deviate from Theodor Nelson's definition and George Landow's theorizations. Its basic characteristic is that it is composed of blocks of text (written, visual, etc.), connected by links forming all sorts of structures (nets, collages, cycles, etc.), and with a possibility for interconnectedness that is, in theory, limitless. Hypertext is also identified with non-sequential writing and multiple authorship, and with the notion that it offers readers multiple reading itineraries.

However, some critical voices, such as that of María José Vega ("Literatura hipertextual"), articulate their disagreement towards this definition of hypertext based on "non-sequential writing" and "textual inter-relation," which is considered insufficient since there are many examples of non-sequential writing displayed on pages of conventional books. For example, the complex annotated editions with their critical commentaries and their cross-references, their references to other readings and texts, their links among words or passages within the same text or of other texts, etc. The reader of these editions also had a variety of itineraries and a freedom of choice. The concept of "non-sequential writing" is also considered imprecise, since writing is necessarily sequential; what is non-sequential or flexible is the textual organization, so it would be more appropriate to talk about texts of a flexible or multiple sequentiality.

These criticisms are not directed to show that print technology already made possible this type of non-sequential writing, but rather to observe that common definitions of hypertext are imprecise. By judging and describing hypertext in comparison to previous forms of texts, these definitions are in fact simplifying the possibilities of those formats of texts derived from print. So the problem with this basic definition of hypertext is not that it ignores its nature, but that it trivializes the history of the book, and therefore, it highlights differential aspects which are not really such a novelty (Vega, "Literatura hipertextual" 11).

Vega also directs her criticism to the fabricated tradition of proto-hypertexts, analyzing the basis for arguments that have found in texts such as Laurence Sterne's *Tristram Shandy* or Italo Calvino's *Il Castello dei destini incrociati* [*The Castle of Crossed Destinies*] prefigurations of hypertexts. Vega deconstructs these arguments, claiming that the fact that these works follow the logic of games and digression, establish an intimate relation with the reader, and meditate on the relevance of the act of narrating, are not reasons enough to consider them proto-hypertexts, since, if this was the case, all literature (where *how* the story is told is as important as *what* is told) could be considered a prefiguring of hypertext.

Vega acknowledges the quantitative leap implicit in hypertext regarding its potential for the creation of different literary structures. However, she wonders if a quantitative growth provides a relevant qualitative difference, "when do we know that what we are actually facing is in fact something other?" (Vega, "Literatura hipertextual" 18). So, in her opinion, hyperliterature, as she calls it, is yet to come; what we have at this point are some tests, some shy beginnings, and timid preparatory experiments. But we have not yet seen the type of literature whose advent Janet Murray prophesized in her book *Hamlet on the Holodeck*.

Antonio Rodríguez de las Heras contributes, in my opinion, with one of the most insightful and useful reflections about hypertext. Using as a model the functioning of human memory, Rodríguez de las Heras describes the art of memory as that of creating abstractions, selections, syntheses, which allow us to recognize the world through a minimum amount of accumulated information. If memory did not register data with a high degree of abstraction, and on the contrary, preserved an exact copy of the image seen, a small change in the object would, on seeing it again, make impossible its recognition (that is why it is sometimes difficult for us to reconstruct people's faces in their absence, but when we see them again we recognize them immediately, even if they have changed their hair, or if we have not seen them in many years). The generosity of the digital container does not invite the user to restrain the contribution of information, thus favouring an information overload which threatens to transform the book of the world into a world trunk: without memory, only register (Rodríguez de las Heras, "El libro digital" 165). The challenge now lies in how to organize this continuous influx of information. Hypertext as a concept seems to fit perfectly into the new information geometry required for the creation of a folded text. From this perspective, hypertext becomes an ideal of writing that can be far more demanding on the author than the traditional linear format of sequential writing. It would not be the mere activity of connecting documents in the World Wide Web that would produce a hypertext, but it would spring from the elaborate architecture of a text conceived to have depth. It is designed and constructed as a unified whole, a textual building that complies with the rules of a useful writing geometry. The reader will decide how deep he or she wants to proceed by unfolding its many layers of meaning; layers that the writer has designed to represent the different levels of synthesis required at each step, allowing the text to retain its internal coherence.

4 Intertextuality and Interactivity

Intertextuality and interactivity are two concepts that have gained popularity with the incursion of hypertext into the field of literary creation. However, their meaning in the corpus of Spanish criticism (and beyond our frontiers) is not unanimous, as there is a multiplicity of coexisting definitions. This section organizes definitions in two poles: the technophile and the technosceptic approach. The purpose of this oversimplification is to underscore the most frequent type of misunderstanding between these two positions, which has to do mainly with the conceptualization of the text and the reader as either active or passive participants in the process of literary communication. In the transfer of concepts from one medium to the other, critics continuously confuse or fail to distinguish between the act of text production and the act of reception; between the referential, material plane of the text as technological artefact, and the symbolic object which the reader constructs in his or her mind through actualization and interpretation. Intertextuality and interactivity are, therefore, conceived as either properties of the text or the reader's interpretative strategies.

4.1 Intertextuality

One of the main topics that concerns both critics and writers of digital literature is the disorientation of the reader in the cyberspace labyrinths. We can trace the origin of this disorientation in the loss of coordinates, both textual and mental, which used to provide a reading context and guide the reader through the text. On the one hand, the advent of digital literature has created a void in the genre structures previously shared by the community of readers. On the other hand, the reader, progressively overwhelmed by an excess of stimuli and information, finds it each time more difficult to approach his or her reading with a clear ideological perspective, one that would provide him or her with a set of stable reading objectives.

A term very frequently discussed in hypertext criticism and which is directly connected with this contextualizing function at risk is intertextuality. Between the reader and the text we find a space of symbolic negotiation which allows, in the first place, the production of the text, and secondly, the possibility of its interpretation. Intertextuality is, therefore, the main writing and reading strategy involved in the construction of this space of encounter.

Several drastic changes affecting writing in the digital space have transformed this space of encounter. In particular, we note two main points of friction which have to do with the blurring of genres, produced by the introduction of many different types of signs in a single "literary" work, and the rupture of sequentiallity, which has affected previous notions of narrativity. The notions of genre and narrativity have been two of the pillars upon which the agreement between writer and reader has been traditionally based, as they are conformed by previous reading experiences with other texts. Described by Julia Kristeva as "the texts' past," the intertextual property is intrinsically connected to the act of memory, but an act which is not only based on the net of textual relations out of which the text is created (and which is an act of memory coming from the writer), but also on the reader's capacity to remember. Thus, intertextuality relies on the literary competence shared by readers and writers.

In practice, it is useful to distinguish between two types of intertextual relations: those that are part of the textual structure, and those which the reader uses as reading strategies. Intertextuality can thus be analyzed as a property of the text: its direct or indirect allusions to other texts, its manifest literary influences, the type of genre to which the text belongs, etc., or as a function of the reader's memory. From a technosceptic perspective, however, it is difficult to understand a purely textual intertextuality. Even the simple expectation of receiving a message from the text can be considered an intertextual operation on the part of the reader, since it is necessary to be familiarized with other texts to have such an expectation. Nevertheless, when technophile critics use the term "intertextuality" in the field of literary studies, and in particular when discussing digital literature, they hardly ever contemplate it as a function belonging to the act of reading, and they most often used it to describe a property of the text. But again we must underscore that, as part of the multiple contextualizing operations undertaken by the reader to make sense out of the text and interpret its meaning, intertextuality is at once a characteristic of the text and the main mechanism required for its reading.

The question that we can ask ourselves is what type of intertextuality does hypertext foster. Spanish technophiles and technosceptics have debated at length about this question, exposing their different backgrounds and conceptual frameworks, each group attributing different meanings to the use of links and their effect on the reading experience.

Strong criticism comes, for example, from the technosceptic critic Cabo Aseguinolaza:

> It could be argued that the kind of intertextuality fostered by the nodes may be characterized as rigid, limited and excluding, since the self-imposing quality of the intertextual paths tend to preclude, because of its actuality (they are materially a part of the work), the purely virtual and unpredictable intertextuality which enriches the interpretation of texts in the printed tradition. In a general sense, textual units that are made accessible by means of the links may be understood as *interpretants*, in a Peircean sense. But interpretants that, in very rough terms, are imposed to the interpreter by the design of the textual machinery. (7)

According to this point of view, when a word is underlined showing that it contains a link, the text hidden behind it is understood as the materialization of a mechanized intertextual association of what would otherwise be, in the print medium, a mental link belonging to the reader. This technosceptic standpoint claims that the superconnectivity of hypertext privileges a type of explicit intertextuality, univocal and without a past. Contrary to Kristeva's intentions, which made of intertextuality the lance against the conception of the text as an autonomous unity of meaning, isolated from other texts, hypertexts present themselves again as a new order of independent, even if interconnected, units. Hypertextual writing incorporates at the same time the text and its context, forming a sort of textual constellation adrift in cyberspace, an unfathomable space where it is no longer possible to take for granted an intertextual framework of shared readings in which writers and readers converge. Given that cyberspace is its natural habitat, hypertext involves a type of writing that is projected towards an uncertain reading future and for this reason it explicitly carries with it all the intertextual references that the author considers relevant. This use of intertextuality becomes, not the text's past but its eternal present, in competition with the free intertextuality evoked by the reader, a reader who is presupposedly forgetful. The need for a reading context in which to integrate the hypertextual information becomes redundant since hypertext already is a self-sufficient and self-explanatory unity.

The structure of hypertext seems to obviate the need to allude to the collective memory of a community of readers by adding to the text all sorts of appendixes which turn the reader's memory into an obsolete resource. When the intertextuality of the hypertext ends up by blocking the free intertextuality evoked by the reader, we can say that the reader has been overloaded with information and has not been able to read the text appropriately. Moreover, the formation of a symbolic object in the mind of the reader is to some extent impeded, not only because it is difficult to integrate all text fragments into a coherent whole, but also because, in the course of link selection, our reading path becomes unique, irretrievable and, therefore, difficult to share with other readers.

Technosceptics are incorporating to their criticism of hypertext their previous understanding of intertextuality as a symbolic property that is based on a rhetoric of absence, a rhetoric that constructed its logic on the existence of a fixed text. The points of indetermination, the gaps in the text, the construction of horizons of expectations for their later verification, all these elements which open the text to the reader's active participation, were only possible in an economy of reading founded on a fixed referential object. The evocative function of the literary text emerged, then, from the space between the lines, among the whirlpool of words that pointed in the direction of what was actually not written. The writer resorted to an aesthetic of absence, which was at the same time a fertile silence full of promises, since he or she could count on the reader's complicity and free association of ideas to fill out what was missing. As Proust would have said, the knowledge of the reader starts where that of the author ends. The literary text had managed to break, by this game of evocation played with the reader, the limits of its own textuality, a textuality that became in this way far more than a mere technology for data storage, for the art of literature (created by both readers and writers) transcended this mnemotechnic function of the text.

But, where does the reader's knowledge begin in a text that never ends? Will the reader perish in a frenzy of never-ending reading? How could we calibrate a text when this is never quite finished, and its definite message always seems a click away? What technophile critics argue is that hypertext brings with it a new economy of reading and writing, in which the principles that at one point served to explain the literary phenomenon, such as Iser and Jauss's concepts related to the evocation of memory need to be reformulated. Critics such as Susana Pajares approach the rhetoric of links from a different perspective. In her opinion, if a word or image is signalled as a link, the reader will understand that it leads to a relevant development of the text. A link is a kind of "meaning in suspense" ("Literatura Digital" 108), it does not have a definite meaning (it is therefore not an *interpretant* but rather a kind of *representamen*). It is in the gap between links, in the movement back and forth done by the reader, where the space for interpretation and collaboration between reader and hypertext lies. The interpretative effort, according to Pajares, is nevertheless doubled. The link forces the reader to think about possible implicatures before and after following the link. This "interpretative excess" or extra interpretative dimension added to the reading process of hypertext makes her think of the lyric quality of links (111), and of an ambiguous and fragmentary language that requires creative reading, not senseless zapping.

Using a pragmatic approach, Pajares compares the reading process of a poem with that of a hypertext. In her opinion, in both cases, the reader produces a multiplicity of weak implicatures, which in the case of the hypertext, are produced twice. Firstly, in a movement of expansion of meaning, from link to node, and secondly, of concretion of meaning, when the reader contrasts the implicatures created by the link with the actual text of the node. Pajares, then, goes on to evaluate the aesthetic effects created in these movements from link to node in both fiction and non-fiction hypertexts. She observes that the interpretative process is similar in both types of hypertext, but whereas non-fiction hypertexts tend to produce descriptive links through "efficient" expressions that limit ambiguity and suggest a few strong implicatures (minimum processing effort + maximum (informative) cognitive effect), in hyperfictions the interpretative effort is deliberately increased by using lyric links that produce a great number of weak implicatures (maximum processing effort + maximum (lyric) cognitive effect). Some non-fiction hypertexts, such as David Kolb's *Socrates in the Labyrinth* (1994) and Diane Greco's *Cyborg: Engineering the Body Electric* (1995), encourage this type of poetic reading (Pajares, "Literatura Digital" 113).

It seems that the "lyric" quality of the link depends on its capacity to suggest a multiplicity of weak implicatures, and the aesthetic success of this promise depends on the intelligent anticipation of the author to the reader's expectations, thus rewarding the invested interpretative effort with the offer of a new, unexpected, but still relevant, implicature, which takes its place among the reader's implicatures in an evocative and enriched context.

Hypertext is, from this perspective, far more demanding for the reader than other literary works constructed sequentially. But is the reader prepared to realize the kind of mental operations Pajares has in mind? What effect will this hypertextual structure have on the mind of the reader?

Faced with the multiple realizations of the hypertext, the reader is inevitably confronted with a problem of information overload, which leads us to approach the faculty of memory in terms of its limitations rather than its evocative virtues. It is not a coincidence that one of the themes of cyberpunk science fiction is the inadequacy of human memory, which is easily overloaded, versus the power of the computerized model (as in William Gibson's *Neuromancer;* Neal Stephenson's *Snowcrash,* or Cadigan's *Synners*). Cyberculture science fiction exposes the changing attitudes we have developed versus the faculty of memory, as we have moved from understanding thought as a narrative flow to conceiving memory as a mere storage function, easily overloaded, or simply an uncomfortable and fearful characteristic of our minds. The structure of hypertext admits a forgetful reader at the same time that places the reader in a relation of dependence with the computer, which assumes an ever increasing information load.

Some hypertext writers (Malloy; Jackson) use links as a way to expose and share their own intertextual connections, evocations, and associations, with the reader, as if their own minds could be poured into an artificial container, without too much manipulation, organization, or embellishment on their part. These narcissistic writers, as they have themselves acknowledged, want the reader to see the world through their eyes, that the reader has access to their memories (Jackson, *Patchwork Girl,* "Think me"). However, this exposure, far from making the reading easier, implies another turn of the screw. What the hypertext writer seems to address is the irrepresentability of the mind's processes, an ever receding subjectivity that is still masked under layers of text, and which still supposes a challenge for the reader to discover and understand. This is possibly the meaning between the lines of this conversation between the artificial intelligence Wintermute and Case, the protagonist of Gibson's *Neuromancer*:

"Can you read my mind... Wintermute?"
"Minds aren't *read.* See, you've still got the paradigms print gave you, and you're barely print literate. I can *access* your memory, but that's not the same as your mind." (165)

The literary texts of the digital era point self-referentially to the keys that would allow the reader to come out safely from the complexity of the technological labyrinth they use to propagate. As I demonstrate in my article "Teaching Digital Literature in Spain" in the second part of this book, the hypertext reader will have to become an agile mutant, able to make quick adjustments in his or her intertextual strategies, to anticipate the type of ideal reader that hypertexts accommodate.

4.2   Interactivity

Closely connected to, and also dependent on intertextuality, interactivity is both a property belonging to the text, which triggers responses and poses new reading challenges, and to the reader, who explores the textual labyrinth and constructs a symbolic object out of the encounter with it. Interactivity within traditional texts is mainly associated with the cognitive processes, such as the creation of intertextual connections, carried out in the mind of the reader, since the mechanical interactivity (turning the page, opening and closing the book) seems to play a basically irrelevant role.

The new forms of digital literature imply a quantitative leap in the type of interactivity, both physical (exploration or manipulation of the text as referent) as well as mental (interpretative effort), they require from the reader. However, instead of approaching these new challenges from a *tabula rasa*, most Spanish critics continue to define digital literature in opposition to its print counterpart, and to approach interactivity from the biased conceptions their relations toward technology impose.

The technophile position of critics, such as José Luis Orihuela and Rodríguez de las Heras, regarding the concept of interactivity is characteristic of the meaning attributed to it by computer scientists. For a programmer, interactivity is a concept that applies to the relation between human beings and machines. In particular it is used to describe those programs that allow the user, by means of an interface, to communicate with the computer in a fashion similar to a dialogue (since this interaction normally follows a question-answer structure). This definition is used to refer to the new function acquired by the reader of hypertexts, who interacts with the digital text by means of the selection of links necessary to proceed with the reading activity.

From the technological pole, the kind of interaction that the print medium allows is, at best, purely "metaphorical." Because it is mainly a mental process, it is considered in some respects less "real" than the one taking place in the digital medium. Hypertext is thus perceived as the textual form that comes closest to a literal fulfilment of interactivity (Ryan). Along the same lines, Orihuela defends the electronic text as the only way to obtain, not a higher degree of interactivity, but interactivity *per se*. Interactivity is understood in terms of navigation, as the activity performed by the reader when exploring a hypertext, selecting paths, and thus actively collaborating in the construction or discovery of the text. From this perspective, a hypertext cannot be read unless there is interactivity, that is, the process by which a reader actively contributes to give shape to the narrative, and "actualizes"[1] a particular reading path. As it becomes apparent, these critics perceive interactivity as a property exclusive to the digital medium.

This conclusion is coherent if we take into account the definition of interactivity from which it departs. From a scientific understanding of information flows, the print medium does not permit the reader any response or emission of feedback back to the text. If we analyze the print medium as a communication technology we observe that the print text offers a type of asynchronic communication between writer and reader. For this reason, the text transmitter, the writer, cannot directly control the context of reception of his or her work; neither does the reader have an open channel of communication with the writer.

From the opposite perspective characteristic of the technosceptics (Darío Villanueva, Fernando Cabo Aseguinolaza, Rodríguez López), using the term "interactivity" to refer to human relations with machines adversely affects its quality. For them, "interactivity" only acquires its true meaning when it is applied to the contact between a minimum of two humans, a live conversation being the most interactive medium we possess. The machine can only offer a simulacrum of interactivity, in which there is no true information exchange. Therefore, any claim that reading hypertext is an inherently interactive experience is regarded with suspicion, since moving from one lexia to the next by clicking a button is not considered synonymous with an increase in communication and collaboration between reader and text.

From the perspective of the technosceptics, normally critics with a purely humanist training, the study of interactivity belongs to the realm of symbolic representation and of the mental processes involved in the concretization or actualization of the text structures into concrete mental pictures or representations. So when discussing the literary work of art, we have to realize that these critics are alluding to the text as a mental symbolic object rather than as a material technological artefact.

What the technophiles choose to ignore and the technosceptics emphasize is that the print text also works as a communicative vehicle with a certain degree of interactivity. The writer shares a common language with the reader, a system of symbolic representation that both need to understand in order for the literary communication to take place, a set of literary conventions and expectations. When reading, the reader must incorporate inside him- or herself the symbolic universe offered by the text, assimilate it to his or her own understanding of the world in order to be able to extract some meaning out of it. In this interpretative process, the text as symbolic object also has the faculty of modifying the understanding that the reading subject has of his or her world and of him- or herself. It is in the transfer of ideas and the modification of mental limits that take place during the reading process that the technosceptic critics establish the terms for their analysis of interactivity.

Radical technosceptics, however, find it difficult to understand the ways in which the text, as material entity or virtual machine, also has the ability to "communicate." Coming from a definition of interactivity that only considers the transfer of information from human to human, the problem is how to include the role of the text as a technological participant in communication. For example, the reader-oriented critic Norman Holland argues that, in the world of literary theory, an error that arises frequently is the confusion of attributing to texts what is really an action performed by the reader. In his opinion, texts are inert objects, inanimate, powerless, and passive. Therefore, they cannot really "do" things, whereas readers can (Holland). Even a critic like Susana Pajares, who has devoted her study to hypertext and who in many respects could be called a technophile—that is, an ardent defendant of digital technology in the field of literature—considers that true interactivity, understood as an exchange between equals in a communicative process, is impossible in hypertexts as well. The word she uses for the reader's activity while selecting links is "exploration," since most often than not, the reader does not have the option of co-authoring the text or altering it in any way (Pajares, "Literatura Digital" 33).

Tracing a middle path between these two perspectives, interactivity can be understood as a field of study that explores the way in which different technological artefacts (the codex, the book, the computer) are used as vehicles of communication between humans, following the communicative model human-machine-human. Interactivity would then be a concept that describes the relationship established between two poles, the technological and the human one, a quality midway between a property of the medium and a process undertaken by the user. Assuming this perspective, we cannot consider the digital technology, or any other, as inherently or automatically interactive, but it rather depends on the use humans make of it.

It is also useful to consider this quality as measurable. There can be different degrees of interactivity, depending on the characteristics of the technology used as much as on the attitude and competence of the user to exploit the interactivity options available. According to this, different technologies permit different degrees of interactivity; however, the degree of interactivity obtained through them also depends on the capacity of the user and his or her degree of familiarization with the technology. We could argue that the notion of interaction applied to print texts as material, technological artefacts is justified from the moment in which we can identify in the text certain strategies which have the power to actively guide the reader response. The work of Wolfgang Iser has enormously contributed to discerning the ways in which the text also "communicates," for example, by the way in which the text moulds an ideal response for an ideal reader. The narrative structures of the implied reader and the narrator are two of the main resources we can use for a study of the interactivity of print texts.

But which are the main resources the digital text uses to trigger or guide a specific response on the part of the reader, beyond the mechanic selection of links? The challenge digital literature poses for critics and teachers regarding interactivity is that digital texts also require an adjustment of the interactive strategies both writers and readers are accustomed to share. The fragmentation and structural complexity of the digital text threatens novice writers or readers with irreparable chaos and total loss of meaning, unless they use their literary competence as a way to build bridges between old and new forms of interacting with the text.

5 Intermediality

Before the arrival of digital literature, intermediality was already a problematic concept, since it could be considered a property of the text (the allusion in traditional written texts to other types of texts and codes, such as textual references to music, films, paintings, etc.; the use of different signs and codes within the same work, as in concrete poetry; the temporal overlapping of different types of texts, as in the case of the scenic arts in general between the script and the actual performance; or combinations of all these types of intermediality within the same work) and a property of the reading process, intermediality would then be a type of intertextual connection, evoked in the mind of the reader, to other types of texts.

The digital text participates in these previous types of intermediality, and adds to them a crucial one: the digital text is intrinsically intermedial from its very technical materiality, at once interface and programming. The different code layers upon which the interface managed by the reader is dependent, those which are used to replicate the literary experience, is an added technological dimension which is lacking in traditional texts and which impinges directly on the reading process.

Recently renewed attention is placed on the least researched of the three classic genres: the theatre, in its electronic variants. Anxo Abuín's *Escenarios del caos: Entre la hipertextualidad y la performance en la era electrónica* [*Stages of Chaos, Between Hypertextuality and Performance in the Electronic Era*] has already become a reference work in this area. Departing from the premises of Calabrese in *Neo-Baroque: A Sign of the Times* regarding the opposition of Classic and Baroque notions inside Western culture—one devoted to order, rule, cause, finitude, etc., and the other to disorder, irregularity, chaos, chance, etc.—Albuín contextualizes digital literature inside the anti-classicist, carnivalesque logic of the hybrid artistic forms that incarnate the sign of our times. He focuses on cinema, theatre, and performance, including their digital counterparts from the perspective of chaos theories, as processes, which entail great complexity and reject a deterministic and linear perspective, in favour of adopting unpredictability and chance as key analytical factors. Albuín's work is imbued with an understanding of intermediality as an analytical practice, which crosses different spaces, media and genres, borrowing concepts from a heterogenic pool of sources in an attempt to find a general frame in which to insert a variety of cultural artefacts.

The complementary movement to analyse digital literature in the context of the arts in general, is to develop a rhetoric of digital literature in its own terms. On-going Spanish research focuses on the concept of intermediality as a key to read digital literature beyond the hypertextual paradigm. The research group "Leethi" at the University Complutense of Madrid, for example, is currently at work revising the aesthetics of visual media in an effort to incorporate a visual sensitivity to their literary approach to digital texts. For this purpose, professionals from different academic cultures (computer design, visual arts) are invited to share their reading responses of selected multimedia texts (among others, the work of Argentinean author Belén Gache, whose *Wordtoys* (1996-2006) offers a rich soil for experimentation on digital literature and intermediality).[2]

6 Conclusion

For a better assessment of the promises of the digital medium, it is necessary to take into account the basis of the old medium's achievements. The virtuality of the printed text was based on a movement of insinuation and concealment that allowed the reader to construct a plurality of meanings present only in potency or virtuality, and thus, transcend the limitations of the medium. As Cabo Aseguinolaza claims, hypertext will have to find its own limits and subvert them in order to be really artistic and literary:

> [H]ypertextual criticism seems to stress just the way in which the new medium has abolished the restrictions of printing. The rhetoric of hypertextuality hastens to show how hypertextuality is capable of materializing and actualizing what was formerly impeded. Clearly

enough, hypertexts still have to seek their own constrictions to make them meaningful. (8)

But before that happens, both readers and writers will have to recover the communal dimension of the reading experience: the community of readers as the space of encounter where to contextualize the reading experience, build a set of conventions, and catch up with each other. Spanish critics contribute to this challenge by pointing to the requirements of this new economy of reading and writing. Rodríguez de las Heras has argued in his essay "El libro digital" ('The Digital Book') that, in order for digital literature to emerge, it is necessary to conceive far more powerful hypertextual organizations than those that we have at this point. In his opinion, the kind of connections that we have now is not really very demanding on the part of the writer, and although this might be sufficient for a web page design, it is not enough for a digital work of literature. What we need, therefore, is far more creativity and experimentation. Only then could it make its appearance as a book without pages, a soft book, polyhedral, navigable, with a new reading excitement and an old frustration for the lost reading coordinates. On the other hand, Susana Pajares demands a greater effort on the part of the reader to extract pleasure out of hypertext; readers will need to improve their literary competence so that they can meet the challenges posed by the new textual structures.

The advent of digital literature in the literary system has brought with it important transformations which affect not only the reading pacts previously shared by writers and readers, but also the relations between teachers and students. The principle upon which the pleasure of the text was founded, which managed the subtle equation between interpretative effort and gained insight, has metamorphosed into a new economy of reading which requires a doubled effort. Teachers and students face a challenge inherent to the newness of the medium and its myriad of polymorphic "literary" manifestations; in particular, the reconfiguration of the concepts of text, genre, reader and author, intertextuality and interactivity, intermediality, together with the added technological dimension.

We, as teachers and critics, will also need, to some extent, to combine the scientific knowledge of the programmatic taste of machines for a specific understanding of information and communication, that is, an exchange of digital data which can be formulated or programmed without any reference to cognizant subjects, with a literary sensitivity that emphasizes the importance of mental processes and their intrinsic value for the creation of shared experiences with other humans. From a combination of these two perspectives, which are indissoluble in the digital text, we will be able to understand more fully the notions of interactivity, intertextuality, and intermediality, less as some intrinsic values of a system, and more as two flexible qualities dependent on both poles, the technological as well as the human one.

Notes

1   Note that the word "actualize" is used by technophile critics to characterize the action by which the reader elicits a specific text through link selection. This word is emptied of the semantic dimension reception critics had attributed to it. For Ingarden, for example, to "actualize" was a mental operation performed by the reader, the action by which the reader created mental representations of the diegesis as the reading activity proceeded.
2   Gache's use of links, which connect different types of texts (visual and aural), is discussed in my essay "Teaching Digital Literature in Spain" (in this book).

Works Cited

Abuín, Anxo. *Escenarios del caos: Entre la hipertextualidad y la performance en la era electrónica*. Valencia: Tirant lo Blanch, 2006.

Abuín, Anxo, and Teresa Vilariño. *Teoría del hipertexto: La literatura en la era electrónica*. Madrid: Arco, 2006.

Alonso, Andoni, and Iñaki Arzoz. *La nueva Ciudad de Dios: Un ensayo cibercultural sobre el tecnohermetismo*, Madrid: Siruela, 2003.

Borràs Castanyer, Laura, ed. *Textualidades electrónicas: Nuevos escenarios para la literatura*. Barcelona: Editorial UOC, 2005.

Cabo Aseguinolaza, Fernando. "Poetry and Hypertext: The Sense of a Limit." *Reading in the Age of Media, Computers, and Internet: International Conference in Honor of Professor Wolfgang Iser's Work*, Sofia, 2000. 17 Apr. 2009 <http://www.liternet.bg/iser/fernando1.htm>.

Cadigan, Pat. *Synners*. New York: Four Walls Eight Windows, 2001.

Calabrese, Omar. *Neo-Baroque: A Sign of the Times*. Princeton: Princeton UP, 1992.

Castells, Manuel. *La Sociedad Red*. Madrid: Alianza Editorial, 2006.

———. *The Information Age: Economy, Society and Culture. Vol. I: The Rise of the Network Society*. 2nd ed. Oxford: Blackwell, 2002.

Echeverría Ezponda, Javier. *Los señores del aire: Telépolis y el tercer entorno*. Barcelona: Destino, 1999.

Fernández Serrato, Juan Carlos. "Tecnologías digitales y literaturas hispánicas." *Liceus*. 15 Apr. 2009 <http://www.liceus.com/bonos/compra1.asp?idproducto=226>.

Gache, Belén. *Wordtoys*. 1996-2006. 15 Apr. 2009 <http://www.findelmundo.com.ar/wordtoys/index.htm>.

Gibson, William. *Neuromancer*. New York: Ace Books, 1984.

Gómez Trueba, Teresa. "La literatura electrónica y sus antecedentes en la cultura impresa." *Liceus*. 15 Apr. 2009 <http://www.liceus.com/bonos/compra1.asp?idproducto=509>.

Greco, Diane. *Cyborg: Engineering the Body Electric*. CD-ROM. Cambridge, MA: Eastgate, 1995.

Hayles, N. Katherine. *Writing Machines*. Cambridge, MA: MIT P, 2002.

Holland, Norman N. "Eliza Meets the Postmodern." *EJournal* 4.1 (1994). 15 Aug. 2009 <http://www.ucalgary.ca/ejournal/archive/rachel/v4n1/article.html>.

Iser, Wolfgang. *The Act of Reading: A Theory of Aesthetic Response*. Baltimore: Johns Hopkins UP, 1978.

Jackson, Shelley. *Patchwork Girl*. CD-ROM. Cambridge, MA: Eastgate, 1995.

Kolb, David. *Socrates in the Labyrinth*. CD-ROM. Cambridge, MA: Eastgate, 1994.

Malloy, Judy. "Electronic Fiction in the 21st Century." *Visions of the Future*. Ed. Cliff Pickover. Middlesex: Northwood, 1992. 137-144.

Millán, José Antonio. *La lectura y la sociedad del conocimiento*. 2000. 15 Apr. 2009 <http://www.jamillan.com/lecsoco.htm>.

———. *Internet y el español*. Madrid: Fundación Retevisión, 2001.

Murray, Janet H. *Hamlet on the Holodeck: The Future of Narrative in Cyberspace*. New York: Free Press, 1997.

Orihuela, José Luis. "El narrador en ficción interactiva. El jardinero y el laberinto." *Quién cuenta la historia: Estudios sobre el narrador en los relatos de ficción y no ficción*. Pamplona: Ediciones Eunate, AAVV, 1999. 15 Aug. 2009 <http://www.ucm.es/info/especulo/hipertul/califia.htm>.

Pajares Tosca, Susana. *Literatura Digital: El paradigma hipertextual*. Cáceres: Universidad de Extremadura, Servicio de Publicaciones, 2004.

Pajares Tosca, Susana. "Ludology meets Hypertext." *Literatures in the Digital Era: Theory and Praxis*. Eds. Amelia Sanz and Dolores Romero. Newcastle: Cambridge Scholars P, 2007. 51-60.

Rodríguez de las Heras, Antonio. "El libro digital." 1999. 15 Apr. 2009 <http://www.inem.es/inem/relint/TTnet/pdfs/libdigi.pdf>.

———. "Nuevas tecnologías y saber humanístico." *Literatura y cibercultura*. Ed. Domingo Sánchez-Mesa. Madrid: Arco, 2004. 147-176.

Rodríguez, Jaime Alejandro. *Hipertexto y Literatura: Una batalla por el signo en tiempos posmodernos*. Santa Fé de Bogotá: CEJA, 1999. 15 Apr. 2009 <http://www.javeriana.edu.co/Facultades/C_Sociales/Facultad/sociales_ virtual/publicaciones/hipertxt-lit/hipertexto_fcs.html>.

Rodríguez López, Joaquín. "Ser o no ser ciberbardo, esa es la cuestión. Diez cuestiones a propósito de la narrativa digital." 2000. 15 Aug. 2009 <http://www.jamillan.com/ciberbar.htm>.

Romero, Dolores. "Spanish Literature in the Digital Domain: Culture, Nation and Narrations." *Literatures in the Digital Era: Theory and Praxis*. Eds. Amelia Sanz and Dolores Romero. Newcastle: Cambridge Scholars P, 2007. 329-341.

Ryan, Marie-Laure. "Immersion vs. Interactivity: Virtual Reality and Literary Theory." 1994. 15 Apr. 2009 <http://www.humanities.uci.edu/mposter/syllabi/readings/ryan.html>.

Sánchez-Mesa, Domingo, ed. *Literatura y cibercultura*. Madrid: Arco, 2004.

Stephenson, Neal. *Snowcrash*. New York: Bantam, 1992.

Talens, Jenaro. *El sujeto vacío: Cultura y poesía en territorio Babel*. Valencia: Universitat de València, 2000.

———, ed. *Critical Practices in Post-Franco Spain*. Minneapolis: U of Minnesota P, 1994.

Vega, María Luisa, ed. *Literatura hipertextual y teoría literaria*. Madrid: Marenostrum, 2003.

Villanueva, Darío. "Sobre *Hamlet en la Holocubierta*." *El cultural*, 1999. 15 Apr. 2009 <http://www.jamillan.com/sobreha.htm>.

Voullaimoz, Nuria. *Literatura e hipermedia*. Barcelona: Paidós, 2000.

Janez Strehovec

Alphabet on the Move

Digital Poetry and the Realm of Language

Digital poetry is an umbrella term which for the flexible purpose of identification often encompasses various multi-media projects at the intersection of digital textuality, hyperpoetry, experimental writing in digital media, net art, software-controlled electronic text-based installation art, text generators, textual software art (code poetry), and text-based computer games with elements generated by the author's very personal approach to the textual material. Some pieces of digital poetry allow the reader to enjoy so-called lyrical atmospheres and qualities; others are even counter-lyrical or post-lyrical. On closer inspection, digital poetry turns out to involve several experimental projects, which are articulated as hybrid entities devoted to in-between cultural, literary and artistic spaces. Attending some of the important events of digital poetry (e.g., *E-Poetry* festival and conference, Paris, 2007) enables one to experience the richness and diversity of today's experimental writing in digital media, which is often about the research in a specific field of, let us say, the cyber'language'[1] shaped by the author's very personal attitude regarding writing in digital media. The common ground of digital poetry performances refers to a variety of forms and genres, spanning from net art and software art (e.g., Eugenio Tisselli's degenerative web site project) to pieces devoted to an author's live performance of reading and interacting with visual displays (e.g., Aya N. Karpinska's and Jörg Piringer's performances[2]). Rather than being a continuation of poetry-as-we-know-it, it is a novel textual and meta-textual, linguistic and not-just-linguistic practice, which has moved away from the printed page and is shaped with the key paradigms of contemporary art and culture. Digital poetry projects (from hyperpoetry and animated poetry to text-based installation and textual VJ-ing) challenge literary theory to redefine and adjust its methodological approach by applying the concepts and theoretical devices taken from other fields, e.g., from Internet studies, studies in techno culture, new media theory and (socio)linguistics. Rather than regarding digital poetry as a purely linguistic phenomenon, my research foregrounds its broader interactions with the key fields of present techno culture and new media art.[3]

Defamiliarizing the Realm of Cyber'language'

Poetry's traditional role of creating lyric atmospheres by imparting intimate feelings and sensations of a so-called lyrical subject and as a place of "a projective saying" (Heidegger) is fundamentally being challenged by information technologies that are able to create their own particular cultural condition, new ways of user-related text organization, and new generations of hybrid and artificial languages. Today we are witnessing how digital media generate a very specific mode of experiencing mixed or hybrid realities, and we can see the particular ways of perceiving, knowing and making culture in a reality of heightened complexity that involves both the given (physical) as well as virtual worlds. Digital media also in a way make language perform differently from the language of traditional print culture as demonstrated by both the artistic examples of text-based computer and video game mods, and—in terms of popular media—bullets on web sites written by means of online journalism. Novel textual practices are emerging in which presentation, linear construction of narrative, depths, and meaning give way to the liquid textscape, blog-based remixability, the multi-sensory textscape experience and special effects (e.g., Amy Alexander's VJ show *CyberSpaceLand* featuring text visuals generated live from search engine queries). Text is undergoing radical shifts in addressing both the author and the reader: Within a new media paradigm, we are facing the linguistic realm articulated in a digital medium with new properties which allow people to write, read, communicate, learn, explore and create in novel ways.

How do we imagine the very nature of digital poetry placed within a broader field of interactive new media art and culture; how do we approach its poetic specificity? Let us say first that digital poetry as a very experimental field of approaching *the realm of cyber'language'* in a very intimate manner belongs to digital literature, which can be considered as a part of new media—meaning it is characterized by new media features such as digitality, interactivity, hypertextuality, dispersal and virtuality (Lister et al. 13). Apart from those features there are a number of others associated with the textual specificity of a new medium. Yet—and that is crucial—digital poetry generated by programming and scripting languages and made possible by a very specific interface (computer screen, or a navigation device such as the mouse or scroll-bar) is by no means merely about technical innovations. It enables us to face textual practice occurring inside the text and in the context of the present cultural production, defined by globalization, multiculturalism, new economy, new forms of experiencing identity, by the issues of gender, community and embodiment, by new forms and new modes of representing the world and its objects, by a new audience which is sometimes closer to the club (DJ- and VJ-) culture than to the

elite culture, by the Internet, aesthetics of special effects and of mosaic, and—
and this is of crucial importance—by the present linguistic practices of online
communication.

In terms of the audience interested in digital poetry, we can encounter individuals who rarely read books, but are more familiar with software, PCs, palms, mobiles and who participate even in the events of club culture. While mentioning club culture, one may also say that digital poetry can be performed in clubs as well and not necessarily in spaces assigned to the elite culture (libraries, university classrooms, cultural centers, etc.). Blurring the difference between the elite and the popular arts also motivates the authors of this poetry, among which we often encounter net artists and programmers who have not undertaken traditional training in the humanities.

By considering the various streams and forms in digital poetry (e.g., its performances within *E-Poetry* biannual festivals, pieces involved in the *ELO Collection, Vol.* 1[4]), we can discover that many of them belong more to the world of new media art than to the world of the book-based literary culture. Due to its new media art features, this practice is also placed beyond the traditional boundaries between two cultures, as they are discussed in Snow's book on the divide between scientific and literary intellectuals (Snow). It seems that Manovich in his *Language of New Media* does not pay enough attention to the digital textuality and digital literary projects—for also in the medium of "linguistic works" events take place, which in a striking way demonstrate key features of the new media. Essential for digital poetry is also its fundamental connection to contemporary art, which nowadays has passed from the established to a supportive function of art in terms of a broader activity including artistic software, a service devoted to solving a particular (cultural and non-cultural) problem, a research, an interface which demands from its user also the ability for associative selection, algorithmic (logical) thinking and for procedures pertaining to DJ and VJ culture, such as mixing, cutting, sampling, re-purposing and recombination.

In any case we can find out that the links between this poetry and net art, software art, browser art and text-based electronic installations are often stronger than their connection to poetry printed in a book and aiming at traditional literary culture. Interestingly, the authors of this kind of creativity do not foreground the question of genre; some of them declare themselves to be creators of digital poetry, others do not; some pieces (e.g., of Giselle Beiguelman's *Poetrica* and Eugenio Tisselli's *Degenerative*) function also in the context of net art, while others (e.g., Camille Utterback's *Text Rain* and Simon Biggs's *Rewrite*) in the medium of (text-based) electronic installations.

Digital poetry as a precarious and therefore also threatening field is based on a text considered an experimental artistic environment for establishing new relations between textual components as well as for striking and challenging experiences of unusual meanings. The readers of such pieces are facing the author's very intimate attitude and her strong emphasis on the language used; in digital poetry, the author tries to establish a relationship with the word-material that is as individualized as possible; we even find cases of the creation of a new language (for example the "text-wurks" of the Australian author Mez). On the other hand, Maria Mencia's *Cityscapes: Social Poetics/Public Textualities* project is basically aimed at extracting a visual text from the city environment, deconstructing, re-purposing and re-mapping it into a different context. The readers/viewers/listeners of this piece are challenged by the author's interesting research on how to integrate digital poetry into the realm of social and urban poetics, into the calligram of the city itself.

> In western culture, the realm of media and advertising has absorbed the language of Visual Poetry, and calligrams have become another official way to engage people in the selling of their products. Reciprocally poetry has also been influenced by this exchange and has moved to other domains away from the page and into the public display. My interest therefore, was to use the language of advertising to create poetic/artistic public work in urban spaces and in so doing to explore the new calligram, that of social poetics, of the neon lights, flickering letters, moving messages and public textualities of city environments. (Mencia)

Rather than dealing with the very intimate contents of modern lyrical poetry, this poetry foregrounds an attitude of social poetics, which is based on the interplay between the language of poetry and the language of commercials arranged within the cityscape's flickering imagery.

What is lacking in digital poetry are the formal demands of the medium of the printed page; in digital poetry the text is displayed on computer screens and stored for further applications in computer storage units, and the demand of alignment as well as the striving for rhymes, assonance and other features of (traditional) poetry forms are often pushed aside. The very lyrical nature of print-based poetry in terms of a very emotional response to an event or occasion, even in a very passionate moment of the lyrical subject, is also often left behind; on the other hand, the demands of the conceptual and purely linguistic and not-just-linguistic experimentation are gaining importance. Such a poetic work is sometimes more about the questioning of the very nature of the medium itself (e.g., software poetry, poetry generators) and about analyzing how the word behaves within the new media paradigm. The state-of-the-art software special effects in terms of attractive 3D visualization[5] are often privileged at the expense of a more innovative use of ordinary language itself.

Although defined as an umbrella and technical term, digital poetry implies the poetic and literary reference, so the question needs to be raised; what precisely is the very literary nature of this kind of poetry? Can it still be considered poetry or has it already developed into something else? In searching for theoretical foundations that can match the issue of the literary nature of digital poetry pieces, I have found a useful device—"literaturnost" ('literariness') which at the very beginning of the 20th century had been introduced in Russian Formalism. Literariness, according to Roman Jakobson, Viktor Shklovsky, Yuri Tynianov, Boris Eikhenbaum, Grigory Vinokur and others, is defined as the sum of special linguistic and formal properties that distinguish literary texts from non-literary texts. The crucial device of literariness is defamiliarization, understood as a series of deviations from "ordinary" language; instead of considering literature as a "reflection" (mimesis) of social reality, Viktor Shklovsky and his Formalist followers considered it as a linguistic dislocation, or a procedure of "making strange." As described by Shklovsky in "Iskusstvo kak priem" ("Art as device" 1917), "ostranenie" ('defamiliarization')—as a typical device of all literature and art—serves to present a familiar phenomenon in an uncommon fashion for the purpose of an aesthetic perception, which is an aim of art. Facing the text with literary features means being struck with both the "artistic" language and the order of things designated by them that deviate from our common expectations based on everyday experience.

In introducing the concept of defamiliarization (for the Formalists, "literariness" and "poeticity" are synonymous) in this essay on digital poetry, I am aware that it works well here only to a certain extent, and that it needs to be continuously refashioned by the use of the new media devices, with a special regard to the software features of digital texts. At the very beginning of the 21st century we are witnessing the blurring of boundaries between disciplines and roles, between institutions and networks; i.e., both literature and everyday life are no longer easily differentiated categories, creating another problem in introducing the "ostranenie." It is also self-evident that Russian Formalists were not concerned with questions of digital textuality, digital literature or the Web in general; however, unlike many traditional literary devices such as form, content, genius, style, aesthetics, lyrical subject, etc., defamiliarization enables one to grasp (and define) the digital literature (and poetry) author's effort in arranging her material in a very uncommon fashion.

Therefore, what are we dealing with regarding this concept of defamiliarization in the field of digital writing? Defamiliarization in terms of digital poetry means that the authors arrange the subject's feelings, sensations, dreams, projections, the language attitude, experience, events and atmospheres in an unfamiliar way in order to ensure a non-habitual and non-automatic perception of an individual's intimate realm as well as of her language, views and ideas.

Briefly, their key aim is in making strange conventionally understood feelings, conditions, human fates, and individual's being-in-the world. They try to hit the reader's attention span in a very persuasive fashion and within a very limited time interval, and because the modern individual is easily distracted, distinctive particularities of language need to be set up in very striking manners. In doing so, the authors use the specificity of new media, their special effects, and they try to organize the 'linguistic' elements in a way that deviates from the language of commercial web sites, online journalism, and Web 2.0 portals, although this often appears to be a difficult procedure. (We should not forget that when we are online, there is everything just a click away from our working environment—also in terms of the language we are dealing with). Along with stylistic and narrative devices (e.g., techno-suspense, techno-surprise[6]), a big emphasis is put on the software-based solutions that often deviate from conventional software applications. Web based textual pieces with artistic or literary ambitions diverge from textual objects applied to ordinary web sites and disturb even the user's perception and cognition (e.g., Mark Amerika's *Filmtext*).

The literariness in digital poetry refers first of all to making cyber'language' strange; we therefore can see that many digital pieces defamiliarize our expectations of how digital texts look like, what they are about, and the order of things performed in them. For example, in Mark Amerika's *Filmtext* genres of film, computer games and text are made strange by presenting cinematic, gaming and textual phenomena in an uncommon fashion. Natalie Bookchin's *The Intruder* defamiliarizes our expectations and ideas about video games and gaming behavior (instead of making a progression to a higher game level and keeping a score, we are interested in gaining the meaning, ideas and feelings of the extraordinary), Komninos Zervos's animated poem *Beer* alienates the visual appearance of the stable lines of the traditional lyrical poem by placing the emphasis on the digital morphing of single nouns and their letters. Eugenio Tisselli's *Degenerative* web site project[7] undermines our belief in a web site as a stable medium, while Simon Biggs's text installation *reWrite* disturbs the reader's habitual expectations of how the authorial text is organized by enabling an artificial condition, which allows her to observe herself reading endlessly self-generating texts,[8] and finally, Michael Joyce's hyperfiction *afternoon, a a story* defamiliarizes the genre of the novel-as-we-know-it. And it is self-evident that each of these projects defamiliarizes also the world, events, language, ideas and scenes referred to in them. In such pieces we are facing strange-making as a distinctive effect achieved by the literary pieces and artworks that are shaped through new media, thereby disrupting our habitual perception of the world while enabling us to see even the cyberspace-based things afresh. In short, digital texts bring something into the language, into its organization (e.g., on web sites), and into reading that did not exist before. And to literariness in terms of new media also belongs the emotional capital of such projects that initiate and stimulate a distinctive form of psychological change and feelings.

Therefore, the digital (poetic) text defamiliarizes our expectations of what digital "language" looks like, of how a special feeling of a digital word is shaped and of what the crucial features of the literary genre are within the paradigm of cyberculture (e.g., feedback loops, customization, the new media-shaped materiality and even physicality—of on the screen displayed text as well as the user's textual control and navigation). Inside the digital medium, the word loses its authority and solidity—which characterized its role in printed texts—and it appears as a raw material for numerous transformations and interventions (made and controlled by software). Text is a textual "moving reserve," a new media-shaped textscape, which challenges both the author and the reader in terms of navigation, orientation, and decision-making. Noah Wardrip-Fruin described these features by referring to *Screen,* his textual Cave Installation:

> The experience of *Screen,* we hope, is one of oscillation. The words are at times objects, and act like graphical objects, and we concentrate on playing them that way. But sometimes the words are words, and we read them as clusters of text—seeing them overlap, hearing them spoken. And sometimes the words are part of a memory, a fiction, and we remember the context in which we heard a word before, we see how the texts are deforming through the play process, deforming more the better we are as players. (Wardrip-Fruin, Interview)

Underlining the sophisticated nature of the new media-shaped textual experience, we can mention also Komninos Zervos's digital poem *Beer* based on the animation of nouns (beer, beef, heel, hell, etc.) by means of digital morphing, which allows a change to letters within words over time, making an instant word that is constantly changing into another word-compound. We can take into account also the (software) intervention with the digital morph (which often replaces the metaphor in print-based modern poetry) and the use of devices such as parataxis, which establish within a single word an actual "stage of tensions" among new meanings, issued from units made of the primary word, now cut to pieces.

Digital poetry often also enables the reader, in the role of the user, to have a very creative and intensive contact with the text—Deena Larsen, in her *Carving in Possibilities* expressed this characteristic with the final call to the reader to "sculpt again" and not to "read again." In the already-mentioned VR text-based installation *Screen,* the text comes to life in relation to the reader's body demanding the bodily interaction with the data-words-bodies. Even devices such as the scroll-bar, mouse and stylus (when using a PDA) enable the reader to handle the written text in a very specific, intimate way and to interfere with the text through an interface (e.g., by means of a mouseover event). In Larsen's *Carving in Possibilities*, words are hidden behind the surface—like the objects temporarily wrapped by the visual artist Christo in his pioneering Land Art projects. The reader is asked to find—by means of the "mouse event" procedure—the covered/wrapped words and make them appear on the screen. By touching various points on the screen, an image of shapeless stone is being transformed into Michelangelo's David. The user's action is individualized; the sequence of textual components adapts to her interventions (this is "customization" which, as a procedure, is well-known in the networked economy) and it always produces or sculpts different sequences of the written, that is to say, accomplishes a different textual event. Larsen's opening line—"I saw precisely what the stone was meant to be"—is a starting point for various textual continuations/derivatives caused by random repositioning of the mouse-touch on the screen.

I have used the word "event" (in Flash vector-based graphics what is talked about is the mouse event), because digital poetry really is about events; it is about creating the text with an emphasized temporal feature, based on two levels—on the internal "unwrapping" of the textual hidden layers as well as on the reader's/user's reading in the form of her interactive intervention into the texts (which is often the case). Beyond the temporal "richness" of the text in terms of its event nature, such a text even demonstrates a very sophisticated structure, based on the relationships between the words and on the special atmospheres connected with these relationships. The author's role lies not merely in projecting the poetry's words, it lies above all in arranging the stage of relationships among words and even within one single word (e.g., in Komninos Zervos's and Mez's texts). Therefore the digital poetry text (designed as an object, browser, textual ambient, text-based computer game, web- installation, piece of software, etc.) in the context of new media innovatively challenges our traditional approach to language.

The Text as Shaped by New Media

In his book *The Language of New Media*, Lev Manovich claimed that

> . . . the printed word tradition that initially dominated the language of cultural interfaces is becoming less important, while the part played by cinematic elements is becoming progressively stronger. This is con-

sistent with a general trend in modern society toward presenting more and more information in the form of time-based audiovisual moving image sequences, rather than as text. (78)

Such a trend is foregrounded even within the important part of the digital textual production, which is organized today in the form of time-based audio-visual moving sequences; in other words, it is based on words in motion that appear as a film of words. The texts themselves have passed into the mainstream film mode, transformed into a kinetic textscape with emphasis on the visual whose main purpose is to attract the hybrid reader-listener-viewer of today as a voyeur, i.e., the staring one. The moving textscape is, metaphorically speaking, designed as a seductive physical entity. In order to fulfill the demands of such an attractive representation, the textscape must be organized and arranged as sophisticatedly as possible (*Screen* as a Cave-Project can serve as a paradigmatic example). Furthermore, it must be possible to satisfactorily perform this textscape exclusively through computer tools—i.e., in order to present the textscape as a seductive entity, it must become a digital text generated specifically by means of different types of software.

The idea of text-film is not coined exclusively by digital culture; it is found already in the historical avantgarde, especially in Marinetti's Futurism, which was based, as far as the poetical practice is concerned, on free, nomadic words, i.e., on the "parole-in-libertà" ('words-in-freedom'). In the manifesto *The Futurist Cinema*, we encounter the idea that "the most varied elements will enter into the Futurist film as expressive means: from the slice of life to the streak of color, from the conventional line to words-in-freedom, from chromatic and plastic music to the music of objects" (Marinetti 131). We can see the actual realization of this idea in certain films, for example in *A Clockwork Orange* (1971) by Stanley Kubrick where textual components made of different symbols and formulae are moving over the screen. In Kubrick's *2001: A Space Odyssey* textual design insertions represent an important component, too.

Moving text is also an essential component of installation art. For example, writings flowing vertically over light emitting diodes (LED) are the trademark of Jenny Holzer's visual art projects; moving text, based on word-objects designed by computer graphics, is also a characteristic of Jeffrey Shaw's electronic installations (for example *The Legible City* and *The Virtual Museum*) as well as of the VR installation *Screen*. In this field, also the Canadian media artist Michael Snow, who in 1982 shot the experimental film *So is this* (16mm, b&w, silent, 45 minutes) as a text-film in which each shot is a single word, was among the pioneers.

The noticeable swing of the text in motion (which, as a rule, emphasizes the visual features because it has to fulfill the imperative of being organized and arranged in an attractive fashion) can be encountered in particular within the digital (visual) culture and within the culture of informing and communicating in the society of information, spectacle and new media—which is also tied to the demands of the new media aesthetics, as well as to the contemporary individual's need to receive information in a form arranged as multimedia, presupposing the coexistence of language, sound, visual, kinetic and tactile effects. By entering the new mediascape, we can find out that the most talked about cultural contents are arranged in a mosaic and hybrid format based on the coexistence of different forms, i.e., that "the logic of replacement, characteristic of cinema, gives way to the logic of addition and coexistence" (Manovich 325).

The text—by no means as something disappearing, but rather as something adapting itself to the aesthetics of new media—has an important place in their midst. We come across it in the "balloons" of comics and in short information bits about pop stars in some music videos, and it appears also in the design of television news based on a mosaic format: "What is evident in current television is that the screen is no longer a 'sacred space' dedicated to a single image. Television has diverged from film in this way—its screen is divided in its presentation of information . . ." (Burnett and Marshall 89). On CNN we thus encounter moving text, flowing underneath visual contents (the so-called bizbar, newsbar, sportbar) which means it is not enough to merely watch and listen—the user must constantly receive a package of information organized in a mosaic way, represented in scriptural, aural, and visual forms. The mosaic design is also the constant companion of web sites, which still contain a lot of entirely linguistic features—arranged in a language characteristic of the web media (the so-called "netspeak") and within the form of bullets with striking visual features.

The "linguistic" element in the textscape (which is often the medium in which digital poetry is generated) is not based solely on kinetic text—i.e., where understanding sequential syntax as well as knowing the syntax of film language are essential to its understanding—it is based also on highlighted visual features, which implies some consideration to the spatial syntax, for within a digital textuality the spatialization of textual components comes to the forefront. In fact, before digital media, the aspirations of Visual and Concrete Poetry for "total textwork" have not been completely fulfilled—in many ways these aspirations have been surpassed and complemented by new elements deriving from the aesthetics of the digital. In any case, it is important that the words inside the textscape are "words-images-virtual bodies," and that they are self-contained signifiers which must be perceived not only considering their semantic function but also by considering their visual appearance as well as their position and motion in space. A user of digital textuality needs to focus at the visual aspect of the text, at the digital word-image itself, not purely using it as a point of departure for his mental "travel" towards something entirely different, to literary worlds with "meaning," which was the topic of the following notion from Roman Ingarden's *The Cognition of the Literary Work of Art*:

> . . . there is the question of the degree to which we really sensibly perceive and must perceive the individual paper and the individual flecks of ink themselves in the concrete reading of a printed book. Are we not rather immediately disposed to apprehend the typical forms of the printed "words" or the typical verbal sounds, without bringing to consciousness what the individual written signs look like? (177)

Unlike this print-based state, in digital textuality the emphasis is not only on the decoding of a meaning. A hybrid reader-viewer-listener of digital text is also interested in what the individually displayed signs look like; therefore, the visual features of a signifier (e.g., its fleck of "new media ink") and the spatial syntax organization of the text units come to the forefront.

One of the new media-based textualities with literary features deploying the moving text(scape) is animated digital poetry set at the intersections of Poetry Avant-garde and Neo-avant-garde, Film, Special Effects, Text-Based Electronic Installation Art, Concept Art, Net Art and Computer Graphics. It includes kinetic and animated poetry, kinetic digital sound poetry, poetry generators, as well as kinetic digital textscapes and installations with poetry characteristics. How can we approach such poetry? What are its main features?

One of the crucial features of the poetry-as-we-know-it (e.g., print-based poetry) is connected with the whiteness of the printed page, the absent, the untold (e.g., Edmond Jabès' account regarding the issue of words in his *Le Parcours*). Hidden text units, i.e., units not yet displayed on the screen, usually keep the readers in suspense. In the case of animated poetry based on moving letters and words, only a small part of the text is in a screen focus, and there is no telling whether or not all the letters and words will appear in the foreground. This means that the reader is faced with the non-trivial effort of having to catch the point of such a work. Interesting examples of such texts are Brian Kim Stefans's piece *The Dreamlife of Letters* and Mary Flanagan's project *[theHouse]*. The latter, as a digital poetry piece which takes the form of a computer-based flowing and spatialized organism, is based on the interplay of moving words and unstable geometric structures (designing the rooms). In her statement, Flanagan suggests that through the process of enacting texts within, alongside, and outside of the text of the computational code, this autobiographical work is regulated by the computational process of the sine wave.

Here, the text is written upon "rooms," and these rooms emerge to create "houses" next to and among the intermingling text. This piece, which is about language and embodiment in terms of moving, very unstable—even nervous and hard-to-catch—structures, is only realized through the user's interaction and navigation. Regarding the spatialization of this piece, one can realize that it intersects both digital poetry and embodiment even in terms of virtual architecture, arranged by means of special effects. Relatively weak and less innovative language of the author's impressions and commentaries give way to attractive spatial visualization; i.e., the linguistic element in such a textscape is to a certain extent deprivileged at the expense of the state-of-the art technical (e.g., software) solutions.

Reading/watching such digital poetry pieces that are articulated in a language owing much to cinema and music video syntax, e.g., to suspense, short and fast cuts, (re)mixing, recombination, and surprise, implicates some essential changes on the level of their perception. Instead of the traditional reader, the digital text user (in terms of hybrid reader/viewer/listener) is being recreated: she is abandoning the merely linear readings, and becomes as capable of complex and non-trivial perceptions and cognitions of such texts as possible; this is connected also to the navigational skills that the user needs in her approach to such pieces. The linear reading gives way to an instable, let us say jumpy perception demanded by the textscape as a sophisticated multimedia-shaped phenomenon that challenges the user to approach it with novel, as a rule hybrid, perceptual acts (e.g., tactile seeing[9]).

On the threshold of the third millennium, it appears that the demands that the viewer of Nam June Paik's video installations was faced with in 1980s and 90s became generalized (these installations often involved dozens of video screens). The viewers had to follow all the screens simultaneously, their gaze had to make an effort to encompass the entirety and, "jumping," they also had to scan and "sail" a landscape of divergent video tapes. They often could not pause and "fall" or immerse just into *one* visual field (screen); rather, they had to cope with the divergence of images (and also these images' temporal divergence) in the entirety of their idiosyncratic appearances. In the daily life of the contemporary net surfer, such an approach is a familiar encounter. The posture at issue is by all means a tough one: It requires adjustable observation of and complex identification with the units of the web site which the surfer navigates either with the cursor or with the scroll bar and, secondly, it requires imaginative surfing of a surface which is now highly heterogeneous and complex and no longer homogenous. The latter is by no means a coincidence; rather, it is a requirement posed by the fundamental cultural paradigm of our day—simultaneous coexistence of divergent cultural contents and formats.

The very principle of plurality and non-conflicting coexistence of heterogeneous elements is characteristically demonstrated by the web site. Within the mass culture of the last decade, the web site has played a similar paradigmatic role as did the music video in the 1980s, shaped by a daring digital morph which provided for the swift transition of images one into another. What gave rise to this morph was the demand that within a few minutes a genuine world of images should be shaped in an extremely compact fashion, with the purpose of defining the locus of the music tape. Crucial to the understanding of the "philosophy" of the web site is its mosaic structure where documents of divergent origin are uploaded and piled, where they coexist and are placed side by side. Each has its own particular identity and exists in its own particular time, yet it easily coexists with other, equally complex documents taken from divergent contexts. Ours is an age of the simultaneity (in Michael Foucault's claim) of images, metaphors, discourses, concepts and scripts, and the computer screen with the graphic user interface providing for the coexistence of windows and even the simultaneity of various application operations is its symptomatic manifestation.

Watching several images at the same time, writing/reading divergent documents written within divergent datascapes, switching smoothly between various approaches—these are the requirements faced by the present-day adjustable user of the "pluriverse" of cultural contents; among them belong also the digital poetry pieces demanding such a sophisticated reading-viewing of a textscape divided on the multiple screens with moving texts (e.g., Maria Mencia's *Cityscapes*).

The Digital Text as a Naked Body

Today, animated digital poetry—as a field with its own specificity—provides us with a new, provocative and challenging form of experiencing 'cybertext' in terms of the word-image-movement that also is testing our senses (Strehovec 2000). However, beyond the efforts towards the organization of words in a form of moving images, cyber'language' also challenges the special effects within the basic form, how the words look like. Referring to the research done regarding the visual features of digital poetic words, one can mention texts by Mary Anne Breeze (Mez), who invented her "mezangelle"-language which combines English letters (English being her native language) with symbols taken from the programming languages and with ASCII symbols and punctuation marks, making the traditional, linear and loud reading procedure rather impossible. Mez uses a broad spectrum of various procedures and textual devices based on investigations of meanings under the condition of artificial juxtapositions, syllable and letter parataxis and interjections of the words. By using interjected words set off in square brackets, [she] also tries to demonstrate a wealth of new and daring associations. By parenthetically splitting words, Mez changes the dynamics of reading and creates new polysemantic structures within one word, as in this part of her *T.ex]/e]/ts:*

> Th[cs]is Mcs.sagc was[h my spacc with text, drench my wonne-tonne-wurdz in silken static and blend yr boundariez] un[der yr thumb, yr noze yr ovariez]liver[N kidneyz N prostrate[tingz]]sendable due to the follow[inge the stuporic superhighwaze]ing reas.on[N off, flik off N on]

Although the applied signs borrowed from the language of code do not work on the level of computing procedures, they grab ones attention through the very sophisticated metamorphosis of language within the new media paradigm, and via the fact that they are blurring the inflexible borders between various linguistic and textual practices. The (silent) reader is curious about the compound of letters that are fenced in within the square brackets (Mez's logo), implying the feeling of being threatened when they are set within non-bracketing clear spaces of the digital textuality.

By encountering this piece—which challenges, among others, both aestheticians and programmers—we come across a sort of textuality that stimulates feelings of the uncanny and can even be located near those streams of net art that deal with the malfunctioning of modern technology. Mez "netwurker's texts" can even be understood as a striking and sophisticated practice of an expanded concept of textuality using netspeak (in terms of David Crystal's analysis from his book *Language and the Internet*), the underlying programming and scripting languages and web visual culture devices. Text as a naked body? How can we come across this metaphor? Challenged by the phenomena of contemporary mainstream visual culture, Fredric Jameson has argued that

> . . . pornographic films are thus only the potentiation of films in general, which ask us to stare at the world as though it were a naked body. On the other hand, we know this today more clearly because our society has begun to offer us the world—now mostly a collection of products of our own making—as just such a body, that you can possess visually, and collect the images of. (1)

The main two emphases of this claim refer to the naked body and seeing in the form of staring; in other words, they draw upon two moments that challenge the thing (and those who produce it) as well as the perception of the viewer to pass into an intensified and enforced state. According to Jameson, it seems that a certain thing can enter the field of the mainstream visual culture precisely when it becomes as interesting, attractive and seductive as a naked, undressed body; the transformation concerns also the very nature of perceiving a certain thing as if it were a naked body, which means that seeing is not enough—that what is required is staring; in other words, a sophisticated process of seeing combined with additional affects and emotions connected with the astonishment at various things, as though they were naked bodies.

It seems that in today's culture a great number of things strive to be presented as naked bodies. It goes without saying that naked bodies (understood in the context of Jameson's aforementioned statement) can also be (fashionably) dressed bodies, as well as landscapes including lakes, mountains and deer, things and images of politics, of economy and the jet set, scenes from sporting events, etc. What is shown or staged can also be (well) dressed, "buttoned up," but it nevertheless functions as a naked body—meaning it possesses the function of attractiveness and seduction and, to put it simply, is for that reason worth staring at.

The demand of the text as a naked body, meant to be stared at, is by no means unknown to digital poetry as a linguistic art within the digital medium, attracting both the process of reading as well as a process of seeing, as is demonstrated by Brian Kim Stefans's "Thanks For Watching" at the end of his animated piece *The Dreamlife of Letters*. In searching within this paradigm, the authors are engaged with the challenge of a poem designed as a 3D object; that is—in terms of the reader's attention—a seductive body inviting the user's full immersion into such a virtual bodily environment. As a poetry project that enables the reader to experience the sensation of a poem as a (virtual) body, we can mention *open.ended* by Aya N. Karpinska and Daniel C. Howe. This text-based installation is designed to reveal itself through continually shifting geometric surfaces. Verses appear on the faces of two separate, translucent cubes situated within one another. To experience this piece, the reader manipulates a joystick or touch-screen to rotate the cubes, bringing lines on various surfaces into view. As cubes and faces and layers are manipulated by the reader, dynamically updated lines move in and out of focus. The structure of the poem allows it to be read in any number of ways; from single verses on cube faces to sequential verses across faces, to juxtapositions of verses across multiple cubes. We are facing a novel reading procedure that can be taken as a point of departure for our further investigation in the field of perception and cognition of digital poetry texts.

Researching digital poetry within a broader context of new media art means taking into consideration all its crucial paradigms as well as cultural turns in today's new media-shaped culture. One of the distinctive features of the present phenomenology of new cultural contents is the striking role of the body within the interface culture, in which the issues of materiality and even physicality come more and more into the foreground. Rather than being pushed aside or left behind as it was within the cyberpunk ideology of the 1980s and 90s, the body of the present nomadic individual armed with the nomadic screenic devices is becoming more and more crucially significant, even in terms of reinventing its novel tasks and functions. The body as our basic organ of having the world (Merleau-Ponty, *Phenomenology of Perception* 146) enters the novel ontological condition of the present mixed reality, determined by the hybridization and merging of in-between spaces and times, which challenge our ways of perception in terms of linking and amalgamating different perceptive acts and procedures. This paradigm, which implies a greater stress onto corporeal, motoric and tactile perception, is crucial also for the present new media art and digital poetry. It seems correct that the perception of new media contents is a dry run for detecting the consequences of this reinvention of the bodily activities within the new media arts and culture.

While we are drawing upon the poem designed as a cube by Aya N. Karpinska, we touch upon the present trend in designing the cultural contents within the 3D, e.g., physical approach, which stimulates the tactile (and haptic as well as motoric perception). Rather than consider the present culture just in terms of its striking visual features, we draw upon its tactility in terms of the mainstream endeavors striving to (re)present the cultural contents within the 3D fashion (e.g., as virtual bodies).

Reading, looking and listening are learned skills; their conventions and procedures are particular to any mass and new medium. Viewers are expected to look at paintings in a white cube in one way, and listen to the symphonic orchestra in Philharmonic Hall in a different way. Also, the new technologies of organizing and processing a text emerge with their own conventions and demands of reading. Along with the hybrid, complex, and heterogeneous nature of digital literary pieces, one can discover a similar complexity and the hybrid nature of procedures devoted to perception and cognition in this area. Reading in terms of decoding symbols for the purpose of deriving meaning gives way to not-just-reading[10] as an essentially more complex activity including both mental and corporeal arrangements. The not-just-reading directs the attention to a broader scope of user's activity. What is the very nature of such an activity? First of all, it is rich in performing features, even in terms of Paolo Virno's claim on virtuosity:

> Let us consider carefully what defines the activity of virtuosos, of performing artists. First of all, theirs is an activity which finds its own fulfilment (that is, its own purpose) in itself, without objectifying itself

into an end product, without settling into a "finished product," or into an object which would survive the performance. (Virno 52)

The crucial point here is the emphasis on the activity without the finished product, i.e., that after reading is terminated, nothing in terms of materiality and physicality is left behind. Aya N. Karpinska has described this new reading experience with the following words: "Instead of forcing the reader to go from left to right, I suggest that she reads front to back, as I am curious about when the transition from surface to depth occurs" ("The Arrival of the beeBox"). The digital poem in a 3D environment addresses the virtual reader, the one who can as an invisible avatar get a chance to enter the textual body of the poem or to possess a poem as a tangible object. Not just to write down a word, but to touch it, to possess it, to manipulate it tangibly are demands on the present individual who is accustomed to being fully immersed in her various everyday tasks. Rather than just read and watch a word, line or sentence, she is interested in grasping a word physically; having the digital word in her palm seems to present her with the full experience of the digital "text" and invites her into the enjoyment of it. Such a condition even implies a tactile feature of digital poetry, simulating bodily interactions between the poem's body and its reader-user: "The ability to rotate the whole poem gives the impression that it is an object, something one could hold between ones hands and gaze into" (Karpinska, "The Arrival of the beeBox").

In referring to Wardrip-Fruin's claim on the three levels of reading enabled by *Screen*, Rita Raley introduces a fourth type of reading in terms of *reading along the z-axis*: "That is, the user does not simply read the words as they circle around her but she also reads through and behind them to the text on the walls. In other words, it is deep reading in this other sense: reading volumetrically, reading surface to depth and back again" (2). However, the reader's experience in a Cave is not just about reading; digital text in a virtual environment is an experience that shapes the reader's more complex behavior: it hits a body and strikingly stimulates its activity. The traditional perspective places the observer outside the event space and excludes the bodily perception, reducing it to an "observation only" event. The 3D immersive text-based environments draw the reader-user into the object of vision/reading, within and among the words, and stimulate its tactile perception:

> The things of the world are not simply neutral *objects* which stand before us for our contemplation. Each one of them symbolises or recalls a particular way of behaving, provoking in us reactions which are either favourable or unfavourable. . . . Our relationship with things

is not a distant one: each speaks to our body and to the way we live. (Merleau-Ponty, *The World of Perception* 63)

In the moment the words come loose in a 3D virtual environment, they are the things Merleau-Ponty refers to; each of them speaks to our body, hits it, and challenges its complex behavior. The reader-user of *Screen* is a reader with a body, and her behavior is physical *par excellence*. And her reading is *not-just-reading*, it is a corporeal experiencing of words-in-motion, which includes kinesthetic and motoric activities, navigation, pushing, lifting and sending back the words, the hand with the data glove controlling the activities. Such an experience of a digital poem or a digital textscape is in the first place novel; it is enabled only by new media technologies (e.g., VR), which transform the reader into the user of an immersive environment and puts her into a kind of cockpit position. And, on the other hand, when the virtual words-images-bodies break loose and become extremely flexible, they are transformed into interactive and impressionable things that enable the new manner in which we approach and interact with them. Such things themselves become actors, affecting change through their observations and reading. They challenge the reader-user to become curious about what happens next, even as an aftermath of her experienced bodily activity in immersive textual environments.

Notes

1   The neologism cyber'language' refers to the language generated and shaped in the on-line communications, the programming and scripting languages, and cyberculture.

2   Cf. their performances at the *E-Poetry* festival in Paris 2007. A video of Karpinska's *Lala* is available at <http://technekai.com/lala/index.html>; information on Piringer's piece can be found at <http://www.epoetry2007.net/artists/oeuvres/piringer/piringer.html>.

3   Since 1997 the author of this essay has been dealing with the theoretical paradigms of, let us say, very experimental forms of digital literature that intersect the literary avant-garde, text-based installation art and various forms and genres of digital arts. In his paper *Text as Virtual Reality*, presented at the first *Digital Arts and Culture* conference in Bergen (1998), he had introduced the term "second order digital literature" in order to refer to digital writing, which is beyond hypertext that, in the 1990s, was regarded as a basic and the most talked about genre of digital literature.

4   This collection is rich in presenting the diversity of examples and trends in digital literature. However, it is weak in terms of the criteria by which the authors were included in it, for many important non-American authors were overlooked.

5   In Jason Nelson's *Dreamaphage* (Version 1, 2003), drag and drop on the screen causes a tunnel graphics effect; bold readable text appears just on certain screens during the user's fast immersion into an attractive visual environment saved on the simulator drive.

6   Both these terms are mine, and are to be explained in my second essay in this book.

7   The key point of this project about the malfunctioning of high-tech is corrupting the website by means of clicking its URL. Each time the site is visited, one of the characters that make up the html code is either deleted or replaced. This causes a step-by-step degeneration, not only of the site's content but also of its basic structure.

8   The essential cues how to approach this sophisticated language installation are found in the author's statement available at <http://www.hosted.simonbiggs.easynet.co.uk/rewrite/statement.htm>.

9   The seeing within the interface culture has ceased to be a pure act of contemplative vision of a distanced viewer; on the contrary, it interacts with one's tactile activities enabling a dynamic oscillation between visual and tactile feedback. Vision is activated by the movement of a hand, seeing (and reading) become tactile, and the new generations of words-images-bodies called onto the screen by means of navigational devices generate a new circle of tactile and kinesthetic activity.

10   I presented my paper "Not-Just-Seeing, Not-Just-Reading (On the perception and cognition of digital literature)," referring to the very sophisticated manner that the reading of digital pieces can look like, at CHArt 2008 24th annual conference at Birkbeck College, Univesity of London.

Works Cited

Alexander, Amy. *VJ Uebergeek CyberSpaceLand Showreel*. 2003. 10 Mar. 2009 <http://www.youtube.com/watch?v=UlM_fxF2VX4>.

Amerika, Mark. *Filmtext*. 2002. 10 Mar. 2009 <http://www.markamerika.com/filmtext/>.

Beiguelman, Giselle. *Poetrica*. 2003-2004. 11 Mar. 2009 <http://www.poetrica.net/english/index.htm>.

Biggs, Simon. *reWrite*. 1999. 10 Mar. 2009 <http://www.hosted.simonbiggs.easynet.co.uk/rewrite/index.htm>.

Bookchin, Natalie. *The Intruder*. 1999. 10 Mar. 2009 <http://www.bookchin.net/intruder/english/html/a_title.html>.

Burnett, Robert, and P. David Marshall. *Web Theory. An Introduction*. London: Routledge, 2003.

Crystal, David. *Language and the Internet*. Cambridge: Cambridge UP, 2001.

Flanagan, Mary. *[theHouse]*. 2006. 11 Mar. 2009 <http://www.maryflanagan.com/house/index.html>.

Heidegger, Martin. *Poetry, Language, Thought*. Trans. Albert Hofstadter. New York: Harper, 1975.

Ingarden, Roman. *The Cognition of the Literary Work of Art*. Trans. Ruth A. Crowley and Kenneth R. Olson. Evanston: Northwestern UP, 1973.

Jabès, Edmond. *Le Parcours*. Paris: Gallimard, 1985.

Jameson, Fredric. *Signatures of the Visible*. New York: Routledge, 1992.

Karpinska, Aya N. "The Arrival of the beeBox: An Exploration of Spatial Text." 2003. 11 Mar. 2009 <http://www.technekai.com/box/beeBoxPaper.pdf>.

Karpinska, Aya N., and Daniel C. Howe. *open.ended*. 2004. 11 Mar. 2009 <http://www.technekai.com/open/index.html>.

Larsen, Deena. *Carving in Possibilities*. 2001. 11 Mar. 2009 <http://www.collection.eliterature.org/1/works/larsen__carving_in_possibilities.html>.

Lister, Martin et al. *New Media: A Critical Introduction*. London: Routledge, 2003.

Manovich, Lev. *The Language of New Media*. Cambridge, MA: MIT P, 2001.

Marinetti, Filippo T. *Selected Writings*. Ed. R. W. Flint. Trans. R.W. Flint and Arthur A. Coppotelli. New York: Farrar, 1971.

Mencia, Maria. *Cityscapes: Social Poetics/Public Textualities*. 2007. 11 Mar. 2009 <http://www.epoetry2007.net/english/artiststxts/mencia.pdf>.

Merleau-Ponty, Maurice. *Phenomenology of Perception*. Trans. Colin Smith. London: Routledge and Kegan, 1998.

―――. *The World of Perception*. London: Routledge, 2004.

Mez, Mary A. Breeze. *T.ex]/e]/ts.* 1995. 11 Mar. 2009 <http://www.netwurkerz.de/mez/datableed/complete/index2.htm>.

Nelson, Jason. *Dreamapaghe.* 2003 (V. 1). 11 Mar. 2009 <http://www.collection.eliterature.org/1/works/nelson__dreamaphage.html>.

Raley, Rita. "Editor's Introduction: Writing.3D." 2006. 11 Mar. 2009 <http://www.uiowa.edu/~iareview/mainpages/new/september06/raley/Writing3D.pdf>.

Shklovsky, Victor. "Art as Technique." *Russian Formalist Criticism. Four Essays.* Ed. and trans. Lee T. Lemon and Marion J. Reis. Nebraska: U of Nebraska P, 1965. 25-57.

Snow, Charles P. *The Two Cultures.* New York: Cambridge UP, 1993.

Stefans, Brian K. *The Dreamlife of Letters.* 2000. 11 Mar. 2009 <http://www.ubu.com/contemp/stefans/dream/index.html>.

Strehovec, Janez. "The Moving Words." *Cybertext Yearbook 2000.* Ed. Markku Eskelinen and Raine Koskimaa. Jyväskylä: Research Centre for Contemporary Culture, 2002. 100-116.

Tisselli, Eugenio. *Degenerative.* 2005. 11 Mar. 2009 <http://www.motorhueso.net/degenerative/>.

Utterback, Camille, and Romy Achituv. *Text Rain.* Installation. 1999. 11 Mar. 2009 <http://www.camilleutterback.com/movies/textrain_mov.html>.

Virno, Paolo. *A Grammar of the Multitud:. For an Analysis of Contemporary Forms of Life.* Trans. Isabella Bertoletti et al. New York: Semiotext(e), 2004.

Wardrip-Fruin, Noah. "Digital Literature." Interview with Roberto Simanowski. 2004. *Dichtung Digital* 6.2 (2004). 11 Mar. 2009 <http://www.dichtung-digital.org/2004/2-Wardrip-Fruin.htm>.

Wardrip-Fruin et al. *Screen.* Quicktime documentation. 2004. 11 Mar. 2009 <http://www.uiowa.edu/~iareview/tirweb/feature/cave/ScreenProfile2004_HiFi.mov>.

Zervos, Komninos: *Beer.* 11 Mar. 2009 <http://othervoicespoetry.org/vol11/zervos/>.

Part Two:
Teaching Digital Literature

Roberto Simanowski

Teaching Digital Literature

Didactic and Institutional Aspects

1 Making Students Fit for the 21st Century

When Nam Jun Paik in the last two decades of the 20th century created video installations confronting the audience with multiple screens which the spectator had to follow by simultaneously jumping from one to another while scanning them all for information, Paik was training his audience for the tasks of the 21st century. With this notion, Janez Strehovec situates our topic within the broader cultural and social context of new media that redefine the areas of economy, sciences, education, and art, stressing the importance of new media literacy in contemporary society. Such literacy not only consists of the ability to read, write, navigate, alter, download and ideally program web documents (i.e., reading non-linear structures, being able to orient oneself within a labyrinthic environment). It also includes the ability to identify with the cursor, the avatar and with virtual space, to travel in spatially and temporally compressed units without physical motion, to carry out real-time activities, and to undertake associative selection, sampling and reconfiguration resembling DJ and VJ culture.

In Strehovec's perspective (in his essay in Part One), the stakes are very high. The aesthetics of the Web teaches the logic of contemporary culture but also the needs of contemporary multicultural society. The mosaic structure of a web site with documents of divergent origin each with its own particular identity and time, the simultaneity of divergent documents, artifacts, and media teaches us, according to Strehovec, to live with the coexistence of conflicting concepts, discourses, and cultures. For this reason it will, as Strehovec holds, also teach us to accept the divergence of life we encounter spatially compressed in modern cities. Such a perspective suggests that the Internet is the appropriate medium for the ethical needs of a globalizing world. It should not be ignored that—in contrast to such rather positive accounts—some scholars have pointed out new forms of "segregation" and "balkanization" on the Internet which foster the "daily me" or "daily we" rather than the attitude of the polyvocal, multicultural, cosmopolitan person (Sunstein; Bell; Doheny-Farina). While this is not the place to debate the pros and cons of these different perspectives,[1] we should pin down two important aspects regarding Strehovec's reference to art history.

1. When Paik remixed content taken from TV, he changed the nature of the material used; i.e., he turned it into art. The effect was the initiation of a meta-reflection about this material and consequently a deconstruction of its underlying claim to represent the truth. Shifting information from everyday life to the realm of art undermines any automatism and certainty in the process of signification effective in quotidian communication. The hope is that such de-automatization eventually also affects the non-artistic discourse and makes people reflect the matters of communication and representation in general; i.e., when they see similar material untouched by Paik next time on TV.

2. While Paik's installations of multiple videos invited questioning and mistrusting the material presented, such teaching took place in a "classroom" accessed only by the interested few of the art-world, especially the art of video installations. A similar paradigmatic role as Paik's video installations can be stated about the music video with its speedy transition between different images, though in this case the classroom was filled with a much broader audience. With the Internet, the classroom has moved to the "streets" and includes, in those countries where electronic media play a central role, everybody who does not shy away from new media.

The role of digital literature in this context may appear to be rather small, especially if one associates it with print literature in contrast to the entertaining mass media cinema, radio and television prevailing today.[2] As reports from the National Endowment for the Arts state, reading has declined among U.S. adults at a rate of 14 % between 1992-2002, in contrast to a 5 % rate of decline the decade before ("Reading at Risk" X). Even when reading occurs, it increasingly competes with other media; i.e., reading time is shared by watching TV, playing video games, or surfing the Web which "suggest less focused engagement with a text" ("To Read or Not To Read" 10). However, as the discussion in the first part of this book has illustrated, digital literature is very different from the old medium of the elite, uniting a variety of media with linguistic, not-just-linguistic and non-linguistic practices. It seems to be the perfect art for the "hybrid-culture," as Karin Wenz puts it in her essay, blurring the boundaries not only between media but also between high- and low-brow culture as well as between the two cultures Charles Percy Snow once distinguished with respect to the natural sciences and the humanities.[3] This hybrid, cross media artefact also seems to be the perfect place to teach *transliteracy*: the ability to read, write and interact across a range of platforms, tools and media.[4] As Dene Grigar concludes a discussion on the future of electronic literature:

> if indeed students spend 10 times more of their energy with fingers on a keyboard instead of a nose in a book, then it stands to reason that we should rethink our notion of literacy and advocate elit [electronic literature] as not only viable but also compelling art form for teaching all aspects of reading, writing, and communicating. ("Electronic Literature")[5]

In addition to blurring the boundaries between cultures, digital literature also blurs the boundary between the student and the teacher who, as Peter Gendolla, Jörgen Schäfer, and Patricia Tomaszek point out, is very often not much more advanced (if at all) compared to the students' knowledge about the subject. While the teacher may know more about the contextualization of digital literature within the history of literature and the arts, the students are likely to possess more *media literacy* regarding achieving, navigating, processing and manipulating data online. This has an enormous effect on the situation in the classroom. Teaching digital literature is not just the continuation of teaching conventional literature with other means; it aims at making the student fit for the 21st century multi-media society and it starts with making the teacher fit for meeting her students.

Given the students' interest in digital media we may, together with Astrid Ensslin and James Pope, also assume a great interest in digital literature as a narrative form which can combine attractive interactivity with engaging narratives delivered via digital media, encompassing the language of books, films, web pages, radio, etc. However, Ensslin and Pope are well aware of the problems that trouble this narrative form: a fractured narrative structure, a confusing navigation system, low level of reader absorption, and the question of narrative closure. While such problems have not allowed hyperfictions to become as popular as scholars expected and predicted in the 1990s, they are unknown in the less narrational genres of digital literature such as kinetic poetry. In contrast to many, though not all, examples of concrete poetry in print, kinetic poetry does not emphasize form and structure at the expense of play and pleasure; it rather allows the words to rediscover their power of seduction, as Alexandra Saemmer puts it in her discussion of Brian Kim Stefans' *The Dreamlife of Letters* (cf. her essay in Part One). Saemmer considers the acoustic, visual, kinetic and interactive voice of digital poetry more closely related to the Surrealist experiences than to Concrete or Lettrist experimentations. In a similar vein, Strehovec (in his essay in Part One) understands Stefans' piece in terms of "voyeurism," for it is as interesting and seductive to the eye as is the naked body. Strehovec argues with Frederic Jameson who, in his seminal book *Signatures of the Visible*, considers the visual essentially pornographic because "it has its end in rapt, mindless fascination:" pornographic films are thus "only the potentiation of films in general, which ask us to stare at the world as though it were a naked body" (1). The endnote in *The Dreamlife of Letters*—"Thanks for watching"—seems to confirm the disconnecting of the (kinetic) visual from careful reading.

However, Saemmer's analysis in Part One demonstrates that it is still possible to undertake a careful reading of moving text beyond staring at it with astonishment and affection. In fact, since such amusing experimentations also more or less explicitly emphasize form and structure of the language involved, they seem to be a perfect link to the *Geist* of the new time: while still being involved in the concept of linguistic signification, with visual, sonic, performative and interactive elements they embed this old cultural practice in newer cultural practices, combining the joy of play with the opportunity of reflection. Digital literature, we may even state, is the inevitable link between the Gutenberg Galaxy and new media. As Noah Wardrip-Fruin puts it: Since computational systems are increasingly used as a means of expression, the careful reading of digital literature will help us understand how to make meaningful, sophisticated use of this means. Digital literature will teach us about our dealing with technology, about textual practices, and about contemporary understanding of art and culture. It does not signify a shift from traditional literary literacy to media literacy, as *information literacy* for the discussion of digital literature does not aim at the sufficient management of information but rather at the critical reflection of the ways information is presented.

While Strehovec points out the link between digital literature and contemporary pop culture, John Zuern holds that digital literature can break some of the powerful enchantments of a culture industry since it alienates our expectations about, for example, what constitutes literature and about how digital technology is supposed to work. As for Strehovec, the stakes are high for Zuern as well. He refers to James Engall's and Anthony Dangerfield's 2005 book *Saving Higher Education in the Age of Money* which urges recovering the university's fundamental mission—the cultivation of imaginative, compassionate, broadly informed citizens—from the increasingly utilitarian, profit-driven co-optation of higher education by commercial interests. Digital literature, Zuern even holds, is a good way to exercise *sophrosyne* because it requires a concentrated effort to assemble evidence, follow up on leads, and weigh alternative interpretations. In a similar vein Saemmer, underlining with Jacques Rancière the "systematic difference" of art and literature compared to regular practices of communication, states that working with digital literature constitutes an excellent way of teaching students to reflect on the use of digital language, media and culture. In contrast to regular web sites that confirm our reading habits, literary and artistic digital works make us aware of the automatisms and standardizations in digital media and let us question them—for instance by boycotting the common rule of immediate satisfaction of the customer's desire for information or by offering seemingly "irrelevant" links (as discussed in Saemmer's essay in Part One). Digital literature can offer a critical approach to the conventions of digital language indispensable for a concept of digital literacy that is not reduced to the mere management of information and acquisition of technical skills.

Such a focus on digital literature as an "alteration of likeness," to apply Rancière's definition of art and literature (14), suggests an analysis of digital literature in the spirit of a semiotic reading rather than with the focus on the social context. While questions relating to how a work of digital literature is produced and consumed—writing technology, authorship, copyright, distribution, access, etc.—certainly need to be raised and are well established as research methods in literary studies, the semiotic analysis is more formal and internally driven, drawing attention to characteristics of language in digital media (letters, links, colors, shapes, sound, processing, interaction) and to codes of meaning. The goal of this approach is to learn how to read a digitally produced sign, how to understand a specific performance within a piece of digital literature. The "reading" this book announces within its title aims at this kind of semiotic analys: reading a given text or artwork respectively for its meaning rather than reading for the social context of its production and perception. Needless to say, such an approach does not prevent the inclusion of the social context into the analysis of the meaning of a particular artwork. While consequently the agenda of this book can be seen in the tradition of hermeneutics typical of literary studies, it is obvious that the interdisciplinary nature of digital literature makes it difficult to locate the discussion of this subject within the traditional academic institutions of literature.

2   Finding the Proper Institutional Home

It may not come as a surprise that a subject connected to so many areas, lacking—to put it this way—the discipline to fit into traditional categories (after all, it sometimes can't even decide whether it wants to be literature or art or just applied technology), is still in search of an academic discipline that understands it as its own genuine subject of research. The contributions in this part of the book (and to a degree also in Part One) report on the institutional obstacles of this search as well as on the almost ideal situations in some other rare instances.

The nature of the obstacles is not only political in terms of institutional agendas and departmental identities, but also even in terms of national politics, as reported by Strehovec about Slovenia. This small nation whose language has always been under threat throughout the course of history is not at the forefront in implementing digital literature into the curricula of literary studies given the dubious relationship of digital literature to language, let alone its general leaning to English as the *lingua franca* of the globalized world. The issue is, as Strehovec points out, of a highly political nature. National ideologists consider national literature the only important subject of the patriotic intellectual and "good" Slovenian, which is in line with the great financial and mental support writers experience in Slovenia. In such a political environment, digital literature cannot expect governmental support and therefore relies fully on individual initiative and idealism.

In France, one reason for the reluctance of literary studies to embrace digital literature is, as Saemmer notes, the competitive examination. Most students in literature departments are being educated as primary and secondary school teachers and eventually have to pass a highly standardized examination, focusing on French language and literature, with a rigid corpus of literary works that contains only contemporary writers who are already canonical. Since digital literature is not based on a business model but is mostly available free of charge, the digital "novelties of the year" do not enter the spotlight of the "Rentrée littéraire"—an annual event in September drawing a lot of media attention to contemporary literature. Certainly, the wrong business model is not the only and probably not the central reason for the lack of attention. Of more importance may be the lack of (a) discipline, as Saemmer concludes her essay: Because of its multimedial, intersemiotic and technological character involving creative and interpretative abilities from text and film analysis to programming, from rhetoric to sound engineering, digital literature could have a place anywhere—and has one nowhere.

What Saemmer reports for France is also true elsewhere: In addition to the intermedial nature of digital literature, the specifics of its distribution turn out to be disadvantageous for its inclusion in literary studies. If then literary studies, as is the case in France and many other countries, is affected by the drastic reduction of financial support, the more likely reaction is the concentration on the "fundamental," classical content of the discipline rather than on new experiments the merits of which are not yet proven and officially established[6] and which, more or less, turn away from language anyway. It may happen, as was the case in German Studies at the U.S.-American Brown University, for example, that a department of literary studies develops an interest in these new experiments precisely because of their experimental character, hoping to attract students by offering cutting-edge-classes on the latest developments in the field of literature. However, if the aptness of such a subject for a literary studies department is questioned, if the interdisciplinary nature of the subject collides with the established regulations for enrollments and course credits (e.g., if such a course on digital literature first of all attracts students from Computer Science, Media, Visual and Performance Studies who don't speak German and don't intend to major in German Studies), if the department realizes all the administrative difficulties and professional consequences of designing interdisciplinary and interdepartmental courses, it will rethink its aspirations to shake up the order of disciplines and refocus on classical, canonized content.[7]

It should be said that the obstacles of including digital literature into literary studies not only derive from the ambivalent role of text in digital literature but also from the organization of literary studies based on specific "national" languages. Works of digital literature very often use English as the *lingua franca* in accordance to the increasing importance of globally accessible cultural expressions and to the decreasing role of language in digital literature. Hence, many examples of digital literature by Germans, for instance, are not in German and hence it is not surprising that Koskimaa's course on digital literature contains only one lecture dealing specifically with Finnish digital literature. Nevertheless, the prevalence of English does not mean that English departments are more likely to include digital literature in their curricula. Thus, Grigar notes for the U.S.:

> English departments that rely on teacher training in secondary education for their bread and butter also neglect teaching elit because, frankly, the demands of testing and classroom instruction leave little room for non-conventional content.

The emphasis is on the delivery of traditional literary content; the lack of access to computers or an overhead projection system in the classroom counts, as Grigar knows from personal experience, for additional obstacles to discuss literature that can't be provided in print.[8]

The situation is easier at universities devoted to cross-departmental cooperation to the extent that courses have not only an interdisciplinary goal in mind, but are also planned and organized by a team of two or three colleagues, as Wenz reports for the Faculty of Arts and Social Sciences at Maastricht University and Maastricht University College. The situation is also easier at departments whose particular focus is, from the first day of their foundation, on the technological and media context in which literary texts are being written, distributed, and read. This is the case with the Department of Language, Literary and Media Studies at the University of Siegen where such a focus soon included questions of how texts are transformed into other media such as film or radio play and, subsequently and consequently, into computer-based media as well as the internet. As a result, the department developed a distinctive profile within the new academic discipline of Media Studies, eventually leading to the foundation of the research group "Literature on the Net/Net Literature" aiming at the analysis of literature in computer-based and networked media. It is also consequential that this research group soon developed an international network and established a transatlantic cooperation with the research on and practice of digital literature carried out at Brown University, of which one result is a joint publication like this book, as well as mutual teaching activities described in detail in the essay by Gendolla, Schäfer and Tomaszek.

The implicit answer to Strehovec's account of the nationalism of literary studies in Slovenia is John Zuern's call (in his essay in Part One) for modernized comparative literature studies attentive to the various forms of expression and figuration not only in different national cultures but also in different media. Zuern underlines that both comparative literature and digital literature already have in common a retooled definition of literature: the former addressing the dominance of national (and more recently Euro-American) conceptions of literary culture, the latter the dominance of the linguistic dimension. Remarkable, though, is Zuern's analogy between the status of the "national" for comparative literature studies and the "digital" for research on computer-based literary texts. Both, Zuern's position could be paraphrased, are myths that need to be overcome for while the "national language" represents a set of linguistic skills all serious students of literature must master, it is also an ideological category configuring our research agendas. Similarly, though the codes and processes that comprise digital textuality are important to the understanding of the subject, the "special pleading for the digital impedes our access to each artwork's 'literary singularity.'" According to Zuern, the preoccupation with the digital "limits the potential of our studies of digital literature to make meaningful contributions to the study of literature broadly conceived as an academic discipline."

Such concerns play less of a role if the study of digital literature is located not in the field of literary but in media studies, which by many scholars is considered the better, more appropriate institutional home for digital literature. While other aesthetic experiments in digital media such as digital composition, painting, animation, or installation are much more integrated into their "natural" institutional homes (Music, Visual Studies, Film Studies or Performance Studies), the hybrid character of digital literature necessitates finding it a new home. The situation becomes clear with regard to the United Kingdom where, as Ensslin and Pope report, digital literature gained entrance to special interest groups of the Poetics and Linguistics Association on narrative and multimodality (PALA). The attention of the PALA, however, does not help the fact that the discussion of digital literature mostly takes place not in the English literature curriculum but in Media and Creative Studies departments.

A different way is pursued in Finland where Raine Koskimaa offers his class on digital literature at the University of Jyväskylä within the Department of Art and Culture Studies at the Faculty of Humanities as a part of the Master's Degree Program in Digital Culture. At this university, the education of techno-culturally savvy humanities graduates is closely connected to the traditional master programs such as art history, contemporary culture studies, or literature. Students majoring in those programs are able to add some digital culture specialization to their "traditional" degrees; i.e., graduating with an MA in literature with expertise concerning the role of literature and literary studies within the contemporary digital culture. This seems to be a promising model to settle the tension between the supra-departmental nature of digital literature and the departmental model of most academic institutions. It is important to note that the Faculty of Humanities at the University of Jyväskylä does not grant hospitality to digital culture as an act of generosity; it grants it in order to update its own structure with the aim of attracting more international students. Such updating seems to be the inevitable answer to the "increasingly flimsy shelter" academic institutions offer, as Zuern (in his essay in Part One) states, to the study of literature and the humanities as a whole. In the same vein as Zuern expects rescue especially from the "revitalization of comparative literature" through the inclusion of new forms of literature or "new horizons for the literary" (as N. Katherine Hayles subtitles her book on electronic literature), others, noting the struggling of English for survival and the rising enrollment in digital media programs, consider the incorporation of technology in English classes "one potent method for saving the Humanities" (Grigar).

The institutional in-between-identity of digital literature translates into every course on this subject concerning content and structure. This is already addressed when Koskimaa (in his essay in Part One), situates digital literature within the triangle of literature, cinema, and games, and admits that some literary cybertexts may be better classified as games or (interactive) cinema. Holding, as Koskimaa does, that "literature" should be acknowledged as a historically changing concept and that the literary world should be kept open to new developments requests courses on the new developments of literature either in literary studies departments or, as is the case at Koskimaa's university, as part of an interdisciplinary digital culture program also offered to and required for majors in literary studies. However, the issue is not only one of different branches of the humanities but also one between the humanities and the technical sciences. Koskimaa asks whether the code is part of the work and to what extent it needs to be factored in to the reading of the work. The counterpart of this question reads: Is there any meaning in the code?

Computer Science teaches students about data structures and algorithms and limits the forms of interpretation to issues such as efficiency, maintainability, and elegance. So also is the observation of Wardrip-Fruin, who stresses that students must also develop "procedural literacy," i.e., be able to read computational processes through an interpretive lens and understand the meaning of computational processes rather than just the way they are programmed. Wardrip-Fruin knows that such literacy is hardly practiced in computer science classes and proposes courses like the one offered by Michael Mateas when he was at Georgia Tech with the goal of *procedural literacy*. To be sure, Wardrip-Fruin is in no way disregarding the knowledge taught in computer science classes, and he also underlines that in order to fully understand the meaning of a computational process, it is often mandatory to understand the technical specifics and to know how the particularities of the given software shapes the work we see. This position, which may appear as an objection to Zuern's warning against a "special pleading for the digital" (though Zuern would certainly agree on the importance of basic programming skills) and which, after all, is to be expected by a professor of computer science whose dissertation on digital literature is entitled *Expressive Processing*, is shared by Koskimaa, himself trained in literary studies, who equally stresses the importance of a general understanding of how computer programs work referring, like Wardrip-Fruin, to Mateas' concept of *procedural literacy*.

Such appreciation of the computational procedure is also the reason why courses on digital literature at Maastricht University offer an additional skills training course teaching the creation of ones own web log, web site, digital video or podcast. The practical experience, Wenz notes in this respect, provides students with a better understanding of both the possibilities and the limitations of digital technology. In contrast to colleges and universities in the U.S., however, Maastricht (and most universities in Europe) does not offer courses in creative writing which then could also include digital media, as is the case for instance at Brown University where a well-known fiction writer (Robert Coover) and a well-known author of digital poetry (John Cayley) organize and conduct classes on writing with/in digital media at the Literary Arts department. As a result, students at Maastricht may increase their digital literacy attending skills teaching classes, but do not venture to produce their own works of digital literature.

While without doubt the understanding of the technological framework is important for an informed, thorough reading of a digital artwork, one also needs to know how to analyze aspects of the work due not to the particularities of the software but to the aesthetic and semantic considerations of the author. Students need to become familiar with the approaches and concepts in both fields—the humanities and arts as well as computer science. This is equally true for their teachers, though it is obvious that the generation of teachers educated in both fields has still to be raised, namely from the current generation of students taught by different teachers who themselves have not yet adequately bridged these two fields. Considering the probable situation in the classroom today, students in a course on digital literature may have to confront the fact that they often know more than the teacher. At the same time, the difference of expectable knowledge among the potential students in such a class presents an additional pedagogic challenge. While students of computer science, for example, will possibly know a lot about information technologies and electronic networks but little about literature and the arts, just as possibly students of literary studies will be familiar with literary theories and philosophical concepts but only have a vague idea of the impact coding has on writing and reading. The question is: How to make this situation productive within the course? What are the most effective steps to involve such student body in the reading of specific examples of digital literature?

3 The Practice of Discussing Digital Literature

Since the 1990s, universities have gradually implemented courses on the general functioning of digital technology and media; i.e., the operating systems of the computer, word and image processing, data management such as research, creation, manipulation, presentation and archiving of information as well as video-conferencing tools. There are quite a lot of opportunities for students today to learn the basic skills of digital technology. However, as stated before, digital literacy must not be limited to the *practical* management of information but should also include the *semiotic* processing of information. In fact, this semiotic processing should be the central task of courses on digital literature: How are semiotic processes influenced by data processing and vice versa? The dual nature of digital literature thereby makes it important to teach a reflective engagement with both languages involved, the natural language that makes the piece at hand a work of *literature* as well as the computational language that makes it a work of *digital* literature.

The task of combining the practice of hermeneutics and programming in courses on digital literature is well understood. Regarding programming skills, these are in many cases, if not in most, practiced during the creation of ones own example of digital literature as part of the class or in additional, parallel skills trainings. Regarding the hermeneutic approach, Wenz notes two general obstacles to the discussion of digital literature in the classroom:

1. The multi-linear, recursive and endless structure of hyperfiction results in different reading experiences regarding the sequence in which students have read the hypertext as well as the proportion of its segments visited.

2. There are hardly any thorough interpretations or commentaries by critics available yet so that students are left completely on their own, unable to confirm the validity and persuasiveness of their readings.

In this context María Goicoechea aptly states that the "disappearance of the fixed text" deeply affects the traditional reading pact between the author and her audience as well as the relationship between the teacher and her students. To rephrase the circumstances with respect to the pedagogic challenge: The teacher is left on her own to not only combine the different experiences of the work (in terms of navigation and interaction) but also to judge the different interpretations of these different experiences. This situation certainly requires didactic sophistication, including the ability to accept different answers and to leave questions open even (or rather: especially) after a thorough discussion with the students

This position is adopted by Zuern whose students raised, with respect to the discussed work *Hermeticon: Pop Spell Maker* by Jason Nelson, all the predictable questions: How are we supposed to read this? What does it mean? To what extent is this literature? As Zuern states, they (he and his students) were in the end "unable, and for the most part unwilling, to answer in any definitive way." What was more important was that the work discussed made everybody address these questions in the first place, and that the attempt to make sense of this work called upon skills in textual analysis, research, and reasoning important to any student of literature: to recognize instances of figuration, including literary tropes and tropes in the work's programming and interface design; to follow up on unfamiliar words, references, and intertextual allusions with research into the relevant linguistic, historical, social, and cultural contexts; to make adequately supported arguments about the implications of the discoveries. Zuern's description of his class on Nelson's *Hermeticon* provides a good example of how the main principle of literary-critical training—to follow up on each aspect of a text that is unfamiliar and strikes us as significant—can be applied to digital literature. Remarkable is not only that Zuern's search for figuration in Nelson's *Hermeticon* looks beyond the text and includes the protocols of Flash's ActionScript programming to find more evidence of *Hermeticon's* tropological activity, but also that the text chunks triggered (together with images) by the user's keystrokes were finally googled. This leads us to Giordano Bruno and the era of Humanism, in which taking individual words and phrases from important literary works was common, reassembling them in new combinations and associating them with completely different persons or situations. With such a cultural background, the aleatoric combinations in *Hermeticon* eventually appear as an updated and ironic version of earlier attempts to read fate by submitting one's reading to chance.

A common starting point for the discussion of the meaning of a particular work is to assign students to explain what attracts them to this particular work. With respect to digital literature, students should also tell how (and how often) they have navigated the work, what they consider the core structure of it, what content they expect behind a certain link. As Ensslin and Pope demonstrate, one way of organizing this discussion is through the use of reading logs as for example Jess Laccetti created as part of her "education pack" for the multilingual and multimedial work-in-progress *Inanimate Alice* by Kate Pullinger and Chris Joseph. It is surprising that these "close reading logs"—which are to be filled out by the students—provide a column for "information" and one for "interpretation," helping students to differentiate between explicature and implicature, but no column for the specific categories of interactive literary hypermedia such as navigation, intermedial interplay and metatextuality. Despite this traditional methodology, which needs to be modified by individual tutors, Laccetti's course on *Inanimate Alice* illustrates very well how such an interactive literary hypermedia work allows discussing various aesthetic and poetic aspects of literature and art. Thus, students' attention is drawn to the timing, emotive effects, and meaning of auditory signals; the strategic location of directional arrows; the use of color; the interplay of music, sound and image; the narratological aspect of the autobiographical genre and the *Bildungsroman*. When students eventually generate (with a user-friendly software) an audio-visually annotated autobiography planner in storyboard form and fill in an autobiography reflection form, the course combines the reflective with the creative.

In a similar way, Koskimaa shows how the hyperfiction *These Waves of Girls* by Caitlin Fisher not only allows teachers to demonstrate hypertextual rhetorics; it also permits introducing modern and postmodern concepts such as autobiographical pact, unreliable narration, dramatic irony, association and intertextuality. The example of digital literature leads to the discussion of aspects important to conventional literature as well. Thus, Goicoechea points out that the hyperlink only makes explicit the baroque use of intertextual allusions that was a general tendency in modernist and postmodernist prose prior to the advent of hypertext. In the same vein, Wenz introduces digital literature not with the focus on its contrast to conventional literature, but rather she uses the hyperlink—and other navigational tools in digital literature such as the threads in Michael Joyce's hyperfiction *Twelve Blue*—as a starting point to discuss the concept of textuality as "interwoven" semiotic structure. As Wenz points out, other hyperfictions—such as Esther Hunziker's and Felix Zbinden's *edinburgh/demon*—can, due to their "cuts"-technique, be discussed with respect to the tradition of film making (i.e., "directors cut," montage). It is obvious that the sonic, intermedial and performative elements of digital literature eventually lead to the question "What is literature?" and to the comparison of the narrative potential in different media such as written texts, images, comics, movies, hyperfiction and digital games. The various genres of digital literature also allow for the connection to other artistic experiments and cultural practices such as sound and visual poetry, happenings, theatre and DJ shows.

However, it is equally obvious that the hyperlink not only represents continuity between conventional and digital literature but also innovative reading experiences or "new reading pleasure at finding unexpected effects," as Goicoechea phrases it. Goicoechea examplifies her notion with the hypertext *Book-Butterflies* by the Argentinean writer Belén Gache, who states in the introduction that writing detains and crystallizes, "kills the words and keeps its corpse . . . like a desiccated butterfly" and then provides eight images of butterflies each linking to various quotes from literary works interconnected only through the reference to butterflies. In a way, this simple string of crystallized words about butterflies decrystallizes the linguistic "corpses" again by their endless combination and confrontation. The pleasure of this reading is—beyond Goicoechea's notion of combining the quotes and recognizing their sources—the endlessness and responsiveness (responding to the reader's click-action) of this combination that exceeds the effect of a similar listing of quotes in conventional literature.

At the Department of Language, Literary and Media Studies at the University of Siegen, the subject of digital literature is approached and discussed within a two-semester seminar. While the first part is an introduction to the role of media in the process of producing, distributing and perceiving literature (i.e., the net of literature or—to apply Pierre Bourdieu's language—the "literary field"), the second investigates the development of new literary forms under the influence of computer technology and discusses important epistemological concepts in this context such as intentionality/chance, performativity/performance, emergence as well as game/play (i.e., net literature and its aesthetics). Interestingly, the first seminar pursues a top-down approach (introducing ideas and concepts to the students), whereas the second favors a bottom-up approach (allowing students self-exploring activities in class). Gendolla, Schäfer, and Tomaszek admit that due to the academic background of its teachers (coming from literary and media studies but not from computer science), this seminar is very much focused on historic contextualization as well as theoretical and aesthetical issues: authorship, structure, perception, meaning, evaluation.

Wenz underlines that teaching at the University of Maastricht is conceptualized as problem-based learning, which means that learning is approached as an enquiry-based, collaborative enterprise starting off with concrete problems and research questions. Part of this concept is, for example, the production of a journal on the subject of digital literature, with self-written articles whose drafts are peer-reviewed within the class. As Wenz explains later, the concept of problem-based learning includes informing the students about the problems the lecturers themselves encounter in their work as researchers. This frankness reflects the experiences inevitably made in a very young research field lacking not only thorough interpretations or commentaries by critics to check the strength of ones own reading, but also established criteria and methods to evaluate the quality of a digital work. The lack of commanding references and criteria on the teacher's side is accompanied by advanced media literacy on the student's side. This combination changes the classroom situation fundamentally and may appear frightening to some teachers. Others—the majority, we hope—will consider it a solid foundation for a long-lasting cooperation between students and teachers negotiating (by way of closely reading the artifacts of new technologies) the old hermeneutic question: What does it mean?

Notes

1 For the relationship of Internet and democracy cf. my discussion of "Online-Nation" in Simanowski (216-245).

2 Of course, we must not forget that literature is a mass medium as well and that in the end of the 18th century its use as a means of distraction had caused disappointment and anger among intellectuals and thinkers of the Enlightenment.

3 Unless stated differently, references to contributors aim at their articles in Part Two.

4 For this definition of *transliteracy* and for its concept cf. the paper by Sue Thomas et al., Professor of New Media at De Montfort University, Leicester, UK, at <http://www.uic.edu/htbin/cgiwrap/bin/ojs/index.php/fm/article/view/2060/1908>.

5   It may not come as a surprise that, in its position statement of 2006 "Resolution on the Essential Roles and Values of Literature in the Curriculum" <http://www.ncte.org/positions/statements/valueofliterature>, the National Council of Teachers of English reacts to the decline in the reading of books by promoting the love of print literature rather than by extending its agenda to include non-conventional forms of literature in digital media.

6   The issue of merits or aesthetic quality is not new to literary studies, as we know from recurring canon-debates. However, while mediocre (or to put it this way: less relevant) conventional literature (and film) is more or less included into curricula on the ground of its popularity and suitability to address issues of form and content, digital literature obviously has to demonstrate at least relevance if it can't claim popularity. As understandable as this reaction might be, it is shortsighted not to discuss new forms of aesthetic expression in digital media until the "masterpiece" has arrived.

7   In the case of German Studies at Brown University, the aspirations originally had been very high and the department was fully aware of what was at stake stating, in its proposal for a new graduate program "German Texts in the Age of Digital Media" in 2002: "Should Brown—hopefully in the not too distant future—rethink the departmental model, we would be among the first ones to welcome such a change and adopt our program accordingly."

8   Grigar points out exceptions such as the English Departments at Duke University and Yale University that show commitment to digital literature by hiring noted theorist N. Katherine Hayles and Jessica Pressman, respectively (2008). We should add that the English Department at the University of California, Santa Barbara, is also aiming at the integration of digital culture, arts, and literature within the core work of a traditional humanities discipline: Alan Liu (chair of the department) in his 2004 study *The Laws of Cool: Knowledge Work and the Culture of Information* impressively demonstrates how, after Adorno, current cultural developments can be discussed critically in an up to date manner, and Rita Raley (director of the department's Literature.Culture.Media center), with *Tactical Media* and other works, provides a critical exploration of art-activism and narratological innovations in new media.

Works Cited

Bell, David. *An Introduction to Cybercultures.* London: Routledge, 2001.

Doheny-Farina, Stephen. *The Wired Neighborhood.* New Haven: Yale UP, 1996.

Engell, James, and Anthony Dangerfield. *Saving Higher Education in the Age of Money.* Charlottesville: U of Virginia P, 2005.

Fisher, Caitlin. *These Waves of Girls.* 2001. 22 July 2009 <http://www.yorku.ca/caitlin/waves/>.

Gache, Belén. *Book-Butterflies.* 1999-2001. 21 Mar. 2009 <http://www.findelmundo.com.ar/mariplib/introeng.htm>.

Grigar, Dene. "Electronic Literature: *Where* Is It?" 2008. 20 July 2009 <http://www.electronicbookreview.com/thread/technocapitalism/invigorating>.

Hayles, N. Katherine. *Electronic Literature: New Horizons for the Literary.* Notre Dame: U of Notre Dame P, 2008.

Hunziker, Esther, and Felix Zbinden. *edinburgh/demon.* 2007. 18 Aug. 2009 <http://www.ref17.net/edinburghdemon/>.

Jameson, Frederic. *Signatures of the Visible.* London: Routledge, 1992.

Joyce, Michael. Twelve Blue. 1996. Eastgate. 18 Aug. 2009 <http://www.eastgate.com/TwelveBlue/Twelve_Blue.html >.

Liu, Alan. *The Laws of Cool: Knowledge Work and the Culture of Information.* Chicago: U of Chicago P, 2004.

National Endowment for the Arts. "Reading at Risk: A Survey of Literary Reading in America." 2004. 20 July 2009 <http://www.nea.gov/research/ReadingAtRisk.pdf>.

———. "To Read or Not To Read: A Question of National Consequence." 2007. 20 July 2009 <http://www.nea.gov/research/ToRead.pdf>.

Nelson, Jason. *Hermeticon: Pop Spell Maker.* 2005. 22 July 2009 <http://www.secrettechnology.com/commercial/hermeticon.htm>.

Pullinger, Kate, and Chris Joseph. *Inanimate Alice.* 2005. 20 July 2009 <http://www.inanimatealice.com>.

Raley, Rita. *Tactical Media.* Minneapolis: U of Minnesota P, 2009

Rancière, Jacques. *Le destin des images.* Paris: La fabrique éditions, 2003.

Simanowski, Roberto. *Digitale Medien in der Erlebnisgesellschaft: Kultur—Kunst—Utopien.* Reinbek: Rowohlt, 2008.

Snow, C. Percy. *The Two Cultures and the Scientific Revolution*. Cambridge, MA: Cambridge UP, 1964.

Sunstein, Cass. R. *Republic.com 2.0*. Oxford: Princeton UP, 2007.

Thomas, Sue et al. "Transliteracy: Crossing Divides." *First Monday* 12.12 (2007). 20 July 2009 <http://www.uic.edu/htbin/cgiwrap/bin/ojs/index.php/fm/article/view/2060/1908>.

Wardrip-Fruin, Noah. *Expressive Processing: Digital Fictions, Computer Games, and Software Studies*. Cambridge, MA: MIT P, 2009.

Noah Wardrip-Fruin

Learning to Read Digital Literature

1 Why Read Digital Literature?

Despite the length of my essay for this volume on the terminology and concepts I use in my thinking about digital literature, a major question remains unaddressed: Why read digital literature?

We might initially answer: For all the same reasons we read other literature. And given that writers work to place their creations wherever there are readers, we can be assured of an increasing literary presence on all the computer-driven screens where we read and write—our laptops, desktops, handhelds, cellphones, console-connected televisions, and so on.

But I believe there are a number of other important reasons at this moment for discussing what we might mean by "reading" digital literature—and learning to perform such readings.

First, as Ted Nelson began arguing in the 1970s, we're living in a world increasingly defined by computer systems—systems designed and implemented by humans. These systems can be designed poorly, or implemented poorly, or designed and implemented to help some people and make life difficult for others . . . but this is the fault of humans, and it can be corrected (and sooner rather than later, if we can learn to spot bad designs before they're widely adopted). To put it another way, "the computer just works that way" is a nonargument. The importance of this knowledge lay behind Nelson's now-famous cry from the front cover of *Computer Lib/Dream Machines*: "You can and must understand computers NOW." When we study works of digital literature—and digital art more generally—in the manner I advocate, we study computational systems explicitly as authored artifacts crafted toward particular ends and embedded in particular contexts, rather than as black boxes that produce neutral outputs "the way the computer works." I believe this represents a crucial form of literacy for our current culture.

Second, in a more specific instance of the above, we're entering a period in which the results of computational processes are increasingly used to form assumptions or offered as evidence. This is one thing if we're forming our assumptions about whether the weekend will be sunny while we're trying to decide whether to have a picnic—but the results of computer simulations are also increasingly used when we're in the process of trying to make more weighty decisions about matters such as city planning and greenhouse gas

249

emissions. To take one of my favorite examples, Jay Forrester's urban dynamics simulations (which inspired *SimCity*) can be used to try to figure out how to build a healthy city, but we need to view any results from Forrester's work through an interpretation of the structures and processes of the simulations— which Garn and others have argued are deeply flawed (for example, by their cities' lack of dynamic interaction with suburbs). We need to learn to ask questions of the designs of simulations that are analogous to the questions we ask when presented with other forms of evidence (e.g., Was the study double blind? What's the n?). Unfortunately, because these questions will often have to do with the unexamined assumptions of the simulation's designers, it may only be possible to pose such questions after literate and informed examination of the simulation's processes. Here, again, learning to read digital literature in a well-rounded manner will help us develop a critical practice that is not limited to inquiry along the lines considered relevant by the designers of such simulations.

Third, and this is particularly important to me as a writer and artist, we should learn to read digital literature because we're increasingly using computational systems as a means of expression and (just as careful reading of exemplary literature is central to the development of most writers) careful reading of digital literature systems is important to our development. Those of us with some computer science coursework under our belts have learned something about reading such systems in terms of things like computability and efficiency. And those of us who've spent some time around computing subcultures have probably learned something about reading them in terms of formal elegance (cf. Maurice Black's *The Art of Code*). But we're only beginning to learn to read computational systems in terms of what they express.

2   Procedural Literacy

In the context of the arts and humanities, most of what I suggest that we study in my essay for this volume is quite familiar. While "data" may be an unusual term for them, we're certainly accustomed to studying text, images, sounds, and so on. Our practices for studying social context, performance, and most other topics I've discussed are well-developed, and already work is taking place that employs them in interpreting digital literature and art.

But there is one aspect that is glaringly absent from our curricula: the study of computational processes. And, as hinted above, we can't address this simply by sending our students to computer science classes. While computer science may teach students about data structures and algorithms, the forms of interpretation explored in such courses are normally limited to issues such as efficiency, maintainability, and elegance. We want our students to have a grasp of algorithms, of processes, but through a very different interpretive lens (and through a set of examples with a different emphasis than those used in most introductions to computer science).

One way to address this would be to make common cause with the group, largely within computer science and digital media programs, that is calling for "procedural literacy." This call is one that, for being associated with computers, has quite a long history. In fact, it follows a strand back into the history of computer science education that can be seen in the 1960s, for example in the observations of Alan Perlis—the first winner of the Turing award (computer science's greatest honor). He proposed that every student (in every discipline) take a first course in programming as part of a general education. Particularly interestingly for our purposes, in 1961 he said:

> Perhaps I may have been misunderstood as to the purpose of my proposed first course in programming. It is not to teach people how to program a specific computer, nor is it to teach some new languages. The purpose of a course in programming is to teach people how to construct and analyze processes. I know of no course that the student gets in his first year in a university that has this as its sole purpose. (Greenberger 206)

Perlis's argument here is cited in several of the writings of pioneering computer science educator Mark Guzdial, who has been working to design first courses in programming that would be appropriate for such use (Guzdial). His results are so far quite encouraging—while the traditional introduction to computer science courses at Georgia Tech have (like those at most major research universities) a high attrition rate, especially among non-majors, his courses have (a) retained students well and (b) succeeded in teaching them about constructing and analyzing processes. However, the types of examples presented and the types of interpretation involved are not ideal for students of digital literature—that is, for developing the ability to perform the sorts of readings advocated in my essay in part one of this volume.

On the other hand, Michael Mateas (while Guzdial's colleague at Georgia Tech) designed a course aimed specifically at digital media practitioners and theorists, with the goal of procedural literacy: *Computation as an Expressive Medium*. Mateas writes:

> By procedural literacy I mean the ability to read and write processes, to engage procedural representation and aesthetics, to understand the interplay between the culturally-embedded practices of human meaning-making and technically-mediated processes. (Mateas 101)

Having read Mateas's syllabus, met some of his students from this course, seen their projects, and talked with Mateas about his overall approach and goals, I believe his course is exceptionally well-designed. (On a technological level, Mateas's course begins by using Processing—a set of abstractions on top of Java designed by artist/programmers Ben Fry and Casey Reas—and then moves on to raw Java). I also think the goal of procedural literacy that he articulates would be especially valuable for those learning to read digital literature, for the following reasons:

- It would be valuable for students to develop an understanding of processes as designed artifacts. Understanding common structures of computational processes in a general sense would open digital media systems to informed modes of interpretation along these lines, even when the source code for the project is not available. Online, Mateas has referred to Kurt Squire's procedurally-focused reading of *Viewtiful Joe* (which I assume is that found in "Educating the Fighter") as a successful example of this.

- Students would emerge being able to communicate more effectively with those who design processes for digital media systems. This would make it more possible to interview artists who use such processes in their work and to engage developer communities more generally. It would also make collaboration with computer scientists and programmers much easier—whether with the goal of creating works of digital literature or of fashioning tools to aid in their analysis (or aid in the communication of results).

- Finally, of course, it would be useful for just about anyone to have practice designing processes, and to have learned some of the helpful concepts and practices such a course could include. Even executing a complex series of find-and-replace operations in a word processor is often easier for those who have had some training in designing computational processes at a general level.

But procedural literacy is not enough.

3 Beyond Procedural Literacy

3.1 Those Despised Specifics

From Perlis's 1961 words to Mateas's more than forty years later, there's a certain disdain for specifics—of particular languages, of particular development environments. As Mateas puts it, "it is not the details of any particular programming language that matters, but rather the more general tropes and structures that cut across all languages" (Mateas 101). Certainly this is true to some extent, but there are also important parts of digital culture, ones quite relevant to those interested in digital literature, that we simply can't access without some understanding of such specifics.

In part this is because some of the most creative computational subcultures (e.g., the demoscene) are focused specifically on work that is interesting and/or difficult precisely in the ways in which it is shaped by the particularities of given computer hardware or software. But even outside such subcultures, many digital media practitioners are actively engaged in reflecting on or working against the specifics of their work environments. The interactive fiction (IF) community, for example, is not organized around difficult feats of programming (the way the demoscene is) but it still is home to practices that reflect engagement with the specifics that Perlis and Mateas would bracket. For example, there is a practice of creating "one room" works of IF, which derives part of its interest from the fact that—for a number of years, ending with the release of Inform 7—all the common IF development environments were object-oriented systems designed around supporting multiple rooms with connections to one another.[1] Authors giving up this fundamental aspect of these tools is difficult to interpret if we're unprepared to consider the specifics of tools. And we'd be at even more of a loss to explain what is virtuosic (and amusing) about creating a work of IF, available for the Z-machine, that includes a chess-playing program.[2] In other words, we need to be able to engage work that is interesting, perhaps virtuosic, because of how it interacts with technical specifics. An introduction for those who would study and make digital literature shouldn't just be about "procedural literacy"—it should also include some engagement with the specifics of particular environments, so that students will learn something about this kind of engagement.

Which brings us to what I consider the good news: there's absolutely no way to achieve the dream of an introduction to procedural literacy that brackets all specifics. For example, as pointed out above, Mateas's course engages the specifics of Processing and then Java. My point is that the engagement with such specifics shouldn't be bemoaned. It's one of the important parts of what students are learning. And we should choose the particular development environments employed, in part, for what they teach about specifics and for the health of their digital media development communities—rather than, for example, some near-evangelical hatred of languages with too much "syntactic sugar." Mateas's choice, of Processing and Java, is a good one in this regard. But there are also others that it would make sense to pursue. For example, now that Actionscript provides a more full language than present in its first version, as well as the ability for code to be written in an external editor, it might make sense to teach a course such as Mateas's using Flash (if working with students in a subfield for which it is a primary tool). In computer music circles, Max/MSP and Jitter—or Pd (Pure Data)—might be the most appropriate choice.

3.2 What about CS?

Given that computer science, as a discipline, isn't very interested in the issues that are primary to practitioners and scholars of digital literature (and digital media generally) it should be no surprise that most who speak of procedural literacy bracket CS almost entirely. And this outlook is supported by the anecdotal evidence of students interested in digital media who take introductory computer science courses—they learn three data structures and four sorting algorithms, briefly wonder what relationship any of it could have to what interests them, and then promptly forget it. But I would argue that we can't afford to completely bracket computer science, because:

- Digital media is built on computer science research results. Students who don't know the basic CS vocabulary in areas related to digital media, and who have no practice reading CS research papers, can't even do a full review of the literature for their field.

- This research is often ongoing. Students who know something of the vocabulary and conceptual framework of CS as it relates to digital media will have a much broader field of examples to consider, potential collaborators, and technologies at their disposal. Those who don't know this are in danger of reinventing the wheel, as they won't even be able to formulate a web search for ongoing CS work related to their own.

This problem remains unsolved. Certainly people like Mateas, who teach procedural literacy courses from an extensive background in computer science, no doubt help their students make such connections. But for our health as a field we need to begin to make appropriate connections with CS in a less ad-hoc way. Simply recognizing that our discipline is closely connected to CS, and that it would be valuable for our students to learn some CS concepts and vocabulary, is doubtless the first step.

Personally, part of my motivation for editing *The New Media Reader* (Wardrip-Fruin and Montfort) was to present CS research papers alongside other fundamental documents for our history as a discipline. And I'm glad to report a last bit of anecdotal evidence from two faculty friends who recommend the book to their students—both report that, while the CS papers are often a struggle for those approaching the book from humanities and arts perspectives, they also work with students attracted to the *NMR* because of its CS content who find themselves challenged as they work through the contributions from artists and cultural critics. If our discipline is inspiring students to come to grips more fully with the approaches and concepts of other fields, we must be doing something right.

4 An Introductory Writing Course

The editors of this collection have asked that I include a note about my own teaching experiences with digital literature, which have largely operated from the creative (rather than interpretive) direction. Though I have taught such courses at New York University, Brown University, the Summer Literary Seminars, and other venues, I have recently moved institutions (to the University of California, Santa Cruz) and am not yet teaching a current course in this area. But I am happy to talk about a past course.

My most recent teaching in the field is a 10-week course titled *Writing for Digital Media* that I taught for two years in the Communication department at the University of California, San Diego. This course presented the particular challenge that the students involved were, with a few notable exceptions, having their first coursework in literary writing of any kind, completely unexposed to computer science concepts (or even the structured text editing used in wikis and similar environments), and without background other than personal experience in the history or present of digital media. Luckily, given the interdisciplinary nature of the department, my colleagues were happy for me to structure the course as a themed introduction to all three areas, emphasizing their connections. So the range of activities in our course meetings included in-class experimental writing exercises, seminar-style discussions of background readings and digital works, lab-style computer tutorials and debugging assistance, and reading/viewing/playing student projects and offering workshop-style critique. While many of these activities were new to the students, registration priority meant that most enrolled students were in their third or final year of the Communication degree program, and already had extensive experience thinking about media forms, representations, institutions, and production processes—an invaluable foundation for our discussions.

The primary emphasis of the course projects was helping students develop a sense of the relationship between writing and procedural systems. Given the background of the students, and my own interests, the most effective way to accomplish this was through an emphasis on writing and games, from Oulipian language games through the structures of mainstream computer role-playing games (RPGs). Outside of course meetings (and preparation for them) student work was organized by five milestones:

1. *A sticker writing project.* This project didn't involve creating a computational system along with writing, but was designed to get students thinking about literary writing in new ways (and practicing the short, situated chunks of writing common to working in many digital forms). It was inspired by projects such as Nick Montfort and Scott Rettberg's *Implementation* and Robert Kendall's *Logozoa,* but with a greater connection to particular locations. Students wrote at least five original texts specific to a place, used stickers to post the texts in that place, took photos documenting the placement (at least one showing context and one with legible text, for each sticker), and then created a blog post about the project. Within this loose format students created works with many structures, ranging from memoir via placement on personally-meaningful objects to scavenger-hunt style directions and low-tech locative narratives.

2. *A story-game project.* The next project required thinking about writing and systems, but employed media for system creation more easily authored and revised (for most students) than digital computation: tabletop board games, card games, and other types of traditional games. These are also media in which many students had experience thinking about structures of rules, because human players are required to uphold the rules of traditional games, and reason through any ambiguities in the rules, whereas computer games hide many of the operations of their rules. Inspired by projects such as *Once Upon a Time* (by Richard Lambert, Andrew Rilstone and James Wallis) and *Betrayal at the House on the Hill* (by Bill McQuillan, Bruce Glassco, Mike Selinker, Rob Daviau, and Teeuwynn Woodruff), students were encouraged to consider both game mechanics that could elicit storytelling from players and those that produced a version of a pre-written narrative through play—though all projects had to include a significant amount of original writing. While, unsurprisingly, the most common project concept was to produce altered versions of familiar boardgames that told stories of college life, the designs and texts were varied and often engaging. Further, during both the design process and

project critique, students began active discussion of how rule systems express ideas both through their structures and the play experiences produced.

3. *A tool tutorial.* The computer role-playing game *Neverwinter Nights* was designed to support player-produced "modules" of content. The included Aurora toolset allows relatively non-technical authors to define spaces, craft character dialogue trees, define quest stages and objectives, place encounters, and so on. A significant online community shares modules they have created, additional objects for use in authoring, and tips on both basic and advanced topics. The game and toolset run on modestly-powered Windows machines (and on emulators) and are available cheaply. This assignment required students to complete an Aurora toolset tutorial, providing a route to (and deadline for) basic competence on the part of non-technical students, while also showing those with more computational experience the route toward extending the tool's behavior through NWScript. For students familiar with computer role-playing games (nearly all of them, given that one course assignment was to play part of the main quest in *Neverwinter Nights*) it also gave insight into some of the common computational structures used to support games of this type, resulting in discussions of how these structures shape authoring and exprience.

4. *An RPG module.* For this project students created at least three speaking characters and two connected spaces in Aurora, using them to structure the experience of a multi-stage story (noted as updates in the reader/player's quest journal), with elements of the story (e.g., characters, locations, events, items) distributed in space, coming to some form (or multiple forms) of conclusion. Students used the largely fantasy-themed elements available in Aurora for purposes ranging from new takes on fairy tales to modern fictions in unusual settings (e.g., a costume party or a hedge labyrinth). Some gave their reader/players traditionally heroic tasks to complete, while others offered more prosaic or ambiguous undertakings, and a few forced genuinely uncomfortable choices on any who wished to reach a conclusion. Simply completing the assignment required a certain amount of procedural thinking combined with crafting language (e.g., ensuring that a character spoke appropriate lines over multiple conversations as the story progressed through stages).

5. *A final project.* Beginning either with their story-game or their RPG module, the course's final project required students to complete a significantly improved version of one. The approach combined that traditional in

writing courses (responding to workshop feedback) with that traditional in game design (playtest, revise, playtest, revise). Many students deepened their engagement with both the writing and the system for their project, and it was with this milestone that the course moved from looking like a collection of assignments to a set of projects that mattered to their authors.

While the course discussed here is rather different from that assumed in the earlier sections of this text—especially in its emphasis on writing computational fictions, rather than interpreting digital literature—I hope these notes are useful. Perhaps one or more of these assignments might be worth adding to a digital literature course, given that experience with creation can offer new insights during interpretation (as I saw when students discussed computer RPGs after using Aurora). Alternately, seeing in some detail what I advocate for training digital literature's creators may shed some light on the reasons I advocate the approach above for training digital literature's interpreters. My hope is that these two aspects of the field will move together in tandem toward a richer engagement with all the elements of digital literature.

Notes

1   An object-oriented approach breaks down a computational process into cooperating objects that usually have defined capabilities, store state information internally, and expose particular interfaces for retrieving and changing that information. Each particular object is an instance of some class (e.g., the room class) which can be subclassed (e.g., for particular types of rooms, like hallways). This is different, for example, from designing in a function-oriented way, which tends to store state information more centrally and is often approached from the perspective of what will happen rather than what the components are. This is sometimes discussed as a difference between a focus on "nouns" and "verbs."

2   The Z-machine is a "virtual machine" for running computer programs, much like the Java virtual machines that allow the same Java program to run on multiple computers (any computer for which there is an implementation of the Java virtual machine). The Z-machine was created by Infocom, and was the machine targeted by their interactive fictions. Its extremely limited capabilities (by today's standards) allowed it to be implemented for 1980s machines from Kaypro, Osborne, Atari, and many others (I've played Infocom games on all three of these). It now runs happily on the lowliest handheld computers, as well as the most powerful

workstations. But its limitations are seen as a bane by some interactive fiction authors, some of whom have begun to target their creations to other platforms.

Works Cited

Black, Maurice J. "The Art of Code." Diss. U of Pennsylvania, 2002.

Greenberger, Martin, ed. *Management and the Computer of the Future*. Cambridge, MA: MIT P, 1962.

Guzdial, Mark. "A media computation course for non-majors." *ITiCSE '03: Proceedings of the 8th annual conference on Innovation and technology in computer science education*. ACM Press, 2003. 104-08.

Kendall, Robert. *Logozoa*. 2006-2009. 21 Aug. 2009 <http://www.logozoa.com/>.

Lambert, Richard, Andrew Rilstone, and James Wallis. *Once Upon a Time: The Storytelling Card Game*. St. Paul: Atlas, 1996.

Mateas, Michael. "Procedural Literacy: Educating the New Media Practitioner." *On The Horizon*. 13.1 (2005).

Nelson, Theodor Holm. *Computer Lib/Dream Machines*. Self published, 1974.

McQuillan, Bill et al. *Betrayal at the House on the Hill*. Renton: Avalon, 2004.

Rettberg, Scott, and Nick Montfort. *Implementation*. 2005. 21 Aug. 2009 <http://www.nickm.com/implementation/>.

Squire, Kurt D. "Educating the Fighter: Buttonmashing, Seeing, Being." *On The Horizon* 13.2 (2005).

Wardrip-Fruin, Noah, and Nick Montfort, eds. *The New Media Reader*. Cambridge, MA: MIT P, 2003.

John Zuern

Pop Spells, Hermetic Lessons

Teaching on the Fringes of the Literary

Compared with works like John Cayley's *windsound*, Judd Morrissey's *The Jew's Daughter*, and Stephanie Strickland's *V:Vniverse*, all of which assemble more or less legible words in ways we typically think of as "literary," Jason Nelson's wacky *Hermeticon: Pop Spell Maker* might appear to many readers as a distant outlier in the category of "literature," if not an altogether alien species. My undergraduate English majors at the University of Hawai'i at Mānoa were certainly skeptical when I included Nelson's piece in their required reading for *Digital Literature: Theory and Practice*," a junior honors tutorial devoted entirely to the analysis and creation of electronic literary texts. The students had all proven themselves to be adaptable, perceptive readers of hypertext, kinetic poetry, and interactive fiction, and many of them were developing considerable skills as authors of electronic literature in their own right. One of them, for example, was exploring the capacity of Flash animation to emulate the pace and inflections of slam poetry, while another was composing sophisticated, fully executable code poems in UNIX, Perl, and Java. *Hermeticon*, however, brought them up short, provoking all the predictable questions: how are we supposed to read this? what does it mean? Why is *this* considered literature? They found the experience of playing with *Hermeticon* intriguing, but wondered if we could really claim that this work is a literary text and not, say, a work of digital art or a toy.[1]

In this chapter I will describe how my students and I worked together to address these questions about *Hermeticon*, questions that in the end we were unable, and for the most part unwilling, to answer in any definitive way. The issues that arose as we grappled with Nelson's work are central to the teaching philosophy I have developed during my ten years of designing and conducting courses that include "digitally born" literary artifacts. While *Hermeticon* dramatically calls our attention to the differences between printed and digital media, as well as the differences between literature and the other arts, our attempt to make sense of Nelson's text also called upon skills in textual analysis, research, and reasoning that should be in the repertoire of any student of literature. In the following sections I will briefly discuss what for me are the three most important of these skills: the students' capacity to recognize and describe instances of figuration in a literary artwork, including tropes in the work's programming and interface design; their capacity (and willingness) to follow up on unfamiliar words, references, and intertextual allusions with research into the relevant linguistic, historical, social, and cultural contexts; and their capacity to make sound, articulate, and adequately supported arguments about the implications of their discoveries. As we will see, Nelson's *Hermeticon*, though arguably on or even beyond the fringes of the literary, offers students an opportunity to exert themselves in all three of these areas, and in doing so it illustrates the value of integrating computer-based texts, fringes and all, into the literary studies curriculum.

Finding Figures

Launched in 2005 on Nelson's Secret Technology web site, *Hermeticon: Pop Spell Maker* initially appears on the screen as an empty rectangular grid while an ominous synthesized bass note pulses in the background. The minimal directions tell the reader to "click on grid and then use your keyboard to create pop spells."[2] When the reader types, each keystroke places an enigmatic fragment of text on the grid, pairing it with a clip from a raucous 1980s television advertisement; for example, the "u" key, calls up the phrase "between the hills" and an ad for Kellogg's Corn Pops. Key combinations produce overlapping pairs and a cacophony of jingles and slogans (fig. 1).

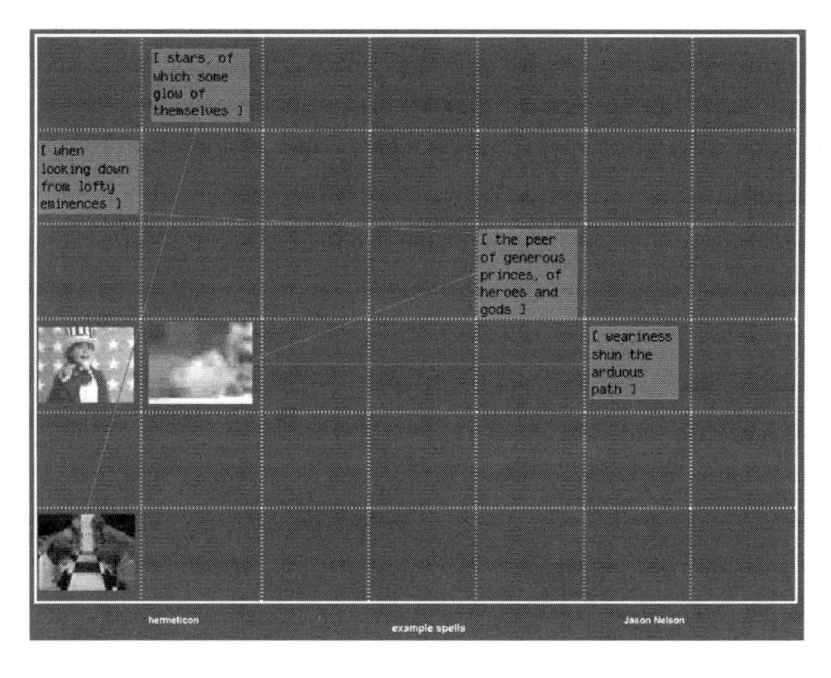

Fig. 1. Jason Nelson: Screenshot from *Hermeticon: Pop Spell Maker.* 2005. Flash and digitized video.

Though in many cases the juxtapositions are striking and evocative, especially in combination with the images, sounds, and movements of the commercials, the pieces of text do not add up to a coherent message, regardless of the combinations the reader types. In fact, the text-video pairs remain only the screen only as long as the keys are pressed; they do not accumulate to fill the grid. *Hermeticon* thus serves as a kind of quirky translation engine that converts whatever words a reader attempts to type into its puzzling, provocative "spells."

The homographic pun of the word "spell" is the obvious place to start an examination of the tropological dimensions of Nelson's piece. Recognizing the play on the verb "to spell" and "magic spell" points students toward one of the work's fundamental motifs: the practice of logomancy, conjuring with words, a motif that is evident in the physical interface and on-screen behavior of the piece. Whatever words the reader attempts to "spell" on the keyboard turn into enigmatic "spells" on the screen. Beyond this literal reference to *Hermeticon's* peculiar design, however, the double meaning of "spell" links the idea of writing with the ideas of enchantment and divination. At this point, some students draw the conclusion that *Hermeticon's* message is that "writing is magical" or that "writing is powerful." As they continue to explore Nelson's piece, and as their further research uncovers the origins of the word "hermetic," the resonance of the title's yoking of the semantic fields clustered around the word "spell" becomes increasingly more nuanced. I will discuss some of these nuances below.[3]

Though it yields somewhat less complex implications, the word "pop" also allows for two different readings: "popular culture," easily interpreted as a reference to *Hermeticon's* sampling of television commercials, and the verb "to pop," which could be used to describe the behavior of the text-image pairs as they spring abruptly onto the screen. The puns on "pop" and "spell" are relatively simple tropes, but parsing such elemental figures is a valuable introduction to the fundamental principles of literary-critical inquiry. The effort to push their reading of a single word beyond a routine, automatic, monological decoding prepares students for more complex interpretive tasks.

When I asked students if they could find other instances of literary tropes in Nelson's text, they pointed to the elaborate metaphors that characterize some of the brief passages of text—"beautiful order and ladder of nature," for example, or "have not a good breastplate of patience"—but given the texts' fragmentary nature, the students found it hard to move from these observations to an explanation, to say nothing of an interpretation, of the work as a whole. Where else, I asked them, could we look for figuration in this text? For if we accept Adalaide Morris's argument that "[d]efinitions of new media poetics that do not account for code miss the synergy crucial to its operations, its realm of discourse, and its self-reflexivity" (9), shouldn't we look at the protocols of Flash's ActionScript programming for more evidence of *Hermeticon's* tropological activity? Without "cracking" the Shockwave file, my students and I could not get immediate access to Nelson's programming, but because I had already introduced them to the rudiments of ActionScript, students had enough background to think about the comparison I proposed between lines like "beautiful order and ladder of nature" and "have not a good breastplate of patience" and Nelson's use of the standard ActionScript techniques for capturing and repurposing users' keystrokes.

Reassigning the user's keystrokes to specific interface functions is a common practice in Flash authoring. It is one way for game designers, for example, to set up the keyboard controls for such actions as moving through space or firing a weapon. *Hermeticon* deploys this technique to generate its juxtapositions of texts and video clips. Can we argue that Nelson's "deviant" application of the key-capture technique constitutes the same kind of "deviance" that defines the literary trope, which in turn, as I suggest in my other contribution to this volume, defines the literary as such? With the widespread adoption of word-processing programs, as John Cayley notes, the keystroke has been

> . . . interiorized as the unremarkable and entirely instrumental, basic gesture of writing (as if writing had not changed, as if the keystroke were a typewriter keystroke). But as we have seen, this gesture exhibits characteristic aspects of the new and potential mediation of writing, and these aspects of mediation have a bearing on poetics—on the way that writing is and will be made—and on our understanding of the very machinery of inscription. ("Inner Workings")

One can argue that Nelson's devious "meta-capture" of conventional key-capture scripting constitutes *Hermeticon's* pivotal trope. *Hermeticon* deviates from our typical interface with the computer keyboard, whether to type words or to fire cannons, in a manner analogous to the verbal text's retooling of the words "breastplate" and "ladder" to suggest, respectively, that the virtue of patience serves as a kind of defense and that nature is a orderly hierarchical structure. Does this "defamiliarization" of the keyboard—to borrow the key term from Russian Formalism's definition of the literary—qualify as a trope that would allow *Hermeticon* to qualify as a literary text? To address this question adequately, students must reconsider the role and, in particular, the source of *Hermeticon's* sparse inventory of words.

Tracking Intertextuality

One of the outcomes of literary-critical training is an instinct to follow up on each aspect of a text that is "unfamiliar and strikes us as significant," to use Hans-Georg Gadamer's cogent formulation for the impetus to interpretation (70). We can cultivate this instinct in our students, but we have to do so deliberately. I suggested that my students submit the phrase "beautiful order and ladder of nature" to Google, and all three results pointed to online English-language editions of Giordano Bruno's 1584 philosophical dialogue *On the Infinite Universe and Worlds*. Other phrases returned the same sites. Further Google searches informed the students that Bruno, a contemporary of Galileo, was one of the founders of humanism, and that his resolutely materialist views to the laws of the physical universe, which called into question divine creation and providence, provoked the Roman Inquisition to imprison him for seven years and then burn him at the stake in 1600.

In itself, this information did not lead to significant insights into *Hermeticon*, but when we supplemented it with more detailed scholarly references, which link Bruno to a culturally specific, decidedly "material" and "interactive" mode of reading, students began to see the scraps of Bruno's dialogue featured in *Hermeticon* as something more than arbitrarily selected "found objects" in a digital collage. In Bruno's time, Lina Bolzoni reminds us, "important literary works were put to uses that to us would be quite unthinkable: they could be condensed, fragmented and recombined at will, individual words and phrases becoming objects (*brevi*) that might be reassembled in new combinations and associated with completely different persons or situations" (124). Bolzoni describes one such use of texts, the group game of *sorti*, a derivation of the Roman bibliomantic practice of the *sortes Vergilianae*, in which books were opened at random, a finger dropped onto a line, and that line then associated in an improvised poetic performance with a randomly chosen person in the group. Playing the game in Naples sometime between 1565 and 1566, Bolzoni tells us, Bruno placed his finger on a line from Ariosto's *Orlando Furioso* describing an unrepentant pagan, and for years afterward interpreted this moment "as a sign of his true character and ultimate destiny" (122). The *sorti* thus served not only as a pastime: falling into a long tradition that includes Augustine's scripture-induced conversion in the Milanese garden, early modern readers sought in the *sorti* advice about present problems and a glimpse of their future lives.[4]

As Espen Aarseth notes in the opening pages of *Cybertext: Perspectives on Ergodic Literature*, the aleatory and combinatory reading practices that digital literature often demands are often compared to early forms of bibliomancy, foremost among them the *I Ching*, "the best-known example of cybertext in antiquity" (9). Following up on the cultural background of the textual dimension of Nelson's piece, my students were more receptive to the suggestion that *Hermeticon* involves its readers in an updated and ironic version of these attempts to read fate by submitting one's reading to chance, situating present-day readers' expectant web browsing and channel surfing within this history of text-based games of chance.[5] Had they not been willing to examine *Hermeticon* in terms of its specific design strategies *and* within the broad context of its literary and cultural allusions, my students would have missed the specific echoes from the cultural history of reading that resonate in their mouse clicks and their fingers' tapping on *Hermeticon's* captured keys. The resonances of the past in Nelson's piece are both intertextual and "intermedial" insofar as they involve appropriations of verbal texts as well as of modalities of embodied engagement with textual materiality.

Proposing Implications

Hermeticon clearly exemplifies the kind of work N. Katherine Hayles includes in "the literary," a capacious category encompassing "creative artworks that interrogate the histories, contexts, and productions of literature, including as well the verbal art of literature proper" (4). In the end, however, our class was left wondering whether *Hermeticon's* cheeky appropriation of the *sorti* by way its intertextuality with Giordano Bruno's treatise, even if it served to quality the work as "literary," was enough to warrant the kind of detailed analysis we had undertaken. Though we never fully dispelled this skepticism, one of *Hermeticon's* subtler visual details added another, somewhat more philosophical interpretive possibility. If we look carefully as we type our spells, we discover that the "normal" alphabetic results of our keystrokes *also* appear on a layer behind Nelson's frenetic video clips and his excerpts from Bruno. Because they are only a few shades lighter than the gray background, these letters can be difficult to see, but the fact that they are still there *at all* reinforces *Hermeticon's* deviation from established interface conventions: the unexpected outcomes of our familiar interaction with the keyboard—the text block and video clips—are, as it were, shadowed and thus thrown into sharper relief by the ghostly presence of the anticipated characters of typical, instrumental, "automatic" typing. *Hermeticon* strikes an unstable equilibrium between the expected and the unexpected, conforming—on its own audio-visual-verbal-kinesthetic terms—with Aristotle's recommendation in Book 22 of the *Poetics* that authors balance the tantalizing strangeness of tropes with the clarity of standard usages (101-102).

Like the *sorti*, in which an existing text is used to compose or divine new messages, *Hermeticon* seems to suggest that reading and writing are ultimately inseparable, recursive processes, and furthermore that neither can escape the influence of languages' relentless, promiscuous, and only partially containable figuration. As an unexpected benefit, this provisional interpretation of *Hermeticon* opened the way for a review of some of the basics of literary theory, to which all English majors in my department's undergraduate program are introduced in our required theory-and-method course. Nietzsche's "mobile army" of tropes, Barthes' "myths," Derrida's "white mythology" all figure writing as a kind of incantatory *spelling* that for good or for ill cannot help but summon the undead tropology of natural human languages. *Hermeticon* dredges these wraiths onto the surface of writing, while the alphabetic script itself—the expected, habituated result of pressing keys—sinks into the gray, half-visible realm of semi-consciousness to which these rambunctious linguistic and cultural spirits are usually relegated. In *Hermeticon* the alphabet as a whole has not so much been replaced as it has been displaced, and the ripples in the wake of this exile of the familiar contributes to this text's seductive, unsettling energy. Just as Early Modern bibliomancy posited reading as an interface between mortal human understanding and a transcendent consciousness at work in the world of human affairs, texts like *Hermeticon* expose the inextricable links between our reading, viewing, and writing practices and the machinic agencies—computational, certainly, but also linguistic, economic, cultural, and political—that so powerfully influence our destinies today.

Conclusion: Digital Literature and the Fate of the Humanities

Digital literature always asks us to think beyond what we assume we already know about the literary without necessarily abandoning any of the knowledge of literary history and strategies of reading we already command. One of the greatest challenges in teaching in this field lies in guiding our students toward a nuanced understanding of the connections between the particular engagement with language that makes any given text a work of *literature* and the particular engagement with computation that makes any given text a work of *digital* literature. If we over-emphasize one or the other of these dimensions of textuality, we will fail to maintain the integrity of the category *digital literature*, not to mention its academic vitality and viability.

In their book *Saving Higher Education in the Age of Money,* James Engall and Anthony Dangerfield challenge educators in the American university system to recover the university's fundamental mission—the cultivation of imaginative, compassionate, broadly informed citizens—from the increasingly utilitarian, profit-driven cooptation of higher education by commercial interests. In light of recent widely publicized scandals involving the presumably well-educated leadership of major American companies, Engall and Dangerfield call for a greater emphasis on questions of values and ethics in college-level teaching. Like many other critics of the corporatization of the university, they argue that a robust interdisciplinary pedagogy can serve as a powerful means to this end, and they recommend the development of courses and curricula in which "subjects such as ethics, aesthetics, rhetoric, linguistics, politics, and science conjoin and are regarded in the light of judgment that weighs conflicting goods and trade-offs, as well as evils, and then acts" (164-165). Digital literary texts, which often combine the techniques of creative writing, graphic design, filmmaking, and computer programming, offer an especially promising point of departure for this kind of teaching. In order to conduct adequate readings of computer-based materials, students need to make a concentrated effort to assemble evidence, follow up on leads, and weigh alternative interpretations; that is to say, digital literature demands an exercise of the *sophrosyne* that higher education in the U.S. is on the brink of abandoning as a central objective of the liberal arts curriculum. To optimize the field's potential, however, teachers need to ensure that students are not simply left to dwell on the differences between digital texts and their printed precursors, but rather that they work to extend these observations into wider-ranging analyses and critiques of contemporary culture. Unless we take this next step, the study of texts on the fringes of the literary will remain a diverting but ultimately irrelevant fillip on our students' utilitarian "degree plans."

Whether or not our students go on to make digital literature—or any kind of literature—a prominent part of their lives, their lives are already enmeshed in what N. Katherine Hayles has called the "complex web" of technologies, institutions, and socio-economic relations with which electronic literature necessarily articulates (42). Teaching digital literature certainly has the effect of dispelling students' entrenched and sometimes reactionary assumptions about what constitutes literature, but can it also break some of the equally powerful enchantments of a culture industry that appropriates the power of networked media to entice readers and viewers into the indentured and indebted servitude of consumerism? By throwing them off balance, confronting them with juxtapositions of stimuli and information that require follow-up and cross-checking, frustrating the expectation that texts should be legible and games winnable, can works like *Hermeticon*, when they are taken (and taught) seriously, compel our students to reflect on the expectations and desires that inform their choices and motivate their actions—as readers, certainly, and perhaps also as moral agents in the complex social worlds in which they will set up their lives? The answers to these weighty questions are well beyond the scope of this essay; they are probably well beyond the scope of any single university course. As we work to integrate electronic literature in the curriculum, however, keeping such questions in the backs of our minds will better equip us to find in the fringes of the literary a reaffirmation of the central goals and fundamental values of the study of literature, even as we push our definition—and appreciation—of literature toward new frontiers.

Notes

1   In her inventory of electronic literary works in the first chapter of *Electronic Literature,* Hayles includes Nelson among those authors "who think of themselves as primarily graphic artists and programmers [and who] write texts to incorporate into their works" (22). As I discuss later in this essay, Nelson's texts readily fall under the rubric of the "literary" Hayles proposes as an alternative to the more restrictive category "literature."

2   When the piece first appeared in 2005, its title was *Hermeticon: An Incantation Engine,* and the directions included the explanation "every letter is a spell part, a conjured hook." When we teach documentation protocols for digital literature, we need to alert students to the mutability of many online texts, a feature that has important ramifications for the claims they seek to make about them.

3   Though students need to be led to this observation, it is useful to note that Nelson's pun on the word "spell" can also be seen as an instance of meta-linguistic self-reference: insofar as it is a trope that relies on homography and/or homophony for its rhetorical (often humorous) effect, paronomasia is itself a kind of spell based on spelling.

4   Other traditions of aleatory reading and writing practices include the *ars magna combinatoria* of the Baroque period as well as the experiments of the *Ouvroir de Littérature Potentielle* (Oulipo). An emphasis the historical range of "radical" treatments of the protocols of written communication helps students to put the "newness" of electronic texts in perspective; it also reminds them that what it means "to write" and "to read" shifts, even if only slightly, depending upon the cultural, philosophical, and religious presuppositions about the power of the word that hold sway in a particular period.

5   The case of Bruno's divination also gave these students the opportunity to think about the diversity of the historical and cultural contexts in which texts have been put to such uses. The *I Ching* reflects a vastly different mindset than the assumptions about fate and textuality embodied in the Roman *sortes Virgilianae,* and important cultural, philosophical, and theological differences pertain even among Early Modern forms of bibliomancy;

members of Bruno's highly educated and politically enfranchised social circle indulging in the *sorti* are playing a very different game from the "däumeln" ('thumbing') of the Bible among bourgeois German Protestants of the same period.

Works Cited

Aarseth, Espen J. *Cybertext: Perspectives on Ergodic Literature.* Baltimore: Johns Hopkins UP, 1997.

Aristotle. *Poetics.* Trans. S. H. Butcher. New York: Hill and Wang, 1961.

Barthes, Roland. "Myth Today." *Mythologies.* Trans. Annette Lavers. York: Hill and Wang, 1984.

Bolzoni, Lina. "Images of Literary Memory in the Italian Dialogues: Some Notes on Giordano Bruno and Ludovico Ariosto." Trans. Lisa Chien. *Giordano Bruno: Philosopher of the Renaissance.* Ed. Hilary Gatti. Aldershot: Ashgate, 2002. 121-141.

Bruno, Giordano. *On the Infinite Universe and Worlds.* Trans. Dorthea Waley Singer. *Positive Atheism Magazine.* New York: Henry Shuman, 1950. 28 Apr. 2009 <http://www.positiveatheism.org/hist/bruno00.htm>.

Cayley, John. *windsound.* 1999. 22 Mar. 2009 <http://www.shadoof.net/in/windsound.html>.

Cayley, John. "Inner Workings Code and Representations of Interiority in New Media Poetics." *Dichtung Digital* 3 (2003). 22 Mar. 2009 <http://www.dichtung-digital.org/2003/issue/3/Cayley.htm>.

Derrida. Jacques. *Margins of Philosophy.* Trans. Alan Bass. Chicago: U of Chicago P, 1982.

Engell, James, and Anthony Dangerfield. *Saving Higher Education in the Age of Money.* Charlottesville: U of Virginia P, 2005.

Gadamer, Hans G. "Writing and the Living Voice." *Hans-Georg Gadamer on Education, Poetry, and History: Applied Hermeneutics.* Ed. Dieter Misgeld and Graeme Nicholson. Trans. Lawrence Schmidt and Monica Reuss. Albany: State U of New York P, 1992. 63-71.

Hayles, N. Katherine. *Electronic Literature: New Horizons for the Literary.* Notre Dame: U of Notre Dame P, 2008.

Morris, Adalaide. "New Media Poetics: As We May Think/How to Write." *New Media Poetics: Contexts, Technotexts, and Theories.* Ed. Adalaide K. Morris and Thomas Swiss. Cambridge, MA: MIT P, 2006. 1-46.

Morrissey, Judd. *The Jew's Daughter.* 2000. 22 Mar. 2009 <http://www.thejewsdaughter.com/>.

Mott, Chris. "Electronic Literature Pedagogy: A Questionable Approach." n.d. 22 Mar. 2009 <http://www.newhorizons.eliterature.org/essay.php?id=3>.

Nelson, Jason. *Hermeticon: Pop Spell Maker.* 2005. 22. Mar. 2009 <http://www.secrettechnology.com/commercial/hermeticon.htm>.

Nietzsche, Friedrich. "On Truth and Lies in an Extra-Moral Sense." Trans. Ronald Speirs. *The Birth of Tragedy and Other Writings.* Ed. Raymond Geuss and Ronald Speirs. Cambridge: Cambridge UP, 1999: 139-152.

Strickland, Stephanie. *V:Vniverse.* 2002. 22 Mar. 2009 <http://www.vniverse.com>.

Peter Gendolla, Jörgen Schäfer and Patricia Tomaszek

Net Literature in the Classroom

Teaching Practice at the University of Siegen

Teaching computer-based and networked literary projects—or more specifically "digital literature"—is not an easy undertaking. It is not simply the continuation of teaching the established literary forms with new electronic means, and it can not represent these new forms comprehensibly with the known didactic methods for the very reason that literature in computer-based media no longer creates firm "objects:" The series of letters on the new surfaces have become mobile; only in the process of "reading" the stories or poems emerge in varying degrees, qualities, and intensities and this also means that the roles of researching, teaching, and learning are becoming blurred in a (still) disturbing way. As a rule, the teacher knows more about the stories, the genres, the authors, cultural backgrounds, and so on; e.g., the various components that so far have comprised the literary field. This continues to remain a central requirement for working with "net literature," which is clearly referring back to these traditions in many ways. But this recognition of intertextual references is merely *one* of the requirements. Already when navigating, for example, within the possibilities of reading or composing the respective literary projects, the advantage lies no longer necessarily with the teacher; often it is the students who are the more experienced users and discover or produce combinations that surprisingly widen the literary field. The students become "teachers" and only in the next step, when poetic qualities are explained—or when the nonsense produced is being criticized—can the teacher again take on his or her customary role. We would like to delineate the interesting, even though sometimes difficult, directions taken in our own teaching at the University of Siegen, as well as with our project partner Brown University in Providence, RI.

1 Literary and Media Studies at the University of Siegen

In the winter semester 2008/09, 12,324 students were enrolled at the University of Siegen (Germany) of whom about 4,900 were studying within the Department of Language, Literary and Media Studies. This makes it the biggest department of the university by student numbers. Research and teaching within this department on the one hand cover the traditionally important areas of *Germanistik, Anglistik,* and *Romanistik* ('German, English, and Romance

Studies'), but on the other hand from its very beginnings in the 1970s, literary studies at Siegen operated with a particular focus on the media in which literary texts are being written, distributed and read (for example, Gumbrecht and Pfeiffer; Kreuzer). This inevitably led to the question of how texts are transformed into films or radio plays—or currently into computer-based media and onto the Internet.

From this starting point, Siegen developed a distinctive profile within the new academic discipline of Media Studies in the 1980s and 90s by focusing on research in media aesthetics and cultural studies. Between 2002 and 2009, a so-called "Forschungskolleg" ('Research Center') has been funded by the *Deutsche Forschungsgemeinschaft* ('German Research Council') entitled *Medienumbrüche* ('Media Upheavals'). It aimed at examining the prerequisites and structures of two "media upheavals:" The first one at the beginning of the 20th century triggered by the new audio-visual mass media, the second one at the crossover to the 21st century that is characterized by the integration and substitution of distinctly analog media with computer-based and networked media. Our ongoing sub-project under the title "Literatur im Netz/Netzliteratur" ('literature on the net/net literature')—we do regard the slash in the title as programmatic—aims at examining literature in computer-based and networked media which we regard as characteristic for such a media upheaval.

2 Degree Schemes in Higher Education

In order to introduce didactic approaches, it is necessary to give some basic information about recent reforms in German higher education. The long-established German university courses and degrees—the "Diplom" ('diploma') for most technical subjects, the "Staatsexamen" (which is the entry qualification for school teachers but also for some other professions in Germany), or the "Magister" in the humanities—had existed in sharp contrast to the Anglo-Saxon tradition of modularized Bachelor and Master degrees with a strictly limited duration of study time. German students, especially in the humanities, were allowed to study without cost as long as they liked; they just had to register for their exams once they had successfully accumulated the necessary credits. This sounds rather anarchic—in particular under German circumstances—and it is pretty obvious that this was not the most economic and efficient system. But on the other hand it allowed students to find their individual areas of specific interest and to go deeper into the matter. Students in the humanities generally had to take only a few compulsory courses (such as an Introduction to Literary Studies, to Medieval Studies or suchlike) but were free to choose most of their classes from a wide range of optional courses, which only needed to cover some areas outlined in the curriculum.

This system, however, had come under pressure in recent years and is currently being replaced by Bachelor's and Master's degrees derived from the English and American model. Officially, this has been done for two reasons: First of all, there had been strong political pressure to reduce the average length of study. In German Studies for example, students averaged 6.5 years to gain their "Magister" or "Staatsexamen" degree. This, of course, has been regarded as too long in comparison with students from the U.S. or other EU countries. Secondly, as a consequence of European integration, efforts have been made to harmonize the degree schemes in higher education in EU countries, the so-called "Bologna Process." By now, BA and MA courses have been introduced step-by-step to replace the traditional German degree system. In reaction to these demands, Siegen's Department of Language, Literary and Media Studies introduced two three-year BA courses as of winter 2002/03. The first one, Language and Communication (LAC), is a course in Linguistics (including language instruction), whereas in Literary, Cultural and Media Studies (LCMS) literature is being taught within the framework of Cultural and Media Studies, which we briefly introduced earlier on. In addition, various 2-year MA courses, among them Literature, Culture and Media and Medienkultur ('Media Culture'), are being offered since fall 2004.

We will not be able to discuss the—to our minds disastrous—results of these reforms here, but we would like to abide by the opinion that these reforms do already have a deep impact on the everyday teaching practice in general and on the teaching of literature in particular. By now, the modularization of courses has been widely realized and the ECTS (European Credit Transfer System) has been introduced in Germany. Therefore German university teachers have to provide an attractive and recurring set of optional modules, and students are making stronger demands for more standardized courses.

3 Teaching Net Literature in the Classroom: Syllabi and Didactic Approaches

By now, literature in modern computer-based and networked media has rather been a subject of mainly scholarly research at Siegen. Teaching activities in the subject matter have been carried out in a rather unsystematic manner so far and have not yet been implemented as a compulsory module in a curriculum. Nonetheless, Peter Gendolla has repeatedly offered seminars and lectures on literature in new media for the last 14 years. His chair in literary studies is known as "Literature, Arts, New Media and Technologies" and is thus explicitly committed to research and teaching of literature in its medial and technological context. Hence, he offered some initial courses approaching the subject matter of "net literature" in the 1990s, such as

- *Literatur auf CD-ROM* ('Literature on CD-ROM'; seminar, 1995): Examples ranged from the first very simple CD-ROM editions of classical writers—which were nothing more than texts by Kafka, Goethe and others and some illustrations—to some more interesting experiments like *otto mops: Auf der Suche nach dem Jandl* (1996) or *Stehender Sturmlauf: Kafka in Prag* (1997) trying to find media-adequate realizations of the originals.

- *Computerlyrik* ('Computer-aided Poetry'; seminar, 1997) exploring early text and poetry generators such as *Ars magna, CAP, POE* or *Delphi*.

- *Literatur im Internet* ('Literature on the Internet'; seminar, summer 1999) exploring new tendencies of writing and reading in networked media. In this seminar students were introduced to topics such as hypertext and hyperfiction, game theory, collaborative writing as well as to theoretic approaches like George Landow's theory of hypertext or Espen Aarseth's cybertext theory.

3.1 *Literatur im Netz* ('Literature on the Net')

From 2002/03, Gendolla and Schäfer jointly offered—in the context of a course program derived from the activities of the Research Center on "Media Upheavals"—various seminars on the topic, beginning with a two-semester seminar *Literatur im Netz* ('Literature on the Net'). As anybody who already taught interdisciplinary classes can tell from her/his own experience, this has positive as well as negative effects. In these particular cases, we had students of Computer Studies who knew a lot more than we do about information technologies and electronic networks but had little knowledge of literature and the arts sitting next to students of pure literary studies who were well acquainted with literary theories and traditions but only had a vague idea of the impact of computers on writing and reading.

What, however, did we discuss with students in the classroom? For the purpose of the first seminar, we used our distinction between "literature on the net" on which we focused in the first semester and "net literature," which was on the agenda in the second semester. We started the seminar with a survey of the media history of literature from ancient epitaphs to the handwritten manuscripts of medieval monks, from the printed books of the *Gutenberg Galaxy* to modern digital computers. Thereupon we examined the impact of computers on literature by discussing the peculiarities of electronic storage and transmission of data. We then referred to traditional aesthetic criteria and asked if they are still in force in selected hyperfictions, collaboratively written texts or computer-generated poems. And then we raised the question whether traditional literary genres such as poetry, prose and drama can be realized in computer-based media and, if yes, how their impact would then change.

After this, we examined how computer-based and networked media have already influenced and changed the literary system. Literature cannot be analyzed without taking into account that verbal objects have always been subject to historically varying communicative practices that are highly dependent on the media in which they are carried out. At this point of our course, we focused on the distribution and post processing of literary texts: How are texts being transferred over time and space? How are they stored and edited in the age of "permanent mutability" (Chaouli 68)?

In the following semester, we focused on what we regard as "net literature" in a stricter sense. We again started with a rather broad approach by discussing various theoretical conceptions of telecommunication networks from physical transport of messages by messengers and the transport of letters by mail to dematerialized telecommunication systems such as telegraphy, telephony or computer networks, but also social and biological networks.

We then raised the question whether new literary forms may be developing under the influence of present-day computer technologies. Although we did not intend a general discussion of theories of literature—this would certainly be too much to expect from students in this context—, we wanted to confront net literature with those four epistemological conceptions we already mentioned in our other essay in this book: *intentionality vs. chance, performativity/performance, emergence* and *game/play*.

3.2 Geschichte der interaktiven Literatur ('History of Interactive Literature')

Whereas we had started our first seminar with a top-down approach by introducing quite complex theoretical conceptions and then trying to apply them to net literature, we gave preference to a bottom-up approach in our second attempt: Since many students had not been in touch with net literature before, this allowed for a beginning with self-exploring activities in class. We then could introduce the theoretical framework on the basis of a thorough knowledge of some exemplary texts. Hence, in our two-semester seminar *Geschichte der interaktiven Literatur* ('History of Interactive Literature'), which we held in

2005/06, we aimed at drawing students' attention to the historical dimension of net literature.

For this purpose, we focused mainly on three tendencies for characterizing and classifying those many literary texts and procedures in which recursive processes can be identified. First, current text generators can be traced back to previous forms of *combinatory literature*. Since the Baroque era, numerous writers were experimenting with literary forms that did not only consider a literary text a symbolic expression of a person's subjectivity but also considered a text as determined by the level of programming and processing of signs. On the one hand, this is reflected in the tradition of word games such as anagrams, palindromes or proteus verses, ranging from Baroque writers such as Quirinus Kuhlmann to 20th century avant-garde poets like Unica Zürn or Oskar Pastior. On the other hand it is presented in mechanical text-generating machines such as Ramon Lull's *Ars Magna* (1305-08), Georg Philipp Harsdörffer's *Fünffacher Denckring der Teutschen Sprache* (1651), which claims to reproduce the entire German-language word formation in a mechanical apparatus, or the (fictive) Grand Academy of Lagado's machine for automatic writing in Jonathan Swift's *Gulliver's Travels* (1726). In 20th century literature, (neo-)avant-garde writers such as the international (though predominantly French) Oulipo group developed a wide range of chance and/or algorithmic procedures for the production of literary texts, which were subsequently implemented into computer-based and networked media. We discussed manifests and texts by François Le Lionnais, Italo Calvino and Raymond Queneau, the creator of the famous sonnet-machine *Cent mille milliards de poèmes* [*One Hundred Million Billion Poems*].

Secondly, *hyperfictions*, too, are not necessarily dependent on computers: If the basic idea of hyperfictions is letting the reader determine how he traverses the text by choosing from different story threads, then this is possible in all storage media in which texts can be divided into segments which are connected to each other by hyperlinks. Starting from Landow's theory of hypertext, we analyzed texts in which readers have the choice between multiple links and thus need to make decisions during the reading process. In print media, this has been done either in permutative novels such as Italo Calvino's *If on a Winter's Night a Traveller* (1979) or Andreas Okopenko's *Lexikonroman einer sentimentalen Reise zum Exporteurstreffen in Druden* (1970). Alternatively, the text segments can be published in loose-leaf form as has been done by Marc Saporta in *Composition No. 1*, by Herta Müller in *Der Wächter nimmt seinen Kamm* (1993) or by Konrad Balder Schäuffelen in his various "lottery novels." We discussed how the reader could either combine the text segments according to set rules or rather intuitively.

It goes without saying that human-human communication has always been possible prior to the installation of computer networks. There have always been *collaborative writing projects* such as the parlor games of the Baroque era, the co-operative writing in 18th century literary salons or the Surrealist "cadavres exquis" ('exquisite corpses'). However, it was not until the implementation of postal systems and of technological transmission media that long-distance collaborations were to become possible, ranging from varying writers' correspondences and the epistolary novels to Mail Art or Correspondence Art projects of the 1960s and 70s, from telephone and fax performances to simultaneous communication via computer networks.

In the summer semester 2006, we continued with analyzing and discussing current tendencies of net literature with a focus on projects in computer-based and networked media. At first, we familiarized the students with the already mentioned media-technological changes of literary production, distribution, and reception (3.1), as well as with the diverse models of interactivity in the computer sciences and also in literary and media studies (e.g., Pflüger; Heibach 68-91; Rettberg) in order to work out the differences to traditional sociological theories of interaction as well as to the usage of the term "interaction" in theories of reception.

Following this, we referred back to Noah Wardrip-Fruin's thoughts on the specificities of "digital literature" in order to give the students an overview covering the wide spectrum of literary works and processes in computer-based media. Wardrip-Fruin's text is a good entry into this field (unfamiliar to most students) because his attempt to determine the typology of this field of knowledge is well suited for the fundamental discussion of the connection of literature to its media with concrete examples.

In order to discuss the different aspects of human and machine "creativity," we at first spent some time with collaborative writing projects like e-mail-novels, where several authors or groups of authors jointly produced literary texts. This engendered particularly the question of the changed traditional conceptions of the author and the attribution of creative processes. When using programmed poetry generators in which literary forms are implemented, this question comes to a head in a special way since the problem arises whether and to what extent artificial "intelligences" are able to create texts to which readers are ready to attribute aesthetic qualities.

The rest of the semester was devoted to the effects of interactivity on literary genres made available by computer-based media. Above all, we discussed the relation of narration and games within literary hypertexts and computer games. In the course of this, we focused on the possibilities of a transmedial narratology that has been particularly questioned by the so-called "ludologists" (e.g., Aarseth and Eskelinen). Attempts to mediate between the narratologists and the ludologists are for one Wardrip-Fruin's efforts regarding "playable media" and "textual instruments," and on the other hand the interactive drama *Façade* by Michael Mateas and Andrew Stern.

3.3 Digitale Literatur und Kunst: Close Readings ('Digital Literature and Art: Close Readings')

For several years we have been cooperating with Roberto Simanowski, who teaches German literature and digital aesthetics at Brown University in Providence, RI. Brown University, one of the renowned Ivy-League universities on the East Coast, is one of the centers where the theoretical and practical discussions regarding digital art and literature are taking place in the U.S. Even though the project partners had already been offering lectures and seminars on digital literature and art for some years, they were exclusively presented at Brown or at Siegen respectively in face-to-face classes. Therefore, the idea emerged to complement our cooperation in research with joint classes so that students from both universities could be included in the discussions, and this as a start led to a one-day initial block-course in Siegen on *Digital Literature and Art: Close Readings* during the winter term 2006/07 for the Siegen students.

Teaching this seminar as a block allowed us to concentrate much more closely on individual literary projects. In particular, it was possible to include longer periods of group-work in which the students were able to first discuss their own experiences and thoughts on the literary projects without a professor's input. Here, we especially aimed at a first descriptive representation of the object before including our guiding questions into the discussion. These had been presented previously already at a first introductory session in order to structure these group-activities. Apart from this, the students earlier had been able to access some theoretical texts and URLs on the BSCW-Server of our University.

Using the examples of the interactive drama *Façade* by Michael Mateas and Andrew Stern, the hyperfiction *Die Schwimmmeisterin* [*The Bubble Bath*] by Susanne Berkenheger, as well as Daniel C. Howe's installation *Text.Curtain*, we discussed above all their continuities and discontinuities relative to "traditional" literature in print media. Continuing, we asked about the intertextual or intermedial relationships to concrete literary forms, structures, elements, conventions, constellations of characters, etc., that are taken over from traditional genres, and then we attempted to find out about those characteristics that can be realized exclusively in digitally networked media. In the course of this we also looked at the relationships between "author," "work," and "reader" and apart from this we were also interested in the technical realization of the projects, as well as the question of the reciprocal "regulation" between human and machine "actors."

The discussion on the interactive installations (or environments, respectively) *Screen* by Noah Wardrip-Fruin, *Text Rain* by Camille Utterback and Romy Achituv, as well as *Listening Post* by Mark Hansen and Ben Rubin led to more concrete questions like, for example, the intertextual relationships between *Text Rain* and the poem by Evan Zimroth on which it is based, or the borders and interdependencies between literature and the fine arts.

4 Teaching Net Literature in a Transatlantic Blended Learning Environment

A follow-up course, *Digitale Literatur und Kunst II* ('Digital Literature and Art II') that broadened the aforementioned cooperative teaching practices, took advantage of the Internet to enable an online cooperation between teachers and students within a collaborative transatlantic teaching framework.[1] What follows are the practical experiences and lessons learned from conducting this cross-cultural class between our seminar group at Siegen and Roberto Simanowski's at Brown University in fall 2008. Since digital literature is created via programmable media and usually produced, published, and read (interacted with) in an online environment, it seemed to be a plausible strategy to teach digital literature in the environment these works participate in. However, performing such a class in a transatlantic teaching framework requires several organizational adjustments. Before presenting the course description along with the methodological approach applied in the Blended Learning class, problems, procedures, and background information related to student groups and logistics will be illustrated first.

4.1 Teaching Procedures

Due to logistical issues—for example, the six-hour time difference and different academic schedules (Brown University's fall term was from September 6th to December and Siegen University's was from October 17th to February 6th)—both partners had to adjust sessions to hold parallel courses. As a consequence, we conducted five transatlantic cooperation sessions where tandem groups discussed their results face-to-face in the U.S. and in Germany separately.

Each of these groups simultaneously undertook special studies for an appointed work of digital literature by using the discussion board for collaborative work conducted in English. The outcomes were then presented to their respective groups in the five (spatio-temporally separated) sessions and presented online as a PowerPoint presentation.

4.2 Teaching Environment

As the central place for online interaction and communication between group members, we provided a secure, asynchronous discussion board. We assumed that students already participate within the Web 2.0 environment and, therefore, shied away from implementing a synchronous communication tool.[2] Instead, students could provide alternative contact information on their member profile. Generally, the discussion board provided space for reflections and discussions while the face-to-face meetings with the teachers served as the place for prompt intermediation.[3] We, as teachers, did not moderate the discussion board but encouraged the students to work together without our direct intervention.

Based on a didactic Blended Learning Model that was developed for the purposes of the class (Tomaszek), the web-based discussion board was understood as a "space for reflection" in which a certain competence could be developed with the help of written-down discussions within small cooperating groups. This was based on the assumption that in a discussion forum critical thought is practiced and that thereby meta-cognition produces knowledge in the reflective process of writing. In this seminar, in which students had to be present, the teaching situation is understood as a space of mediation. In this mediational space, activity- and transfer-oriented knowledge is acquired that can be implemented or applied on the basis of a research oriented development of competence.

Generally, it was the teachers' goal to turn students into researchers, critics, and self-directed discussion board moderators in the online environment. Within this environment, students were engaged to develop their own thoughts, views, and insights.

This is also advantageous because German students wouldn't have had enough language skills to react spontaneously and adequately to an American student's comments. We observed this phenomenon in the final session that was held via an online video-conferencing system in real-time. Here, German students had difficulties organizing their ideas and reacting promptly to the American students. Implementing the asynchronous discussion board proved to be the most effective way for students to do their research collaboratively. It provided opportunities to consider the matters discussed in the face-to-face environment, and the depth of the student responses reflected this. They were able to draw enlightening connections that ranged from programming knowledge related to n-grams when discussing Wardrip-Fruin's *News Reader* to discussions of Shklovsky's theory of "defamiliarization" when talking about Utterback's *Text Rain*. These inputs and links to external information and experiences definitely enriched the students' discussions held on the discussion board. While discussing asynchronously on the provided discussion forum, students had more time to elaborate on answers and to draw on knowledge they already had and made use of to adopt for the given assignments.

The discussion board was open for all students to elaborate on the projects and accompanying research questions. Moreover, the face-to-face classes that were held each week while the discussion board was open provided another source of inspiration, insights, and knowledge. Via the online communication system, students shared what they learned in the face-to-face meetings with their counterparts. This dynamic broadened the classroom-facilitated, intercultural collaboration between students from different courses of studies to foster multifocal perspectives. The teachers accompanied the process in face-to-face sessions and commented on outcomes by posing questions and giving valuable hints to direct the students towards new perspectives.

4.3 Methodological Course Description

To conduct the class in Germany and the U.S. successfully, a methodological approach, divided in four phases, was developed:

- *Phase 1:* Teachers at both universities conducted face-to-face classes discussing identical topics within six weeks (spatio-temporally separated) in Germany and the U.S.

- *Phase 2:* The students were divided into five groups, which usually consisted of one American student and three to four German students. These groups were designed so that participants could draw on their varying backgrounds to contribute their ideas to a pool of collective group knowledge.
Each group discussed one work in-depth by answering research questions provided by the instructors. Furthermore, students were asked to read assigned academic papers to complete their presentations. These presentations were prepared by the students from both universities collaboratively and presented face-to-face to their respective classes in the same week (spatio-temporally separated) both in Germany and the U.S.

- *Phase 3:* The second phase served as a preparation for a final online-session conducted via a synchronous video conferencing system at the end of the seminar. Here, students were asked to adopt what they learned.
- *Phase 4:* This was a phase of reflection and documentation. The groups prepared final PowerPoint presentations, which they uploaded to the online class forum.

Students need to be familiar with a number of divergent works to be able to discuss the varieties of digital literature and to approach new reading and interpreting strategies successfully. The online environment helped to meet that need by providing a discussion board for time permitting in-depth discussions.

In the face-to-face sessions, teachers used their literary and cultural studies perspective to help students develop abilities for testing concepts of "traditional" literary theory critically. Moreover, students were asked to describe as well as to evaluate the structures, forms, aesthetics, and techniques of selected works of digital literature in respect to their theoretical and methodological competences within assigned research questions (Schäfer et al. 69). In the realtime sessions, the class discussed intermediality, multilinearity, interactivity, and programming as features of digital literature and art with reference to specific examples.

Students worked collaboratively in groups on their group assignment. They explored the Web for related information, read academic papers provided by their instructors, and discussed their findings and observations in the online class discussion forum.

4.4 Syllabus and Research Questions

Five thematic foci were agreed upon for the joint seminar sessions with exemplary literary or artistic projects in each case:

Session 1: Interactive installations I
Project: Camille Utterback and Romy Achituv: *Text Rain*

Research questions:
– How does Utterback and Achituv transform Zimroth's poem "Talk, You"?
– Could this poem be replaced by another text?
– What are the main differences between fixed texts and texts in motion?

Session 2: Interactive installations II
Project: Scott Snibbe: *Deep Walls*

Research questions:
- What are the main differences between traditional ("inter-passive") and interactive art?
- How are we to understand the grammar of interaction, the (spatial and temporal) structure and the applied symbols of Deep Walls?

Session 3: "Playable media" and "textual instruments"
Project: Noah Wardrip-Fruin et al.: *News Reader*

Research questions:
- How does Wardrip-Fruin define "playable media"?
- What are the differences to computer games on the one hand, to literary texts on the other hand?
- How are "instrumental texts" differentiated from "textual instruments"?

Session 4: Digital photography
Project: Andreas Mueller-Pohle: *Face Codes*

Research questions:
- What are the roles, features, functions of photography in traditional literature?
- Is the text imprinted on the faces the "genetic" makeup of the image itself or rather the fingerprint of the photographer?

Session 5: Mapping Art, body liberation and surveillance
Projects: George Legrady: *Making Visible the Invisible;* Mark Napier: *Black and White;* Josh On: *They Rule;* Golan Levin: *The Secret Lives of Numbers;* Martin Wattenberg: *Shape of Song;* Greyworld: *The Source*

Research questions:
- Are there relationships between maps in general, mind maps, concept maps and mapping art?
- What is the common ground, what the difference between the aesthetics of mapping art and the aesthetics of readymades and photography?

Along with the research questions, students were given links to theoretical papers provided in an electronic reader in the online discussion board. These academic readings formed the common theoretical ground for the tandem groups' research and analysis.

4.5 Student and Course Performance

As a result of divergent methodological approaches that the students from Germany and the U.S. adopted in their research, the overall discussions were enriched by their differing views and complementary perspectives that brought a panoply of meaning to the projects and a wide range of insights into the research questions.

The board messages of Brown University students demonstrate that the student groups approached the course material differently: Brown University students worked critically with an established hypothesis on digital literature and art that they had developed together in class. This hypothesis served as a starting point for all other evaluations and discussions on primary and secondary literature and allowed to prescind the topics on various levels. In contrast, German students used secondary texts mainly as a source to understand the assigned work of digital literature and to apply the terminologies used in an academic paper correctly. Thus, they worked closely with the given academic papers without prescinding from the contents read. Thanks to the collaboration with students from other educational backgrounds, the transatlantic Blended Learning class helped them to experience other approaches for dealing with works of digital literature and its accompanied research papers.[4]

5 A Résumé for the Future

As we have said in the beginning, the teaching of digitally networked literature is not an easy undertaking; it is in no way fully developed; it has no completed curricula with canonical projects, let alone differentiated methods. Of course the reasons lie in the fast changes of the new literary forms, as well as in the constant technical changes of the media systems within which they are being "written." If we, however, take net literature as the testing field for the emerging forms of communication in a global electronically networked world, then a characterization and sedimentation of digital literature corresponding to the traditional canonizations will not surface since the literary arts are about to become *opere aperte*, open works of art in a still further reaching sense than Umberto Eco once had suggested. Authors and readers, teachers and students read and write together with programs, fluidly creating texts. Whether great art or great kitsch emerges from this will be decided—as it always has been—through criticism and the further history of their reception.

Translated by Brigitte Pichon and Dorian Rudnytsky

Notes

1. Students from Brown University were majoring in a variety of subjects: Chinese, Music Theory, Management, and Digital Aesthetics; Literary Systems; Literature and languages or Computer Science. German participants were mostly students pursuing a Bachelor or a Master of Arts in Literary, Cultural and Media Studies. The overall students experience with digital literature, art, and new media ranged from basic competences in programming to theoretical knowledge acquired in classes on interactive literature.

2. Instead, students could provide alternative contact information on their member profile. In fact, 59 percent of the German students used other communication systems (for example, E-Mail, *Skype*, *ICQ*, *Messenger*) to work together on their assignments. These communication systems were used by German students who couldn't meet face-to-face and who wanted to discuss issues in real-time with online tools that allowed them to ask questions and get answers promptly. Due to the time difference, American students didn't participate in these real-time discussions; they used the discussion board instead.

3. Asynchronous communication systems such as the discussion board allow the time for thoughtful discussions and preparations; moreover, these discussions are permanent and able to be reviewed. Such detailed examinations of the classes' subjects couldn't have been conducted on synchronous face-to-face communication channels, as words are ephemeral and cursory with unclear conversation threads.

4. An evaluation of the students' learning activity at the end of the seminar was conducted by using a coding scheme developed by Anna Veldhuis-Diermanse to analyze message content in computer-supported collaborative communication systems. With the help of this coding system, it was possible to observe cognitive, meta-cognitive, and affective learning activities performed by our students in the discussion board. A content analysis of the posts revealed that 53 percent of the discussions were related to a cognitive learning activity, 24 percent to a meta-cognitive activity, and 23 percent were within an affective learning activity (Tomaszek). The results highlight a concentrated student performance in which participants focused on their group-discussions by presenting concepts, reasoning, arguments, visions, and conclusions by relating these to their learning process and research goals.

Works Cited

Aarseth, Espen J. *Cybertext: Perspectives on Ergodic Literature*. Baltimore: Johns Hopkins UP, 1997.

Chaouli, Michel. "Was bedeutet: Online lesen? Über die Möglichkeit des Archivs im Cyberspace." *Digitale Literatur*. Ed. Heinz Ludwig Arnold and Roberto Simanowski. Munich: Text + Kritik, 2001. 65-74.

Eskelinen, Markku. "Six Problems in Search of a Solution: The Challenge of Cybertext Theory and Ludology to Literary Theory." *The Aesthetics of Net Literature: Writing, Reading and Playing in Programmable Media*. Ed. Peter Gendolla and Jörgen Schäfer. Bielefeld: Transcript, 2007. 179-209.

Gumbrecht, Hans Ulrich, and K. Ludwig Pfeiffer, eds. *Materialität der Kommunikation*. Frankfurt a.M.: Suhrkamp, 1988.

Hayles, N. Katherine. *Electronic Literature: New Horizons for the Literary*. Notre Dame: U of Notre Dame P, 2008.

Heibach, Christiane. *Literatur im elektronischen Raum*. Frankfurt a.M.: Suhrkamp, 2003.

Kreuzer, Helmut. *Veränderungen des Literaturbegriffs: Fünf Beiträge zu aktuellen Problemen der Literaturwissenschaft*. Göttingen: Vandenhoeck & Ruprecht, 1975.

Landow, George P. *Hypertext 3.0: Critical Theory and New Media in an Era of Globalization*. Baltimore: Johns Hopkins UP, 2006.

Pflüger, Jörg. "Konversation, Manipulation, Delegation: Zur Ideengeschichte der Interaktivität." *Geschichten der Informatik*. Ed. Hans Dieter Hellige. Berlin: Springer, 2004. 367-408.

Rettberg, Scott. "All Together Now: Collective Knowledge, Collective Narratives, and Architectures of Participation." 2005. 28 Aug. 2009 <http://www.retts.net/documents/cnarrativeDAC.pdf>.

Schäfer, Jörgen, Sigrid Schubert, Kirstin Schwidrowski, and Christian Eibl. "Digitale Literatur und Kunst: Blended Learning zu ästhetischen Prozessen in und mit Informatiksystemen." *E-Learning und Literatur: Informatiksysteme im Literaturunterricht*. Ed. Jörgen Schäfer and Sigrid Schubert. Siegen: Universi, 2007. 61-78.

Tomaszek, Patricia. "Netzliteratur in der Lehre: Fachliche Kompetenzen vermitteln und erwerben durch kooperatives Blended Learning." University of Siegen: 2008. TS.

Veldhuis-Diermanse, Anna. *CSCLearning? Participation, Learning Activities and Knowledge Construction in Computer-Supported Learning in Higher Education.* Diss. Wageningen Universiteit, Netherlands, 2002.

Wardrip-Fruin, Noah. "Five Elements of Digital Literature." In this book.

Karin Wenz

Digital Media@Maastricht University

Problem-Based Learning as an Approach to Digital Literature

The Faculty of Arts and Social Sciences at Maastricht University and the University College offer courses with an interdisciplinary goal in mind. These courses are planned and organized by a team of 2-3 colleagues, who are specialists in the field. I myself do not teach a separate course on digital literature but do give an introduction to digital literature and art as part of my courses on digital media and on narrative media, and also an introductory lecture in a colleague's course on media and the senses.

Teaching at Maastricht University and Maastricht University College is based on Problem-based learning (PBL). PBL assumes that effective learning can only take place if the student is actively participating in the learning process. Learning is approached as an enquiry-based, collaborative enterprise starting off with concrete problems and research questions. Literature read together in class is not simply summarized; students are asked to focus on the solving of research questions collectively, in small-scale groups of twelve to fifteen students.

Problem-based learning simulates research processes understood as collaborative activities: "There is no essential difference between doing research and studying in a PBL-setting. Instead of 'problem-based' we could therefore also speak about 'inquiry-based' learning" (Wesseling 17). As students can choose a course freely, we assume that the group is sharing a common interest in the topic, its research questions, and problems related to it. Both students and teachers participate in a learning process that is student-centered in the sense that the learning process of the students lies at the center in the design of the courses as well as in the development of the curriculum as a whole.

The lecturer and the colleagues supporting him or her in the design of the course are responsible for the choice of central themes and problems, the construction of tasks and assignments, and the selection of literature. Additionally to meeting in small tutorial groups twice a week, a lecture will be offered weekly to introduce students to the field and frame the learning process. In the case of digital literature, those lectures introduce students to the discussion of concepts as well as genre. An introductory lecture deals with the debate of such concepts as "digital literature" (e.g. Simanowski, Block et al.), "electronic literature" (Electronic Literature Organization, ELO) and "net literature" (Gendolla and Schäfer). The characteristics of digital literature are discussed in the broader context of characteristics of digital media in general, the debate on interactivity and ergodic literature (e.g. Aarseth; Landow; Manovich).

Examples are read and discussed together. The genre we start off with is hyperfiction. We read Michael Joyce's *Twelve Blue* in class together, which as a classic is a good starting point to introduce the concept of textuality as "interwoven" semiotic structure, as *Twelve Blue* uses threads in its literal meaning as navigational tools beside hyperlinks. The thread and the metaphoric use of the term to describe textual connectedness is a starting point to discuss not only textuality but also to relate it to the concept of hypertext. All students use the Web a lot; however, in most cases they are confronted with digital literature and art for the first time in this course. Hyperfiction offers them a start in a familiar environment, offering surprising navigational tools and dynamic connections of the different narrative parts, which leads to an experience in between fascination and frustration (cf. Bootz 2007).

Another example of hyperfiction introduced in a lecture is Esther Hunziker and Felix Zbinden's *edinburgh/demon* (2007). The example is problematic for use in an English class as it combines text in German with only some English textual fragments. I introduce *edinburgh/demon* not to discuss the storyline or the content of this hyperfiction but to discuss the relation of hyperfiction to its historical precursors, to other media, as well as its intermedial possibilities. One of the authors, Esther Hunziker, described her art practice in an interview in 2007. She claims that working with found footage, with fragments, recycling and re-constructing material lies at the basis of her art. With this statement, she relates her work to precursors since the avant-garde. Montage, collage—but also reusing material several times in different contexts and thereby setting it into a new perspective are strategies used by Hunziker and Zbinden. The artists offer two ways to interact with the artwork: a free choice between the 80 pieces integrated in *edinburgh/demon* or, alternatively, following one of the "cuts," which offer a pre-selection of the pieces. The description as "cuts" puts them into the tradition of filmmaking, where a different version of a movie is offered under the tag "director's cut." In filmmaking, the director's cut usually refers to a version that is longer in comparison with the standard edition that has been shortened due to practical reasons.

The "cuts" offered here have a different function. Although the director's cut usually is the most complete version of the artwork, the selections of parts of the artwork here highlight specific topics and play with expectations of the user.

The artists practice working with fragments; recycling and re-constructing material is reflected in the material basis of *edinburgh/demon*. This hypertext combines text, music, photographs, videos, and a computer game as well as static, dynamic, and generated text. The multi- and intermedial possibilities hypertext offers are used fully.

Other genres introduced are digital poetry, MUDs, interactive drama, installations and the cave, and digital performances. Even though the distinction following traditional literary genre as well as categories based on technical conditions is problematic, they are used to help students to become familiarized with the works introduced, but in the discussion afterwards they are also problematized. The genre of performative digital poetry is a rather new and surprising one, which uses performances either on stage or in virtual environments to perform readings of digital poetry combined with dance, sound and/or lightshows. As we are dealing with many examples including media and installation art, the use of caves, and digital performances, the discussion in class always ends up with a general debate around the question: "What is literature?"

In the course on narrative media, this question is not central; rather, it is the comparison of the narrative potential of media as written text, images, comics, movies, hyperfiction and digital games. Topics central in this course—beside an introduction to narratology—are transmedial storytelling, adaptation, and media-specific problems.

Even though digital literature can be classified as being hybrid in all respects—not only because of its multi- and intermedial quality but also because of its genre-transgressing features—the question of genres is introduced in both courses. The concepts hypertext and hyperfiction are not only theoretically presented but also practically analyzed, and examples are read in class. Examples of digital poetry are shown, and set in relation to sound poetry and visual poetry. Videos of digital performances are discussed in their relation to happenings, theatre and DJ shows. In the case of digital performances in virtual environments (for example in *Second Life*) and their post-editing, as in recent works by Alan Sondheim, the relation to machinima (game videos) is highlighted. Both courses on digital and narrative media are not only focused on digital literature, but give an introduction to the general field and the crossover between literature, art, and partly also computer games. In digital media, all traditional forms come to be options of art and design again, as the example of Hunziker and Zbinden has shown. This is a perfect case to show how not only analogue media are digitized and integrated but also which interactive and processing characteristics of digital media as text generators, mouseover effects, visualization, and linking have been used to build a work of digital literature.

In the case of digital media, this leads to a double coding. One coding can be understood as culturally based, based on cultural artifacts which belong to the sphere of art as well as to the sphere of popular culture. The second coding belongs to the technological sphere; the specific features of digital media and the underlying programming. The term hybrid culture refers to this intersection as well as to the convergence of forms and meanings. This convergence combines forms from traditional areas of art, mass communication, and popular culture employing digital media. Hybridization is a phenomenon resulting from the increased mediation of vast areas of human experience, which is dependent on the storage and processing capacities of digital media. Therefore, hybrid culture is closely linked to the development of digital media, which is shown in class using the example of digital literature. The lectures are the only activity in which lecturers are central. However, the lectures are also supportive of the students' learning process not only by providing a theoretical framework but also by informing students about the problems the lecturers themselves encounter in their work as researchers. Therefore, a close relationship between the lecturer's research and the teaching activities is required.

In the field of digital media, we can take a previous knowledge and at least some basic skills of the students for granted. PBL tries to mobilize their previous knowledge, challenge them and help them to develop a deeper understanding of their own practice and experiences. This is also the reason why I first introduce hyperfiction and do not start with the historical roots of digital literature in kinetic poetry for example. The—on a first glance—most familiar cases are introduced first; from there we move on to those with which no prior knowledge and experience can be expected.

Some courses at Maastricht University offer an additional skills training session to the 2-hour lecture and 4-hour tutorial group meeting weekly. This skills training session may consist of, for example, creating a personal web log, designing a web site, or producing a digital video or a podcast. Thereby students do not only deal with a topic theoretically but also gain a better understanding of the possibilities as well as the limitations in the use of digital media. The practical experience supports a critical discussion in class as theoretical texts are evaluated on the background of the practical work experience. However, in the 6 years I have been teaching at Maastricht University, the practical skills sessions only one time resulted in a creative writing project, for which a student simulated an interview with Jean Baudrillard on the topic of virtuality paralleled with an essay in which she discussed his writings (also academically). Students have a platform to publish, perform and discuss their own literary works; however, they have not produced any work of digital literature yet. The reason for this is that we do not offer courses in creative writing (neither for analogue nor for digital media), nor do we have a traditional faculty structure with a division into disciplines and a literature department, but follow interdisciplinary goals in research as well as in teaching.

Even though lecturers pre-structure the learning process, students are supported in a way that makes it possible for them to take responsibility for the content and the process of the learning activity in the course of the class. These working formats allow for a diverse, stimulating and challenging program, but they require thorough preparation for classes by the students. Simply showing up without being prepared does not allow for active participation and formulating research questions collectively, as students need to interact with each other in the sessions. The sessions consist of two main parts. Students will read (ideally in advance) a short text (1-2 pages) written by the team of lecturers on a problem and a topic related to the course's theme and will freely brainstorm. This leads to a collection of ideas and a discussion of previous knowledge. They inform each other about the experiences made and will formulate some questions. These questions are then used to find a solution for the problem formulated in the short text provided by the lecturer, called the assignment. The questions are formulated by the students under the supervision of a lecturer who will guide them in this rather free, creative process. They are a guideline for the preparation of the following meeting in which the literature the lecturers suggest for each assignment will be prepared individually by the students with the goal to find answers for the questions formulated as a result of the brainstorming. Students report back to the group what they think are possible answers. This meeting has to dive much deeper into the material and has to be distinguished from a mere brainstorming. The texts have to be read critically and the suggestions of the authors read have to be discussed in comparison. Students take turns at being the discussion leader in these discussions so that the lecturer can step back and only support the discussion with additional information or guide it when needed. Then, the discussion of the texts is again followed by the reading of a new assignment and a new brainstorming session. During the brainstorming process, students need to leave familiar grounds and enter a domain without authorities that may serve as external sources and provide security. Students learn to get comfortable with a certain degree of uncertainty. The goal is that they achieve confidence from their collaboration with each other. PBL is understood as open-ended and only predetermined very little by lecturers. However, the function of the lecturer is important when students start to raise questions such as, for example, "what is literature," thereby helping them to reformulate a question like this into, for example, "what is specific about digital literature." A more general discussion on art or literature is also offered in an additional lecture.

Apart from a field or a case that is central for a course, research methodology is also introduced. For example, narratology is introduced and applied in the course on narrative media, while in the course on digital media, virtual ethnography is presented to the class as one possible method to investigate such social software as *Facebook*, *MySpace* or *YouTube*, the practices we can observe there, and the communities using it. The concrete works of digital literature and digital art are analyzed by using semiotics as the framework.

Collaboration is not only central in class meetings but also important for staff members in the process of developing a course. Collectively, the faculty enables but also constrains a student's learning process by selecting topics and case studies, decides which practical skills training to offer, formulates assignments, and selects the sources students should read. Within these constraints, students are free to define their own interests.

The type of students' assessments is liberal, ranging from rather traditional written exams (rarely used in the humanities) or academic essays, to projects such as web sites or web logs and video comments on a topic related to the course's theme. Regardless of the format chosen by the student, there must be an explicitly formulated research question and the conclusion should provide an answer to it. The PBL is a simulation of research but not by providing a safe environment excluded from the central problems of our society. As Wesseling puts it:

> A PBL-faculty is not a closed system; it is not internally focused on purely academic problems. A PBL-faculty will "resonate" with its societal environment, also in terms (subsets) of major problem areas. In other words, a PBL faculty will try to be in "sync" with its environment and change with it over time. (21)

This means, for example, that dependent on the development of research topics and the formulation of a new research program as well as through the interests of new staff members, the courses offered by the faculty are continually modified. External partners who offer help with skills training or offer a place for an intern are equally relevant as important cooperation partners outside of academia. The goal is to perform in multi- or interdisciplinary teams. Therefore, already the planning of courses is not left to an individual researcher alone but to a team from the very beginning. Not only students improve group-learning skills in a PBL setting; staff members do this as well.

As academic writing skills are central to doing research, teaching will also address problems of composition and peer review processes. In special courses, students are asked to prepare a journal, decide on, for example, creating a special issue on digital literature in Europe, write individual articles, but during the writing process they have to send their draft versions to the group to receive constructive feedback, think about the journal's structure, and write the introduction together. These journals can be sold to the other students and faculty members if the group wishes to do this.

In the beginning, there usually is a resistance to freely brainstorm in a group you do not already know very well, as well as a resistance to hand out a draft of a paper to the fellow students and deal with critique. However, the experience of working collaboratively on a project—let's say for example, a journal—is very fruitful and rewarding in the end. Students learn to deal with diversity as well as cultural differences, as the population of our students, especially in the master programs, is international and highly diverse. This diversity is a resource that PBL tries to use as a catalyst in collaborative projects as well as in brainstorming on themes in the tutor groups. The very positive effect this didactical system has for the students and the learning process has simultaneously a slightly negative downside for the faculty members. We do not have only a single small group of students interested in a course, which means that the course—which already takes 6-8 hours weekly when teaching one tutor group—adds up to 10-12 hours weekly when 18 or more students are interested in the topic and this large group therefore has to be split into two or even more smaller ones. PBL is very time-intensive not only for the students but also for the staff members. To offer faculty some flexibility, the courses are planned and offered for a longer period and not only for a single study year; an example being the course on narrative media that has been taught by me for five years now, with only the literature and the examples used annually updated. The first year needs a lot of investment by preparing the course and the lectures; however, the following years are less time consuming, as the program is not changed as long as a staff member is interested in the topic and the course attracts enough students and receives positive evaluations.

Many students perceive digital literature as new, surprising, and challenging. However, they also complain about the time factor in preparing, especially works of hyperfiction for class. Contrary to a printed work of fiction, hyperfiction does not come with a clear ending. Sometimes the reader does not know whether he or she has read everything or missed some important parts which are needed to understand the narrative fully. Thus, every student arrives in class with a different reading experience depending on the sequence in which they had read the hypertext. Some stop early, being annoyed by an interface or bored by coming back to the same fragment all over again. Furthermore, for many works of digital literature there is no interpretation or commentary by critiques yet so that students are unsure whether their interpretation of the work is valid and convincing.

For digital poetry performances the problem lies in the quality of videos available online. Thanks to Scott Rettberg, there are videos available with a higher quality now; however, the first ones were posted on youtube, filmed with a mobile phone camera, lacking in focus and being difficult to understand because of background noise. This problem is not new and is a reminder of the academic discussions of happenings, for which documentation was difficult to find and often missing. Regardless of the didactical method used, the field of digital literature is challenging in teaching, partly because of time constraints, partly because of the problem of documentation and accessibility.

Works Cited

Aarseth, Espen J. *Cybertext: Perspectives on Ergodic Literature.* Baltimore: Johns Hopkins UP, 1997.

Block, Friedrich W., Christiane Heibach, and Karin Wenz. "Introduction." *p0es1s: The Aesthetics of Digital Poetry.* Ed. Friedrich W. Block, Christiane Heibach, and Karin Wenz. Ostfildern: Cantz, 2004. 11-36.

Bootz, Philippe. "The Problem of Form: *Transitoire Observable*, a Laboratory for Emergent Programmed Art." *The Aesthetics of Net Literature: Writing, Reading and Playing in Programmable Media.* Ed. Peter Gendolla and Jörgen Schäfer. Bielefeld: Transcript, 2007. 89-106.

Joyce, Michael. *Twelve Blue.* 1996. Eastgate. 18 Aug. 2009 <http://www.eastgate.com/TwelveBlue/Twelve_Blue.html>.

Gendolla, Peter, and Jörgen Schäfer, eds. *The Aesthetics of Net Literature: Writing, Reading and Playing in Programmable Media.* Bielefeld: Transcript, 2007.

Hunziker, Esther, and Felix Zbinden. *edinburgh/demon.* 2007. 18 Aug. 2009 <http://www.ref17.net/edinburghdemon/>.

Landow, George. *Hypertext 3.0: Critical Theory and New Media in an Era of Globalization.* Baltimore: Johns Hopkins UP, 2006.

Manovich, Lev. *The Language of New Media.* Cambridge, MA: MIT P, 2001.

Simanowski, Roberto. "Digitale Literatur: Definition und Typologie." *Dichtung Digital* 1.1 (1999). 8 Apr. 2009 <http://www.dichtung-digital.de/Simanowski/28-Mai-99-1/typologie.htm>.

Wesseling, Lies, and Ger Wackers. "Problem Based Learning." *Transformations in Media Culture: Coursebook Module 1, Master Media Culture.* Ed. Reneé van de Vall. Maastricht 2008. 13-34.

Raine Koskimaa

Teaching Digital Literature through Multi-Layered Analysis

1 Digital Literature in the Context of Digital Culture Studies

I am teaching digital literature as a part of the curriculum in the Master's Degree Program in Digital Culture at the University of Jyväskylä. The program belongs to the Department of Art and Culture Studies within the Faculty of Humanities. It was started in 2005 as a response to a twofold challenge: there was an obvious demand for techno-culturally savvy humanities graduates, and there was a need to broaden the international student recruitment. From 2003 onward, there had been a Professor of Digital Culture planning and organizing the program. At that time, one academic program in digital culture already existed in Finland (University of Turku), which offered both BA and MA studies in Finnish, but in our survey in the field we did not find any other programs explicitly with "digital culture" in their title. There were programs like *Digital Media*, *Digital Communication*, *Digital Aesthetics* and such, which often come close to our notion of "digital culture," but usually with one clear distinction: the MA Degree Program in *Digital Culture* at the University of Jyväskylä is strictly theoretical, and research oriented. In comparison, most of the other related programs in Finland (and also internationally) have a strong practical/applied element in them.

The structure of the program reflects the variety of major subjects offered within our Department. All of them—art education, art history, contemporary culture studies, literature, and museology—are also available as major subjects for the students in the digital culture program (with the restriction that the student's BA degree has to be such, that major studies in a given subject are possible). Naturally, the student may also major in *Digital Culture*. There are no obligatory minor subject studies, but there are a substantial number of so-called core studies courses, which are obligatory for all students regardless of their major. It has been considered an important aspect of the program to offer the possibility to engage in any of the majors (like art history, literature, etc.) parallel with the core studies emphasis on digital culture. This means that students may graduate from our program as an MA in, for example, literature with expertise in digital culture, and a unique understanding of the role of literature and literary studies within the contemporary digital culture. Most of the courses are open to regular students (not attending the MA program), who may add some digital culture specialization to their "traditional" degrees. This ensures that digitalization processes within particular fields of art and culture studies may be addressed within the MA studies.

The students majoring in digital culture, on the other hand, gain a deeper understanding of digital culture phenomena and related research methodology (e.g. social network analysis, close reading of hypertext works). In digital culture we recognize, following Charlie Gere, that digitality "encompasses both the artefacts and the systems of signification and communication" of our contemporary life (12). Digitality here refers to "the whole panoply of virtual simulacra, instantaneous communication, ubiquitous media and global connectivity" (11). In these studies, all those phenomena that do not neatly fall into the traditional disciplinary fields—and the majority of originally digital formations belong to that category—can be properly addressed. Cybertextuality and computer games, as well as online virtual worlds and social networking sites, are prominent issues in major studies within digital culture. Teaching is closely related to ongoing research projects, so that students experience up to date teaching in the quickly developing field. It is also an aim to get the students engaged in research projects during their MA studies, so that they already have some experience of research work when they graduate.

With a subject like digital culture that in essence is so fundamentally global it is highly beneficial to have a truly international student body. Seminar discussions, which are an important part of the studies, are unquestionably enlightening for everybody, teachers included, when issues such as democracy in/of the Internet are discussed between participants coming from five, six different continents.

The students have their background mainly in the humanities, but not necessarily in literary studies. The course on *Digital Literature* begins with a historical overview of writing as technology. Then we have lectures on avant-garde writing (Futurism, Dadaism, Surrealism), followed by lectures on later experimental writing such as mail-art, concrete poetry, sound poetry, and especially the Oulipo. The theoretical considerations begin with the concept of hypertext and its applications to literary expression. Heavy emphasis is laid on the presentation of cybertext theory, which, in a sense, forms the backbone of the whole course. The last part of the course is devoted to various forms of digital literature, beginning with text adventure games and proceeding to hypertext fiction, text generators, e-poetry, and various sorts of web-based literature. There is also one lecture dealing specifically with Finnish digital literature. All of these lectures are accompanied with demonstrations, where the students have a chance to access and read the works dicussed by themselves. Finally, there is a concluding lecture situating digital literature as part of the larger media landscape.

In addition to the specific course on digital literature, issues such as hypertext and cybertext theory, interactive media, programmable media, procedural literacy, multimodal analysis, are integral parts of other core courses like theories of digital culture and digital art. Issues directly related to digital literature and its research thus form one of the main strands of the whole program.

2 Theory Embedded in Analysis: The Case of *These Waves of Girls*

Pedagogically, when it comes to teaching digital literature, my main strategy is to embed as much as possible of the relevant concepts and contexts into the analyses of specific works. In what follows, I'll present one such analysis (or at least a portion of it) of the work *These Waves of Girls* by Caitlin Fisher. *These Waves* won the first prize in the fiction category awarded by the Electronic Literature Organization in 2001. In the category of electronic literature, Fisher's work can be further characterized with such labels as web fiction, hypertext fiction, and multimedial fiction. Multimediality in *These Waves* relies heavily on the combination of text and visuals. Pictures and colors are fundamental part of the signifying structure of the work. There are also sound effects, and parts of the text can also be listened to as audio files. What I especially attempt at demonstrating to the students is the way in which hypertextuality is used in this specific work. What is there in the work that wasn't possible in the traditional text format? For this end we have to pay attention to the narrative aspects of the work, as well as to its hypertextual structure. Also, I'll introduce concepts such as autobiographical pact, unreliable narration, and dramatic irony in connection to certain aspects of the work. Finally I will try to draw all these elements together and show how they playfully interact with one another to form a unique work of art.[1]

2.1 Autobiography and Unreliable Narration

These Waves is written in the form of a confessional autobiography about a girl coming to terms with her lesbian identity. The so-called (auto)biographical pact dictates that in biographical narration the events are recounted honestly—of course, the capabilities of human memory set limits to truthfulness of the facts told and also there are certain things which may be omitted, but still, there should be no intentional forgeries of events, and definitely no lies.

Even if it is a question of fiction, as with *These Waves*, if it uses the autobiographical form, the readers suppose that the narration is truthful *in the fic-*

tional world. But the narrator deliberately makes this assumption questionable. At one point she teases the audience by asking herself if things really happened the way she tells them:

> The desire to write is the desire to fool you, seduce you. Here I am—again—always getting the girl, saying the right thing or (toss this in for effect) something deliciously, winsomely wrong. Look over there—that's me, at four. . . . (desire_to_write)
>
> I write, but it doesn't need to be my life, exactly. It lets me fill in the parts I forget. One name. One moment. A hand on my thigh that reminds me of all the other hands. Of yours. (hand_on_my_thigh)

The narrator asks if it is believable that she really was that successful in her courting with other girls. Couldn't it rather be that she tells *how she hopes things would have been*? Thus, we as readers have to decide if we want to read the story as a realistic narration where the things mainly have happened the way they are told, or if we treat the set of small stories as imaginative figments of the narrators imagination who is just making it all up as she goes. This is a classroom example of unreliable narration, as it forces us to ponder about the reliability of text we read.

It is quite common these days to subscribe to some sort of constructivist perspective on life writing; one's life story is always, to some extent, constructed in the act of writing. Raymond Federman, an author who has used (and misused!) autobiographical form and written extensively about it, takes a more radical approach, however. Referring to Louis-Ferdinand Céline, he claims that "a biography is something one invents afterwards" (88-89). It is not only a question of "filling in the parts I forget," but conjuring up a whole life, an act so creative by nature that there is no use for the distinction between autobiography and fiction. As readers we get to ponder about the nature of remembering, of telling stories about one's life; how does it change our reception of a story if we believe it is about the author's own life, or does it really matter? One of the genuine accomplishments of Fisher's work is to bring forth these questions in a tangible, and still discreet, way.

What is more relevant for our discussion here, though, is the way how this whole thematic is buried deeply within the hypertextual structure of the work.

2.2 Hypertextual Rhetorics

It is quite possible that the reader never faces the question about the reliability of the narrator; in fact, it requires a considerable amount of patience to even find the two nodes explicitly posing the question. If one goes through the labors of systemically charting the hypertextual structure of *These Waves*, one quickly sees that there are certain nodes which are very densely linked to other nodes ("Mr_Anderson," and "Vanessa," for example, both have more than ten links leading out from them), while the majority of the nodes have fewer—but still several—links leading to and from them, and then there are nodes with only one link connecting them. Both "the_desire_to_write," and "hand_on_my_thigh" belong to those almost isolated nodes. When reading *These Waves*, one is frequently finding herself faced with "Vanessa," whether she likes that or not, but it requires the reader to stumble to the one link out of "Butterfly," in order to visit "desire_to_write" even once. Here we are facing a completely different situation compared to reading traditional print fiction where all pages and paragraphs are constantly available.

2.2.1 Dramatic Irony

In print fiction, one underlying assumption is that a story is read in a linear manner from start to finish, including everything in between. In hypertext fiction this assumption does not hold. The whole idea of hypertext is that there is no linear text, but a set of interconnected text chunks. Thus, it is problematic if there really are such things as a beginning and an end, but it is actually not often that the reader really reads all of the text contained in the work (in many works it is actually impossible to read all of the text as some text chunks may be made mutually exclusive; reading one makes the other unavailable). This means that there may be readings where this teasing about the reliability of the narrator does not play a role at all. Proceeding, this takes us to the concept of dramatic irony, to a situation where a part of the audience is totally ignorant of something (the doubts the narrator casts on her own reliability) and reads the narration at face value, while another part of the audience does notice this modifier, thus simultaneously gaining a richer understanding of the text and of the narrator; at the same time also savoring the extra pleasure of knowing that there are ignorant fellow readers who never "got it."

In print fiction, dramatic irony mostly depends on sophisticated techniques such as the use of foreign languages, complicated reasonings, references to other works of art, etc., to divide the readership into those getting the joke, and to those not getting it (Vladimir Nabokov being one of the masters of this practice). While all these techniques, naturally, are available also to a hyperfiction author, she may additionally use the hypertextual strategy of hiding something in the hypertextual structure of the work. It may happen quite simply as in the just-given example (a text node with only one link leading to it), so that only a superficial reader is left out of the revelation (and even she can accidentally stumble upon the crucial text fragment), or in a more complex manner, where, for example, a certain set of text fragments have to be read in a certain pre-defined order to "get the joke" (as in Michael Joyce's *afternoon*).

This quite clearly demonstrates how the hypertextual structure (how the nodes of a work are interconnected with links) may be used as a device for a narrative trope like dramatic irony. Hypertextual structure and narrative structure, however, are two separate levels of hypernarrative, and the former is the basis for the narration and sets certain limits to it; it does not, however, determine the narration in any way. Thus, in order to analyze a hypertextual fiction, the analysis of the hypertextual structure is necessary (in order to understand how it works), but it is not enough, as the narrative components in the work cannot be reduced to the hypertextual infrastructure.

2.2.2 Linking and Compulsive Memory

When we analyze traditional narrative text, we mainly pay attention to the linguistic and narratological properties of the text, but when dealing with hypertextual works, we also have to look at the hypertextual structure, and then see how these separate layers work together. There is one instance in *These Waves* where the juxtaposition of narrative and hypertextual structures create an engaging effect. In a part titled "Neil," there is a recollection of an obviously traumatic experience where a schoolboy drives his fist through the safety glass in a door frame, hurting himself badly and bleeding violently. The narration is cut into short pieces following each other through a series of directed links symbolized with an arrow. Each of the rightward arrowed links takes the reader forward along the sequence, and the leftward arrows take her back to the previous node. At one point <Neil4.htm>, however, clicking the left-arrow will not take the reader to the previously read node <Neil3.htm>, but to the first node of the sequence <Neil1.htm>, to the node where the accident is first described. Thus here <Neil4.htm>, where the chaos of other kids in the school bus is described, the link does not work in the expected way, but instead returns the reader back to the accident. In this way, the hypertextual structure is used to create the effect of the compulsive return of the traumatic memory.

2.2.3 The Associative Structure

During the relatively short history of hypertextual practices, there has been a strong connection to the idea of associative writing. For Vannevar Bush, the inventor of the hypertext system, the idea was to have a device with which it would be possible to record the reader's associations during the reading, and also making these recorded associative structures available to other readers. Ever since, one of the main functions for hypertext links has been to serve as a means for pointing out and making associations. George P. Landow wrote in his highly influential book *Hypertext* (1992), summarizing the thinking of Vannevar Bush:

> Bush wanted to replace the essentially linear fixed methods that had produced the triumphs of capitalism and industrialism with what are essentially poetic machines—machines that work according to analogy and association, machines that capture the anarchic brilliance of human imagination. (18)

As an example of associative linking in *These Waves*, we can take the page <Wake_up_fairy4> which ends with the following paragraph:

> I ate my lunch from a blue and yellow astronaut lunch box and liked my thermos to be broken so I could shake it and hear glass. I sipped my warm warm drink looked a long time at the teachers and memorized their license plates and that's why *I* was late.

There are two links in this paragraph, of which the first one is attached to the anchor phrase "shake it and hear glass"—if the reader clicks on this link, she will end up in the page <Neil1> which starts:

> Neil gets off the schoolbus, runs to the door of his building on Howard Avenue, trips on the step and pushes his arm through the security glass.

The sound of glass in the broken thermos activates in an associative manner the memory of the event in the school bus. Here the association is easy to follow as there is the explicit motive of broken glass in both cases; in many other instances the connection is not nearly this evident.

Regarding Fisher's work, one is tempted to say that it is a paradigmatic example of the associative hypertext. It is a work of autobiographical reminiscences (whether it is a "true" autobiography or a fictional one is not relevant here), where the hyperlinks are mainly to be used as a means to point out the interconnections, overlaps, and coincidences between several episodes recounted by the narrator. The hypertext serves both to simulate the associative working of the (narrator's) memory, and to present a way for the reader to follow potential associations.

2.2.4 Temporal Order and Strange Loops

Traditional realistic narration follows the causal and temporal logic, where later events are prepared for by the previous ones, and later things cast new light on older things and give a (new) meaning to them. This kind of logic is hard—if not impossible—to maintain in hypertext. *These Waves* does not even try to do it but, rather deliberately, plays totally against it. There is, potentially, an extremely clear-cut temporal framework at hand; the school grades, from the first class to junior high, etc. But despite even this scale, the work very strongly resists the causal-temporal ordering. Things do not necessarily follow each other because something happened before: The logic of order might arise from the retrospective perspective of the narrator, or things may not actually be (causally) related at all.

Another way to work against the linear order (both temporal and causal) in *These Waves* is the case of "nested frames." The screen is divided into two parts by using the frames option of html coding; in one part there is the menu, and in another there is the current page. Usually, by clicking on a link (in the menu or in the text itself), the contents of the current page change. In "Vanessa," there is an exception though; instead of just changing the text, it reopens the whole screen in the right-hand side frame. There is still the same text on the screen (even though in a smaller frame this time) and it is possible to click on the same link once again, resulting in reproducing the whole screen once again inside the frame (fig. 1).

This creates the same kind of experience as putting two mirrors opposite to each other and then seeing your own reflection in an infinitely ever-smaller scale. In visual arts, this kind of illusion is called *mise-en-abyme*, while in fiction Brian McHale has called the similar effect as "strange loops" (*Postmodernist Fiction* 119-121). There is a sense of short-circuiting in the way these screens are piled inside each other, and instead of linear development, it is basically a circular structure, endlessly starting all over again. As such it is a denial of change, and it can be seen as referring either to the similarity of days following each other where nothing happens but things just repeat themselves, or once again, there may be the more sinister interpretation where one is always in danger of sinking too deeply into one's thoughts and memories and stories, ending up in a coma or trance-like pathological state, unable to break free from the stasis.

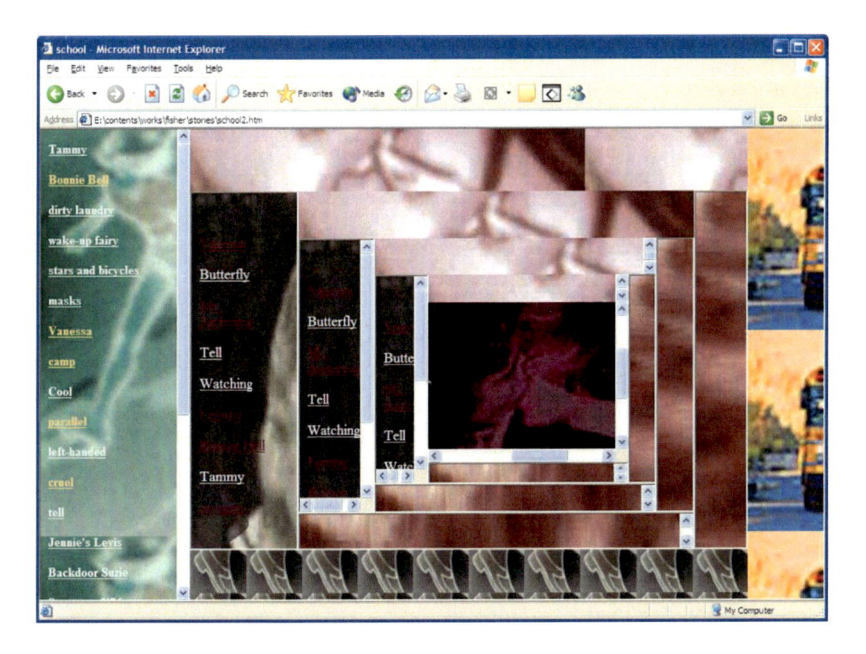

Fig. 1. Nested frames.

2.3 Personal and Social Relations

These Waves of Girls is, as the title suggests, a collection of stories about girls' lives. The basic unit here is the school class, inside of which there are the strict rules of friendship. There is the best friend, the other close friends, those who are not friends at all but rather enemies, and then the older school kids, to whom there is usually a distance; things related to them only are heard through somebody whose older sister/brother is in the upper class. Maybe the most important way to demonstrate the trust in the best friend is to share secrets, of which there are a plenty. About those who are not friends there is always a multitude of rumours and gossip that gets circulated and inevitably distorted along the way. And here is another motivation for the hypertextual structure (the first being the simulation of the associative workings of the human memory)—following the hypertextually linked story fragments is very much like hearing a piece of gossip here and there. Some of the things are very hard to come by, whereas some stories you'll hear over and over again.

Another level of secrecy comes from Tracey's (the protagonist) sexual identity, her knowing early on that she likes girls more than boys. In addition to all the usual secrets between preteen and teen girls, she has the great secret of the not-yet-out-of-the-closet lesbian. As a coming out story, *These Waves* has the strong feeling of deliverance, of letting out all the things that the narrator had to keep inside herself while still a girl. The hypertextual structure collapses the two temporal levels together, so that the self-conscious older narrator and still unsure narrated girl blend into each other—even when coming out with the truth, she is still hiding the revelation in the labyrinth of the hypertext, in the entangled web of girls' secrets.

According to Marleen Barr, history writing has been so thoroughly dominated by the male perspective that the act of women writing about their own lives and experiences unavoidably takes on the form of fabulation; as something that exceeds or expands the limits of what is seen as "normal" and factual (*Feminist Fabulation*). Seen from this perspective, *These Waves* can be read as a feminist fabulation giving voice to the others (women, lesbians, kids) suppressed in the culturally dominant male histories. The fabulation here would also refer to the free imaginative mode of remembering where the factualness of the autobiographical narration is called into question; it is fabulation inside the frame of one's (the narrator's) own life story.[2]

In a more formal way, linear narratives are often seen as totalistic modes of expression; the point of view adopted by the narrator dominates over the story, and all other points of view are either excluded or subsumed under its control. Multilinear narration, like in *These Waves*, works in another way, or at least it can be read in another way. Whereas linear narrative can be seen as power discourse, multilinear narration bears the potential of challenging this by building up a network of rivaling voices of others and avoiding the one dominant ideology altogether. Instead of one linear narrative, there are all the associative linkings and branchings, reflecting the multitude of possibilities in life.

> It's always like this for me—this way or that way? If I kill the butterfly, will I become a dentist? If I press it on page five instead of six, then what? . . . At eight, I realize all of these things happen at once. 79 on the math test? No problem. One Tracey has 92, another 40. These are the living Traceys. Some Traceys can't even walk—smashed in an airplane tragedy; some Traceys are in the Ice Capades. ("Parallel")

These Waves of Girls is ultimately in many ways a quite a traditional *Bildungsroman*, a story of the growing-up of a girl into a full-fledged individual within the society. But it is also a growing-up story of hypertext fiction. Instead of developing and polishing technical and programmed qualities of the new digital media, it takes the technology available and uses it for its own ends. When reading *These Waves*, one is not so much invited to appreciate the latest developments of dynamic web coding; instead, it makes one ponder about the invented and constructed nature of the narrated past or the ideological power relations working within society. Even though the claims that hypertext resembles in some concrete way the synaptic network of brain functions is already discarded, *These Waves* manages—in a more symbolic way—to depict the activity of remembering, and of working out mental constructions of the past, the identity, and the self. It also uses the hypertext structure as a means to reproduce the feeling of secrecy, whispered gossips, and the ever-circulating rumors playing such an important role in schoolgirls' lives. It manages to breathe life into its technical platform, a feat that justifies its position as an exemplary model of digital literature.

Notes

1 A more extensive analysis of *These Waves of Girls* is presented in Koskimaa, "These Waves of Memories."

2 It is worth noting, that the title of the work may be seen as an allusion to the novel *The Waves* by Virginia Woolf, who is one of the most important figures in feminist writing, and who is also known for her highly associative writing style. A more thorough comparison between *These Waves* and Woolf's writing would yield a wholly new article.

Works Cited

Barr, Marleen. *Feminist Fabulation: Space/Postmodern Fiction*. Iowa City: U of Iowa P, 1992.

Federman, Raymond. *Critifiction: Postmodern Essays*. Albany: SUNY Press, 1993.

Fisher, Caitlin. *These Waves of Girls*. 2001. 28 Apr. 2009 <http://www.yorku.ca/caitlin/waves/>.

Gere, Charlie. *Digital Culture*. London: Reaktion Books, 2002.

Joyce, Michael. *afternoon. a story*. CD-ROM. Watertown: Eastgate Systems, 1987.

Koskimaa, Raine. "These Waves of Memories: A Hyperfiction by Caitlin Fisher." *Dichtung Digital* 6.3 (2004). 28 Apr. 2009 <http://www.dichtung-digital.org/2004/3-Koskimaa.htm>.

Landow, George P. *Hypertext: The Convergence of Contemporary Critical Theory and Technology*. Baltimore: Johns Hopkins UP, 1992.

McHale, Brian. *Postmodernist Fiction*. London: Methuen, 1987.

Rettberg, Scott, ed. *State of the Arts: The Proceedings of The Electronic Literature Organization's 2002 State of the Arts Symposium & 2001 Electronic Literature Awards*. Los Angeles, CA: ELO/UCLA, 2003.

Woolf, Virginia. *The Waves*. Cambridge: Cambridge UP, 2008.

Astrid Ensslin and James Pope

Digital Literature in Creative and Media Studies

Introduction

Despite an increasing number of critical, applied (pedagogic), and empirical studies on digital literature performed in the UK (e.g. by Ensslin and Bell; Pope), formalized, systematic teaching is only now—with the take-off of the Web 2.0 and open source technologies—beginning to emerge in the tertiary education sector. That said, at the time of writing this evolution is mostly taking place in Media and Creative Studies departments rather than the "traditional," critical English literature curriculum. For example, London Metropolitan University offers some study of hypertext in its MA in Creative and Cultural Industries, while the impact of digital media on literature appears in the Digital Culture and Technology MA at King's College, London. While we shall avoid dwelling on the speculative reasons for this general reluctance within British literary studies, we focus on recent developments in Creative and Media Studies in the UK. After all, these seem to be the academic environments within which scholars, practitioners and computer scientists are showing the greatest willingness to experiment with new forms of teaching as well as combined methodologies that integrate learning and teaching strategies from various academic disciplines.

Our contribution looks at representative curricular strategies and teaching methods developed and applied recently at DeMontfort University (Leicester, East Midlands), Bangor University (Wales), as well as the Universities of Leeds (North England) and Bournemouth (Southern England). The main focus of our case studies will be on how digital literature (mostly fiction) is being used to help students build knowledge and skills in the areas of digital literacy, multimodal narrative analysis, stylistics, creative writing in the native and foreign language classroom, and in the creation of original digital fictions.

Case Study 1:
Digital Literacy, Multimodal Analysis, and Ludic Interaction

In what follows, we shall give an example of how skills in digital literacy, multimodal narrative analysis, and ludic interaction have been and may be taught by using an award-winning, multilingual digital work-in-progress, *Inanimate Al-*

ice, by Kate Pullinger and Chris Joseph.[1] At the time of writing, four episodes of *Inanimate Alice* are complete ("China," "Italy," "Russia," and "Hometown") in English, French, Spanish, Italian, German, and Afrikaans, and six further sequels are to follow "later."[2] We shall focus mostly on Jess Laccetti's exemplary "education pack," which she created and tested at De Montfort University and which was implemented, for instance, at Bangor University by Ensslin in a First Year module, "Introduction to New Media." The education pack, which is available from the *Inanimate Alice* web site and hence a kind of paratext to this fiction, contains teaching materials and methods on the inter-relationship between story and medium (Lesson Plan 1); homodiegetic narration, autobiography and multimodality (Lesson Plans 2 and 3); and character development in the tradition of the Bildungs- and Künstlerroman (Lesson Plan 4).

By way of an introduction, *Inanimate Alice* is a story about "a young girl growing up in the 21st century" (Pullinger and Joseph). Each episode is "a self contained story" (Pullinger and Joseph), and Alice's biography is told from the age of eight to young adulthood. As a first person narrator, her voice guides the "reader" through this modular *Entwicklungsroman*, and she develops her technological expertise and cosmopolitan experience in the process.[3] The language of the narrative changes from that of a child to that of a mature adult, and so does the way she interacts with her changing social and geographic environments. Whereas, in "China" (Episode 1), she is still a young girl without much awareness of the political implications of her father's professional role in the oil industry, the two following episodes convey to the reader the affluent yet socially excluded situation of her parents, the domestic role of Arab women, and the personal risks resulting from being foreigners in a socially and politically restrictive environment (Saudi Arabia and Russia). During their stay in an Italian skiing resort (Episode 2), the narrative harks back to the family's actual residence in Saudi Arabia, where Alice has her own private tutor, Ayisha, with whom she communicates via her handheld device, Ba-Xi. Like an *idée fixe* or a *Dingsymbol*, the gadget recurs in each episode, taking on increasingly sophisticated shapes and functionalities. In its quasi-techno-utopian function, it works as an intermedial reference to the Apple iPhone and other multi-functional, contemporary handhelds, and Alice uses it to create her animations and to communicate with her imaginary friend, Brad—an animated character whom she herself has programmed. Episode 3 ("Russia") contains the first dramatic turning point in Alice's life, when her parents are expelled from Russia for political and economic reasons, the details of which are left to the reader's imagination and intertextual frame of reference. Episode 4 sees Alice and her parents settled into a murky working class home in suburban Middle England, where she goes to school for the first time and experiences the challenges and peer pressures of socialised teenage life.

Each episode contains a vibrant interplay of multimodal features. Sound and image are interwoven with written language so as to create an unusual reading experience. Despite the potent audiovisual effects, which could potentially render the text as a film rather than a literary artefact, the reception process is nonetheless guided primarily by *linguistic* narrative discourse, which is organized in a linear way. Arrow signs are used to indicate links—in the sense of a page turn—to the next section, and the size of the text chunks is kept to a minimum (one to three short sentences) in order to facilitate screen reading. Importantly, Pullinger and Joseph further integrate ludic interactivity: each episode contains short games, the rules of which readers have to identify by trial and error (cf. fig.1 for an example from Episode 2, "Italy"). Suspense and the drive to "read/play on" are thus created textually (through language processing), semiotically (by following signs), multimodally (through emotive audiovisual effects) and ludically (through games that challenge the reader's combinatory creativity, motoric nimbleness, and logical reasoning).

Fig. 1. Screenshot from *Inanimate Alice*, Episode 2 ("Italy").

Due to its wide range of aesthetic, ludic and narrative techniques, combined with a unique mixture of traditional and innovative storytelling strategies, the pedagogic potential of *Inanimate Alice* is considerable. To provide students with an analytical toolkit and to teach them a critical stance towards the effects of "multiple modes of presentation," Laccetti recommends Luesebrink and Fisher as preparatory or in-class reading. For class work, she suggests that students should initially be made to discuss the semiotic differences between various modes of representation and to show Episode 1 of *Inanimate Alice* to the group afterwards. Depending on classroom conditions, students may be put into small groups to navigate the episode on their own. The session is rounded off with a discussion on "sensory inputs," and Laccetti gives directions as to where to draw students' attention: e.g. the timing and emotive effects of auditory signals; the strategic location of directional arrows and their relative distance to written text; the meaning of silence and isolated noise; the use of colour in meta-art;[4] the distracting effect of background noise and music in gaming; and the use of multiple modes to indicate macrostructural elements in the story, e.g. climax, peripety and close.[5] For coursework, students are required to send their responses to further critical and analytical questions to the class blog.

Lesson Plans 2 and 3 deal with narratological aspects as well as the autobiographical genre in relation to the digital medium. For preparatory reading, Laccetti suggests Jahn for narrative stance, Sullivan for "Hypertextualising Autobiography," and Terziu or John for multimodality. In class, students are asked to tell stories about their own lives in order to introduce them to homodiegetic narration. Based on the reading tasks, students are then taught the differences between homodiegetic and heterodiegetic narration. This is followed by a joint viewing of *Inanimate Alice*, Episode 3, "Russia." Students are then encouraged to navigate the story in pairs, filling in close reading logs as they go along.[6] This is followed by a class discussion on the interplay of music, sound and image in the same episode (e.g. the effects of darkness and light accompanied by music; the thematic, functional use of music to signal gaming mode vs. reading mode; elements of visual design and visual grammar, e.g. sharpness of image, positioning of the viewer, presence and absence of participants, and spoken vs. written language). In the critical follow-up, students are encouraged, amongst other things, to think about how the story might be improved by modifying certain multimodal elements. In the following session, students create an audio-visually annotated autobiography planner in storyboard form and fill in an autobiography reflection form. To draw students' awareness to copyright issues, a handout on "copyright and fair use guidelines for school projects" is distributed and discussed. To complete their multimodal autobiographies, students may use the user-friendly iStories software.[7]

Lesson Plan 4, finally, explores character development and the extent to which *Inanimate Alice* can be considered to be following the tradition of the *Künstler-* or *Bildungsroman*. Hader serves as a short introduction to the essential features of the *Bildungsroman*, and students are encouraged to apply these to episodes from their own life and media experiences. *Inanimate Alice* is then discussed in class against the previously established theoretical background. Amongst the methods used are prediction making, character trading cards and character analysis compared with real-life reports and statistics on technology-oriented teenage culture in the Western world.[8]

In all, Laccetti's education pack contains a host of templates for handouts and further suggestions for class activities, which cannot be explained in full detail here.[9] She pitches her teaching materials at a teenage audience that is not familiar with narrative or semiotic theory, for which reason various aspects of her approach may, at first glance, appear somewhat naïve and mundane to an audience of university lecturers. That said, given that digital literature in the UK tends to be taught in Media and Creative Studies rather than as part of literary curricula, the chosen level may be considered appropriate for First Year undergraduates that are both lacking in and keen on developing digital literacy and basic narratological knowledge. When implemented at Bangor University in spring 2008, students engaged with the material enthusiastically and some even highlighted the teaching unit on *Inanimate Alice* as particularly enjoyable and insightful in their module evaluation questionnaire.

Case Study 2:
Creative Writing in the Literary Foreign Language Classroom

The second case study reports on an educational action research project that was carried out by Ensslin in autumn 2004 at the University of Leeds, School of Modern Languages and Cultures. The project was dedicated to testing and fostering intrinsic motivation, developing advanced communicative competence in a foreign language (German), medially extended literary competence and spatial, macrostructural thinking through creative collaborative writing in the digital medium, as well as to teaching critical awareness along the lines of poststructuralist and hypertext theory (cf. Ensslin "Reconstructing the Deconstructed;" "Literary Hypertext in the Foreign Language Classroom;" *Canonizing Hypertext*).[10]

A "formal" classroom environment for collaborative, digital creative writing was chosen to facilitate classroom discussion and peer feedback. The classroom contained three computers, around which the small "teams" (approximately four students each) arranged themselves. Although some students tended to be in the same team every time, there was no strict seating order, so that team constellations varied according to individual preferences. Each of the ten class sessions lasted two hours. The 13 participants were Level 2 students of various Modern Languages programmes (e.g. German and French, German and Spanish, English and German), who took part in the project as a voluntary extracurricular activity. A project web site was created to publish student writings, and to provide access to the hypertexts read in class and the project timetable.

The project syllabus was organized around eight proper seminar sessions, which were framed by two audit units, in which student performance was recorded by means of questionnaires, structured interviews and story-writing tests. The seminar sessions were centred around specific aspects of narrative theory, hypertext theory, stylistic text analysis across literary genres, and web editing with Macromedia Dreamweaver.

None of the students had encountered literary hypertext before, nor were they familiar with the technological concept of "hypertext." Therefore, participants were first introduced to the concept of hypertextual networks and some literary examples. They were given three hypertexts (Nils Ehlert and Wolfgang Bauer's *Jetzt? Oder der höchste Augenblick*; Gavin Inglis's *Same Day Test* and Geoff Ryman's *253, Or: Tube Theatre*) to read jointly in three separate, rotating groups. During the reading process, participants were asked to discuss—in the foreign language—what they thought the texts were about.

Afterwards the whole group exchanged ideas and impressions, at which point the tutor explained the concept of (proto-)hypertext. The students were then given copies of an authentic hypertext map, which was taken from Ehlert and Bauer's web site. The example served to illustrate the structural components of hypertext and provide a model upon which students could then base their own hypertext maps. For the subsequent, preparatory activity, they could choose from a selection of hypertext metaphors commonly used in hypertext theory and fiction (e.g. "labyrinth," "patchwork quilt," and "spider web") as the starting point for their own associative (mind) maps. The students had to label their nodes and links in terms of how they interlinked with each other—again in the foreign language. At the end of the session, the mindmaps were collected, scanned and put on the project web site. The reading task for the following week was a section from Kuhlen on hyperlinks.

Session 2 was dedicated to literary genres. During the first 15 minutes, the students were asked to discuss what they had read about linking structures on the basis of the hypertexts they had read so far, and to what extent they considered a taxonomy of links feasible. To introduce students to literary genres in an inductive manner, they were given excerpts from Theodor Storm's poem "Die Stadt" ('The City'), Arthur Schnitzler's drama *Reigen* ('Hands Around'), and Alfred Döblin's montage novel *Berlin Alexanderplatz*. In teams, students discussed how the three texts could be distinguished in terms of structure, content, and language. In pairs, they then transformed the texts into different genres, turning, for instance, *Reigen* into narrative prose, and "Die Stadt" into dramatic dialogue. The products were read out to and commented on by the other team members. Afterwards, they were collected, corrected and published on the project web site. For homework, the students read a section from Landow on collaborative authorship.

Whereas, in the two initial sessions, students wrote with pen and paper, Session 3 introduced Dreamweaver web editing software, which would, from that point onwards, serve as their main writing platform. The session started with a revision of the reading task, which focused on collaborative authorship and how it could be employed to help learners improve their literary and communicative competence. Then they went into their usual groups to tackle their first web editing tasks. After a period of exploring background and font colours and sizes in Stefan Maskiewicz's *ColoRama*, they were introduced to the basic applications of Dreamweaver: text editing, colouring, linking, as well as inserting images and tables. For homework, students had to read various excerpts from Genette and Stanzel to prepare for an introduction to narrative point of view.

In session 4, the students learnt about and experimented with narrative perspectives and aspects of focalization. Again, during the first minutes they were asked to recapitulate and discuss the reading assignment. After that, they were presented with a number of short passages from various English and German novels. In their teams, they discussed the excerpts with respect to narrative situation and focalization. The results were consolidated in a succeeding plenary discussion. Then the students were asked to apply what they had learnt to their own writing, by creating new short hyperfictions and experimenting with narrative perspective and focalization techniques. The Dreamweaver documents were opened and continued. The writing was again followed by peer feedback. For homework, the students had to read passages from Ludwig about metre, rhyme, and stanza.

Session 5 introduced students to metrical feet, stanza forms and rhyme schemes. To apply the theory, the teams were given a number of stanzas from various English and German poems, which they had to analyze in terms of metre and rhyme. The results were discussed with the whole group. Then, the usual writing teams were formed, and students were asked to add to their existing hypertexts elements of verse. They were also encouraged to start thinking beyond the limits of their own "private" hypertexts, to read what the other teams had written and link parts of their own writing to other participants' documents where appropriate. For private study, students were asked to read further digital fictions via links provided on the project web site.

Between sessions 5 and 6 there was a half-term break, after which a revision of all theory covered so far was deemed necessary. Students also reflected on further digital narratives they had read over the holidays (Mark Amerika's *Grammatron* and Stefan Maskiewicz's *Quadrego*). In a succeeding theory section, students learnt about stanza forms and poetic genres. They were once again given text samples for analysis and subsequently wrote their own poems in German, following the conventions they had just learnt about. Unsurprisingly perhaps, most of them chose non-rhyming or humoristic genres such as haikus and limericks. The poems were subsequently read to the other team members and integrated as new lexias into the existing hypertext network. For homework, they had to read definitions of stylistic features such as trope, metaphor, metonymy, simile, anaphora, and epiphora.

In session 7, figures of speech and tropes were focused on. First, students looked at and revised previously written texts, helping each other to find better formulations and to correct grammatical errors. After that, they discussed the texts they had read for homework with additional input and explanations given by the instructor. The teams were then given a number of short texts, which were full of rhetorical figures and imagery. Jointly, they had to find examples of the stylistic means they had been taught. Subsequently, they were asked to create lexias which contained text types that typically feature a lot of rhetorical features. The teams discussed what sort of texts that could be, and concluded that they would try fictitious conference speeches. It turned out that, statistically, they found metaphors, parallelisms and assonances particularly convenient for their purposes.

There was no preparatory reading for the final project session, as it served as an opportunity for project members to complete and further embellish their hypertext. Students were also asked to write a report on how their motivation levels had developed throughout the project.

To summarize and conclude from the results of the study, hypertext can be said to support constructivist objectives such as subject-orientation, process-orientation, learner autonomy, intrinsic motivation and deep learning insofar as it serves as an efficient tool for organizing, structuring, synthesizing, storing and making accessible information via learner-friendly templates, logically organized linking structures and navigational aids. Furthermore, the results of the case study support the assumption that hypertext enhances deep learning through collaboration, which again encourages the joint construction of knowledge, intrinsic motivation through immediate social discourse with peers and peer as well as tutor feedback. What is more, learners bear responsibility for their own texts, which are published after undergoing peer-review, thus being empowered and rewarded for expressing their ideas creatively and independently of any external motivational stimuli, such as assessment.[11]

Case Study 3:
Masters Level Analysis and Creation of "New Media Narratives"

To introduce the third case study let us first take a look at the theoretical underpinning to the teaching of digital literature in the Media School at Bournemouth University. The drive there has been to integrate empirical research (some of which is reported in Pope)[12] with the formal teaching on the MA in Interactive Media, and within the BA degrees in TV Production, Interactive Media, and Scriptwriting. The aim has been to not only enliven the debate as to digital literature's future, but also to generate innovative and fruitful practice.

One motivation has been to "lift" digital literature out of the creative and critical ghetto it would appear to have migrated into (incidentally, the term "interactive narrative" is often used to open the form out to students of film, interactive media, and creative writing, and to emphasize that one of the core interests is the use and effect of interactivity in narrative creation and reception). After early excitement about the possibilities for the form, and subsequent negativity, we seem now to be in a phase where creative experimentation continues on the Web, but digital literature (which term includes hyper-fiction and other types of interactive narrative) has not expanded into wider recognition via commercial projects, or gained a wider audience beyond the academy and the artists themselves.

There is however clearly a great interest amongst students in the concept of a narrative form which can combine interesting interactivity with engaging narrative, delivered via digital media, encompassing the language of books, films, web pages, radio, and so on. Students at undergraduate and Masters level show us that the form is not an evolutionary "dead-end" — it will continue to develop rather than fade into obscurity to become only of historical interest, though there is long way to go before it is going to be able to "cross-over" to gain a wider audience. Clearly, the problems of fractured narrative structure, confusing navigation systems, low levels of reader absorption, and the question of narrative closure still trouble the form. Even the more successful examples currently available, for example Megan Heyward's *Of Day, Of Night*, or Andy Campbell's *Dreaming Methods* output, still have not quite solved the problem of the interactivity/narrative tension around which many theorists and critics debate. Most recently Ryan is saying, "[i]t will . . . take a seamless (some will say miraculous) convergence of bottom-up input and top-down design to produce well-formed narrative patterns" (99), and perhaps she has a point: it is still difficult to build interactivity into a sophisticated narrative which can generate reader absorption without the interactivity disturbing the reader's engagement, as students all find when they read and discuss digital literature in class. But we believe it can be done, and the clues to solving this problem are out there, in the works mentioned above for example, in the ideas and work being generated by students, and in the data produced by reader-oriented empirical studies (Pope). Key factors reported by readers include the need for always-meaningful links, narrative-driven navigation, constant context signposting, use of screen-conventional navigation iconography, and interface design that merges schema for form and content (cf. Pope, and also Douglas and Hargadon).

The theoretical and creative approach adopted in the case studies reported below is that this is a whole new form where we should strive to incorporate understandings from literature, theatre, film, gaming, graphic design, human-computer-interface usability, and reader-response (reception) theory. In order to begin to shift digital literature out of this critical stalemate and creative lonely corner, the approach at Bournemouth is that it cannot be understood simply by reference to the theories and practices of one antecedent tradition.

In a twelve week sequence of part-lecture/part-workshop sessions in a unit called Narrative and New Media, these Interactive Media students are asked to consider how new media are changing narrative forms: in particular they explore narrative structures, interactivity and narrative, closure, and reader satisfaction, since these have been identified in the literature and in empirical studies (Pope) as key issues for readers when they encounter interactive fiction. Through lectures, discussion of "old" media narrative, analysis of current digital literature, and creation and production of original narratives, this unit is an attempt to blend theory with practice, and break down conceptual/theoretical barriers. Students follow a critical and creative "path" from analyzing linear, non-digital, non-interactive narratives, towards the practice of analyzing and using non-linearity, digital media and interactivity.

As many scholars have noted (e.g. Birkerts; Miall; Ryan; Walker), narrative structure in hyper-fiction can very quickly become too fractured and confusing, apparently without cause and effect relations to drive the narrative. To begin the analysis of this aspect, lectures on narrative theory in sessions 1 and 2 are followed by the students being asked to bring to the session an example of a narrative, from any medium, which they consider to be non-linear (i.e. where "conventional" chronology and/or cause and effect relations may be disrupted) and which they consider to be successful.

Each student presents a case for the "success" of the piece they have chosen, essentially to stimulate discussion around what features they find in an engaging narrative structure. In discussion, "successful" usually means having the well-recognized dramatic qualities of anticipation, tension, excitement, fear, surprise, relief, resolution, and so on. "Conventional" media are discussed first since these students, despite being well-qualified in multi-media design, or perhaps being experienced film editors, or web-developers, have almost without exception never come across interactive fiction (evidence, at least in this small "sample," that digital literature has not yet lost its "underground" status).

Having identified what is considered to be desirable in narrative structure, students are better able to analyze the multi-structures of interactive pieces such as *afternoon, a story* (Joyce), *Of Day, Of Night* (Heyward) or *The Virtual Disappearance of Miriam* (Bedford and Campbell). Non-linearity in non-interactive forms builds a useful bridge towards a consideration of interactivity in narrative, and so some input on the history of literary experimentation is provided, looking for example at Modernism, and works by writers such as Saporta or Borges.

Alongside these sessions (probably 3 and 4, though flexibility is allowed depending on student interest), students are asked to write a non-linear short story, beginning to think about the challenges faced by writers who might want to confront narrative "convention" in areas such as structure, narrative voice, character, and closure. The stories are read and discussed in-session, and issues of potential development into digital media with interactivity are approached. Students will then be introduced to current examples of digital literature and they will be made aware of the critical debate around narrative, interactivity, reader-satisfaction (referring to Douglas, and Murray for example), and the importance of interface design.

In the middle two or three sessions, the students are asked to find an example of an interactive digital narrative, demonstrate it in class, and comment on its "success" or otherwise. The aim here is to examine how, in interactive narrative, features such as narrative structure, narrative voice, character development, drama, and closure are all delivered via and affected by the interface: this is an area of digital literature which we argue the critical literature has largely overlooked. Students discuss the challenge of creating an interface which facilitates easy, quick, intuitive navigation, which displays the fictional world in a comprehensible way, and which will generate a meaningful, absorbing narrative with the dramatic "hits" they have already identified as being desirable. Nielsen's guidelines for navigation are referred to as well as studies from human-computer interface usability research (e.g. Pace), proceeding from the belief that narratology in this medium must integrate usability into its field of concern.

The twelve week sequence culminates in the assessed project, which requires students to write, design, and produce an interactive narrative of their own, either an entirely original piece, or an adaptation of a story from another medium (adaptation of course raises its own interesting questions, and one fascinating example was an interactive version of the film *Amélie*). The students combine this project with the assessment for their design unit, allowing a fruitful conjoining of theory and practice.

Some excellent results have been seen, and we will now refer to one specific example which seemed to illustrate how positive has been the pedagogic approach adopted. *The Mobius Case* by Rutger van Dijk uses Flash software to create a highly visual, readily navigable narrative about two people whose relationship is shattered by a tragic night out and an accident, which might or might not have been caused by the male protagonist.

One key to the success of this piece is a navigation system, which combines effective usability with narrative coherence. The illustration (fig. 2) shows the time line feature across the top of the screen: this can be used simultaneously as a menu of scenes from the story, allowing therefore total non-linearity of reader experience and narrative progression, and as a place-marker, since it keeps track of very scene viewed.

Interactivity, and thus movement around the narrative, is also offered by various hot spots in images, animations, sound tracks, and words, with the time line "filling up" as each scene is visited, no matter how it is arrived upon. We have found in this piece, and in empirical studies, how reader satisfaction is increased when navigation system, interactivity design, and narrative progression are tied tightly together.

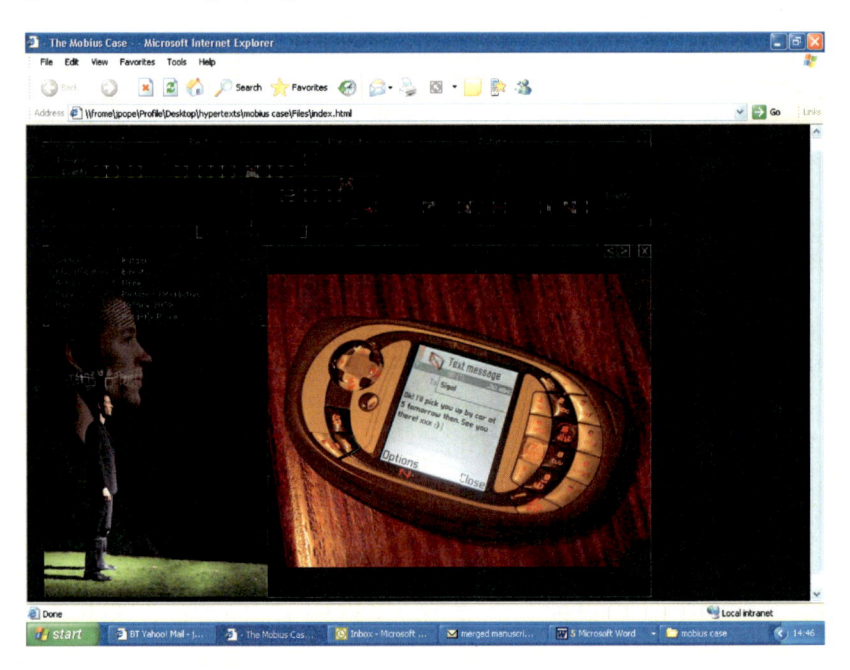

Fig. 2. Screenshot from *The Mobius Case*, with interactive timeline at top of screen.

The "opposite" of this equation is found in Joyce's "classic" hypertext novel, *afternoon, a story*, in which navigation is obscure, and any relation between a reader's navigation choices and the narrative's development is very difficult to discern without the sort of academic study carried out by the likes of Walker and Douglas. *The Mobius Case*, on the other hand, offers what Ryan calls ontological interactivity (i.e. a "deep" interaction in which the user can affect the progress and content of the received narrative), while also providing clear navigation and context. An example of this possibility for the user is a video sequence in which the couple are driving to a night out in town: the reader/user can choose which kind of music the couple hear in their car, and depending on which music is chosen, a different mood for the video scene is thus created. Undergraduate students at Bournemouth University when discussing the piece have commented that the choice, for example, of fast and wild electro music for the scene can lead the reader to feel that the driver was responsible for the imminent crash; choosing the calm classical music by contrast might make the reader feel that the crash happens "out of the blue." This, we argue, is a subtle, non-confusing provision of interactivity which does alter the delivery and reception of the narrative in a significant way.

To conclude this case study, interested readers might wish to note that Bournemouth University is developing its teaching of digital literature into further areas in and beyond Higher Education, using the research data referred to above (Pope) and the experience of the teaching outlined. For more information on this "extension" research and teaching, cf. Pope's blog at <http://www.genarrator.blogspot.com/>.

By way of a general conclusion, as with the very nature of digital literature our overall approach to teaching is to experiment within parameters, which we are beginning to establish, for what is likely to work well for narrative and for readers. No doubt our approaches will change as new examples appear on the Web, or perhaps in book shops under the banner "Digital Literature." We will eventually have enough digital literature out there to begin to discuss narrative for its own sake rather than, as at present, being rather sensitive to the medium and its challenges. At the present time we are trying to find out what can be done to tell accessible, navigable, psychologically involving narrative, as well as to analyze it comprehensively and meaningfully: it is all still so new, despite those who would say it's already had its day.

Notes

1 Amongst numerous other international successes, *IA* has been the winner of the "Premio per l'arte digitale" (Italian Ministry of Culture); cf. <http://www.brad-field.info>.

2 Cf. <http://www.inanimatealice.com>. Only "Episode 1: China" is available in Afrikaans at present.

3 Clearly, the term "reader" in the conventional sense can no longer capture the multi-faceted receptive process of digital interactive narratives such as *IA*. Similarly, the concept of digital fiction itself has "fuzzy edges" (Pauli) as it combines the creative potentialities of computer technology in such multifarious ways that it may be conceived of in terms of a continuum between fiction and computer game rather than either of the two *in abstracto*. On the other hand, we contend that digital fiction should be seen as a creative genre in its own right, which makes it more than just the sum of its constituent elements.

4 In analogy with the concept of metadrama (drama within the drama), the term "meta-art" is used here to emphasize the "metamedial" character of Pullinger and Joseph's work.

5 For further suggestions and teaching methods on *IA's* Episode 1, multimodality and digital narrative, cf. Laccetti.

6 The close reading logs are divided into two columns, one of which documents "information" while the other adds the students' "interpretation." This helps students develop an understanding of what differentiates explicature from implicature, i.e. what is explicitly said in the text from what readers infer, using their knowledge of the world and the context. Clearly, one could argue that interactive literary hypermedia require further categories such as navigation, intermedial interplay, and metatextuality. Laccetti here seems to suggest a basic, traditional methodology that is up to individual tutors to modify.

7 *iStories* is available for download at <http://www.istori.es>.

8 Laccetti recommends a 2005 press release by *The Pew Charitable Trusts* as reading material.

9 For further information cf. Laccetti.

10 The project predated the explosive popularization of Web 2.0 applications and was therefore still arranged and carried out in line with the creative and communicative facilities offered by Web 1.0 technology.

11 For a more in-depth evaluation of the Leeds Hypertext Project, cf. Ensslin, *Canonizing Hypertext*.

12 Empirical study of the responses of 36 readers to a range of hypertext fictions, conducted at Bournemouth University and locales in Dorset, UK.

Works Cited

Amélie. Dir. Jean-Pierre Jeunet. UGC and Miramax, 2001.

Amerika, Mark. *Grammatron*. 1997. 18 Mar. 2009 <http://www.grammatron.com>.

Bedford, Martyn, and Andy Campbell. *The Virtual Disappearance of Miriam*. 2000. 18 Mar. 2009 <http://www.dreamingmethods.com/uploads/dm_archive/objects/html/t_object_342657_268084.html>.

Bell, Alice. "'Do You Want to Hear About it?' Exploring Possible Worlds in Michael Joyce's Hyperfiction, Afternoon, a story." *Contemporary Stylistics*. Ed. Marina Lambrou and Peter Stockwell. London: Continuum, 2007. 43-55.

———. *The Possible Worlds of Hypertext Fiction*. London: Palgrave-Macmillan, 2010. Forthcoming.

———. "Ontological Boundaries and Conceptual Leaps: The Significance of Possible Worlds for Hypertext Fiction (and Beyond)." *New Narratives: Theory and Practice*. Ed. Ruth Page and Bronwen Thomas. Lincoln: U of Nebraska P, 2009. Forthcoming.

Birkerts, Sven. "Digital Storytelling: Is It Art?" *Synapse* 1997. 27 Feb. 2002 <http://www.hotwired.wired.com/synapse/braintennis/97/31/index0a.html>.

Campbell, Andy. *Dreaming Methods*. 18 Mar. 2009 <http://www.dreamingmethods.com/>.

Döblin, Alfred. *Berlin Alexanderplatz*. Berlin: Fischer, 1929.

Douglas, Jane Y. *The End of Books, or Books Without End? Reading Interactive Narratives*. Ann Arbor: U of Michigan P, 2000.

Douglas, Jane Y., and James Hargadon. "The Pleasures of Immersion and Engagement: Schemas, Scripts and the Fifth Business." *Digital Creativity* 12.3 (2001): 153-166.

Ehlert, Nils, and Wolfgang Bauer. "Jetzt? Oder der höchste Augenblick." *Literatur.digital. Formen und Wege einer neuen Literatur.* Ed. Roberto Simanowski. CD-ROM. München: DTV, 2002.

Ensslin, Astrid. "From (W)reader to Breather: Cybertextual Retro-intentionalisation in Kate Pullinger et al.'s Breathing Wall." *New Narratives: Theory and Practice.* Ed. Ruth Page and Bronwen Thomas. Lincoln: U of Nebraska P, 2009. Forthcoming.

———. "Respiratory Narrative: Multimodality and Cybernetic Corporeality in 'Physio-cybertext.'" *New Perspectives on Narrative and Multimodality.* Ed. Ruth Page. London: Routledge, 2009. 155-165.

———. *Canonizing Hypertext: Explorations and Constructions.* London: Continuum, 2007.

———. "Of Chords, Machines and Bumble-bees: The Metalinguistics of Hyperpoetry." *Language in the Media: Representations, Identities, Ideologies.* Ed. Sally Johnson and Astrid Ensslin. London: Continuum, 2007. 250-268.

———. "Breathalyzing Physio-cybertext." *Proceedings of the Eighteenth Conference on Hypertext and Hypermedia, ACM, September 10-12, 2007.* Ed. Simon Harper et al. Alpha: ACM, 2007. 137-138.

———. "Literary Hypertext in the Foreign Language Classroom: A Case Study Report." *Language Learning Journal* 33 (2006): 13-21.

———. "Hypermedia and the Question of Canonicity." *Dichtung Digital* 36 (2006), 18 Mar. 2009 <http://www.dichtung-digital.org/2006/1-Ensslin.htm>.

———. "Women in Wasteland: Gendered Deserts in T.S. Eliot and Shelley Jackson." *Journal of Gender Studies* 14.3 (2005): 205-216.

———. "Reconstructing the Deconstructed: Hypertext and Literary Education." *Language and Literature* 13.4 (2004): 307-333.

Ensslin, Astrid, and Alice Bell. *New Perspectives on Digital Literature: Criticism and Analysis. Dichtung Digital* 37 (2007). 6 Aug. 2008 <http://www.brown.edu/Research/dichtung-digital/editorial/2007.htm>.

Fisher, Caitlin. "Electronic Literacies." *Light Onwords, Light Onwards.* Ed. Bruce W. Powe, and Stephanie Hart. 2004. 18 Mar. 2009 <http://www.nald.ca/fulltext/ltonword/part3/fisher/fisher.pdf>.

Genette, Gérard. *Narrative Discourse: An Essays in Method.* 1972. Trans. Jane E. Lewin. Ithaca: Cornell UP, 1980.

Hader, Suzanne. "The Bildungsroman Genre: Great Expectations, Aurora Leigh, and Waterland." *The Victorian Web: Literature, History, & Culture in the Age of Victoria*. Landow, George P. 1996. 18 Mar. 2009 <http://www.victorianweb.org/genre/hader1.html>.

Heyward, Megan. *Of Day, Of Night*. CD-ROM. Cambridge, MA: Eastgate, 2004.

Inglis, Gavin. *Same Day Test*. 1999. 18 Mar. 2009 <http://www.bareword.com/sdt/>.

Jahn, Manfred. *Narratology: A Guide to the Theory of Narrative*. 2005. 18 Mar. 2009 <http://www.uni-koeln.de/~ame02/pppn.htm#N3.3>.

John, Barbara. "The Sounding Image: About the Relationship between Art and Music—an Art-historical Retrospective View." *Media Art Net*. n.d. 18 Mar. 2009 <http://www.medienkunstnetz.de/themes/image-sound_relations/sounding_mage/1/#ftn1>.

Joyce, Michael. *afternoon, a story*. 1987. CD-ROM. Cambridge, MA: Eastgate, 1990.

Kuhlen, Rainer. *Hypertext: Ein nicht-lineares Medium zwischen Buch und Wissensbank*. Berlin: Springer, 1991.

Laccetti, Jess. *Inanimate Alice Pedagogy Project: Lesson Plans and Education Resource Pack*. 2007. 18 Mar. 2009 <http://www.inanimatealice.com/education/edupack.pdf>.

Landow, George P. *Hypertext 2.0: The Convergence of Contemporary Critical Theory and Technology*. Baltimore: Johns Hopkins UP, 1997.

Ludwig, Hans W. *Arbeitsbuch Lyrikanalyse*. Tübingen: UTB, 1994.

Luesebrink, Marjorie. "Literature in a Hypermedia Mode." *PopMatters*. Interview with Thomas Swiss. 2000. 18 Mar. 2009 <http://www.popmatters.com/a-and-i/000909.html>.

Maskiewicz, Stefan. *ColoRama*. 2004. 18 Mar. 2009 <http://www.leeon.de/showroom/toolbox/colorama/colorama.htm>.

———. *Quadrego*. 2001. 18 Mar. 2009 <http://www.quadrego.de/start.htm>.

Miall, David S. "Trivializing or Liberating? The Limitations of Hypertext Theorizing." *Mosaic (Winnipeg)* 32.2 (1999). 8 May 2009 <http://www.powen.org/researcharticles/Miall-hypertext_theorizing_limitations.pdf>.

Murray, Janet H. *Hamlet on the Holodeck: The Future of Narrative in Cyberspace*. New York: Free Press, 1997.

Nielsen, Jakob. "The Art of Navigating through Hypertext." *Communications of the ACM* 33.3 (1990): 296-310.

Pace, Steven. "A Grounded Theory of the Flow Experiences of Web Users." *International Journal of Human-Computer Studies* 60.3 (2003): 327-363.

Pauli, Michelle. "Down with Alice." *Guardian.co.uk*. 2006. 18 Mar. 2009 <http://www.books.guardian.co.uk/digitalliterature/story/0,,1966934,00.html>.

Pope, James. "A Future for Hypertext Fiction," *Convergence: The International Journal of Research into New Media Technologies*. 12.4 (2006): 447-465.

———. *Genarrator*. 18 Mar. 2009 <http://www.genarrator.blogspot.com>.

Pullinger, Kate, and Chris Joseph. *Inanimate Alice*. 2005-2008. 18 Mar. 2009 <http://www.inanimatealice.com>.

Ryan, Marie-Laure. *Avatars of Story*. Minneapolis: U of Minnesota P, 2006.

Ryman, Geoff. *253: Two Five Three or: Tube Theatre*. 1996. 18 Mar. 2009 <http://www.ryman-novel.com>.

Schnitzler, Arthur. *Reigen. Liebelei*. Frankfurt a.M.: Fischer, 1960.

Stanzel, Franz K. *A Theory of Narrative*. Trans. Charlotte Goedsche. Cambridge: Cambridge UP, 1984.

Storm, Theodor. "Die Stadt." *A Book of German Lyrics*. Ed. Friedrich Bruns. E-book. 2005. 8 May 2009 <http://www.ibiblio.org/pub/docs/books/gutenberg/etext05/8glyr10.txt>.

Sullivan, Laura. "Hypertextualizing Autobiography." *Kairos: A Journal for Teachers of Writing in Webbed Environments* 1.3 (1995). 9 May 2009 <http://www.english.ttu.edu/kairos/1.3/coverweb/Sullivan/kairos.recipe.html>.

Terziu, Fatmir. "How the Relationship between Soundtrack and Image Contributes to the Meaning of the Documentary." 2007. 18 Mar. 2009 <http://www.fatmir-terziu.blogspot.com/2007/06/how-relationship-between-soundtrack-and_28.html>.

The Pew Charitable Trusts. "Teens Forge Forward with the Internet and Other New Technologies." 29 July 2005. 8 May 2009 <http://www.pewtrusts.org/our_work_report_detail.aspx?id=23330>.

Dijk, van Rutger. *The Mobius Case*. 2005. 18 Mar. 2009 <http://www.media.bournemouth.ac.uk/studentshowcase/work/mobius/Main.swf>.

Walker, Jill. "Piecing Together and Tearing Apart: Finding a Story in *afternoon*." 1999. 9 May 2009 <http://www.jilltxt.net/txt/afternoon.html>.

Alexandra Saemmer

Digital Literature—In Search of a Discipline?

Teaching Digital Literature in France: A Short Overview

Academic research on digital literature was initiated many years ago; researchers and teachers like Jean-Pierre Balpe and Jean Clément at University Paris 8 have provided major contributions to the understanding of electronic poetry, hyperfiction and text generation. They have also managed to integrate digital literature into university courses in Information and Communication Sciences. But most of the Departments of Literature have not supported these educational experiments. Whereas a certain number of specific literary methods undoubtedly prove suitable for the analysis of poetry and narrative texts in electronic media (semiotics, gender and cultural studies, biographical or even thematical approaches), literary studies in France are quite reluctant to deal with digital literature. Of course, the competitive examination system that is inherent to France could account for this reluctance: as it is the case in other countries, French universities do not only educate researchers, but also primary and secondary school teachers. At the end of their studies, they must pass a highly standardized competitive examination, essentially focusing on knowledge in subjects like history of the French language and literature, grammar and rhetoric. A corpus of literary works is drawn up annually to help students get prepared for this examination. Some contemporary writers are included in this corpus, but on the condition that they are already canonical and considered "classic" authors. In France, literary studies actually struggle for life—this profound crisis, linked to a drastic reduction of financial support for literary teaching and research, causes in many places a re-concentration on the contents considered as "fundamental:" the history of French literature and language, traditional narrative and poetic forms and figures.

The ambiguous status of digital works, between literature, visual and performing arts, does not facilitate their integration into one specific discipline either. Thanks to its many specificities—including hypermedia—digital literature involves many creative and interpretative abilities, from film analysis to programming, from rhetoric to sound engineering. As a result, digital literature in French universities could have found a place anywhere, but to date found almost none. The teaching of digital literature undoubtedly requires multidisciplinary approaches: a pedagogical network integrating the visual arts, literary studies, musical studies, information sciences, communication sciences, and IT. Digital literature thus makes us dream about a university no longer divided into several disciplines, but providing students with networks of skills. Although there are only a few courses entirely dedicated to digital literature at French universities up to this day, the interpretation of animated or generated artworks and hyperfiction can be successfully integrated in many different pedagogical contexts, thanks to its multidisciplinary character. Three specific classroom situations will be presented in this article.

Digital Literature in Methodology and ICT Courses

Courses about the general functioning of computers and their operating systems, word and image processing, the search and retrieval of information in databases and online catalogs have been gradually implemented in French universities from the 1990s (the number of hours ranges from 21 to 48 hours per student; these courses are primarily intended for beginner students, but sometimes also exist in the second and third degree—Master and PhD).

Initially, these courses have often been part of the programs offered by the academic disciplines, the contents thus varying a lot from one department to another. For example, in the ICT courses provided for the students in literature at the University Lyon 2, the emphasis is laid not only on general information retrieval, but on specifically literary electronic resources (*Frantext* for example, a database that allows searching for keywords or grammatical structures in literary texts; the online library *Gallica*, which offers a digitalized version of thousands of classical literary works; the critical edition of literary texts through digital media, such as the project *Les dossiers de Bouvard et Pécuchet de Gustave Flaubert*). Students are also familiarized with a critical approach to the information retrieved from the Internet, and with tools helping them to structure their ideas (mind-mapping programs and bibliography software, such as "Notes de lecture," an application specifically developed for literary students). In Performing Arts (cinema, theatre, dance and photography), critical and practical approaches of image processing, multimedia integration and web sites designing have been privileged in the programs of this course.

Since 2002, the Ministry of Education has been trying to establish a framework for these courses ("Referentiel C2i") in order to provide all students in French universities with a certain number of common "basic skills." The following skills are put forward on this list: research, creation, manipulation and management of information; retrieval and data processing; data management, backup and archiving; oral presentation of a research work; video-conferencing tools; communication rules on the internet; collaborative work; critical approaches of the problems and challenges of ICT: usage rights and duties, legal and ethical aspects. The students can validate the acquisition of these skills by passing a "certification" called C2i, following the B2i for college and high school students. In some universities, ICT and Methodology courses have thus become transdisciplinary (for example at the University Lyon 2).

Many of these skills listed by the "C2i repository" prove to be purely technical. Admittedly, a certain number of core skills are necessary to maintain a general "information culture." But if we want students to acquire not only technical mastery, but also real "information literacy," the sole teaching of technical manipulations will not be sufficient. As Jean-François Lyotard comments in his visionary book *La Condition postmoderne* [*The Postmodern Condition*], the transmission of knowledge should not be limited to information, but involve all the procedures able to improve the possibilities of connecting the fields that the traditional knowledge management isolates with jealousy (86).

How could "information literacy" be defined? The location of information and its intelligent archiving certainly are a part of it, but so are the history of computer networks and their evolution, their technical foundation (from the first hypertexts to RSS) and their socio-cultural implications (from the first inter-university networks to social networks like *Facebook*). Of course, students must still learn how to find and to forward information; but they also need methods to evaluate information, to interconnect it and to make it evolve in their cultural context. This knowledge, which is not simply about skills, could be summarized as "cyberculture." As defined by Claude Baltz, who teaches cyberculture at the University Paris 8, "there is no information society without cyberculture," because "we need appropriate conceptual tools to think about the complexity and the common (non)consistency of the information society." Baltz's courses are mainly intended for Master students. But a certain number of cybercultural contents can be successfully integrated into Methodology and ICT courses for younger students.

Digital literature plays an important role in this context.[1] If we consider, according to Jacques Rancière, art and literature as a "systematic difference" compared to regular practices, as an "alteration of likeness," digital art and literature constitutes an excellent way for students to reflect on the use of digital tools, supports and interfaces in our society, to question the issues, utopias, advantages and dangers of the "digital revolution."

1. The Internet is wide open to self-publishing. Certain forms of digital art and literature seem particularly appropriate to discuss the democratization of the access to writing, its chances and its dangers. Everybody can *proclaim himself* a writer on the Internet—the possibility for writers to escape the traditional selection by book publishers enables the public to decide what kind of literature is worth reading; the success of literary blogs like *Le tiers livre* by François Bon or *Le Bloc-Notes du Désordre* by Philippe de Jonckheere proves that the online public is able to make good choices. Although these forms of self-pub-

lished literature do not confirm Alain Finkielkraut's concern about the disappearance of "scripta manent," (*L'inquiétante' extase*) critics are certainly right to deplore the lack of literary quality in a certain number of open writing spaces and the explosion of narcissistic self-reflections.

Thus, anybody can *be* a "writer" on the Internet—but in huge parts of the world, people do not even have access to electricity. In his recent artwork *Still Moving*, Maurice Benayoun proves in a very tactile way that the geographical landscape is entirely reconfigured on the Internet: one day, he recorded the frequency of three words ("nervous," "anxious" and "excited") in each country of the world by using *GoogleNews*. Each emotion has its color on an interactive landscape, which was represented on a huge deflated balloon. The more one specific word was cited, the more irregular was the relief of a country: the highest "mountain of emotions" formed in Paris; the central parts of Africa remained mostly excluded from this landscape.

As Philippe Lejeune (*Cher écran*) and more recently Bernhard Rieder ("Membranes numériques") have shown, the former from a literary point of view and the latter in a sociological and philosophical approach, the success of self-publishing tools like blogs, often linked to "social networks" (*MySpace*, *Facebook*), also tackles the issue of online privacy, questioning the new contours of the cyber-subject both closed ("my"space) and open to intrusion. The photo-diarist Louise Merzeau for example, links her web site to other photo-diaries. She comments: "The memory network thus becomes a network of memories, whose cohesion develops and then diminishes every day" (135). In this respect, the hyperlinked web site does not only constitute a complex representation of the author's artistic and social networks, but connects this area to the "world."

Many students know social networks such as *MySpace*, many of them have created a profile on *Facebook*. They tell their everyday adventures and impressions; they talk about private, cultural or political issues. The technical manipulation of these collaborative tools cannot constitute an objective of academic ICT courses any longer. Anyway, students rarely reflect on the private *and* public characters of their online spaces, and on the new modes of writing and mediation in these networks.

In order to help them become aware of these "cybercultural" questions, the diary "Kinjiki" seems to be an interesting pedagogical support. Ophélia has regularly been updating her "online diary" since August 2001 (many online diaries are abandoned after a few months). Her web site called "Kinjiki," "The prohibited colours" (inspired by the title of a novel by Yokio Mishima), does not only impress the reader by its literary and graphic quality. The metatextual problematization of many issues related to personal online publication also accounts for a close reading of "Kinjiki" during a course dedicated to cyberculture. As it is, Ophelia is fully aware of the presence of readers, of "all these eyes looking over her shoulder," and of their influence on web writing. She thus thematizes with accuracy the paradox of "intimate" writing on the Internet. In a certain number of her articles, she also reflects on the "truthfulness" of intimate writing, on the impossibility to capture events with words—these remarks incite students to think critically about our culture of testimony, about the (mis)use of pictures or videos as a "track of reality."

The surprising lack of hyperlinks in "Kinjiki's" texts brings into discussion an important utopian aspect of the cyberculture. At the beginning of the electronic networks, some philosophers, writers and artists, largely inspired by the research that was led in the field of artificial intelligence, dreamt about the imitation of neural networks on a digital medium. In fact, hypertext techniques facilitate the complex interconnection of data, and can thus be considered as ideal tools for all diarists who try to capture and to actualize the "reality" of their daily moods in their online texts. Therefore, the absence of hyperlinks in many online diaries seems paradoxical. In his book *Cher écran*, Philippe Lejeune imagines an online diary whose links would not be added, but would serve to "weave" the text itself (383). He cautiously adds that such a text may not be a diary any more: the author of a diary can hardly have the hindsight to frame a network between the events, characters, thoughts or intertextual allusions *while* writing them. In case the author wants to construct a more global hypertextual structure between his articles, he would have to distance himself from his every day perception. The reflective aspects of the hypertext would then turn his diary into an autobiography.

In "information literacy" courses, it seems essential to explain not only the function of hyperlinks in online writing spaces, but also their consequences on the reading process. I therefore propose that students imagine a hypertextual structure for "Kinjiki's" online diary, and reflect on the impressions that such a structure would produce on the reader. Students can observe that a hypertext is simultaneously seducing and disturbing, performative and frustrating: as the reader hesitates between the activation and non-activation of a hyperlink, he does not read the text itself. The dual function of the hyperlink (a linguistic sign to be read, and a "bottom" to be manipulated) causes a cognitive disorder that explains why digital reading is often considered as difficult and tiring. A critical and creative reading of literary diaries like "Kinjiki," thematizing a certain number of issues related to hypertextual and intimate writing, allows one to explore these cybercultural topics in both a theoretical *and* a sensitive way— a pedagogical method that proves more efficient than purely theoretical explanations.

2. Many literary and artistic creations on digital supports thematize or problematize the issue of navigation and reading processes in cyberspace. Of

course, the forms and figures of argumentation on digital media can also be explored on commercial web sites (including online advertising) and information portals (online press). Whereas these web sites tend to confirm our reading habits, a certain number of literary and artistic digital works offer a critical approach of our usages; they make us aware of our automatisms, our expectations, and make us question the conventions and rules of digital argumentation. Here are some examples for how this can be carried out:

- Visitors of web sites generally seem very eager. For instance, many visitors make circular movements with the cursor on the screen before and during the reading process (Yves Jeanneret, Anne Béguin et al.). Artistic web sites often force visitors to take their time: for example, *Revenances* by Gregory Chatonsky imposes a very slow rhythm of navigation on its visitors; if a visitor wants to exit the page, a pop-up window tries to make him aware of his impatience.

- Online visitors are accustomed to discovering new effects of the interface after each click; in *The Subnetwork*, Gregory Chatonsky also offers manipulable areas—but the consequences on the interface are not immediately visible.

- Usually, the visitor of a web site wants to progress rapidly towards a specific aim. *Explication de texte* by Boris du Boullay questions this childish "frenzy" by immersing the visitor in a hypertext in which each and every click has the same effect on the interface. The visitor turns around and around, always discovering the same words.

- Our e-mail box is regularly invaded by spams. Spampoetry by Philippe Boisnard parasites these forms, generally regarded as parasitic, by literary proposals.

- When French students are in search of information, they consult *Google*. *The Church of Google* shows the dangers of this monopoly in a satirical way. The anonymous author(s) of this project explain: "We have compiled a list of nine proofs which definitively *prove Google* is the closest thing to a 'god' human beings have ever directly experienced."

- More and more Internet users check their popularity on *Google*. *GoogleMirror* holds up a distorting mirror to them.

- Students are rarely aware of *Google's* page ranking. *The Google adwords happening* by Christophe Bruno reveals the ranking practices in a striking way.

Whereas the access to information and knowledge is increasingly dominated by a small number of companies, whose evolution and influence on the presentation of data is largely conditioned by commercial interests and attention to the immediate satisfaction of the customer's desire, these literary and artistic projects constitute precious places of resistance and subversion.

The *techniques* of information literacy grow easier to learn every day—students do not need specific courses to use them in accordance to the rules established by software companies, information providers and research engine developers. But "cybercultural" knowledge is also based on an awareness of the challenges and opportunities of the information society. The major aim of "information literacy" courses will thus be to inspire not only sophisticated, but creative uses of the network technologies.

Teaching Digital Literature in Information and Communication Sciences

For the moment, only a few Information and Communication departments explicitly include digital literature and arts in their curricula. "Multimedia creation" however, sometimes called "hypertextual writing," "online publishing" or "web site analysis," is already part of the curricula in most of these departments. Students are both familiarized with the programming languages of digital creation (e.g. XHTML, XML, JavaScript, PHP, Action Script), the software used in this field (e.g. Flash, Dreamweaver, Front Page, Final Cut), CMS (Content management systems), and with theoretical approaches of digital writing (from sociological and cognitive approaches to semiotics).

The acquisition of technical skills required for online publishing does not really constitute a problem for the students: all of them regularly use computers. Many of them have already experimented with blog formats. The widespread uses of CMS, blogs and Wiki tools, where the form and the content are generally separated, have in fact played an important role in this familiarization, but the standardization of formats also leads to uniformity. In my Master courses devoted to "hypertextual writing and online publishing," I often observe that students tend to copy the standard format of blogs, with their wide margins around the content window, their endless blocks of text and their calendar tools, even if they are just supposed to build a simple HTML page. Their practice of customizable home pages like "Netvibes," which no longer contain internal content, but are based on an architecture entirely generated from outsourced information (compiled RSS files), reinforces this tendency to consider the "form" of the text as a negligible detail.

Actually, formatting is absolutely present in CMS, blog and wiki tools. But the formats are ready-made; they are imposed by the provider and can only be changed if the author knows how to re-program them. Students are rarely aware of that restriction in these online publishing tools, where "the discourse is no longer anchored in the device, but the device anchors the discourse" (Ertzscheid). Thus, the "second text" (Souchier) provided by the pre-manufactured format, might turn into a "second voice" and disrupt the message. Students in Information and Communication Sciences must obviously be familiar with blogs, CMS and wiki techniques. However, it seems necessary to enable them to question these standardized formats, and to adapt them to their real needs.

After a general introduction to online publishing, I ask Master students to select two web sites: one that seems particularly convincing to them and a second one that seems particularly "negative." Few students cite blogs or wiki portals as positive examples. They are spontaneously interested in web sites provided by cultural institutions, such as museums or concert halls experimenting with the possibilities of digital media in more creative ways. At this moment in the course, students do not yet have the structured theoretical tools they need to justify their choices. Some of them proceed in a quite intuitive way, explaining their positive impressions by the "beauty" of the colours, the "aesthetics" of the animations, the "correctness" of the links; other students use analytical grids, currently available on educational sites,[2] to evaluate the quality of a web site in more "objective" ways; in these analytical grids, they sometimes find general qualifiers such as "the efficiency of the links," the "appropriateness between content and form." But what is an "efficient" hyperlink? Students need specific criteria to identify, evaluate and use the structures and forms of the argumentation of digital writing. In order to make them explore the possibilities of multimedia and hypermedia argumentation, a theoretical and practical approach to the forms and figures in digital literature seems appropriate.

Obviously, online advertising is also experimenting with the forms and figures of interaction and animation. But nowhere else on the Web is the panoply of forms and figures as diverse as in digital literature and arts. A rhetoric and semiotic approach of these forms and figures helps students identify which parts of an argument are in accordance with the general grammatical rules of the hypermedia discourse and the reader's expectations (for example, the activation of a link on a word giving access to a definition of this word), and which parts may be considered as a transgression (for example, the activation of a link on a word leading to an expression only "metaphorically" connected to this word). All these figures are not inherent to the linguistic and iconographic forms of multimedia, but rise from the reader's perceptions; consequently, they allow us to question the reading and writing habits and expectations on digital supports in a very effective way.

Online advertising and web design are largely inspired by digital arts and literature. With communication students, it is therefore particularly interesting to analyze how certain figures in hypermedia art become standardized, loosing their transgressive strength, supporting the advertising argument. In *Community of words* by Silvia Laurentiz and Martha Gabriel, the interactor is for example invited to enter a poem in a certain form. The computer calculates the relevance of each word: the result is visually rendered by a bigger or smaller size of the word in an interactive 3D environment. The aesthetic surface of this poetic device vividly recalls the use of animated text on the site Kenzo Parfums. From a technical point of view, the graphic realization also recalls interactive and multimedia "tag clouds."

Obviously, digital literature and art cannot be reduced to figures and forms of interaction and animation. Besides the "cybercultural" aspects that a certain number of works thematize in an utopian or disenchanted way (cf. the pedagogical elements mentioned above, which can also be discussed with students in Information and Communication Sciences), some artistic proposals focus on one of the main features of the digital media: the fragility of the device. Formats, software, operating systems and the speed of computers are subject to change; text animations that moved on the screen in a reasonable way a few years ago, are impossible to decipher nowadays. Only the program remains stable over time; the updates of the program depend on the computer with which they are actualized. Theoretical discussions thematizing the problems linked to the conservation and archiving of digital creations are only starting; the technical solutions (video screenshots or programs transforming old formats into more recent ones) do not always seem convincing. Future communication and information specialists should be aware of these problems. Admittedly, they also could discuss these with documentalists or librarians. But nobody theorizes the fragility of digital creations with the same rigor and radicalism as the poet Philippe Bootz ("Reader/Readers"). His creations allow us to show this fragility to students in a very striking way.

At the University Paris 8, Jean-Pierre Balpe, Jean Clément and Philippe Bootz have played a decisive role in the integration of digital literature in the curricula of Information and Communication Sciences. Two courses explicitly devoted to digital literature and poetry are proposed to the students in this discipline. Crystallizing the questions, the potential and the problems of digital media, digital literature will, sooner or later, play an equally important role in other departments of Information and Communication Sciences.

Teaching Digital Literature in Visual Arts

Unlike literary studies, visual arts have included for a certain number of years seminars on the aesthetics and practice of digital arts in their curricula—from the first academic year until Master and PhD degrees. The term "digital arts" often includes diverse practices such as video art, digital photography, performances and installations with digital supports, electronic music, web design and graphic arts. As the border between text and image is blurred in many contemporary art movements (Fluxus mixes up texts and images, Concrete poetry is exposed in art galleries, Sound poetry is often associated with performance arts, etc.), theoretical discussions and practical experimentations with textual forms and figures are generally included in Art courses. On the one hand, it is important to work with students on the affiliations between the "historical" avant-garde movements and the digital artistic forms. On the other hand, it is essential to discuss the specificities of digital arts and literature.

Fig. 1. Martin Chabannes, *Color Control.*

The first specificity, which is spontaneously cited by students, when asked to define digital arts, is the possibility of an "interaction" with text and images. The forms and figures of interaction on digital media must be analyzed with precision. Such case studies are necessarily based on "close readings" of digital works, that sometimes take the form of an oral presentation, but also result in practical experimentations: in the teaching practice of visual arts, aesthetic theory and experimentation are inextricably linked (the corpus of digital works chosen by my students at the University of Saint-Etienne for oral presentations, and their practical experimentations can be visited on <http://www.elektronikarts.blog.fr/>). For example, I asked students to conceive a practical experimentation based on one specific figure of manipulation. Martin Chabannes decided to reflect on the figure called "neantism:" the reader can interact with an animated word ("pouvoir"/"solitude") by replacing the cursor, getting the impression that these manipulations have some influence on the background videos; in fact, this power given to the reader is only an illusion.

At the beginning of digital art courses, I can observe that for many students, it seems very difficult to transgress the rules of commercial and advertising online argumentation. As in Information and Communication Sciences, a juxtaposition of selected digital works with advertising or commercial web sites thus proves useful. This comparison enables students to become aware of a frequent figure in digital arts and literature: the "detournement" of usual online practices which is often based on a critical reflection on the reader's expectations.

A second specificity of digital arts and literature concerns the relationship between art and technology. This issue is as important to discuss with art students as the relationship between text and image, or the affiliation with avant-garde movements. In my digital art courses, I generally introduce this relationship by discussing the "technological sublime" concept. The term first appears in certain analyses of the history of technology: in some contexts, technical progress has replaced religious eschatology, becoming a source of myth and transcendence. The "technical sublime" also plays an important role in science fiction literature and cinema (in the film *Ghost in the Shell* for example, a bodiless consciousness resists political domination by surviving on the Internet), and in posthumanist philosophy (for example *How We Became Posthuman* by N. Katherine Hayles); in all these approaches, technology is supposed to open the door to a new existence transcending the normality of the present time.

How could the idea of "technological sublime" spring up from a digital creation? The program cannot exceed the duality of 0 and 1. Nevertheless, some artists mystify the relationships between the animated words and images, the sounds and manipulation gestures in a digital artwork, in order to advocate an "unrepresentable," something that words could not tell and yet, that one could "feel" by experiencing the work. On the screen surface, the "unrepresentable" could be explored through inter-mediality. As regards the relationships between the artistic work and the computer, the "unrepresentable" would become "sensitive" throughout the incidents and interferences proper to the potential instability of the electronic device (digital devices being inherently instable, the results of calculations on the screenic surface undergo changes: Whereas the program remains the same over time, the speed of computers increases, software and storage tools disappear). Surrounded with mystery, this instability is not only reflected in certain artworks, it is literally over-exploited, as it is intended to give access to this "technological sublime" discussed above, in which the machine itself would provide novelty.

The fragile, ephemeral character of digital art and literature can be experienced in *Revenances* by Gregory Chatonsky, a digital work thematizing the "technological sublime" in a particularly subtle way. The reader, who moves in *Revenances* like in a video game, i.e. by manipulating the mouse buttons and the arrow keys, sometimes goes through walls and windows as if they had no consistence; at other moments, objects and walls strangely resist the mouse movements; as the cursor comes into contact with the bed, the chairs, or a photo floating in space it results in the projection into another space-time, that of the video world. There, the reader is supposed to meet a "revenant" (the French word for "ghost"), but this mysterious encounter does not only take place on a thematic level, or through the combination of heterogeneous media, it is also intrinsically linked to the characteristics of the electronic device. Thus, in *Revenances*, it seems to be in the contact between the clashing temporalities of 3D manipulations and the video loop, as well as in the passing from a plug-in to another, Cortona for the 3D and Flashplayer for the video, that Gregory Chatonsky perceives the possibility of a *gap*, a space where "revenances" would be welcome—even if this gap becomes apparent only as the Cortona icon appears and acts like a smuggler from one world to another—as the device visibly overflows into the artwork.

There is always a risk of rupture when the device overflows its boundaries—on Mac computers, for example, the Cortona plug-in cannot be correctly run, and a major part of the work remains inaccessible to the reader. Given the theme of *Revenances*, this decomposition is likely to be accepted by the artist as a particularly sublime intrusion of the device. A definitive disappearance being the opposite of a "revenance," Gregory Chatonsky nevertheless recommends the reader to run this artwork on a PC: he needs the metaphorical community of images, sounds and words to fascinate the reader, to make him believe in mysterious overflows of the electronic device on the work.

I generally show the PC and the Mac version of *Revenances* to my students, and I ask them if we should consider the Mac version as "incomplete" or "bugged." This question, quite destabilizing for the students, allows discussing some fundamental questions about the concept of ephemeral, recycling and conservation in contemporary art.

Confronted with the instability of the digital artworks that sometimes profoundly alters the media surface (some animated poems of the beginnings of digital literature now cross the screen so quickly that they cannot be read any more), the writer has three options:

- He requires the "right" technical environment for his work—a requirement that, over time, will increasingly be faced with the impossibility of maintaining old machines, obsolete software and operating systems;
- He agrees to create ephemeral, uncontrollable works. He may thus decide to let the work slowly fade away on the internet, accept its changing

forms and updates, assuming not only the fact that the incident and the unexpected partake in the interpretation of such a work, but considering "obsolence" as a main aesthetic principle of electronic literature and art: a literally disenchanted vision of the work and the world, where the "here and now" will never come back again; in order to illustrate this approach, the digital poem *La Série des U* by Philippe Bootz and Marcel Frémiot can be experimented with students on different computers: some connections between sound and visible forms are conserved in any digital environment, other manifestations profoundly change from one machine to another;

- The writer "re-enchants" its work, investing it with the spirit of sublime and nostalgia. This neo-symbolist trend constitutes the aesthetic principle of digital works like *Revenances* by Gregory Chatonsky, or *Twittering* by Talan Memmott. Gregory Chatonsky evokes the influence of the film *Histoire(s) de cinéma* by Jean-Luc Godard on *Revenances*: on a structural level, these digital creations work with the "mystery" as an aesthetic category.

The aesthetics of the ephemeral and the aesthetics of re-enchantment are based on the use of specific rhetorical *figures*. The aesthetics of the ephemeral are mistrustful of the great indifferent mixture of meaning and materiality; they naturally tend to *a-media* figures, where no meaningful relationship can be established between the acts of manipulation, the animated words and images and the linguistic or iconographic content. The aesthetics of re-enchantment are based on a re-theologization of the relations between meaning and materiality, claiming for the existence of the "unspeakable," the "non representable," which cannot be said, but experienced through manipulable inter-mediations. The aesthetics of the ephemeral and of re-enchantment in digital literature are two very different ways of writing the loss of traditional narrative structures and meaning in the early 21st century. They re-invent aesthetic and literary traditions that must be discussed with art students.

Because of its *intersemiotic* character integrating fixed and animated images, video and sound, program and technical supports, digital literature will perhaps always *remain* in search of *one* specific discipline. But the effective integration of a reflection on digital literature in French curricula, from ICT courses to visual arts, should not obscure a more fundamental problem: the reluctance of literary studies towards the new forms and figures of literary writing on digital media. Writers like François Bon, well known in literary circles for his "paper" novels, but also experimenting with digital formats (*Le tiers livre*), have nevertheless an important influence on the acceptance of digital literature. A gradual integration of digital literature in the curricula of literary studies will hopefully give a certain number of animated, interactive and programmed digital works the place they deserve, within the canons of 20th and 21st century literature.

Notes

1 In his book *Cyberculture*, Pierre Lévy yet emphasizes the role of digital arts and literatures (173).
2 For example <http://docinsa.insa-lyon.fr/sapristi/index.php?rub=1004>.

Works Cited

Baltz, Claude. "Elements de cyberculture." 23 Feb. 2009 <http://www.boson2x.org/spip.php?article129>.

Benayoun, Maurice. *Still Moving*. 23 Feb. 2009 <http://www.still-moving.net/>.

Boisnard, Philippe. *Spampoetry*. 23 Feb. 2009 <http://www.databaz.org/xtrm-art/?p=56>.

Bon, François. *Le tiers livre*. 23 Feb. 2009 <http://www.tierslivre.net/>.

Bootz, Philippe. "Reader/Readers." *p0es1s: The Aesthetics of Digital Poetry*. Ed. Friedrich W. Block, Christiane Heibach and Karin Wenz. Ostfildern: Hatje-Cantz, 2004. 93-121.

Bootz, Philippe, and Marcel Frémiot. *La Série des U*. 23 Feb. 2009 <http://www.collection.eliterature.org/1/works/bootz_fremiot__the_set_of_u/index.htm>.

Bruno, Christophe. *Le Google AdWords Happening*. 23 Feb. 2009 <http://www.iterature.com/adwords/index_fr.html>.

Chabannes, Martin. *Color Control*. 23 Feb. 2009 <http://www.eiki42.free.fr/color_control/>.

Chatonsky, Gregory. *Revenances*. 23 Feb. 2009 <http://www.incident.net/works/revenances/>.

―――. *Sous-terre/The Subnetwork*. 23 Feb. 2009 <http://www.incident.net/works/sous-terre/>.

Boullay, de Boris. *Explication de texte*. 23 Feb. 2009 <http://www.lesfilmsminute.com/explication/>.

De Jonckheere, Philippe. *Le Bloc-Notes du Désordre*. 23 Feb. 2009 <http://www.desordre.net/blog>.

Dord-Crouslé, Stéphanie, dir. *Les dossiers de Bouvard et Pécuchet*. Digital Edition. 23 Feb. 2009 <http://www.dossiers-flaubert.ish-lyon.cnrs.fr/>.

Ertzscheid, Olivier, "Dispersion, dissémination et diversion: Les 3 mamelles du 2.0?" 23 Feb. 2009 <http://www.affordance.typepad.com/mon_weblog/2007/01/dispersion_diss.html>.

Finkielkraut, Alain, and Paul Soriano. *Internet, l'inquiétante extase*. Paris: Mille et une nuits, 2001.

Frantext. "Base textuelle." 23 Feb. 2009 <http://www.atilf.atilf.fr/frantext.htm>.

Gallica. "Bibliothèque numérique." 23 Feb. 2009 <http://www.gallica.bnf.fr/>.

Google Mirror. 23 Feb. 2009 <http://www.elgoog.rb-hosting.de/index.cgi>.

Hayles, N. Katherine. *How We Became Posthuman: Virtual Bodies in Cybernetics, Literature, and Informatics*. Chicago: U of Chicago P, 1999.

Information Literacy. 23 Feb. 2009 <http://www.informationliteracy.org.uk/>.

Jeanneret, Yves et al. "Formes observables, représentations et appropriation du texte de réseau." *Lire, écrire, récrire: Objets, signes et pratiques des médias informatisés*. Ed. Emmanuel Souchier, Yves Jeanneret, and Joëlle Le Marec. Paris: Bibliothèque Centre Pompidou, 2003. 91-158.

Kenzo Parfums. 23 Feb. 2009 <http://www.kenzoparfums.com/FR/kenzo.html>.

Kinjiki. 23 Feb. 2009 <http://www.kinjiki.free.fr/>.

Laurenitz, Silvia, and Martha Gabriel. *Community of Words*. 23 Feb. 2009 <http://www.turbulence.org/spotlight/cm/community-of-words.htm>.

Lejeune, Philippe. "Cher écran." *Journal personnel, ordinateur, Internet*. Paris: Seuil, 2000.

Lévy, Pierre. *Cyberculture*. Paris: Odile Jacob, 1997.

Lyotard, Jean François. *La condition postmoderne*. Paris: Minuit, 1979.

———. *The Postmodern Condition: A Report on Knowledge*. Minneapolis: U of Minnesota P, 1984.

Memmott, Talan. *Twittering. E-Poetry Festival 2007*. Performance. 23 Feb. 2009 <http://www.epoetry2007.net/>.

Merzeau, Louise. "Au jour le jour: Autour d'une expérience de journal photographique sur le web." *Traces photographiques, traces autobiographiques.* Ed. Vray, Jean-Bernard Vray, and Danièle Méaux. Saint-Étienne: Publications de l'Université de Saint-Étienne, 2004. 131-136.

Ministère de l'enseignement supérieur et de la recherche. Le Référentiel C2i niveau 1. 23 Feb. 2009 <http://www2.c2i.education.fr/sections/c2i1/referentiel/>.

Mortier, Anne-Marie. "Notes de lecture. A program for Bibliography. 23 Feb. 2009 <http://www.sites.univ-lyon2.fr/lettres/ndl/index.php>.

Ghost in the Shell. Dir. Mamoru Oshii. Toho, 1995.

Prudhomme, Brigitte. "Evaluation de l'information présente sur Internet." 23 Feb. 2009 <http://www.docinsa.insalyon.fr/sapristi/index.php?rub=1004>.

Rieder, Bernhard. "Membranes numériques: des réseaux aux écumes." 23 Feb. 2009 <http://www.archive-esic.ccsd.cnrs.fr/docs/00/26/75/60/PDF/article_phiteco_rieder.pdf>.

Souchier, Emmanuël. "L'image du texte: Pour une théorie de l'énonciation éditoriale." *Les cahiers de médiologie* 6 (1998). 23 Feb. 2009 <http://www.mediologie.org/collection/06_mediologues/souchier.pdf>.

The Church of Google. 23 Feb. 2009 <http://www.thechurchofgoogle.org/>.

María Goicoechea

Teaching Digital Literature in Spain

Reading Strategies for the Digital Text

1 Introduction

The convergence with Europe and the information technologies are transforming the teaching of literature in the Spanish universities. The inclusions of digital literature as a new subject in the university curricula is still, however, a rarity. In the following pages I will draw a picture of the state of affairs in Spain regarding the teaching of digital literature, and I will share some teaching strategies I have implemented in my everyday practice as well as my reflections for a future pedagogy of digital literature.

Generalizing, we could say that the literary system is being transformed in three main aspects (Romero López, "Retos de la enseñanza" 146):

1. The digital medium is being used to preserve and edit literary texts, including in them graphic material, links with related texts, dictionaries, etc.

2. Digital literature makes its appearance with new generic characteristics, new creators (who combine their knowledge of literary resources with the technological mechanisms of digital text production), and new readers capable of enjoying reading texts on the screen.

3. The methodology of teaching literature is changing to include the use of computers as learning tools.

It is fundamentally this third aspect that has received wider attention in the Spanish context, as it is made apparent in the recent publication *Enseñanza virtual y presencial de las literaturas*, edited by Pilar García Carcedo. The Spanish universities are at the moment more concerned with the adjustments that the Bologna Treaty and the European convergence require than with revising the notion of what is literature in the digital era. In the last years the European Union has been developing the Common Space for European Education, whose purpose is to homogenize degrees in order to facilitate the mutual recognition of studies among countries of the Union and the greater mobility of students. To accomplish this objective, a system of uniform credits has been introduced, the European Credit Transfer System (ECTS), which permits the integration of theoretical and practical learning and places its emphasis on the learning process of the student.

Spanish teachers have to adjust their predominantly theoretical teaching perspective to incorporate a more practical approach that places the student's independent learning experience at the centre of the teacher's planned activities. This implies that the teacher will have to include in the organization, orientation, and supervision of the students' work a mixed system of virtual and presential learning. It is for this reason that information technologies have been predominantly perceived as tools for the teaching of literature[1] rather than transforming forces of the very concept of literature. In most cases, we are teaching with the tools of the 21st century (through virtual learning environments such as WebCT or Moodle, for example) the content of 19th century literature curricula.

There also exists a conservative tendency in a large portion of the Spanish academia and the publishing industry that covertly censures digital literature, since they perceive these new creations as a threat that challenges their own intellectual and economic interests. The threat experienced is, in a certain sense, real since most Humanities Departments are suffering a profound transformation. The five-year degree needs to be comprised into a four-year one, and many teachers fear the extinction of their courses. Some of the eliminated subjects will be offered at a postgraduate level, but there are also subjects and even whole degrees (as it is the case of Classical and Romanic Philologies) that risk their very existence. In this context, it is very difficult to integrate a new subject into the curricula.

Nevertheless, digital literature courses have begun to make their appearance in the university curricula since approximately 2001 when José Luis Orihuela, at the University of Navarra, a private institution, introduced his course *Non-Linear Writing* as an elective course as part of the Communications Degree. Nowadays we find similar courses offered as elective courses at postgraduate levels in the Communications, Humanities and Art Degrees of different universities. The University of A Coruña, for example, offers one of the most prestigious Master studies, *Master in Digital Creation and Communication*, which includes several courses related to Digital Literature, including Orihuela's *Non-Linear Writing*, L. Hernández' *Digital Worlds*, and R. Campos' *Audiovisual Language and Script*. Two other pioneer universities are the Open University of Catalonia, a virtual university which offers a *Master in Literary Studies in the Digital Era*, and a postgraduate course entitled *Literary Studies and Digital Literature* with Laura Borràs Castanyer as main architect of its curricula design, and the University Carlos III of Madrid, whose Humanities Degree enjoys one of the most avant-garde curricula of the Spanish territory. Professor Domingo Sánchez-Mesa and his colleagues have designed the following elective courses:

Literature and Cyberculture, Literature, Film and Videogames: Cyberculture, and *Theatre and Cyberculture.*

The Fine Arts Degree of the University Complutense is the only degree in Madrid's largest university with a subject entitled *New Digital Narratives*; however, the title is misleading since its approach is thoroughly artistic, being a course dedicated to the study of the new technologies of digital printing. The new English Studies Degree of the University Complutense of Madrid, which is in the process of being approved, does not include Digital Literature as an independent subject but as a final section of an elective course on *Literary Theory and Criticism.* However, a new subject called *New Technologies for Literary Research* has been included as a weak sign of modernization. I have designed the course *The Reader in Cyberspace: Cyberculture and Literature* which, hopefully, will be soon offered at the postgraduate level. The course program has been adapted to fit the requirements of the European Credit Transfer System[2]

De facto, introductions in the curricula are actually made by individual teachers who include digital literature as a last chapter in the literary history courses they currently teach. As it is in my case, I dedicate the last chapter in the syllabus of *Classic Works of Gothic Fiction in English* to Cybergothic, where we discuss among other topics the digital narratives of Cybergothic and Technoromanticism, Shelley Jackson's hypertext *Patchwork Girl* as a revision of Mary Shelley's *Frankenstein,* the Gothic tropes in William Gibson's *Neuromancer* and Pat Cadigan's *Synners,* etc. We also use this opportunity to reflect upon the main critical concepts introduced by cyberculture and their relevance for literary studies: such as the new forms of production and reception/interaction in cyberspace; the blurring of the roles between writer and reader; the revision of the concept of genre and intermediality; and digital metaphors of the body, the text, and the machine.

Other actions directed to popularize digital literature and encourage creators have been the organization of Digital Literature Prizes, such as the Digital Literature International Prize "Ciutat de Vinaròs," organized by the research group *Hermeneia* at the University of Barcelona (UB), and the Microsoft-Leethi Prize "Literatures in Spanish from Text to Hypermedia" organized by the research group "Leethi" ("Spanish and European Literatures from Text to Hypermedia") at the University Complutense of Madrid.

These are attempts to place digital literature in the university discussion forums, to compel critics to reflect upon the definition of digital literature and the new criteria it demands for its evaluation, and, in the case of the Microsoft-Leethi Prize, to foment digital literatures in Spanish. The general objective of the Leethi group regarding the organization of the First Pan-Hispanic Digital Literature Prize was actually to use it as an opportunity of learning and research. More precisely, we were interested in:

1. Searching parameters of classification and evaluation:
   - What is digital literature? Will it evolve as a new art form or is the digital platform the new medium to which all literature will move?
   - How are we going to deal with the intermedial nature of the digital text? The problem of genres.
   - How are we going to assess the creative use of the digital medium?
   - How are we going to evaluate the intrinsic literary value we expect of the works?
   - Which characteristics intrinsic to the digital medium are we going to evaluate: design, readability, accessibility?
2. Elaborating a digital literature collection of canonical texts.
3. Promoting the discussion and elaboration of pedagogical methods for teaching literature in the new medium.
4. And finally, promoting the digital edition of literary texts.

For these purposes, the prize is divided in three modalities:

A. Electronic Edition of literary works in Spanish.

B. On-Line Didactics of literatures in Spanish.

C. Creation of Digital Literature in Spanish.

The contributions received for the creative modality came mainly from university spheres and, with a few remarkable exceptions, they denoted an amateurish style that made us conclude that digital literature in Spanish was still in its infancy. This is part of the reason why it is difficult to justify its inclusion in the university curricula, since many teachers believe that we still need to wait for more conclusive examples. As Dolores Romero has remarked "where digital literature is concerned, one can be a pioneer but we still do not know who the geniuses will be" ("Spanish Literature" 338).

2 Teaching Strategies for Introducing Digital Literature

The same paradoxical situation that takes place in the realm of digital literature criticism, where the corpus of critical works far exceeds that of "canonized" digital literature, reproduces itself in the field of Spanish digital literature pedagogy. I have reflected upon the new challenges that digital literature will pose in my teaching practice even before digital literature has made its "official" appearance in the curricula. In the following sections I will share some of the reflections I have made regarding the introduction of digital literature in our literature classes and provide some teaching examples I have used for this purpose. I will focus on some of the points of friction that teachers and students encounter when approaching the electronic texts, and I will propose some practical reading strategies that can help instructors improve their practice of teaching digital literature.

2.1 Adjusting Our Intertextual Reading Strategies

The reader's experience of previous texts constitutes one of the most important reading strategies that are applied to new texts. The high interconnectivity allowed by the digital medium has produced textual structures that have boosted the use of expansions, appendixes, side notes, digressions, background information of all sorts, deforming the genre frames to which the reader is accustomed. Students' first reaction to this characteristic of digital texts is normally one of disorientation and anxiety. It is therefore useful that the teacher establishes a connection with printed literary texts that provoke in the reader a similar reaction and that he discusses the type of reading strategies that the students have already been using with this type of text (cf. section 3.1.). By making these reading strategies (which are normally applied at the unconscious level) explicit, the teacher is helping the students build a transition between the already-known literary experience and the new, allowing them to make the necessary adjustments.

It is thus worth noticing that the movement towards an explicit intertextuality increasingly overloaded—in the form of citation, collage, side notes, bibliographical references, references to music, film, and other cultural products—has been for many decades the general tendency in printed texts, both academic and literary. The academic style today is identified by dependence without precedent on quotations and references as a way to give credibility to the arguments presented. This requisite, inherited from the positivist scientific method, turns the accumulation of knowledge into a writing style. In the literary field, the baroque use of intertextual allusions has characterized modernist and postmodernist texts.

In this respect, cultivated readers already possess the tools needed to cope with an excess of intertextual relations that they are not always able to identify, while still enjoying reading. They have become used to filter relevant information from a sea of data by projecting onto the text patterns of meaning and reading objectives, and by taking into consideration the different levels at which the text is signifying, such as the subliminal and subconscious level. Information is processed without too much conscious effort, with the hope that it will occupy its place in the puzzle retrospectively or be discarded. The overloading of information, however, originates when the reader is confronted with a surplus of new information, which s/he does not know how to cast aside or contextualize in an integrating structure. In this case, the readers need to adjust their reading strategies; they need to learn to discard information or glide over it without exerting themselves too much. This ability is necessary in a variety of texts, both printed and digital. Two good places to start a discussion of print versus digital reading strategies are the digital works of Jim Andrews, *The Idea of Order of Key West Reordered*, and Young-Hae Chang and Marc Voge (Young-Hae Chang Heavy Industries), *Dakota*. These two digital texts are examples of what Jessica Pressman has referred to as "digital modernism,[3] a type of digital literature that uses central aspects of modernism. Jim Andrews' work, for example, remediates a poem by Wallace Stevens by digitalizing the sound of its reading and allowing the reader to manipulate its display in two modes, the normal and the glitched one. *Dakota*—a flash animation based on capitalized black text over a white background flashed at varying speeds synchronized to jazz music—is, according to its author, based on Ezra Pound's *Cantos* part I and II. In both cases, the works align themselves with literary modernism's aesthetic practices, at the same time that promote an awareness of their distinctively different, digital nature and the types of reading practices they require.

The next step can be to reflect upon the screen literacy level the student has already achieved in his/her previous navigating experience. One activity designed to discuss the issue of screen literacy and the experimental nature of many digital texts in this respect is the comparison of their reading instructions.

The teacher needs to emphasize that greater familiarity with digital literature in general also fosters the development of a literary competence that will allow the reader to construct mental maps of the document structure more easily. Moreover, one can also learn to trigger effects by exploiting the interactive buttons, and to avoid redundancy by paying attention to the clues about navigation offered by the screen (such as recognizing the address of a link one has already visited, and stopping the loading of the page to return quickly, etc.).

We see how, progressively, our previous knowledge of digital texts begins to be incorporated to our intertextual reading strategies. However, not every reader manages the conventions of the new medium with the same degree of dexterity. Landow highlighted the importance of such conventions, and proposed hypertext and hypermedia authors to use a set of techniques, some sort of user manual, to help readers face the main problems they encounter:

1. The lack of orientation, which inhibits them from reading efficiently and obtaining pleasure from the reading experience.

2. The lack of information with respect to what type of data each link is going to yield, which produces the encounter with non-required or already read information.

3. The need for information regarding the overall functioning of the document, which will help the reader feel more at ease.

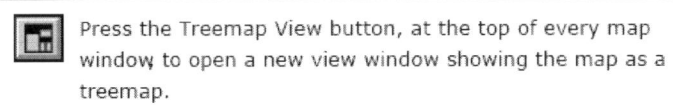

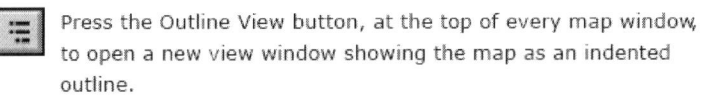

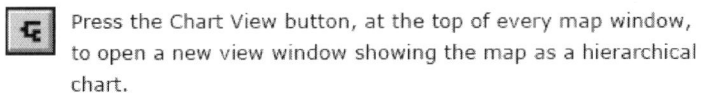

Press the Treemap View button, at the top of every map window, to open a new view window showing the map as a treemap.

Press the Outline View button, at the top of every map window, to open a new view window showing the map as an indented outline.

Press the Chart View button, at the top of every map window, to open a new view window showing the map as a hierarchical chart.

Fig. 1. Reading Instructions for Shelley Jackson's *Patchwork Girl*.

In general, digital works of literature are improving in their use of reading instructions and orientation tools, even if in some cases, as Shelley Jackson's *Patchwork Girl* reading instructions, they revert into another sort of information overload (fig. 1). The Spanish work *Diorama* by Santiago Ortiz presents an interesting structure, which reminds us of Rodríguez de las Heras' understanding of the ideal hypertext architecture. The tags above the cube inform about the type of information each link yields: a theme, a quotation, a commentary of the author, an external link, a drawing, picture or image, the title of a book, or an interactive application. Before entering the document, the reader also receives some instructions regarding the actions s/he can elicit with the mouse and the functioning of the document. The actions the reader can perform include rotating the cube (the three-dimensional space where we find the links interconnected), accessing the link information, isolating related topics inside the cube, or accessing content through the upper menu (fig. 2).

The beauty of this system is that the spatial orientation is always maintained, since the link information appears superposed over the former screen, so the reader can always keep track of his/her previous step. Moreover, the highly mobile structure of this work actively helps the reader by recombining links on the screen according to their degree of thematic relevance. If the proposed organization of the material does not fit the user's purposes, the reader can parallely create his/her own interface by connecting previously unrelated links, actualizing, erasing, and creating new contents for his/her personal use.

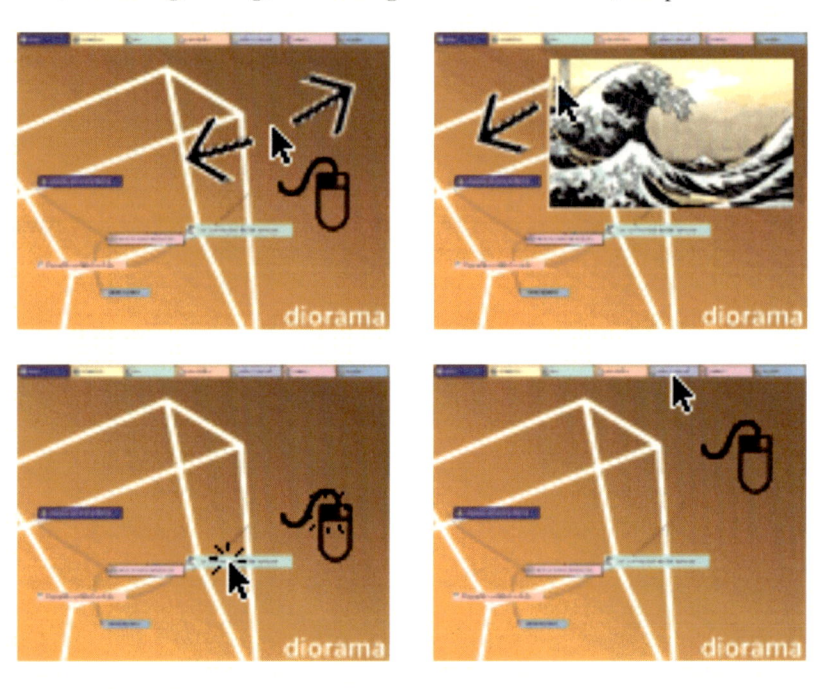

Fig. 2. Navigation instructions of *Diorama* by Santiago Ortiz.

2.2 Rupture of the Concept of Genre. Reading Strategy: A Synesthetic Approach

Midway between the essayistic and the literary style, *Diorama* blurs the concept of genre, as it also happens with *Patchwork Girl* and many others. Readers are obliged to review their previously known categories for texts and to conceive of a different one to incorporate the newcomer—at the same time as they become familiarized with its reading instructions, which varies from one document to another. Therefore, many things have to be relearned anew when approaching a different digital work. Like a new Sisyphus, the reader will have to start all over again with each new work, adjusting to new reading instructions, new rules and configurations, new mixtures of registers, styles, and types of text, new combinations of text and image, of movement, speed, music, and—in the most extreme cases—the reader is even proposed literature without words. This final proposition, which would dynamite all previous conceptualizations regarding the literary, has been implicitly made by several collectives that have included works such as *Sisyphus* under the rubric of "digital literature." We propose the classroom analysis of this piece to introduce students to the debate regarding the differential nature of digital literature with respect to print literature, and to reflect upon the new reading strategies that these type of works call for their interpretation.

The award-winning artist Antoni Abad[4] created his piece *Sisyphus* as a representation of his fight against himself. Later transformed for the Internet, the work acquired new meanings as its two screens were staged by different servers, one based in Barcelona and the other in its antipodean cousin, Wellington, New Zealand.

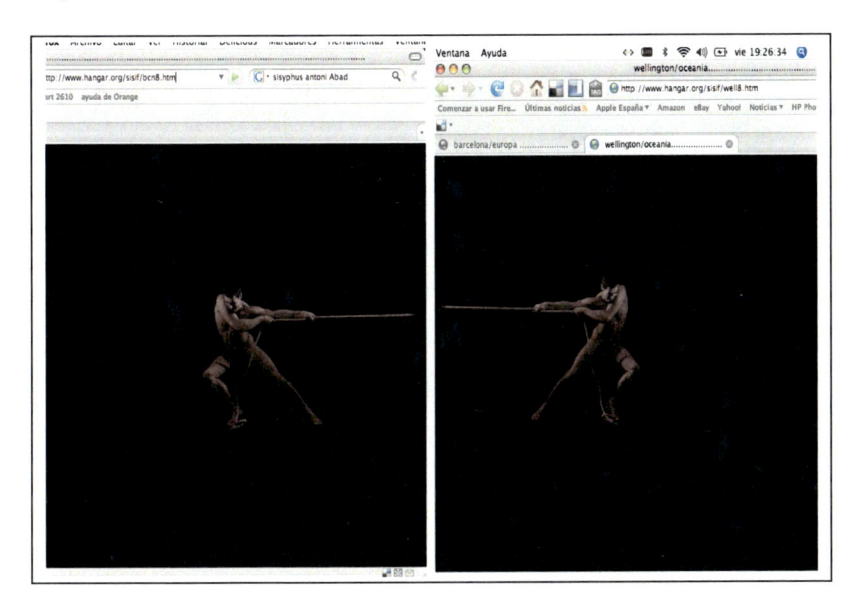

Fig. 3. *Sisyphus* by Antoni Abad.

Classified by the research group Hermeneia as an example of digital literature, this netart work exposes the actual blurring of boundaries between different forms of art and their convergence in the Internet. Of course, its classification as literature is polemic. The argument for considering these pieces digital literature is grounded on theories regarding the intermedial nature of the digital text and its integration into the still predominantly wordy matrix of Internet. The Electronic Literature Organization, for example, admits as digital literature computer art installations that ask viewers to read them or otherwise have literary aspects. The nature of these literary aspects is, however, left unspecified. Antoni Abad's *Sisyphus* is also included in their directory and described as a multimedia work.

When words share a space with other types of signs, the question becomes: How many words do we need to make a multimedia work a work of literature? How do we assign a literary value to these new formations? A closer look into *Sisyphus* allows us to realize the central function that words play, even if they are not the words of its author but of its curator, Roc Parés, glossing the work. Without Parés' singular commentary, which appears when clicking the image of the rope at the center, the piece would lack a fundamental context in which to make sense (fig. 4). Beginning with a quote from Paul Virilio regarding his aesthetics of disappearance, this text also provides clues for the work's reading ("Sisyphus is nowhere, it only exists when someone asks for it, in this sense it resembles a stretch or a word. In order for it to work it needs people to go and visit it.")

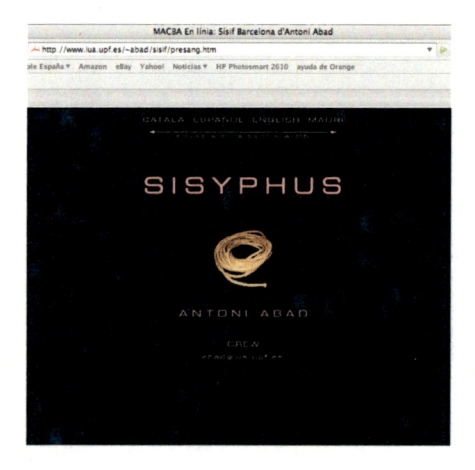

Fig. 4. *Sisyphus* by Antoni Abad, entry page.

We could also say that literature only exits in the mind of the reader. So, if we suspend our criticism for a moment and take up the challenge of reading Abad's work as literature, we would arrive to the conclusion that we need to exercise different ways of approaching the visual text in conjunction with the linguistic. These approaches or transformations of our perceptive habits can be useful to understand other pieces of digital art that combine different media. For example, in order for the work *Sisyphus* to be seamlessly "converted" into literature, the spectator might need to modulate his/her mind to a synesthesic mode of perception: "see" words when looking at an image, in a way that consciously imitates the mental dislocations of people living with this neurological condition, the synesthetes[5], who see a color when they look at a number, or hear a tone when they look at a color.

Son of a sculptor and a writer, Antoni Abad is surely another synesthete, claiming through his work the liberation of art from established media supports. Internet appeals to him for its tendency towards minimalism, as he is compelled to transmit the biggest amount of information through the minimal amount of signs. Compressing information in this way, he is also demanding on the part of his spectators a similar way of decoding, one which is able to produce as much information as possible from the minimum amount of input.

The use of a type of reading that unites different types of signs (symbolic, indexical, iconic, etc.) would multiply the signifying possibilities of the work. Interpreting the images the visitor elicits in conjugation with the title of the piece and the curator's commentary would require a synesthetic approach to the image as text, reading its parts in a syntagmatic order, placing our interpretations in relation with other texts, contextualizing the piece in its wider textual reference, the Internet.

Proceeding in this manner, Abad's work would be invested with a relevant meaning inside the conceptual frame of cyberculture. Let us now analyze the classical reference of the title and its relation with the specular images that appear. As we see, the myth of Sisyphus is juxtaposed to the myth of Narcissus, since two identical naked figures fight against each other. Thus, the struggle against oneself manifested by the artist in this piece is placed in the context of digital communication, producing a variety of messages which acquire even deeper significance when inserted in the on-going debate about digital art: a discourse in which the themes of solipsism and recurrence in the digital work of art have already received critical attention (cf. section 3.2).

Abad's simulation of two narcissuses drilling the planet from one point to the other, made virtually real through the collaboration of different institution at opposite ends of the world, expresses one of the crucial paradoxes of cyberculture, a medium which has an incredible potential for interconnectivity, at the same time that it isolates the individual from direct contact with others, triggering a self-referential movement. Thus, there are thematic reasons that legitimize the inclusion of Abad's piece inside a collection of works that reflect the preoccupations of cyberculture, even if its classification as a piece of digital literature is not accepted.

To sum up, it needs to be said that this radical proposition on the part of Hermeneia is characteristic of a period of change in the literary paradigm that puts every previous certainty into question. The literary experience becomes then a total projection on the part of the reader, a process independent of the medium that triggers it, a special sensitivity that translates the world into words—a movement, in short, that will definitively conflate the writer with the reader.

2.3 Rupture of Narrativity. Reading Strategy: The Principle of Serendipity

The minimalism of Abad's work contrasts significantly with the artistic manipulations of written texts, which appear in a baroque profusion of different shapes and structures in digital literature.

Fig. 5. *Book-Butterflies* (1999-2001) by Belén Gache.

A common feature to many of them is the rupture with traditional narrative forms, making obsolete the reader's intertextual habit of presupposing a linear structure for texts. The narration loses its temporal dimension, debilitating the plot and character construction. This might leave in the reader a sensation of loss, of provisional nature. However, if we try to search for its positive aspects, we will discover a new reading pleasure at finding unexpected effects. This idea (pointed out by Laura Borràs Castanyer as she recapitulates over her teaching experience with hypertext (67)), can be applied, for example, to the work *Book-Butterflies* (1999-2001) of the Argentinean writer Belén Gache. Gache's introductory statement—"Writing detains, crystallizes. In a way it kills the word and keeps its corpse. An ethereal corpse like a desiccated butterfly"—prepares us for an ephemeral reading experience in which there is not the possibility of retracing one's steps. Clicking on the image of a butterfly elicits a quote from a literary work whose only suture point with previous or following quotes is its reference to butterflies.

The principle of serendipity can be described as the chance discovery of a literary effect. But, as it happens with chance discoveries in science, the reader must be trained to recognize them, to have a sense of fulfilment when they appear. The ideal reader of a text such as this one could obtain pleasure out of at least two operations: the construction of an imaginary narrative, threading the quotes into a meaningful chain[6], and the recognition of the quotes' sources, contrasting the personally constructed story with the previous readings the original texts once evoked. However, for the average reader, only the first operation is readily available, since the second corresponds to either a very erudite reader, well-versed in world literature and with an extraordinary memory, or to the personal reading history of the author herself. We can yet include a third possibility, the pleasure obtained in the nonsensical quality of the chance chain of quotes. Teachers might use Gache's text or a similar one to discuss the type of reading the student has applied when confronted with a non-linear, alleatory combination of textual fragments or links, and the type of reader s/he is depending on his/her degree of acceptance of incoherence and chaos.

As many other hypertext theorists have pointed out (Coover, Clement, Landow, Pajares), this reading strategy, which obliges the reader to play with analogies and metaphor, to read using selective perception, and find generalizing themes, is closer to a poetic reading than to a narrative one. This poetic reading requires a reader who is well prepared to deal with ambiguity, open-endedness, and lack of closure; a reader who, in short, has so many intertextual resources himself or herself as to be able to project a literary structure, be it meaningful or carnivalesque, over an amorphous collection of quotes.

3   Recycling Our Interactive Reading Strategies

Digital literature vindicates its amorphous, monstrous nature. As we can observe in the following two fragments from works by Antoni Abad and Shelley Jackson (cf. fig. 6 and fig. 7), the lack of narrativity, of interconnection between text fragments or events, is frequently thematized:

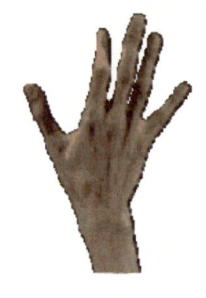

... stretch by stretch I have renegotiated my life as if it were an intermittent space for ruined illusions and stretch by stretch I have suppressed in it all the commas likely to accumulate oxygen and all the full stops that would provide it with a new liberating space in order to organize it like a sort of perpetual vomiting of gratuitous acts lacking in the slightest sense of organization with no other richness than its own which stems from its purest captivating gesture in its brutal, absurd audacity incapable of reorienting it towards a territory minimally doted with sense as emptying my existence of reasons and projects which generate illusions and new perspective I recognize that I have reached the supreme level and paradoxically of being finally possessed by life through the neurotic contemplation of my most primitive functionality and from that I am sure I will reach happiness beyond my wildest dreams thanks to the quantification of time measured stretch by stretch. ...

Fig. 6. *Minor Measures* (1994) by Antoni Abad (continuous video projection, text).

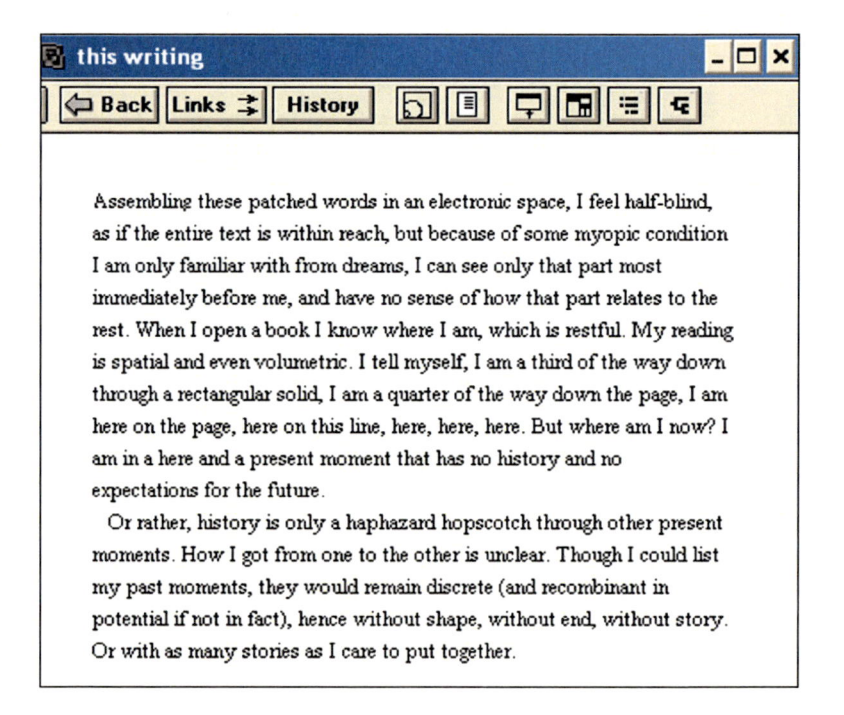

Assembling these patched words in an electronic space, I feel half-blind, as if the entire text is within reach, but because of some myopic condition I am only familiar with from dreams, I can see only that part most immediately before me, and have no sense of how that part relates to the rest. When I open a book I know where I am, which is restful. My reading is spatial and even volumetric. I tell myself, I am a third of the way down through a rectangular solid, I am a quarter of the way down the page, I am here on the page, here on this line, here, here, here. But where am I now? I am in a here and a present moment that has no history and no expectations for the future.

Or rather, history is only a haphazard hopscotch through other present moments. How I got from one to the other is unclear. Though I could list my past moments, they would remain discrete (and recombinant in potential if not in fact), hence without shape, without end, without story. Or with as many stories as I care to put together.

Fig. 7. *Patchwork Girl* (1995) by Shelley Jackson. Sequence of links: Title Page Broken accents> Phrenology> X> This writing> Dreams.

The lack of sense, the disarticulation, the *collage*, they work, as these authors observe, as mantras that leave the mind blank, empty of wishes, projections, objectives and reasons, and they prepare it for the assimilation of our most purely physiological reality as well as of those hidden aspects of our psyche.

Too much emptiness, nevertheless, can revert into a totally trivial experience. In the following sections I will discuss two possible reading strategies that can avoid the pitfalls of the loss of sense and of intersubjective coordinates.

3.1   The Loss of Meaning. Reading Strategy > Dream-Reading

The excess of indetermination, produced by textual fragmentation and lack of structure, augments the difficulty of some of the functions normally undertaken by the reader, such as the creation of cohesive hypotheses and their later verification. The data that fail to find a space into a meaningful structure, become irrelevant, and revert into information overload. A competent reader will, therefore, be the one who has acquired the skills to deal successfully with it, by being able to construct a manageable symbolic object[7] that has found a balance between chaos and order, redundant and relevant information, ambiguity and determinate meaning.

Both fragments point self-referentially toward the new reading strategies that would allow the reader to manage chaos, inside and outside the text. Abad's text alludes to the strange paradox of being finally possessed by life as he becomes aware of his own machine-like functioning, of the cyborg in him ("through the neurotic contemplation of my most primitive functionality"). Through the video projection of a hand repetitively measuring space-time stretch by stretch, Abad represents the mechanical aspect of our body systems for apprehending the real. Reading should not be more complicated than that: a self-referential awareness or contemplation of our own pulsations as we advance, stretch by stretch, through the text.

Jackson seems to describe a complementary mode of reception when she refers, in the following link entitled "Dreams," to the solution for apprehending the textual skein she has created: "the answer, of course, is to look with my dream eyes, not the eyes of my body." Dream-reading is not so much a matter of rational classification or remembrance of textual fragments or passages, but of trusting memory's ability to recall them from a subconscious reservoir once they become a marked feature by contingency with other pieces of the puzzle. This type of subliminal reading or unconscious scanning is the dream-reading of Bachelard (1960), which Barthes describes as: "a homogeneous (sliding, euphoric, voluptuous, unitary, jubilant) practice" (37). This mode of reception is also considered by Gabrielle Schwab as a way of creating an interface or a transitional space where primary modes of experience (subconscious, irrational) can connect with secondary modes (rational, conscious). Schwab has termed texts requiring this mode of reception as "transitional texts," for example experimental modern and postmodern texts, such as Joyce's *Ulysses*, Pynchon's *Gravity's Rainbow*, or Cortázar's *Rayuela* ("Reader-Response").

The reading cyborg that emerges as the ideal reader of digital narratives has not made its appearance from a cultural void. On the contrary, its literary competence has been nurtured in print narratives that have stretched previously conceived boundaries regarding literary aesthetic conventions. These transitional narratives have fostered a way of reading characterized by a high degree of self-reflexivity, an over abundance of apparently futile information, a synesthetic mixture of different artistic genres, and sensitivity towards technological metaphors that long preceded the digital medium. It goes without saying that digital literature students would greatly benefit from reading such print literature as a vaccination against the pitfalls of ambiguity and information overload.

3.2 The Fear of Solipsism: Reading Strategy—Building Context

We should not ignore, however, that the authors of the previous extracts, Abad and Jackson, either driven by an aesthetic choice or forced by the constrictions of the new medium, have renounced compliance with the implicit covenant upon which readers bestow a great amount of reading pleasure: The expectation that the writer will make the artistic effort of providing with unity and coherence a sequence of events, of creating a virtual reality which is symbolic, meaningful and explanatory, a titanic effort which the reader appreciates and contrasts with the apparent meaningless sequence of ordinary events in real life.

When the reader assumes this role traditionally performed by the writer, as well as other navigating functions, s/he certainly develops an authorial personality that was previously lacking in more traditional texts. Too much projection on the part of the reader over the indeterminate and fractures structures of digital texts can lead, however, to a dominant reading lacking in intersubjectivity. The world of the text is too indefinite to present a counterpoint to the narcissist projection of the reader's subjectivity. Eventually, we, as solitary readers, might suffer from a solipsistic reading, a reading that reflects without distortion our own self-image and desires, and denies access to otherness.

The fear of a solipsistic fall is another common theme in many hypertextual narratives. For example, the multimedia artist Dora García's work *Heart-*

beat, is a hypertext story dealing with a disease or vice that can also afflict the cyborg reader in front of the computer (fig. 8):

> Secretly and without anybody noticing it until now, a new fashion has spread among our youngsters: the vicious habit of listening exclusively to the beatings of their heart. Those who call themselves "heartbeaters" suffer from an altered perception of the real, of the external world, which is reduced to a mere echo of their internal spaces. This intimate percussion influences thoughts and behaviours, and is addictive.

Fig. 8. *Heartbeat* by Dora García.

If training at complex information processing, experienced by readers familiarized with "transitional texts," is invaluable when transported to hypertext or hypermedia reading, there is another activity belonging to the reading experience that is more necessary than ever in the context of digital literature: Contextualizing individual interpretations of texts inside bigger frames of reference, such as the communities of readers and the critical discourses generated by the digital medium: the critical discourse of cyberculture.

For example, the teacher of digital literature can use this work by Dora García to introduce students to these frames of reference by showing them that what they are reading is not a digital text adrift in cyberspace, but actually a text well-anchored to a community of readers and a critical discourse. *Heartbeat* belongs to the digital literature corpus compiled by Hermeneia in collaboration with the community of readers created around it. Therefore, it will be important to remark the agglutinating function of certain sites, such as Hermeneia's, whose webpage functions as a meeting point for a community of readers interested in digital literature. García's text also shares with other artistic products of the digital age a set of anxieties and common themes. The theme of narcissism, as we have seen in other works, is a recurrent preoccupation in cyberculture criticism. We can introduce, at this point, more philosophical or critical discussions of cyberculture to enrich the student's reading experiences: for example, Lee Scrivner's article "The Echo of Narcissism in Interactive Art and Hypermedia," Michael Heim's "The Erotic Ontology of Cyberspace," or Mark Dery's "Escape Velocity."

4 Conclusion

Digital literature shares with other artistic products of the digital age a set of anxieties and common themes that entangle the reader into the critical discourse of cyberculture. The digital literature touches upon the paradox of simultaneous superconnectivity and isolation, showing the reader the dangers inhabiting the very same medium the text uses to propagate. The digital artist warns the reader of the progressive dissolution of that communal dimension reading, as well as other human practices, once enjoyed. Taking heed of this warning, it is up to us what kind of cyber-readers we want to become: those who fall into a cacophony of voices, in which everybody "talks" (writes) but nobody "listens" (reads), or those who want to find a balance between their personal projections and interpretations, and the communal experience shared by a community of readers. The teacher of digital literature has an important role introducing students not only to the peculiarities of digital literature and to the critical corpus produced in its wake, but also to the wider discourse the phenomenon of cyberculture has created: a contextual frame in which notions of identity, community, art, information, virtualization, boundaries, etc., have acquired new meanings.

It is in this context where apparently incomprehensible works have worked out a space for interaction and communication. As signs which only acquire meaning in relation to other signs, cyberculture artefacts respond to a meaningful web of concepts, no matter how disperse and isolated the digital work of literature appears in the wild sea of cyberspace. Teachers of literature, as lighthouses, have the responsibility of guiding students safely to port: the appreciation of the literary experience no matter where it is found.

Notes

1 For some Spanish examples of the use of new technologies for the teaching of literature visit the following link: <http://www.hermeneia.net/eng/espais/didactics.html>.

2 I discuss the experience of analyzing different digital narratives as part of Gothic fiction in the following articles: "*Patchwork Girl*: la reescritura del mito de Frankenstein en la era digital" and "Unravelling the Mysteries of Cybergothic: A Stylistic Analysis of Iris Carver's 'Unscreened Matrix: K-Goths and the Crypt'."

3 For Jessica Pressman "'Digital Modernism' is an identifiable organizing principle for a subset of electronic literature that shares a common, conscious modus operandi: these works use central aspects of modernism to highlight their literariness, authorize their experiments, and situate electronic literature at the center of a contemporary digital culture that privileges images, navigation, and interactivity over narrative, reading and tex-

tuality" (303). As products of a contentious and even anomalous position inside cyberculture, this type of texts represent only a portion of electronic literature, which, precisely for its nostalgic flair, can be used as an appropriate nexus between the students' experience of printed texts and the digital medium.

4   Antonio Abad (born 1960), winner of the Prize ARCO Electrónico in 1999, has been the first Spanish artist to sell his net-art to an institution (the healthcare foundation Sanitas bought his work 1,000,000 presented in ARCO in February 1999).

5   Curiously enough, it has been recently discovered that synesthesia is much more frequent than it was previously thought, occurring perhaps in one of 200 people. According to neuroscientist V.S. Ramachandran, from the University of California, San Diego, synesthesia is much more common in artists, poets, and novelists (Zandonella).

6   For example, a random selection of quotes from texts by Severo Sarduy, Chuang-Tzu, and Elena Poniatowa can yield the following sequence or interpretation of links: Wings of a butterfly imitating a dead leaf> A man dreaming he is a butterfly> A lover feels her happiness has gone when she sees her partner desiccate a butterfly.

7   The term "symbolic object" is used in reception theory to refer to the specific "concretization" the reader has made of the text in the act of reading. According to this theory, the convergence of text and reader brings the literary work into existence. The structure of the literary text is differentiated from the actual symbolic object or mental realization of the text that the reader has constructed while reading.

Works Cited

Abad, Antoni. *Sisyphus*. 1995. 21 Mar. 2009 <http://www.iua.upf.es/~abad/sisif/presang.htm>.

———. *Minor Measures*. 1994. 21 Mar. 2009 <http://www.iua.upf.es/~abad/sisif/Abad1994ang.html>.

Andrews, Jim. *The Idea of Order at Key West Reordered*. 10 Apr. 2009 <http://www.vispo.com/stevens/stevens.htm>.

Bachelard, Gaston. *La poétique de la rêverie*. Paris: P.U.F, 1960.

Barthes, Roland. *The Pleasure of the Text*. Trans. Richard Miller. Oxford: Basil, 1980.

Borràs Castanyer, Laura. *Textualidades electrónicas. Nuevos escenarios para la literatura.* Barcelona: Editorial UOC, 2005.

Cadigan, Pat. *Synners.* New York: Four Walls Eight Windows, 2001.

Chang, Young-Hae, and Marc Voge. *Dakota.* 2002. 10 Apr. 2009 <http://www.yhchang.com/DAKOTA.html>.

Dery, Mark. *Escape Velocity: Cyberculture at the End of the Century.* New York: Grove P, 1996. 1-18.

Gache, Belén. *Book-Butterflies.* 1999-2001. 21 Mar. 2009 <http://www.findelmundo.com.ar/mariplib/introeng.htm>.

García, Dora. *Heartbeat.* 21 Mar. 2009 <http://www.aleph-arts.org/art/heartbeat/index.html#>.

García Carcedo, Pilar, ed. *Enseñanza virtual y presencial de las literaturas.* Granada: Grupo Editorial Universitario, 2008.

Gibson, William. *Neuromancer.* New York: Ace Science Fiction, 1984.

Goicoechea, María. "Unravelling the Mysteries of Cybergothic: A Stylistic Analysis of Iris Carver's 'Unscreened Matrix: K-Goths and the Crypt'." *Sites of Female Terror.* Estudios de la mujer, vol. VI. Navarra: Editorial Aranzadi, 2008. 75-88.

―――. "*Patchwork Girl:* la reescritura del mito de Frankenstein en la era digital." *Estudios de la Mujer: Discursos e Identidades,* vol. V. Madrid: Universidad Complutense de Madrid, 2005. 165-171.

Heim, Michael. "The Erotic Ontology of Cyberspace." Ed. David Trend. *Reading Digital Culture.* Malden: Blackwell, 2001. 70-86.

Jackson, Shelley. *Patchwork Girl.* CD-ROM. Cambridge, MA: Eastgate, 1995.

Landow, George P. "What's a Critic to Do? Critical Theory in the Age of Hypertext?" *Hyper/Text/Theory.* Ed. George P. Landow. Baltimore: Johns Hopkins UP, 1994. 1-48.

Ortiz, Santiago. *Diorama.* 2004. 21 Mar. 2009 <http://www.moebio.com/santiago/diorama/>.

Pressman, Jessica. "The Strategy of Digital Modernism: Young-Hae Chang Heavy Industries's *Dakota.*" *MFS Modern Fiction Studies* 54.2 (2008): 302-326.

Romero López, Dolores. "Spanish Literature in the Digital Domain: Culture, Nation and Narrations." *Literatures in the Digital Era.* Newcastle: Cambridge Scholars P, 2007. 329-341.

Romero López, Dolores. "Retos de la enseñanza de la literature española ante la convergencia: experiencias con los créditos ECTS y las tecnologías digitales." *Enseñanza virtual y presencial de las literaturas*. Granada: Grupo Editorial Universitario, 2008.

Schwab, Gabrielle. *Subjects without Selves*. Cambridge, MA: Harvard UP, 1994.

Scrivner, Lee. "The Echo of Narcissism in Interactive Art and Hypermedia." *Literatures in the Digital Era*. Newcastle: Cambridge Scholars P, 2007.

Zandonella, Catherine. "Probing the Picasso Lobe. What Scientist are Learning; What Artists Know." *Update. New York Academy of Sciences Magazine*. March/April (2006): 6-11.

Janez Strehovec

In Search for the Novel Possibilities of Text-Based Installations

Teaching Digital Literature within New Media Studies in Slovenia

Let us begin this section with a short description of a very basic feature of Slovenian culture and the current condition of scholarship in the humanities and social sciences, bearing in mind that this account is based on my personal experiences. Let me first explain that in Slovenia (as a small Central-European and post-socialist country) even today at the beginning of the 21st century we are still facing a very traditional, pre-modern and archaic attitude towards poetry (and literature) as an exclusive field, promoting and fostering national identity. What is at issue here is a kind of surplus, that certain superimposed value applied to the literature and above all to the poetry of this small nation (only two-million people), the language of which used to be constantly under threat throughout the course of history (in one period by the German language, in another by the Serbian and also the Croatian languages), and in the present by English as the lingua franca of the globalized world. Therefore, it is considered to be self-evident that national policy should support and foster its "literati."

Beyond the Privileged National Literary Culture

The intimate link between the issue of national identity and its literature appears to be an obstacle in the Slovenian approach to contemporary arts and culture, shaped as they are by new media and the impact of popular culture. The national ideologists often preach that national literature is the only worthwhile pursuit of the intellectual, and it is even considered as a kind of "patriots' club" where only the right, "good" Slovenians congregate. Of course this (in many ways self-evident) privileging of national literature, tied as it is to the printed medium of books, has many positive side effects. The position of authors (including poets) is quite good; there are a number of journals published, authors are awarded grants, library fees and prizes. Slovenia is probably the easiest place in the world to have your poetry published and even to get paid for it, although afterwards such books often just gather dust on library shelves.

On the other hand, and outside of the art and literature scene limited by the ideology on national literature, there are many internationally successful authors in Slovenia who are active in the field of new media art (for example, Marko Peljhan, Janez Janša, and Vuk Ćosić, who was among the pioneers of net.art).[1] There are also a number of institutions and internationally active organizations devoted to it, for instance the multimedia centre Kibla (Maribor), the gallery Kapelica in Ljubljana and the Kiberpipa, the cultural centre, computer lab and internet cafe also in Ljubljana, to name just a few. And all of them are supported by the National Ministry of Culture and by local organizations, which are to a certain extent open to new movements in digital arts and culture. Unfortunately, this interest has not been taken up by the Slovenian universities in Ljubljana, Maribor, Koper and Nova Gorica where new media art and even new media theory is only slowly being incorporated into the curricula, and this holds especially true for digital literature.

In Slovenia, there are no simple and creative connections between research and teaching—a number of successful researchers at various institutes win international acclaim for their work, yet have virtually no opportunity to present their findings within the framework of university teaching, a state of affairs which is unimaginable for their English or American fellow researchers and professors. On the other hand, the professors at the universities (especially those in the fields of social sciences and the humanities) are so taken up with their teaching responsibilities that they often have to completely neglect their research work.

Although my position within the Slovenian academia is relatively weak, I was sometimes able to find research institutions willing to support my research projects in the theory of contemporary art and digital textuality (I conducted those as the principal researcher). I also published seven scientific monographs in Slovenia between 1985 and 2007; the last one was *Besedilo in novi mediji* [*Text and the New Media*], dealing both with Web 2.0 textuality and the issues involved with the sophisticated reading of digital texts. Since it is legally possible in Slovenia to have the status of a private researcher (an individual has the same rights in terms of applying for grants, as does a scientific organization), I have spent eleven years being listed as such.

Should they get enough works published, private and institutional researchers have the option to gain university titles, which at least ensures them the appropriate affiliation with which they can present themselves when cooperating internationally, although in practice they do not give any lectures and are engaged only as mentors of post-graduate students and doctorate advisers. Thus, I am habilitated as an associated professor of New Media at the University of Ljubljana, but I am working only as a researcher and offer mentorship and consultations to small groups of postgraduate students at the University of Ljubljana and at the University of Primorska (Koper) on a part-time/contractual basis. In April 2006, I sent a proposal in writing to the Dean of the Faculty of Arts in Ljubljana suggesting that Digital Literature be introduced as a new subject into the university curriculum (within the framework of the Bologna renovation of university programs), but this attempt has failed. I have never received any answer, although such a subject might have synchronized well with the programs of various other Departments (e.g., Slovenian Studies, Library Science, Comparative Literature and Literary Theory).

However, this suggestion was better received in the Department of Slovenian Studies at the Faculty of Humanities Koper. Thus, a subject entitled *Digital Texts* was listed among the elective subjects in the 2008/09 curriculum for undergraduates, and will be available in 2010/11 for post-graduates as well. However, not enough students applied at the beginning of 2008/09 and so the lectures were not held. In that same department, another of my subjects, *Phenomenology of Reading,* is also available as an elective, incorporating within its syllabus subject matter related to the reading of digital texts.

At that Faculty, the writer Andrej Blatnik (PhD), who teaches Creative Writing, covers the subject of digital literature in one of the thirteen lectures that comprise his course. That actual lecture (which incorporates both practice and theory), however, is held by Peter Purg (PhD), who is more familiar with the problems of new media art and culture. Some digital literature contents are to be included in Blatnik's forthcoming course at the Department of Library and Information Science and Book Studies (Faculty of Arts, Ljubljana) as well, with the further cooperation of Purg.

Since I have dedicated a number of years to the theory of digital literature and web textuality, I have incorporated the findings of my research into the obligatory subject *Theory of New Media,* which is aimed mostly at the post-graduate students of the New Media and Video course at the Academy of Fine Arts and Design (University of Ljubljana) and at the students of the *Theory and Philosophy of Visual Culture* course at the Faculty of Humanities Koper; occasionally it catches the interest of post-graduate students from other departments (e.g., Faculty of Arts, University of Ljubljana) where it can be studied as an elective subject. Since the subject draws 12-14 students each year, there are no lectures as such. The course is taught in the form of individual consultations (mostly based in forms of E-teaching and learning) and the final is given either in the form of an oral exam, a written text assignment, or a combination of both. Some students have a great affinity to digital literature; thus in September 2008, a candidate received her PhD under my supervision, where an important part of her doctoral thesis was dedicated to the digital poetry of the Slovene author Jaka Železnikar. (By the way, my new PhD candidate from the University of Primorska is engaged with the topic of the digital texts authorship.)

Approaching the Experimental Streams of the Cyberlanguage

The question that arises here is how to present digital literature, and especially digital poetry, to the students. In my essay "Alphabet on the Move" (in this book) I argue that I do not consider digital literature as a form of continuation of literature as we know it, but rather as an emerging field, shaped in close connection to new media arts and software and the internet culture. Due to the profile and the preferences of the students, who are especially interested in media installations and hybrid fields at the intersections of various artistic genres and forms, the consultations are directed towards the analysis of those works which are questionable and non-self-evident in their literary nature. During the first few consultations, the students are introduced to hyperfiction and hyperpoetry (Shelley Jackson's piece *my body—a Wunderkammer* is used as an example) where I point out to them the phenomena of perception and cognition of hyperfiction producing the effects of "techno-suspense" and "techno-surprise" (Strehovec, "The Moving Words" 103). The first term describes the uncertainty when the reader, full of expectation, clicks on the hyperlink, while the other refers to the reader's sensations when she "lands" at the unit of text after that click. Here we are dealing with the reader who is not "safe," but who is instead exposed to deviations from her expectations. The students are also familiarized with the basic viewpoints from George P. Landow's *Hypertext Theory* and the contemporary, mostly post-structuralist theory of intertextuality (by referring to the key concepts and paradigms from the works by de Saussure; Bakhtin; Kristeva; Barthes; Genette; Riffaterre[2]).

After a short introduction to hyperfiction, which is the most representative of the experimental tendencies in literature as we know it, we move onward to those hybrid text-based projects which characteristically demonstrate what is happening with cyberlanguage in the paradigm of new media and technoculture. As far as availability is concerned, the easiest content to present to the students is content available online, as they can access it at any time from their personal computers. The following projects, therefore, function as a starting point for our dialogues on the key paradigms of digital literature in the context of new media art:

- Noah Wardrip-Fruin et al.: *Screen*
- Mark Amerika: *Filmtext*
- Natalia Bookchin: *The Intruder*
- Komninos Zervos: *Beer*
- Brian Kim Stefans: *The Dreamlife of Letters*

- Camille Utterback and Romy Achituv: *Text Rain*
- Jon Thomson and Alison Craighead: *Trigger Happy*

When it comes to *Screen*, a text-based installation placed on a VR platform Cave, we direct our attention towards the question of the digital word as a flexible signifier and the reception of this word within the framework of corporeal, very intimate and decidedly tactile perception of text units, as the reader, as interactive user, is able to touch the words with a data glove, take them out of the text and place them in new contexts. As a challenge for the new forms of perception and cognition of digital text, we use the piece *Text Rain* by Camille Utterback and Romy Achituv as an interactive installation in which participants use the familiar instrument of their bodies, to do what seems unbelievable—to lift and play with falling letters that are not falling randomly, but form lines of a poem about bodies and language. Reading the phrases in the *Text Rain* installation becomes a physical as well as a mental endeavour. By confronting this piece, the students are also challenged to think about the possibilities of how the text-based installation is formed, and with the idea that they themselves take into account the cyberlanguage as a demanding scope of their own art-making.

We treat *Filmtext* as an example of a web-based textual installation, as its author Mark Amerika argues that "with FILMTEXT I take this surf-sample-manipulate research practice right into the belly of the beast, interfacing Hollywood with hypertext, video games with literary rhetoric, interactive cinema with image *écriture*" ("Expanding the Concept of Writing" 9). *Filmtext* demonstrates that text making in terms of the new media paradigm is surf-sample-manipulate research practice; rather than being an Artist or Author, the textscape producer could be defined as a (new media) researcher dealing with the issues of the cyberlanguage.

Natalia Bookchin's *The Intruder* is presented as a piece that demonstrates the blurring of the borders between two (within the modernist paradigm strictly separated) fields—the elite, high art (e.g., Borges's literature) and the popular culture genres (e.g., video and computer games). The author was inspired by Borges's tale of two brothers in love with the same girl (*La intrusa*, 1966) to create a multimedia story narrated through ten computer games, which according to the software used make references to some classic, but nowadays very outdated video games from the 1980s, such as *Pong, Kaboom, Laser Blast, Outlaw, Jungle Hunt,* and *Gal's Panic*. When encountering this project, the students are made aware of the fact that *The Intruder* alludes to the feminist approach of the author, where the hero of Borges's text is understood as an intruder and a disturbing element in a world controlled by men; in the last unit of the game, she is even put in the role of a moving target at which shots are fired from a circling helicopter. This project is presented to students in order to demonstrate that the video (and the computer) game platform could also be a proper one for artistic or literary appropriation in terms of repurposing, refashioning and recombination as crucial procedures in (new) media art. By facing such a game patch, we are struck with the present condition of contemporary art, which is shaped with the culture of mixes, recombining, sampling, rapprochements, hybrid forms, in-between spaces, side-by-side integrations of separated fields and repurposing of state-of-the-art technological platforms. Today, when the realms of art and literature (on the Web or beyond it) are just one or two clicks away from the worlds of the commercial, political and social, the artists (and the digital literati) are urged to reinvent their very personal poetics that could even include positive attitudes regarding the possibilities opened up by state-of-the art technologies and the tactics of, let us say, the present economical survival kit.

A similar experience awaits the students when they encounter the first-person shooter game *Trigger Happy* by Jon Thomson and Alison Craighead, where the reader in the role of the player shoots at an excerpt from Foucault's text "Qu'est-ce qu'un auteur?" ('What is an author?'), implying that we are dealing with a gamescape where the words function as the moving target. Instead of shooting at a fleet of alien spaceships gradually coming closer, which was the idea of the original arcade game *Space Invaders*, the game was modified in this instance; here the player aims her gun at quotations from the aforementioned essay, which disappear word by word whenever the player hits. The text that critically analyses the figure of the author is thus literally destroyed, while simultaneously the students are made aware of the opportunities that video and computer games present for new media storytelling.

Brian Kim Stefans's piece is illustrative in so far as the author shows us that moving letters are in fact primordial, atom-like units of digital text-based pieces; they are used as a tool in a game of association played with the words brought onto the screen, while at the same time the words and letters function also as decidedly visual signifiers, where their appearance on the screen makes use of film aesthetics (Strehovec, "Attitudes on the Move"). Rather than applying only the concepts of literary theory shaped by Poststructuralism, some concepts from film theory like suspense, stain, and dissolve seem to be useful in describing the crucial points in the temporal organization of the digital "parole in libertà." In this regard, the digital poem *Beer* by the Australian author Komninos Zervos is similar. Zervos was one of the first to emphasize the importance of software for the making of digital poetry by entitling his cycles according to genre as Shockwave-, Flash-, and Java(script) Poetry. The software is by no means a neutral tool; on the contrary, it shapes the way one perceives and considers the cultural contents, something that is also demonstrated by digital poetry.[3]

Towards the "Mouse Reading"

Digital literature belongs to the world of new media and technologies and is confronted with the philosophy of this world, so the students are familiarized with the current cultural trends, shifts of paradigms in contemporary philosophy and criticism, and with the most progressive tendencies and streams in the (new) media art, which is often evolving with the procedures and devices of remixing, sampling, repurposing, and recombination

The students are familiarized with the projects and ideas by way of dialogue. When it comes to art students, the teacher first gets acquainted with their primary field of interest and the profile of their work, research and study to date, and then encourages them to imagine how they themselves would respond to the cultural and artistic problems faced by the authors of the projects dealt with within the course. Since theory has an important role in contemporary art and literature, they are asked to try their hand at writing statements about such pieces. They are also given a short assignment requiring them to read individual examples of digital literature and then they are asked to write about what attracted them to that particular piece, what the core structure of the project is like, how they read the piece, how many times they have re-examined a section of the text, what kind of software was used, and which solutions and procedures they would use in such a project had they been inspired with the same idea.

The software problem is presented to them by means of so-called code poetry (the stream in digital poetry, represented by many important pieces by Alan Sondheim), which directs one's attention to the code applied to new media art and literature, and even to the processes of creating malfunctionings of the code (well-known in Jodi's net art). Referring to the software art piece *Failed Fractals*, José Carlos Silvestre argues that this is a code poem, "because you can't just run the code and watch: you must know what it is trying to do and why it fails. The code itself is important. Of course, you couldn't just read the code or about the code, either, you also have to run it" (*Failed Fractals*).[4]

The students of my course at the Academy of Fine Arts and Design also find out that contemporary storytelling can express itself with the help of mobile phones and GPS devices, which means that they are introduced to the world of the key paradigms of today's mobile culture and challenged to think about the role of the narrative and lyric in it. At the same time, certain hardware and software solutions are suggested to them. They are stimulated to think about the possibilities of the inclusion of "cyberlanguage" in their forthcoming installations, for the language beyond the printed page is a striking and questionable field, which challenges the readers with novel approaches and solutions.

Although my elective courses *Digital Texts* and *Phenomenology of Reading* at the Faculty of Humanities in Koper have not yet been taught, I would like to point out some key elements emphasized in the syllabus of *Digital Texts*. The subject (meant as a first-term subject for 2nd or 3rd year students of the first stage of the Bologna *Slovenian Studies* course and encompassing 180 hours) understandably focuses on the issues presented in the description given earlier in this paper; it is an introduction to the analysis of the key paradigms of digital literature within the framework of new media, with special emphasis placed on the treatment of the expanded concept of post-printed text, consisting of groups of signs from diverse origins. The Internet is presented as the source for the new lexis: neologisms, compound words starting with the prefix 'cyber' or including signs such as "@" and "dot.com," acronyms (for example, ASAP), emoticons and smileys, signs taken from programming and scripting languages. Then follows the (mostly socio-linguistic) analysis of the language of chat rooms, blogs and emails, for which David Crystal's *Language and the Internet* is used as key reference.

In both *Phenomenology of Reading* and *Digital Texts*, we will also be directing our attention to the reading of texts which in terms of their interruptive, nervous and jumpy nature demand the tactile and motor activity of "mouse reading," a term I coined describing reading accompanied with the *click and drag* activities. As a historically important milestone pioneering reading beyond a (white) printed page, Eduardo Kac's holopoetry is spotlighted as well, because "a holopoem must be read in a broken fashion, in an irregular and discontinuous movement, and it will change as it is viewed from different perspectives." (131) Such a reading of various pieces belonging to the broader field of electronic and digital literature demands interruptions during the individual reader's spontaneous immersion within the textscape, due to the necessity of constantly returning to one's starting point; as such, this, let us say, "artificial" reading, will also demand of the students that they re-read and then stop for a while at certain points in the text in order to write down their impressions, thoughts and such findings as they were able to capture while traversing the textual environment.

Notes

1 In terms of political background and attitudes, it is very hard to imagine that Slovenian authors of the (new) media art are being included among the right-wing intellectuals.

2 Graham Allen's *Intertextuality* (2000) is used here as an introductory companion.

3 Today, specific software could be discussed even in terms of mind-changing, e.g., the popular PowerPoint presentations shape both the visual and the mental way of how to present and discuss a particular problem. The description of the sophisticated mind's efforts in defining a problem gives way to attractive schemes, keywords and bulleted lists, and (moving) images.

4 The *Failed Fractals* refers to the noise that occurs when the author has drawn in the Julia-set quadratic fractal; the computation has failed because the applied numbers were too large and quickly exceeded the memory allocated. This means that the code is trying to describe something (i.e., a fractal which only exists in computers and does not model real-world phenomena) suggesting infinity, but stumbles upon the material limitations of a computer.

Works Cited

Allen, Graham. *Intertextuality*. London: Routledge, 2000.

Amerika, Mark. "Expanding the Concept of Writing: Notes on Net Art, Digital Narrative and Viral Ethics." *Leonardo* 37.1 (2004): 9-13.

———. *Filmtext*. 2001-2002. 17 Apr. 2009 <http://www.markamerika.com/filmtext>.

Bookchin, Natalia. *The Intruder*. 1999. 17 Apr. 2009 <http://www.bookchin.net/intruder/english/html/a_title.html>.

Crystal, David. *Language and the Internet*. Cambridge: Cambridge UP, 2001.

Jackson, Shelley. *my body—a Wunderkammer*. 1997. 17 Apr. 2009 <http://www.collection.eliterature.org/1/works/jackson__my_body_a_wunderkammer.html>.

Kac, Eduardo, ed. *Media Poetry: An International Anthology*. Bristol: Intellect, 2007.

Silvestre, José C. *Failed Fractals*. 2008. 17 Apr. 2009 <http://www.bogotissimo.com/ff>.

Stefans, Brian K. *The Dreamlife of Letters*. 2000. 17 Apr. 2009 <http://www.ubu.com/contemp/stefans/dream/index.html>.

Strehovec, Janez. "The Moving Words." *The Cybertext Yearbook 2000*. Ed. Markku Eskelinen and Raine Koskimaa. Jyväskylä: Research Centre for Contemporary Culture, 2000. 100-116.

———. "Attitudes on the Move: On the Perception of Digital Poetry Objects." *CyberText Yearbook 2002-2003*. Ed. Markku Eskelinen and Raine Koskimaa. Jyväskylä: Research Centre for Contemporary Culture, 2003. 39-55.

Tisselli, Eugenio. *Degenerative*. 2005. 17 Apr. 2009 <http://www.motorhueso.net/degenerative>.

Thomson, Jon, and Alison Craighead. *Trigger Happy*. 1998. 17 Apr. 2009 <http://www.triggerhappy.org>.

Utterback, Camille, and Romy Achituv. *Text Rain*. 1999. 17 Apr. 2009 <http://www.camilleutterback.com/movies/textrain_mov.html>.

Wardrip-Fruin et al. *Screen*. 2002. 17 Apr. 2009 <http://www.uiowa.edu/~iareview/tirweb/feature/cave/ScreenProfile2004_HiFi.mov>.

Zervos, Komninos. *Beer*. 2002. 17 Apr. 2009 <http://www.allenandunwin.com/writingexp/files/beer.swf>.

Contributors

Astrid Ensslin is Lecturer in Digital Communication at the School of Creative Studies and Media, Bangor University (Wales). She is founding editor of *Journal of Gaming and Virtual Worlds* and author of *Canonizing Hypertext: Explorations and Constructions*. Further publications include *Language in the Media: Representations, Identities, Ideologies* (co-edited with Sally Johnson) and articles in *Language and Literature, Dichtung Digital, Journal of Literature and Aesthetics, Gender and Language, Corpora, Sprache und Datenverarbeitung* and *Zeitschrift für deutsche Philologie*. At present she is working on two books entitled *The Language of Gaming: Discourse and Ideology* and *Creating Second Lives: Reading and Writing Virtual Communities*, and co-directing (with Alice Bell) the Leverhulme Digital Fiction International Network.

Peter Gendolla is Professor of Literature, Art, New Media and Technologies at the University of Siegen. He also is Director of the Cultural Studies Research Center *Media Upheavals* and directs the sub-project *Net Literature*. With Georg Braungart and Fotis Jannidis he is editing the *Jahrbuch für Computerphilologie* and *Forum Computerphilologie*. He is currently completing a book on aesthetic difference and is co-editing the forthcoming book *Beyond the Screen: Transformations of Literary Structures, Interfaces and Genres*. He is also co-editor of *The Aesthetics of Net Literature* (2007), *Wissensprozesse in der Netzwerkgesellschaft* (2005), *Formen interaktiver Medienkunst* (2001) and *Bildschirm-Medien-Theorien* (2001).

María Goicoechea teaches English Literature at the Complutense University of Madrid. Her doctoral dissertation is entitled *The Reader in Cyberspace: A Literary Ethnography of Cyberculture* (2004). Her research interests include literary theory, ethnography, and cyberculture. Her recent publications in English are "What (cyber)reading for the (cyber)classroom?" (2009), "The Posthuman Ethos in Cyberpunk Science Fiction" (2008) and "Androids, Gynoids and Cyborgs: Applying Bem's Theory of Psychological Androgyny to CyberFeminist Reader-Response Criticism" (2007).

Raine Koskimaa works as a Professor of Digital Culture at the University of Jyväskylä, Finland. He teaches and conducts research especially in the fields of digital textuality, programmable media, and game studies. He has published widely around the issues of digital culture, digital literature, hyper- and cybertextuality, game studies, reader-response studies, media use, and narratology. His *Digital Literature: From Text to Hypertext and Beyond* (2000) is available at <http://www.cc.jyu.fi/~koskimaa/thesis>. He is the co-editor of the *Cybertext Yearbook* Series <http://www.cybertext.hum.jyu.fi>, and a member of the Literary Advisory Board for the Electronic Literature Organization and the Review Board for *Gamestudies*.

James Pope teaches English literature, narrative theory, and creative writing at Bournemouth University. Research interests include reader-responses to new-media fiction, and the relationship between writing software and narrative form. To pursue this research, he is currently developing dedicated software for interactive writing, details of which are at <http://www.genarrator.blogspot.com>. He is currently working on creating original interactive fiction, and has written on the subject of interactive fiction in several online and print publications, including *Convergence* and *Dichtung Digital*. He is also a published author of six novels for teenagers, including *Spin the Bottle* (1996) and *Semi-Perfect* (2001).

Alexandra Saemmer is Associate Professor of Information and Communication Sciences at the University Paris 8. Her current research projects focus on semiotics and aesthetics of digital media, reading and writing on digital supports. She is author and editor of several books and articles on electronic literature and arts, digital semiotics, and the relationship between contemporary literatures and arts. Her books include *Matières textuelles sur support numérique* (2007), *E-Formes 2: Les literatures et arts numériques au risqué du jeu* (co-editor, forthcoming); *E-Formes 1: Ecritures visuelles sur support numérique* (2008, co-editor), *Les Lectures de Marguerite Duras* (2005, co-editor), *Duras et Musil* (2002). She is also author of e-poetic creations: <http://www.mandelbrot.fr>, <http://www.revuebleuorange.org/oeuvre/tramway>.

Jörgen Schäfer is a Postdoctoral Research Fellow at the Cultural Studies Research Center *Media Upheavals* at the University of Siegen. He is currently completing a monograph on literature in computer-based media and is co-editing the forthcoming books *Beyond the Screen: Transformations of Literary Structures, Interfaces and Genres* and *Medien der Literatur: Ein Handbuch*. In recent years, he has been the author of *Exquisite Dada: A Comprehensive Bibliography* (2005) and the co-editor of *The Aesthetics of Net Literature* (2007), *E-Learning und Literatur* (2007), *Wissensprozesse in der Netzwerkgesellschaft* (2005) and *Pop-Literatur* (2003).

Roberto Simanowski is Assistant Professor of German Studies and Digital Aesthetics at Brown University and editor of *Dichtung Digital,* an online journal for digital aesthetics. He is author and editor of several books and articles on literature and culture in the 18th century, nationalism, the literary salon, media theory and digital culture. His most recent books include *Digitale Medien in der Erlebnisgesellschaft* (2008), *Transmedialität: Studien zu paraliterarischen Verfahren*

(2006, co-editor) and *Interfictions: Vom Schreiben im Netz* (2002). His forthcoming book *Against the Embrace: The Recovery of Meaning Through the Reading of Digital Arts* will be published in 2010.

Janez Strehovec is Principal Researcher and Associate Professor for New Media at the University of Ljubljana and the University of Primorska, Koper. He is author of seven books in the field of cultural studies and aesthetics published in Slovenia. His most recent book is *Besedilo in novi mediji* [*Text and the New Media*] (2007). He has also published in journals such as the *Journal of Popular Culture*, *CTheory*, *Afterimage*, *Dichtung Digital*, *Organdy Quarterly*, *Cybertext Yearbook*, *Glimpse*, *Digital Creativity*, and *Technoetic Arts*, and has presented papers at conferences in Europe, Mexico, Australia, Singapore and the United States. He is currently preparing the book *The Software Word* on the philosophy and aesthetics of digital texts.

Patricia Tomaszek (MA) is a research assistant at the Cultural Studies Research Center *Media Upheavals* at the University of Siegen. Since 2007, she is also working as a research associate for the Archive-it Project the Electronic Literature Organization maintains in collaboration with the Library of Congress digital preservation initiative to archive works of electronic literature. *about nothing, places, memories, and thoughts* a cut and randomly mixed poem-dialogue with Robert Creeley, was published in *Drunken Boat* (2008).

Noah Wardrip-Fruin is Assistant Professor of Computer Science at the University of California, Santa Cruz. He is a member of the Expressive Intelligence Studio and a vice president of the Electronic Literature Organization. His digital media projects have been presented by conferences, galleries, research facilities, arts festivals, and museums. He is author of *Expressive Processing: Digital Fictions, Computer Games, and Software Studies* (2009) and has edited four books, including *Second Person: Role-Playing and Story in Games and Playable Media* (2007), with Pat Harrigan, and *The New Media Reader* (2003), with Nick Montfort.

Karin Wenz is Assistant Professor for Media Culture at the University of Maastricht (The Netherlands) since September 2003. Her disciplinary profile is in media culture and semiotics with a focus on digital culture, especially digital literature, the interrelation between games and art, fan cultures and online communites. Her most recent books are *Stile des Intermedialen* (co-edited with Ernest W.B. Hess-Lüttich, 2008) and *p0es1s: The Aesthetics of Digital Poetry* (co-edited with Friedrich W. Block and Christiane Heibach, 2004).

John Zuern is Associate Professor of English at the University of Hawai'i at Mānoa. His work on digital literature and the application of computer technology in university teaching have appeared in *Computers and Composition, Literary and Linguistic Computing, Text Technology, dichtung-digital.org,* and in the collections *Virtual Publics: Policy and Community in an Electronic Age* and *Cultural Critique and Global Corporation.* In 2003 he edited a special issue of the journal *Biography* on online life writing. His chapbook of Flash poetry, *Ask Me for the Moon: Working Nights in Waikiki,* was featured in *The Iowa Review Web* in 2005. He has also coordinated technology-based development initiatives in public housing facilities in Honolulu and for the Hawaiian Language Immersion Program in the Hawai'i public school system.

Medienumbrüche

SIGRID BARINGHORST, VERONIKA KNEIP,
ANNEGRET MÄRZ, JOHANNA NIESYTO (HG.)
Politik mit dem Einkaufswagen
Unternehmen und Konsumenten als Bürger in
der globalen Mediengesellschaft

2007, 394 Seiten, kart., 28,80 €,
ISBN 978-3-89942-648-9

ALBERT KÜMMEL-SCHNUR, JENS SCHRÖTER (HG.)
Äther
Ein Medium der Moderne

2008, 404 Seiten, kart., zahlr. Abb., 33,80 €,
ISBN 978-3-89942-610-6

RAINER LESCHKE, JOCHEN VENUS (HG.)
Spielformen im Spielfilm
Zur Medienmorphologie des Kinos
nach der Postmoderne

2007, 422 Seiten, kart., 33,80 €,
ISBN 978-3-89942-667-0

Leseproben, weitere Informationen und Bestellmöglichkeiten
finden Sie unter www.transcript-verlag.de

Medienumbrüche

ANNEMONE LIGENSA, DANIEL MÜLLER (HG.)
Rezeption
Die andere Seite der Medienumbrüche

Januar 2010, ca. 300 Seiten, kart., ca. 25,80 €,
ISBN 978-3-8376-1026-0

NANETTE RISSLER-PIPKA, MICHAEL LOMMEL,
JUSTYNA CEMPEL (HG.)
**Der Surrealismus in der Mediengesellschaft –
zwischen Kunst und Kommerz**

Dezember 2009, 278 Seiten, kart., 27,80 €,
ISBN 978-3-8376-1238-7

JÜRGEN SORG, JOCHEN VENUS (HG.)
Erzählformen im Computerspiel
Zur Medienmorphologie digitaler Spiele

Januar 2010, ca. 500 Seiten, kart., ca. 39,90 €,
ISBN 978-3-8376-1035-2

Leseproben, weitere Informationen und Bestellmöglichkeiten
finden Sie unter www.transcript-verlag.de

Medienumbrüche

MANFRED BOGEN, ROLAND KUCK,
JENS SCHRÖTER (HG.)
Virtuelle Welten als Basistechnologie für Kunst und Kultur?
Eine Bestandsaufnahme
Februar 2009, 158 Seiten, kart.,
zahlr. z.T. farb. Abb., 16,80 €,
ISBN 978-3-8376-1061-1

JÖRG DÖRING,
TRISTAN THIELMANN (HG.)
Mediengeographie
Theorie – Analyse – Diskussion
Februar 2009, 654 Seiten, kart.,
zahlr. z.T. farb. Abb., 39,80 €,
ISBN 978-3-8376-1022-2

RAINER GEISSLER,
HORST PÖTTKER (HG.)
Medien und Integration in Nordamerika
Erfahrungen aus den Einwanderungsländern Kanada und USA
Februar 2010, 280 Seiten,
kart., zahlr. Abb., 28,80 €,
ISBN 978-3-8376-1034-5

MARCUS HAHN,
ERHARD SCHÜTTPELZ (HG.)
Trancemedien und Neue Medien um 1900
Ein anderer Blick auf die Moderne
Februar 2009, 410 Seiten, kart.,
zahlr. Abb., 33,80 €,
ISBN 978-3-8376-1098-7

INGO KÖSTER, KAI SCHUBERT (HG.)
Medien in Raum und Zeit
Maßverhältnisse des Medialen
Februar 2009, 320 Seiten, kart.,
zahlr. z.T. farb. Abb., 29,80 €,
ISBN 978-3-8376-1033-8

MICHAEL LOMMEL, ISABEL MAURER QUEIPO, VOLKER ROLOFF (HG.)
Surrealismus und Film
Von Fellini bis Lynch
2008, 326 Seiten, kart., 29,80 €,
ISBN 978-3-89942-863-6

MICHAEL LOMMEL,
VOLKER ROLOFF (HG.)
Sartre und die Medien
2008, 228 Seiten, kart., 23,80 €,
ISBN 978-3-89942-816-2

ISABEL MAURER QUEIPO,
NANETTE RISSLER-PIPKA (HG.)
Dalís Medienspiele
Falsche Fährten und paranoische Selbstinszenierungen in den Künsten
2007, 416 Seiten, kart., 36,80 €,
ISBN 978-3-89942-629-8

DANIEL MÜLLER,
ANNEMONE LIGENSA,
PETER GENDOLLA (HG.)
Leitmedien
Konzepte – Relevanz – Geschichte,
Band 1
November 2009, 352 Seiten, kart., 28,80 €,
ISBN 978-3-8376-1028-4

DANIEL MÜLLER,
ANNEMONE LIGENSA,
PETER GENDOLLA (HG.)
Leitmedien
Konzepte – Relevanz – Geschichte,
Band 2
November 2009, 294 Seiten, kart., 28,80 €,
ISBN 978-3-8376-1029-1

K. LUDWIG PFEIFFER,
RALF SCHNELL (HG.)
Schwellen der Medialisierung
Medienanthropologische Perspektiven – Deutschland und Japan
2008, 226 Seiten, kart., zahlr. Abb., 29,80 €,
ISBN 978-3-8376-1024-6

Leseproben, weitere Informationen und Bestellmöglichkeiten
finden Sie unter www.transcript-verlag.de